Job #:121111

Author Name:Lester

Title of Book: Grammar and Usage in the Classroom

ISBN #:9780205306558

Grammar and Usage in the Classroom

SECOND EDITION

Mark Lester

Eastern Washington University

New York • San Francisco • Boston
London • Toronto • Sydney • Tokyo • Singapore • Madrid
Mexico City • Munich • Paris • Cape Town • Hong Kong • Montreal

Vice President: *Eben W. Ludlow*
Editorial Assistant: *Grace Trudo*
Executive Marketing Manager: *Lisa Kimball*
Editorial Production Service: *Chestnut Hill Enterprises, Inc.*
Manufacturing Buyer: *Suzanne Lareau*
Cover Administrator: *Jennifer Hart*
Electronic Composition: *Omegatype Typography, Inc.*

Internet: www.ablongman.com

Library of Congress Cataloging-in-Publication Data
Lester, Mark.
   Grammar and usage in the classroom / Mark Lester.—2nd ed.
      p. cm.
   Rev. ed. of: Grammar in the classroom. New York : Macmillan, c1990.
   Includes index.
   ISBN 0-205-30655-1
      1. English language—Grammar. 2. English language—Grammar—Study and teaching. 3. English language—Usage—Study and teaching. 4. English language—Usage. I. Lester, Mark. Grammar in the classroom. II. Title.

PE1112.L45 2000
428'.007—dc21   00-042104

Printed in the United States of America

Contents

3 *Basic Sentences and Their Diagrams   71*

PART II • *Usage*   *303*

PART III • *Glossary of Grammar Terms*   *376*

To the Instructor

Grammar and Usage in the Classroom is an extensive revision of *Grammar in the Classroom* (hereafter: first edition). In revising the first edition, I have made the book more accessible and more relevant to the needs of the students using the book. Based on my work with school districts, in-service teachers, and the hundreds of students I have taught using the first edition, I have made the following changes in content:

- *The separation of grammar and usage.* Some school districts still teach grammar in the conventional manner, but most teach grammar on a much more ad-hoc basis in response to particular usage problems. Teachers therefore need a model of how to address student usage problems more effectively and with a minimum of grammatical machinery.
- *More material for English as a second language (ESL) students.* This edition includes much more ESL material for two reasons: (1) the first edition was used in many ESL programs, and (2) most mainstream secondary classrooms now include a number of students whose first language is not English. Teachers of these students need at least a basic knowledge of how to respond to typical ESL problems.
- *Increased coverage of verb forms and tense.* I found that students using the first edition had great difficulty with both traditional verb terminology and with the modern approaches to the verb given in later chapters. In the first edition, the topic of verbs and tenses is a kind of *leitmotif* running through many chapters. In the second edition, I have pulled all the verb and tense issues together (including the passive) in Chapter 4, "Verb Forms, 'Tense,' and Helping Verbs." I have given a more thorough and helpful treatment of this confusing area.
- *Less emphasis on sentence combining.* While I am still an advocate of sentence combining, it is clear that for a variety of reasons sentence combining has not been successfully adopted in secondary English or ESL programs. I have reluctantly concluded that the first edition's heavy emphasis on sentence combining is flogging a horse that may not be actually dead but that is in intensive care.
- *Replacement of "classical" transformational grammar with a more modern descriptive grammar.* With deemphasis on sentence combining, there is no

strong rationale for retaining the introduction to "classical" transformational grammar. Like many others in the field, I have been quite taken with the descriptions of English provided by generalized phrase structure grammars (GPSG). I have used this approach with a number of classes and have been quite impressed by how natural it seems to students. (A particularly good grammar of English using this approach is C. L. Baker's *English Syntax*.) Accordingly, in Chapter 7, "Redefining Verb Complements," I have used an informal version of GPSG to extend the inadequate analysis of verb complements in traditional grammar. This chapter also has an extensive treatment of phrasal verbs—a notorious problem for ESL students.

- *Glossary of grammatical terms.* The first edition did not have a comprehensive glossary of grammatical terms. As a result, I found that students would forget the specifics of a term, especially one presented in a previous chapter. To help students remember all the terminology, the glossary in the second edition gives a brief definition and a simple example of every technical term used in the book.

The approach in the second edition is similar to that of the first edition, only more so. I think that the aspect of the book that students most liked was the practical tests and the hands-on exercises with answers in the back of the book. I have considerably expanded both the number of tests and the number of self-correcting exercises. Most of the additional tests grew out of problems my own students encountered with the material. To give just one example, students often have trouble distinguishing *that* beginning relative clauses from *that* beginning noun clauses. In the first edition, I mentioned in passing that they can paraphrase the relative pronoun *that* with *which*, but they could not use *which* as a paraphrase for the *that* beginning noun clauses. In the second edition, I formalize this as a test and reinforce it with an exercise. The second edition also has a summary at the end of each chapter of every test used in that chapter.

I have added an occasional "Teaching Tip," which addresses the reader as a teacher rather than a student. The teaching tips give suggestions for how the material under discussion might be taught more effectively.

Acknowledgments

I want to thank the following reviewers: Russel K. Durst, University of Cincinnati; Melvin J. Hoffman, Buffalo State College; and George Dorrill, Southeastern Louisiana University.

To the Student

This book is designed to give you two things: (1) a solid knowledge of grammar and the skills to teach it to your students; and (2) a broad understanding of the causes and treatments of usage errors—grammar mistakes such as subject–verb agreement errors, sentence fragments, and apostrophe errors.

An important feature of this book is that it does not treat you as just a student; it treats you as a prospective teacher who must in turn teach what you have learned to your students. There is a world of difference between being a student and being a teacher. As a teacher you must have an active rather than passive command of the terms and concepts of grammar. It is not enough, for example, that you can recite the definition of the parts of speech. You must be able to identify the parts of speech correctly in your students' writing and, meeting your students at *their* level of understanding, be able to lead them to do the same.

Accordingly, the book relies heavily on practical, operational tests that help you and your students identify grammatical constructions and usage errors. For example, we can identify nouns by tests that zero in on the three distinctive features that only nouns have: only nouns have plurals, only nouns can follow the article *the,* and only nouns can be replaced by pronouns. These simple, practical tests will get you out of many tight spots. The tests are also wonderfully helpful to your students. With the tests, they have effective tools for grammatical analysis and for dealing with their own usage problems.

Every test in the book is reinforced by one or more exercises. It is only by hands-on work with many sentences that you will gain an active command of the tests. A big word of warning: since the answers to all the exercises are provided, there is a temptation to check your understanding of a test by running through the answers without first doing the exercises by yourself. The danger here is that you will think that you have understood the test when you have not. The devil is always in the details. No two sentences are exactly alike. It is only by working through many examples on your own that you can truly internalize the tests and will be able to use the tests with new sentences. Remember, when you are in front of a class, you will not have the option of going back and checking your notes. Either you know it then and there in front of everyone, or you do not know it at all. Your students will have no doubts about which is the case.

Finally, a brief overview of the book's organization follows. The main text is divided into three parts. The first and largest part is **Grammar**. The second part is **Usage**. The third part is a **Glossary of Grammatical Terms**.

Part I: Grammar

The grammar portion of the book includes seven chapters.

Chapter 1: Teaching Grammar and Usage

Chapter 1 is the most important chapter in the book for prospective teachers because it explains the current chaotic state of teaching grammar and usage. Most school systems have come to the conclusion that they need to teach more grammar and usage; there is complete disagreement on how much grammar and usage to teach and how best to teach it. Prospective teachers need to be fully informed about the controversies surrounding grammar and usage. Prospective teachers need to have worked out for themselves a rationale for teaching grammar and usage, and be able to articulate it and defend it. (You can count on being asked to do so in job interviews.)

Chapter 2: Parts of Speech

Chapter 2 covers the seven parts of speech and how to identify them.

Chapter 3: Basic Sentences and Their Diagrams

Chapter 3 describes the structure of sentences and how to diagram them.

Chapter 4: Verb Forms, "Tense," and Helping Verbs

Chapter 4 gives a detailed analysis of verbs and how they are used.

Chapter 5: Phrases

Phrases are groups of words that act as a single part of speech. Prepositional phrases, for example, act as adjectives or adverbs.

Chapter 6: Clauses

Clauses contain a subject and a verb. This chapter is mostly about dependent clauses, clauses that cannot stand alone.

Chapter 7: Redefining Verb Complements

This chapter borrows concepts from modern grammar to explain a wide variety of structures that are outside the boundaries of traditional grammar.

Part II: Usage

The Usage section is an alphabetical listing of the major usage problems, such as apostrophe errors, sentence fragments, run-on sentences, subject–verb agreement errors, and pronoun errors. The Usage section also deals with three topics that are especially difficult for non-native speakers: articles, participles used as adjectives, and the use of the progressive tense.

Part III: Glossary of Grammar Terms

The Glossary contains a brief definition of every term used in the book, along with an example. One of the real problems in learning grammar is the terminology. There are lots of terms, and some of the terms are quite confusing. The Glossary helps remove some of the burden of remembering all the jargon.

I

Grammar

1

Teaching Grammar and Usage

This book deals with two closely related topics: grammar and usage. For most people, the term "grammar" means the rules of the language as set down in a grammar book. If we violate these rules, we produce sentences with "usage" errors such as sentence fragments, run-on sentences, subject–verb agreement errors, pronoun errors, and the like. Until the 1960s, the value of teaching grammar in schools was seen as self-evident: Students needed to know the rules of grammar in order to find and correct the usage errors that violated those rules.

Beginning in the early 1960s, however, two factors conspired to deemphasize the importance of grammar and to fragment the existing consensus on what grammar was and how it should be taught.

- *Research questioning the value of grammar teaching.* A number of research studies in the 1950s and 1960s cast doubt on the usefulness of teaching grammar as a way to help students control writing errors. Study after study found no correlation between students' conscious knowledge of grammar rules and their ability to write well or even to avoid usage errors. By far the most influential attack on the value of teaching grammar appeared in a National Council of Teachers of English (NCTE) publication, *Research in Written Composition* (1963), by Richard Braddock, Richard Lloyd-Jones, and Lowell Schoer. For many schools, this widely quoted statement from their study legitimized the abandonment of traditional grammar teaching:

  In view of the widespread agreement of research studies based upon many types of students and teachers, the conclusion can be stated in strong and unqualified terms: the teaching of formal grammar has a negligible or, because it usually displaces some instruction and practice in composition, even a harmful effect on improvement in writing. (37–8)

- *New types of grammar.* The development of structural linguistics in the 1950s provided a competing approach to grammatical analysis that undercut the validity of traditional grammar as a subject matter. As its name implies, structural linguistics is concerned with the structure or form of words and sentences. For example, in structural linguistics verbs are defined, not by meaning as they had been in traditional grammar, but by the fact that verbs have a distinctive past-tense form. Many of the advocates of structural linguistics loudly proclaimed that traditional grammar, mired in its Latinate traditions, was hopelessly inaccurate and unscientific. At the end of the 1950s it appeared that schoolroom textbooks would continue to teach grammar, but that the grammar would be based on structural linguistics instead of traditional grammar.

  However, just as structural approaches were beginning to bear fruit, transformational grammar, a radically new approach based on information theory, burst onto the scene. Transformational grammar is based on a highly abstract set of rules that can be manipulated to produce all the grammatical sentences in a language. Transformational linguists were quick to ridicule structural linguistics as (guess what) hopelessly inaccurate and unscientific. For most secondary schools, this was one revolution too many. Caught between the linguistic criticisms of traditional grammar on the one hand and the instability of competing modern linguistic theories on the other, most secondary schools said, "a plague on both your houses," and, following Braddock, Lloyd-Jones, and Schoer's advice, simply abandoned the teaching of grammar.

Two generations have now grown up since the early 1960s and, if nothing else, we have learned that ignoring problems of writing error does not make them go away. Our students make the same subject–verb, sentence fragment, and apostrophe errors that they always did, but now we have no shared vocabulary for talking to students about their errors.

In response to the increasingly vociferous criticism that high school and even college graduates cannot write acceptable formal English, schools have responded in two different ways:

- *Back to basic grammar.* Some schools have returned to various versions of traditional grammar instruction. Sometimes this takes the form of systematically dividing up the topics of traditional grammar by grade level. For example, grade 6 does parts of speech, grade 7 does the sentence and its parts, grade 8 does some portion of clauses and phrases.

  Most schools, however, find that there is such turnover in students from year to year that they cannot assume that students bring any predictable level of grammar knowledge to the classroom at the beginning of each school year. As a result, these schools are forced to teach grammar on a very hit-or-miss basis as determined by the level of the students, the time available in the curriculum, the interests of individual teachers, and, of course, the belief system of the current principal.

The current state of grammar teaching is chaotic. Grammar instruction is mandated in some states but not in others. Most (but not all) schools now make at least some attempt to teach grammar, but there is great uncertainty and disagreement on what to teach and how much time to spend on it. It is not uncommon for different schools in the same district to use totally different approaches. Unfortunately, it is all too common for teachers in the same building to disagree strongly about how to teach grammar, resulting in an unstable patchwork of temporary compromises that seems to change each year.

- *Direct focus on usage.* Some schools and individual teachers have taken the exact opposite approach. They have no confidence that teaching grammar to students enables the students to apply that knowledge to their own usage errors. Accordingly, they focus directly on usage problems as they arise in the classroom. This approach assumes that while students may be ignorant, they are not stupid. If students are given enough examples of a particular usage error (preferably drawn from the students' own papers), with the proper coaching they can be led to see what the errors are and how to correct them.

  Although this approach has had some real successes, it is far from easy to implement. Perhaps the biggest problem is the burden it places on individual teachers. Rather than depending on a textbook to provide the grammatical content and pedagogical structure of a lesson plan, teachers must, on the spur of the moment, draw on their own knowledge for all the relevant grammatical terms and concepts that students need to address usage problems. Many teachers are not sufficiently comfortable with their own level of grammatical knowledge to undertake such open-ended interactions with their students.

This book is designed to prepare prospective English teachers to function (and even flourish) in these unsettled times. The book gives prospective teachers both a solid foundation in English grammar and a methodology for teaching it effectively (Part I), and the book shows how to address the common usage problems directly, with a minimum reliance on formal grammar (Part II).

Part I: Grammar

The main problem with teaching grammar from the teachers' standpoint is its unfavorable cost–benefit ratio: it takes so much time for such meager results. A good deal of the problem in teaching grammar comes from the conventional methodology it employs. A typical grammar lesson begins with an abstract definition ("A noun is the name of a person, place, or thing"), followed by a few examples, and a set of worksheets. Some students, of course, are able to succeed with this approach. Unfortunately, most students quickly flounder and lose interest. Robert DeBeaugrande, in an article entitled "Forward to the Basics: Getting Down to Grammar," (*College Composition and Communication* 35: 348–67) describes the problems with this approach:

> As long as school grammar is couched in vague or technical terms, it is not "basic" enough to help students with genuine literacy problems, and we will achieve very little by going "back" to it. Such grammar is like a ladder with the lower rungs taken out: the real beginner can't get anywhere. Students who don't happen to figure out by themselves, through lengthy induction, what the basic terms mean, won't profit much from grammatical instruction. If school grammar succeeded in past times, the student population was much narrower and more uniform than what we have today; it was much easier to rely on hidden presuppositions about things we couldn't explain very well. (359)

This book gives an alternative method of teaching grammar that has proven to be much more successful than the traditional "drill and kill" methodology. The approach is based on the premise that all of us have an enormous intuitive knowledge of English that we can tap into to help us gain a conscious understanding of what we are already doing unconsciously.

As an example, let us take the definition of noun. As we mentioned above, the traditional definition of noun is "the name of a person, place, or thing." In one sense, the traditional definition is perfectly accurate: nouns are indeed the names of persons, places, or things. The problem with the definition is that it is not very operational. That is, we cannot use the definition as a kind of tool to distinguish nouns from other parts of speech. For example, the word *blue* is the name of a color, yet in sentences like "My new coat is *blue*," *blue* is not a noun. *Running* is the name of an action, but in the sentence "I am *running* for treasurer," *running* is not a noun.

In this book, three operational tests are given for **common nouns.** (Common nouns are the names of groups, as opposed to **proper nouns,** which are the names of individuals. *Student* is a common noun; the name of a particular student—*Charley Brown*, say—is a proper noun. Proper nouns with their capital letters rarely pose part-of-speech identification problems.) The first two tests are quick and easy, but not perfect.

1. The test: if a word can be used immediately after *the*, the word is a noun. For example, we can tell that *student* is a common noun because we can say *the student*. This test works with 99 percent of common nouns. It fails only with abstract nouns (such as *justice* and *beauty*) in certain sentences, for example, *The justice* is important to every society; *We all admire the beauty*. (Note: Throughout this book, an asterisk [*] is used to indicate that a sentence is ungrammatical.)

2. Pluralization test: if a word can be made plural, the word is a noun. For example, we can pluralize the word *student: student—students.* This test is less reliable than the *the* test because there are a number of nouns that are not used in the plural, for example, *lightning—*lightnings; baggage—*baggages; dust—*dusts.*

Although these two tests are not perfect, they are easy to use and have the great advantage that they do not give false positives; that is, if a word can be used with *the* or made plural, then it MUST be a noun.

As an illustration of the usefulness of these two tests, here is a sentence that contains an italicized word often mistakenly classified as a noun:

I went *home.*

We can tell that *home* is not a noun in this sentence by applying the two tests:

The test:
*I went *the home.*

Pluralization test:
*I went *homes.*

Despite the fact that *home* is the name of a place, *home* is not a noun in this sentence. (It is actually an adverb: *home* tells where the writer went.)

3. Pronoun replacement test: if a word AND ALL OF ITS MODIFIERS can be replaced by a pronoun, then that word MUST be a noun. Conversely, if a word and its modifiers cannot be replaced by a pronoun, then the word CANNOT be a noun. This is the most important of the three noun tests because it has zero exceptions both positively (applied to nouns) and negatively (applied to words that are not nouns). Unfortunately, it is the most complicated of the three tests to use.

Here is the pronoun replacement test used negatively to the word *home:*

Pronoun replacement test:
I went *home.*
         it

Since the pronoun *it* cannot replace *home, home* cannot be a noun.

Here is the pronoun replacement test used positively to the word *woman:*

A well-dressed young *woman* glanced into the mirror.

Pronoun replacement test:

A well-dressed young woman glanced into the mirror.
         She

Since the pronoun *she* can replace the noun *woman* and all its modifiers, *woman* must be a noun.

In practice, students would apply the first two tests to see if they get a clear-cut answer before they bothered with the more cumbersome pronoun replacement test. In this particular case (as in most cases), it is obvious from the first two tests that *woman* is a noun and no further testing is required:

> *The* test:
>
> *The woman* glanced into the mirror.
>
> Pluralization test:
>
> Well-dressed young *women* glanced into the mirror.

Sometimes, however, the pronoun replacement test is the only one that will work. For example, in the sentence

> John hates *proofreading,*

what part of speech is *proofreading*? It is actually a noun, but neither of the first two tests can establish that fact clearly:

> *The* test:
>
> ?John hates *the proofreading.*
>
> Pluralization test:
>
> ?John hates *proofreadings.*

The pronoun replacement test, however, establishes beyond any doubt that *proofreading* in this sentence is a noun:

> Pronoun replacement test:
>
> John hates *proofreading.*
>   it.

The point of these examples is to show that students can be given highly reliable tests that they can use on their own to take the guesswork out of grammatical analysis. The tests are not always simple (like the pronoun replacement test), but even the more complicated ones can be easily mastered with a little practice and reinforcement.

The grammar portion of this book is essentially a battery of comparable tests for all the standard grammatical topics. It is important that you, as a teacher, become comfortable with these tests. (If nothing else, you will have your own techniques for grammatical analysis that will get you out of innumerable tight spots.)

Some Suggestions about Teaching Grammar

If you are in a teaching situation where you are expected to teach grammar in a systematic manner, supplement the students' textbook with appropriate tests from this book. One of the many advantages of the tests is that most of them are self-contained. That is, most of the tests do not require any other grammatical knowledge or terms. For example, the *the* test for nouns requires no other information to make the test work.

Whenever possible, use the students' own writing as a source of examples. Next best is to use whatever they are reading as a database.

Rather than give rules, give the students ample examples, break the class into small groups, and let them work out the rule from the examples. When they create the rule, there is a sense of ownership. If nothing else, they will remember it much better.

Treat grammar rules as helpful generalizations, not revealed truth. Encourage students to find exceptions and see if they can find any pattern to the exceptions. That way students are working with the rules rather than seeing exceptions as invalidating the rules.

Minimize the time spent doing parts of speech. It is too atomistic, and students do not see any benefit from it. Put the following chart on the board. It is adequate for most parts-of-speech identification purposes:

Noun:	the _____
Verb:	will _____
Adjective:	very _____

The key to grammatical analysis is the verb. Every sentence (and every clause) must have a verb. The verb can be used to find the subject, and the verb controls the complement. Once students are taught to find verbs, they can fill in the rest of the sentence. Once students know what to look for, have them identify all the verbs in their own writing and in whatever they are reading.

Diagramming is very helpful. It gives students a way to visualize the grammatical relationships in a sentence. Once students get the hang of diagramming, they enjoy its puzzle-solving nature. It is the one aspect of grammar that students find (kind of) fun. It lends itself very well to small groups.

Part II: Usage

The Usage portion of the book is arranged alphabetically by usage topic. Each topic is a self-contained presentation of tests that can help students gain

control of that particular usage error. The treatment of the major usage errors—
apostrophes, article usage, fragments, run-ons, and **subject–verb agreement**—
are essentially minichapters that also deal with the causes of the errors.

Addressing usage error by focusing directly on the causes and treatment
of that error with minimal use of grammatical terms and concepts has been
the topic of much pedagogical research. The landmark book in the usage-
based approach is Mina P. Shaughnessy's *Errors and Expectations: A Guide for
the Teacher of Basic Writing* (New York: Oxford University Press, 1977). It is undoubtedly the single most important book ever written about the problem
of writing errors. The book examines the truly impressive writing problems
of nontraditional students who entered the City University of New York
through an open admissions policy. Her conclusions, based on an error analysis of 4,000 placement exams, are summarized below:

> I have reached the persuasion that underlies this book—namely that B[asic]
> W[riting] students write the way they do, not because they are slow or non-
> verbal, indifferent to or incapable of academic excellence, but because they are
> beginners and must, like all beginners, learn by making mistakes. These they
> make aplenty and for such a variety of reasons that the inexperienced teacher
> is almost certain to see nothing but a chaos of error when he first encounters
> their papers. Yet a closer look will reveal very little that is random or "illogi-
> cal" in what they have written. And the keys to their development as writers
> often lie hidden in the very features of their writing that English teachers have
> been trained to brush aside with a marginal code letter or a scribbled injunc-
> tion to "Proofread!" Such [teacher] strategies ram at the doors of their incom-
> petence while the keys that would open them lie in view. (5)

Three ideas about the causes of error are implicit in this passage:

1. *Learning to write standard English is like acquiring a new dialect or language.* Basic writers, even though they are native speakers of English, do not
command the special forms and conventions of written English, which are
sufficiently different from the conventions of the oral language to constitute
a separate dialect. In this sense, basic writers exhibit many of the behaviors
of second-language learners.

2. *Errors are a necessary part of the learning strategy.* Basic writers make
errors of a certain type as a necessary consequence of their learning process.
As basic writers change and become more competent, the nature of their errors also changes. These errors, then, are a sign of development and progress.

3. *Errors are the result of a deliberate strategy.* Basic writers do not make
errors on purpose, but the errors they make are a necessary consequence of
the strategies that they have adopted.

We shall now explore each of these three causes in more detail.

Causes of Usage Errors

1. *Learning to write standard English is like acquiring a new dialect or language.* We are all quite tolerant of the errors that beginners make. In language, we expect young children to make numerous mistakes as they grapple with the eccentricities of the adult language. We are sympathetic to the difficulties an adult learner of English as a second or foreign language goes through, especially if we have had to struggle with someone else's language ourselves. Mina Shaughnessy wonders why we do not show the same tolerance and sympathy for our students making the transition from the oral language to the written language. She argues that we do not appreciate how wide a gulf separates our students' everyday oral language from the requirements of formal written English and how hard it is for them to bridge that difference.

Many of our students are much more comfortable with the oral language than the written language. When these students write, what they are really putting down on paper is self-dictated oral language that is meant to be heard, not read. Often what looks wrong to more experienced writers sounds fine when it is read aloud. Here are some features in the oral language that students often attempt to replicate in the written language.

- In the oral language, we show that two ideas are closely related by putting them inside the same pronunciation unit and saying them together. Students sometimes transfer this technique to writing. They try to show that two ideas are closely related by writing them together as a single punctuation unit. That is, they deliberately create what would be called a run-on sentence to make the ideas sound right. For example, in the run-on sentence

  *Money is not happiness it can't buy love or trust.

  the student is trying to capture the close relation between the two ideas. The first idea (*money is not happiness*) is a generalization that the second idea (*it can't buy love or trust*) then supports. The student doesn't want to separate the ideas with a period, in part because it would force the two ideas to be said as two different sentences. In fact, when the run-on is spoken as a single sentence, it sounds fine.

- In the oral language, we use pauses for emphasis. In the written language, students sometimes try to achieve the same dramatic pause by creating a fragment—a piece of a sentence punctuated as a separate sentence, for example,

  I carelessly switched off my computer. Without saving my paper first.

  Again, when the sentence is spoken, the pause implied by the fragment sounds correct. By putting *without saving my paper first* in its own sentence, the writer has created the dramatic pause that emphasizes the importance of the information in the fragment.

The reverse situation is when basic writers are not aware of distinctions made in the written language that have no counterpart in the oral language. A simple example is the need to distinguish in the written language between common and proper nouns because of the requirement to capitalize the latter. There is nothing in the oral language that corresponds to a capital letter.

A major problem for nearly all basic writers is the use of apostrophes to distinguish the singular possessive -*s* from the plural possessive -*s* and from the plural -*s*. The three grammatically different -*s*'s are pronounced exactly the same: *boy's, boys',* and *boys*. Since the oral language gets along fine without distinguishing the three different uses of -*s*, a student might ask why it is so important to distinguish them in the written language.

2. *Errors are a necessary part of the learning strategy.* If learning formal written English is like learning a new dialect or language, then we would expect to see basic writers behave like all other language learners, and this is exactly what they do. We know from studies of how children acquire their first language and how both children and adults acquire a second language that language learning takes place through a kind of trial-and-error strategy in which broad generalizations (unconscious rules) are overly applied at first, then successively refined and narrowed to produce increasingly more accurate output.

For example, when children are first working out the rules for the past-tense forms of regular English verbs, they invariably overgeneralize and apply -*ed* to irregular verbs, producing such "errors" as *hitted* and *comed*. These errors are not random. Forms such as *hitted* and *comed* reflect what linguists call "intermediate" rule systems. In order for children to reach a final rule system that is compatible with the adult system, they have to work their way through successive intermediate stages. Thus the errors produced by these intermediate rules reflect necessary stages in their learning process. It is not that errors cause improvement; the errors are a necessary by-product. Learning cannot take place without the intermediate rule systems and the errors that they unavoidably generate. To a large degree, then, the errors that basic writers make are the result of students' working their way through the intermediate stages from the rules of the oral language to the rules of the written language. We expect that as basic writers gain more experience with the written language they will gradually gain control over writing errors, as is indeed the case.

3. *Errors are the result of a deliberate strategy.* Obviously, basic writers do not deliberately choose to produce errors. Basic writers are not passive. Their strategies are their best attempts to make sense out of what they are doing. If they had a better strategy, they would use it. Any strategy, even a poor one, is better than no strategy at all. In other words, students will not abandon even a clearly inadequate strategy until they can put a better one in its place. This fact accounts for a good deal of the persistence of certain common errors.

What Can We Do to Help Students Eliminate Usage Errors?

One reason the grammar-based approach to helping students control usage error is relatively ineffectual for many basic writers is that it is too difficult for basic writers to convert a grammar book's abstract grammar information into practical strategies for solving their own usage problems. We have all seen students go through a grammar workbook perfectly, and then fail completely to apply what they have just learned to their own writing.

The biggest single problem that basic writers have in developing successful strategies for coping with errors is simply their lack of exposure to formal written English. The one characteristic that is uniformly true of successful writers is that they read extensively. We would think it absurd to expect a student to master a foreign language without extensive exposure to it. Yet we often expect our students to produce formal written English when many of them have had virtually no experience with it. As Shaughnessy has pointed out, basic writers have such little familiarity with formal written English that what they produce themselves can be a grotesque parody of it. In the long run, probably the best thing we can do to help our students is have them read, paraphrase, and discuss significant amounts of well-written nonfiction that can serve as a model of what formal written English is.

In addition to providing more exposure to formal written English, what specific things can we do to help our students gain control over their usage errors?

The key to eliminating usage errors is to help students find the errors. Once they have found the errors, fixing them is usually easy. The problem is finding them in the first place. The usage-based approach helps basic writers by modeling strategies that most successful writers have already developed on their own for finding errors. Rehearsing these strategies for finding writing errors gives basic writers practical ways of controlling their own errors.

For the most part, the strategies for finding usage errors presented in this book have grown out of an analysis of the causes of these errors. Following are two examples.

Subject–Verb Agreement Errors.   The unit on subject–verb agreement is based on research that shows that two specific situations cause the vast majority of subject–verb agreement errors. The single most common cause of subject–verb agreement error is the sheer complexity of the subject phrase. The longer and/or more grammatically complicated the subject phrase is, the more likely the student is to make the verb agree with the nearest semantically strong noun. For example, in the sentence

> A group of expensive yachts with brightly colored sails *was/were* coming into the harbor.

there is a strong tendency to make the verb plural to agree with either of the plural nouns *sails* or *yachts* rather than with the actual singular subject *group.* In other words, when we get to the verb, we are most likely to make it agree with the most prominent noun, usually the nearest, semantically strongest one. Knowing this, we can help students monitor for subject–verb agreement by modeling the strategy of always jumping to the BEGINNING of the sentence to see if the first noun could serve as a plausible subject of the verb. If it can, it is probably the subject.

Fragments.   Research shows that fragments are typically a comment on or explanation of the previous sentence. Sometimes the fragments are merely afterthoughts, and sometimes they are set apart for emphasis. For example, in the fragment

> My buddies frequently go to Reno. *Where they usually lose their shirts.

the fragment is a comment on the first sentence. Most fragments are easily corrected by merely attaching them to the preceding sentence. Before doing that, of course, the basic writer must be able to identify the fragment as a fragment. In a grammar-based approach, we would help students identify fragments by teaching them to recognize their incomplete grammatical structure. Unfortunately, it takes a good deal of grammatical knowledge to be able to do this. In the example above, the fragment contains both a subject and a verb, yet it is still a fragment because of the *where.* (The fragment is actually an adjective clause beginning with an adverb [technically, a relative adverb] rather than the expected relative pronoun—a structure that is not even addressed in most traditional grammar books.)

The usage-based approach to fragments is not based on consciously identifying the grammatical structure of the fragment, but is instead based on identifying what it is about fragments that makes them so hard to spot. The key to identifying fragments is the fact that they cannot stand alone; what makes them hard to see is the fact that we unconsciously attach them to the preceding sentence, in which case they are no longer fragments. The trick, then, is to help students isolate the fragment from the preceding sentence. A test that has proven to be quite effective is to turn a suspected fragment into a noun clause by putting *I know that* or *I realize that* in front of it. Any grammatically complete statement will produce a grammatical sentence when paraphrased in this manner. However, fragments will produce ungrammatical sentences:

> *I know that *where they usually lose their shirts.*

> *I realize that *where they usually lose their shirts.*

The whole point of this test is to separate the fragment from the sentence on its left—the sentence on which it is dependent. By paraphrasing the fragment in this manner, the writer is forced to look at the fragment in complete isolation from the previous sentence. When the fragment is thus isolated, every speaker of English knows that it cannot stand alone, and therefore it must be a fragment.

This book provides this kind of hands-on test for the more common writing errors. Our experience has been that if students discuss the tests, work through the exercises, and compare notes with each other, they will have techniques that really do give them the ability to find their writing errors. There is one proviso: the teacher must take writing errors seriously. If students are held completely accountable for correcting their own errors after they have learned the techniques for finding the errors, then the students will take error correction seriously and be reasonably successful at it. On the other hand, if students are graded solely on the content of their writing with no consequences for uncorrected writing errors, then the tests will slide into oblivion.

Teaching Grammar and Usage to Non-Native Speakers

We conclude this chapter with some comments about teaching grammar and usage to non-native speakers.

First of all, not all non-native speakers are alike. Non-native speakers bring to English their own language experiences. At one extreme are immigrants from developing countries who are not even literate in their native language. At the other extreme are students who are already highly competent writers in their own language.

A second variable is the amount and type of exposure they have had to English. Some students will be starting from scratch. Some will have lived in the United States for years and have fair oral fluency. (Many of the students that Shaughnessy writes about were native-born Americans whose English was somewhat limited because their dominant home language was not English. These native Americans have some of the same language problems that immigrants have.) At the other end of the spectrum, some immigrants (especially from Asia) will have almost no oral ability, but they have studied English since childhood and may have more conscious knowledge about some aspects of English grammar than their American teachers do. (For example, I actually overheard a Japanese high school student questioning her American teacher about the uses of the hortatory subjunctive.)

A third variable is the reason students are learning English. Students who hope to stay in the United States have a very different motivation from students who need English for purely utilitarian reasons and have no interest in acculturation. Students who foresee a need to communicate actively in English are much more likely to be concerned about errors than students who need only the passive skills of reading and understanding spoken English.

The kinds of errors that non-native speakers make reflect to a large extent their writing ability in their native language. Non-native speakers who

are competent writers in their own language usually have relatively few problems with the common usage and punctuation errors that native basic writers make. Conversely, non-native speakers who are basic writers in their own
language will exhibit most of the same problems that basic native speakers
have, and they will benefit from the same treatment.

What distinguishes all types of non-native speakers from native speakers is difficulty with areas of grammar that are highly idiosyncratic to English.
These areas pose few problems for native speakers, and, consequently, they
are usually given minimal treatment in non-ESL textbooks. Chief among these
problems are articles (the use of *a/n, the,* and *some*), verb tenses, and phrasal
verbs (compound verbs like *give up*), all of which are treated extensively in
this book.

Finally, here are some suggestions about teaching grammar and me-
chanics to non-native speakers that you may find useful.

*Improving non-native speakers' reading ability is key to improving their gram-
mar.* Many grammar errors go away by themselves as students gain reading
fluency. One study found that the most effective way of improving non-native speakers' grammar was to require intensive reading (supported by discussion and some journal writing). Even though grammar issues were never
discussed directly, students who did extensive reading fared better on grammar tests than students who had focused on grammar exclusively.

Some problems that non-native students perceive as grammar problems
are really vocabulary problems that can only be addressed through extensive reading. The most important instance of this is preposition usage: knowing which prepositions go with which verbs in forming ordinary prepositional
phrases. For example, we look *at* a picture; talk *to* a friend; eat *with* a knife and
fork; and drive *by* the post office. In America we live *on* Elm Street, but in
England people live *in* Elm Street. There is simply no way that a non-native
speaker can predict which preposition to use in all these adverb prepositional
constructions. The only way that non-native speakers can learn these is
through extensive reading. Having non-native students keep a journal of their
own preposition errors and surprising uses of prepositions from their reading is also very helpful.

Be sensitive to cultural differences. For example, be wary of asking "yes"
or "no" questions. For many students from Asia and elsewhere, the only answer they can give a teacher is "yes," even if they have no idea what the question was. Asking non-native students if they have understood your
explanation can be very misleading if they can only say that they did, whether
they did or not. To see if they actually have understood what you are saying, ask them to explain it back to you in their own words.

Another cultural difference is the boundary between individual and
group responsibility. Many students are from cultures in which group col-
laboration is more acceptable than in ours. If you want students to work in-
dividually, you need to make the ground rules very clear. A particularly

difficult concept for many non-native students is what we mean by the term *plagiarism*. Most non-native students (and many native ones as well) genuinely do not understand the rules governing quoting or paraphrasing the work of others. Time spent on this issue can head off some major problems later.

If it is worth saying, write it on the blackboard. Much of what we say to non-native speakers is not understood. If it is written down, they can copy it and work out the meaning later.

Be tolerant of errors in areas that are highly idiosyncratic, especially articles, phrasal verbs, and choice of prepositions. Improvement in these areas will be glacially slow no matter what you do.

If at all possible, have non-native speakers work with native-speaker peers. Many non-native students have surprisingly little contact with their American peers and are quite uncomfortable initiating the contact themselves.

Have students keep a record or journal of errors and constructions they have had trouble with. Using this journal at conferences is a highly productive way of meeting individual needs. It also gives students who are shy about using English a topic they can talk about.

2

Parts of Speech

The foundation of traditional grammar is the classification of each word in a sentence by its part of speech. The conventional seven parts of speech are **noun, adjective, pronoun, verb, adverb, preposition,** and **conjunction.** (Often grammar books mention an eighth part of speech, the **interjection.** Interjections are exclamations such as *Oh* or *Well* that play no grammatical role in the sentence. We will ignore interjections from this point on.)

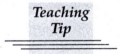

Teaching Tip

When discussing parts of speech with students, never discuss the part of speech of a word in isolation. Instead, have a student put the word in a sentence and then put the sentence on the board so that everyone can stay focused on it. The reason for putting the word in a sentence (besides buying a little time for you to think about it) is that many words can be used with different meanings and as different parts of speech. Unless the word is nailed down in a sentence, you may be defining one use of the word while students are thinking of a completely different meaning. For example, the word *chain* can be either a noun or a verb, depending on the context. However, when we put it into a sentence, its part of speech is fixed:

Noun: The *chain* is rusty.

Verb: We had to *chain* the dogs.

The seven parts of speech fall into two very different groups called **open classes** and **closed classes.**

Open Classes	**Closed Classes**
Noun	Pronoun
Adjective	Preposition
Verb	Conjunction
Adverb	

The terms "open" and "closed" refer to the membership eligibility of the parts of speech. Think of each part of speech as a club. The open classes are large public organizations that freely admit new members. Their total membership is huge—so large, in fact, that no one knows how many there are at any one moment. On the other hand, closed classes are small, private clubs with exclusive, limited memberships. The membership list for the closed classes has not changed in hundreds of years and is not likely to change for hundreds of years into the future.

We identify the members of the two different classes in quite different ways. Let's use the **pronoun** as a typical example of a closed class and the **noun** as a typical example of an open class. The main way we identify a pronoun is by referring to the membership list of the pronoun club. If a word is not on the list, it is not a member of the pronoun club. This "definition by membership list" is feasible with pronouns because the list is small and stable.

With an open class like nouns, this listing approach is impossible. Not only are there too many words to list conveniently without carrying around what would amount to a dictionary of nouns, many of the words in the four open classes can belong to more than one class, as we saw with the example of *chain*. So even if we found the word *chain* in our list of nouns, we could not be sure that the word was actually being used as a noun in any particular sentence. For words in the open classes, we can only identify their part of speech by identifying some features common to all the words in each of the four classes that distinguish them from the other part of speech classes.

In traditional grammar, nouns and verbs are defined by meaning: nouns are names; verbs express action. The remaining two classes, adjective and adverbs, are defined by their role as modifiers: adjectives modify nouns; adverbs modify the other three open classes, verbs, adjectives, and other adverbs.

In this book the traditional definitions are supplemented by operational tests based on the common, distinctive features that characterize each of the open classes. These tests give students a more hands-on way of determining the part of speech of words in the open classes. These operational tests typically fall into one of the following three types:

1. *Word-form tests.* Open-class words often have distinctive endings by which the class can be identified. For example, nouns have plural and possessive endings, and verbs have past-tense endings.

2. *"Tip-off" word tests.* Certain words can occur only with specific open classes. For example, *the* can be used only with nouns and *will* can be used only with verbs.

3. *Substitution tests.* Certain types of words can substitute only for specific open classes. For example, the pronouns *it* and *they* can substitute only for nouns and their modifiers.

Nouns

> **Traditional definition:** A **noun** is a word used to name a person, place, thing, or idea.

There are two types of nouns: **proper nouns** and **common nouns.** Proper nouns are the names of specific individuals.

- Specific persons: *Alfred Newman, Senator Blather, Aunt Sally, Charlie Brown, Dorothy*
- Specific places: *Chicago,* the *Atlantic Ocean, Mexico, Walden Pond, Oz, Kansas*
- Specific things: *The New York Times,* the *Public Broadcasting Service,* the *Xerox Corporation*

Proper nouns are easy to recognize because they are typically spelled with initial capital letters.

Common nouns do not refer to specific individuals. Instead, they refer to categories.

- Persons: *student, child, woman, ballet dancer, father*
- Places: *city, attic, picnic grounds, sidewalk, country, planet*
- Things: *book, computer, cloud, anteater, dragon, moisture*
- Ideas: *patriotism, justice, confusion, friendship, love*

Common nouns are the names of categories, whereas proper nouns are the names of individuals within those categories—as we can see by comparing the nouns in the following lists of common and corresponding proper nouns:

Common Nouns	Proper Nouns
caveman	Fred Flintstone
politician	Senator Blather
country	Canada
cat	Garfield
program	*Gilligan's Island*
movie	*Gone with the Wind*

Identifying Common Nouns

Students rarely have difficulty identifying proper nouns as nouns—in part because proper nouns are distinctively names of individuals or entities and in part because proper nouns are spelled with capital letters. Accordingly, we will focus on helping students identify common nouns. There are two simple and highly useful tests for identifying common nouns: the *the* test and the plural test, which we will discuss here. There is also a third test for nouns—pronoun substitution—that is 100 percent reliable. However, this test is a bit more complicated than the first two tests because it identifies not just the noun, but the noun together with all its modifiers. We will introduce this test when we get to the section on pronouns [see "Redefinition of Third-Person Pronouns" on page 38].

The **the** Test

> **The *the* test for common nouns.** If a word can be used with the definite article *the*, then that word is a common noun.

The simplest way to test whether a word is a common noun is to see if the word can be used with the definite article *the*. For example, we can use *the* with all the common nouns listed above:

> the caveman
> the politician
> the country
> the cat
> the program
> the movie

The *the* test is quite reliable, but it is not foolproof because it has at least three problems.

   1. Some abstract nouns (for example, *honesty, caution, justice*) are rarely used with *the*:

> *The honesty is the best policy.

> *He threw the *caution* to the winds.

> *We all seek the *justice*.

However, even these nouns can be used with *the* if the noun is followed by a modifier (underlined in the following examples):

People are distrustful of *the honesty* of politicians.

He abandoned *the caution* <u>that had served him so well</u>.

We all demand *the justice* <u>guaranteed us under the Constitution</u>.

2. *The* is often separated from the noun it modifies by other modifiers (adjectives). For example, in the phrase *the old man, the* is separated from the noun *man* by the adjective *old*. The fact that *the* is next to *old* does not mean that *old* is a noun; *the* is not modifying *old*. Rather, both *the* and *old* are modifying the same noun, *man*. If in doubt, we can test which word *the* modifies by pairing it up with the words that follow. That is, we can paraphrase *the old man* as *the man, not as *the old*. The paraphrase tells us that *man* (not *old*) is the noun that *the* modifies.

3. When we paraphrase words in a sentence, we must be careful that we do not inadvertently change one part of speech into another. For example, in the following sentence, notice the words *book* and *ticket:*

The travel agent will *book* a *ticket* for you.

In this sentence, the word *book* is a verb. The fact that we can say *the book* does not show that *book* in this sentence is a noun. All it shows is that *book* CAN be used as a noun in some context. However, when we try to use *the* with *book* in the context of this sentence, it is ungrammatical:

*The travel agent will <u>the</u> *book* a ticket for you.

Our inability to use *the* with *book* tells us that in this particular sentence, *book* is not a noun.

Now, let's try a comparable paraphrase with the word *ticket.* When we paraphrase the sentence with *the* before *ticket* (substituting *the* for the modifier *a*), the result is perfectly grammatical because *ticket* is a noun in this sentence:

The travel agent will book <u>the</u> *ticket* for you.

The moral is that when doing this test or any other paraphrase test, we must be very careful not to change the part of speech of the word being tested by taking it out of the context of the original sentence.

Noun Exercise #1: Identifying Nouns by the the *Test* _____

Below are pairs of related words. One word in each pair is a noun; the other word is another part of speech. In the space provided, try the *the* test on each word. Write NOUN under the word that passes the *the* test. The first question is done as an example. (Answers to this exercise are on page 390.)

   0. defend/defense <u>*the defend/the defense   </u>

                                          Noun

1. authority/authorize _____
2. lengthen/length _____
3. concession/concede _____
4. discover/discovery _____
5. perform/performance _____

Noun Exercise #2: Identifying Nouns by the the Test _____

Underline the common nouns. Confirm your answers by inserting *the* in front of every common noun. Make whatever changes are needed to make the sentence sound right. Some nouns will sound better if you add a modifier after the noun. The first question is done as an example. (Answers to this exercise are on page 390.)

   0. Formulation of problems is essential.

      Answer: <u>Formulation</u> of <u>problems</u> is essential.

      Confirmation: *The* <u>formulation</u> of *the* <u>problems</u> (that we face) is essential.

   1. Instrument measures velocity.

   2. They registered protest against ruling.

   3. I was attracted to fabric by texture.

   4. Machines recorded discontinuity.

   5. Problems were uncovered after inspection.

   6. Departure of friends is always sad.

   7. Waiter brought us phone.

   8. Moon was just rising over hills.

   9. We all admired drawing she got on trip.

   10. They bought safe to protect valuables.

A second identifying characteristic of common nouns is their ability to be used in the plural, which is usually formed by adding either *-s* or *-es*, for example:

Singular	*Plural*
cat	cats
dog	dogs
hero	heroes
box	boxes
spy	spies (note the spelling change)

There are two groups of nouns that form their plurals differently. One group is made up of native English words that have preserved old ways for forming plurals, for example:

Singular	Plural	Singular	Plural
man	men	ox	oxen
goose	geese	calf	calves
woman	women	sheep	sheep
child	children	deer	deer

(*Deer* and *sheep* really are plural, as we can tell when they are used as subjects of plural verbs—for example, "The deer *are* in the forest," "the sheep *are* in the fields.")

The other group are borrowed words (usually from Greek, Latin, or Hebrew) that have kept the plural forms used in their language, for example:

Singular	Plural
radius	radii
thesis	theses
cherub	cherubim

The Plural Test

> **The plural test for common nouns.** If a word can be used in the plural. then that word is a common noun.

If a word can be used in the plural, then we are certain that the word is a noun. The plural test is thus a highly reliable test for nouns.

Unfortunately, there is a catch. A large group of nouns, called **mass** or **noncount nouns,** is always used in the singular. The plural test thus fails to apply to them. Some examples are *lightning (*lightnings), homework (*homeworks),* and *water (*waters).* (For a detailed treatment of mass or noncount nouns, see "Articles" in the Usage part.) Despite this group of exceptional nouns, we can still say with complete accuracy that IF a word can be made plural, then that word must be a noun.

Noun Exercise #3: Identifying Nouns by the Plural Test _____

Underline the singular common nouns. Confirm your answer by making them plural. Make whatever changes are needed to make the sentence sound right. You will often need to change the verb to make it agree with the new plural subject. The first question is done as an example. (Answers to this exercise are on page 390.)

0. The battle was fought fiercely

   Answer: The <u>battle</u> was fought fiercely.

   Confirmation: The *battles* were fought fiercely.

1. The experiment with the mouse was going well.

2. The policeman told us that the bridge was out.

3. The lawyer argued for the claim.

4. The poem appeared in the new anthology.

5. Snow White took out a finger bowl for the dwarf.

6. The governor held a press conference.

7. A flower was poking up through the snowbank.

8. My dream was very unsettling.

9. The fly was buzzing around in the window.

10. The speech put the audience to sleep.

To summarize, both the *the* test and the plural test are highly reliable ways to identify common nouns. If a word can be used with *the* or can be made plural, then we are completely confident that the word is a common noun (always provided that we have not otherwise changed the meaning of the word). However, there are common nouns that the tests fail to identify. The *the* test fails to apply to a few abstract nouns, and the plural test fails to apply to all mass or noncount nouns. Because there is a large number of mass nouns, the plural test is somewhat less useful than the *the* test. Nevertheless, these two tests give us an easy way to identify quickly the vast majority of common nouns. The tests also have the advantage that as long as they are used properly, they will never give a false positive. That is, if a word can be used with *the* or can be pluralized, we can be absolutely sure that the word is a common noun.

Noun Exercise #4: Identifying Nouns _____

Underline all of the nouns in the following sentences. Label all proper and common nouns. For common nouns, confirm your answers by one of the tests for common nouns. The first question is done as an example. (Answers to this exercise are on page 391.)

0. Chicago is known as the windy city for obvious reasons.

   Answer: <u>Chicago</u> is known as the windy <u>city</u> for an obvious <u>reason</u>.

   　　　　　Proper noun　　　　　　　　　common noun　　　　　common noun

   　　　　　<u>Chicago</u> is known as the windy <u>city</u> for an obvious <u>reason</u>.

   Confirmation:　　　　　　*the* windy city　　*the* obvious reason

   　　　　　They are known as the windy <u>cities</u>　　for obvious <u>reasons</u>.

1. A good plumber can fix any sink ever made.

2. A pound of hamburger will not feed us.

3. College professors are always looking for grants.

4. The good fairy granted her wish to play quarterback.

5. Economists were issuing dire predictions at regular intervals.

6. Napoleon's army advanced rapidly on Moscow.

7. He forgot to telephone his office about the meeting.

8. His interpretation of the law was challenged in court.

9. The class grimly wrote yet another essay.

10. A student showed a drawing he had purchased in Venice.

Adjectives

> **Traditional definition: An adjective** modifies a noun
> or a pronoun.

(As a clarification of this traditional definition of adjective, the indefinite pronoun *one* [and a few other indefinite pronouns] can be modified by adjectives. For example, in the sentence

> I would like *the other **one.***
>
>   adj   adj   indef pronoun

the adjectives *the* and *other* both modify the indefinite pronoun *one.* The use of adjectives to modify indefinite pronouns is so limited that we will concentrate on the much more common use of adjectives to modify common nouns.)

The term *adjective* is used collectively to refer to all types of noun modifiers that come before the noun. (Adjectives can also be used after certain verbs, for example, "The answer was <u>correct</u>." Adjectives used in this manner are called **predicate adjectives.** Predicate adjectives are discussed in detail in Chapter 3.)

The Pair Test

> **The pair test for modifying adjectives.** If a word can be paired up
> with a following noun, then that word is a modifying adjective.

A simple way to identify modifying adjectives is to pair up each adjective, one at a time, with the noun it modifies. For example, in the sentence

I ordered the special deep-dish, Chicago-style pizza.

we can pair up each adjective with the noun *pizza:*

> *the* pizza
> *special* pizza
> *deep-dish* pizza
> *Chicago-style* pizza

This test shows that there are four separate adjectives modifying *pizza:*

> I ordered *the special deep-dish, Chicago-style* pizza.

Modifiers that fail this test are not adjectives; typically they are adverbs that modify adjectives. For example, in the sentence

> I like very spicy pizza.

we can tell that *spicy* is an adjective because we can pair it up with the noun *pizza:*

> *spicy* pizza

However, when we try to pair up *very* with the noun *pizza,* the result is ungrammatical, telling us that *very* is not an adjective modifying *pizza:*

> **very* pizza

(*Very* is actually an adverb modifying the adjective *spicy* (*very spicy*).

Teaching Tip

Some students are confused by the *a/an* distinction when using the pair test. Give them several examples—*a ripe apple / an apple; an old banana / a banana*—and have them state the rule for using *a* and *an*. (The choice between *a* or *an* is determined by whether the word immediately following begins with a vowel or a consonant sound.)

Adjective Exercise #1: Identifying Modifying Adjectives by the Pair Test

Underline the adjectives. Confirm your answer by applying the pair test. The first question is done as an example. (Answers to this exercise are on page 392.)

0. The first movie was about these tiny armed soldiers.

   Answer: <u>The</u> <u>first</u> movie was about <u>these</u> <u>tiny</u> <u>armed</u> soldiers.

   Confirmation: the movie, first movie; these soldiers, tiny soldiers, armed soldiers

1. My first class is in an old theater.

2. Tall prickly weeds were choking out the vegetable garden.

3. A horrid new crime wave was sweeping the entire kingdom.

4. Several discount department stores had specials on the upright freezer.

5. An old sun-burned man was leaning against the weathered fence.

6. The wine store specialized in very expensive French wines.

7. We had a nice evening with some old friends.

8. The desperate company finally called in an outside consultant.

9. An ominous dark shadow passed by the open window.

10. Aware of his weak backhand, John relied on his excellent first serve.

There are two major classes of adjectives used as noun modifiers, which we will call *determiners* and *descriptive adjectives*. If a noun is preceded by both a determiner and one or more descriptive adjectives, the determiner always comes before the descriptive adjective(s).

Determiners

The term **determiner** refers to a group of modifiers that (with the exception of **number words** and **quantifiers**) are mutually exclusive; that is, only a single determiner modifies any one noun. For example, *the* and *a* are both determiners, but they are mutually exclusive. We can say *the book* or *a book*, but we can never say **the a book* or **a the book*.

Determiners can be broken down into five mutually exclusive subclasses:

Articles: *the* (definite); *a* and *an* (indefinite)

Demonstratives: *this, that, these, those*

Number words:

    Cardinal numbers: *one, two, three, . . .*

    Ordinal numbers: *first, second, third, . . .* ; plus other words indicating order: *first, last, . . .*
        (Note that ordinal number words are exceptional in that we can combine them with *the* and possessives: *the first game, the Three Stooges, my last question, Rudolf's first wife, . . .*)

Possessives:

    Nouns: *John's, Mary's, . . .*
    Pronouns: *my, your, his, her, its, our, their*

Quantifiers: *some, much, many, several, . . .*

Adjective Exercise #2: Classifying Determiners _____

In the following sentences, all the determiners have been underlined. Under each determiner, indicate which of the five subclasses the determiner belongs to. The five subclasses are Article (Art), Demonstrative (Dem), Number word (#) Possessive (Poss), and Quantifier (Quant). The first question is done as an example. (Answers to this exercise are on page 393.)

0. I took the first bus that came by.

  Answer: I took the first bus that came by.
                  Art #

1. There were several messages on our answering machine.

2. This test will cover the last chapter.

3. We delivered two packages to that address.

4. I left my wallet at home.

5. There were ninety-nine bottles of beer on the wall.

6. John's car was an old Ford with two cracked windows.

7. Most computers are now hooked up to a server.

8. I ordered some coffee and the last piece of pie.

9. All roads lead to Rome.

10. I didn't have much money with me.

Descriptive Adjectives

Descriptive adjectives—words such as *tall, beautiful, angry,* and *green*—are open-class adjectives. More than one descriptive adjective can be used with the same noun. For example, in the following sentence, no less than three descriptive adjectives modify the noun *cat:*

  Six *thin gray Siamese* cats were outside the door.

Notice that the three descriptive adjectives are not separated by commas. Generally, multiple descriptive adjectives modifying the same noun are not separated by commas. (However, see "Commas and Coordinate Adjectives" in the Usage part for a situation in which descriptive adjectives must be separated by commas.)

  Most descriptive adjectives share an important distinctive feature that helps us recognize them: they are **gradable. Gradable** is the technical linguistic term for adjectives that have **comparative** and **superlative** forms. Here are some examples of sentences with comparative and superlative adjectives:

  Comparative: Sally took a *smaller* piece than Sue did.
  Sally has a *more sensitive* personality than Sue.

Superlative: Sally took the *smallest* piece of all.

                  Sally has the *most sensitive* personality in her class.

As you can see, there are two different patterns for forming the comparative and superlative. One-syllable adjectives and a few two-syllable adjectives (especially ones of native English origin) tend to follow the Old English pattern of *-er* and *-est* endings. Most two-syllable adjectives (especially ones of French origin) and all adjectives of three or more syllables follow the pattern of using *more* and *most* with the adjective. Here are some examples of each type:

-er/-est Pattern	*more/most* Pattern
brave, braver, bravest	ambitious, more ambitious, most ambitious
calm, calmer, calmest	careful, more careful, most careful
cruel, crueler, cruelest	generous, more generous, most generous
nice, nicer, nicest	impatient, more impatient, most impatient
rule, ruder, rudest	loyal, more loyal, most loyal
shy, shyer, shyest	serious, more serious, most serious
witty, wittier, wittiest	vicious, more vicious, most vicious

Gradable adjectives that are not used in the comparative or superlative forms are said to be in their **base form**. The base forms of most gradable adjectives share a feature that is helpful in identifying them: they can be used with the word *very*, for example,

Sue is a *very brave* child.

Samantha is a *very ambitious* singer.

We can further confirm that *brave* and *ambitious* are gradable adjectives by using them in the comparative and superlative forms:

Base:	very brave	very ambitious
Comparative:	braver	more ambitious
Superlative:	bravest	most ambitious

The fact that an adjectives can be used with *very* is a simple way to identify gradable adjectives.

The *very* test for gradable adjectives: If a noun modifier can be used with *very*, then it is a gradable adjective.

Adjective Exercise #3: Identifying Gradable Adjectives _____

In the sentences below, all of the adjectives have been underlined. Identify the gradable adjectives by putting *very* in front of them. Confirm your answers by writing the comparative and the superlative forms under each gradable adjective. The first question is done as an example. (Answers to this exercise are on page 393.)

  0. From space, the Earth is a beautiful blue sphere.

      Answer: From space, the Earth is a *very* beautiful *very* blue sphere.

      Confirmation: more beautiful, most beautiful

                                    bluer, bluest

  1. A cold wave suddenly crashed over the wet deck.

  2. The weary firefighters slowly collected their grimy equipment.

  3. His nervous laugh seemed to fill the room.

  4. The unpleasant ceremony finally came to an end.

  5. All work and no play makes Jack a dull boy.

  6. A large ornate chandelier hung in the center of the large room.

  7. Holmes investigated the mysterious disappearance of Lady Greer's rare manuscript.

  8. We paddled the heavy boat across the still waters of the pond.

  9. The tired children were waiting in a long line.

 10. The heavy rain caused severe damage.

     Most descriptive adjectives are gradable, but some are not. Descriptive adjectives that are not gradable are called **absolute adjectives.** Here are some examples of absolute adjectives:

     the *main* idea
     a *wood* fence
     false teeth

Notice that we cannot use any of these adjectives with *very* or in the comparative and superlative forms:

Base:	*very main idea	*very wood fence	*very false teeth
Comparative:	*mainer/ *more main	*wooder/ *more wood	*falser/ *more false
Superlative:	*the mainest/ *the most main	*the woodest/ *the most wood	*the falsest/ *the most false

     Unlike gradable adjectives, absolute adjectives refer to properties that do not admit of any degree. An idea is either the main idea or it is not—some ideas are not "more main" than other ideas. Compare *main* with the gradable adjective *important*. There are degrees of being important. Some ideas are very important. Some ideas are more important than others, and one idea is the most important idea of all. In other words, gradable adjectives like *important* refer to properties that have degree—things can be more or less important. Absolute adjectives do not have degree. They are all or nothing, not more or less. As a result, they cannot be used with *very* or in the comparative and superlative forms, because the property to which they refer is absolute; either it is present or not—it cannot be there to a degree. Absolute adjectives are much more difficult to recognize as adjectives than gradable adjectives are because we cannot use absolute adjectives with *very* or put them into the comparative or superlative forms as we can with gradable adjectives.

Adjective Exercise #4: Identifying Absolute Adjectives _____

In the sentences below, all of the adjectives have been underlined. Underline absolute adjectives by underlining them a second time. Confirm your answer by showing that the base form cannot be used with *very* and that the comparative and superlative forms are also ungrammatical. The first question is done as an example. (Answers to this exercise are on page 394.)

0. I wore my best cotton shirt.

Answer: I wore my best cotton shirt.

*very cotton shirt; *more cotton shirt; *the most cotton shirt

1. They must think that I am a complete idiot.

2. We listed the chief reasons for going ahead with the project.

3. He finally got a full-time job at the plant.

4. The students finally found the correct answer to the problem.

5. My uncle raises giant pumpkins on his farm.

Let us now summarize what we know about adjectives. Adjectives are words that precede and modify nouns (and a few indefinite pronouns). There are two main classes of adjectives, determiners and descriptive adjectives. If a noun is modified by both classes, the determiner always precedes the descriptive adjectives. Determiners consist of five subclasses:

Articles: *the; a/an*
Demonstratives: *this, that, these, those*
Number words:
    Cardinal numbers: *one, two, three, . . .*
    Ordinal numbers: *first, second, third, . . .*
Possessives:
    Nouns: *John's, Mary's, . . .*
    Pronouns: *my, your, his, her, its, our, their*
Quantifiers: *some, much, many, several, . . .*

With a few exceptions, only one determiner can be used with each noun, whereas any number of descriptive adjectives can modify the same noun.

An important characteristic of descriptive adjectives is that most of them are gradable, which means that an adjective can be used with *very* in the base form, or it can be put into the comparative and superlative forms. The comparative form is either *-er* or *more;* the superlative form is either *-est* or *most.* A quick way to identify gradable adjectives is the *very* test.

Not all descriptive adjectives are gradable. Descriptive adjectives that cannot be used with *very* in the base form or that cannot be put into the comparative and superlative forms are called absolute adjectives.

Adjective Exercise #5: Identifying Nouns and Modifying Adjectives

In the following sentences, underline all nouns and pronouns twice and their modifying adjectives once. Remember, we can have nouns without modifying adjectives, but we can never have modifying adjectives without a noun. The first question is done as an example. (Answers to this exercise are on page 394.)

0. My dentist has some expensive new equipment.

   Answer: My dentist has some expensive new equipment.

1. His first book was about rural development in upstate New York.

2. The topic interested only a few specialists.

3. Eighteenth-century Latin grammar is the source of modern grammar.

4. The unexpected rainstorm completely ruined my new shoes.

5. A successful swindler often has polite manners.

6. The purchasing committee debated endlessly about the kind of computer.

7. His insulting behavior almost created a major diplomatic incident.

8. The possible junior partnership interested my sister.

9. Watson gave Holmes a far-fetched explanation of Lady Danforth's mysterious disappearance.

10. My cousin actually won a valuable prize in a publisher's sweepstake.

11. I made only one mistake, but it was a bad one.

12. Our new car gets poor mileage.

13. I'll have the roast chicken and a tossed salad.

14. The vacant lot was covered with countless unsightly, rank weeds.

15. A good salesperson can get by with a winning smile and pressed clothes.

16. The witness's confusing statement hindered the entire investigation.

17. That was my first consideration.

18. The committee was impressed by the candidate's broad knowledge.

19. A dozen people were packed into that old stationwagon.

20. We finally found the right key in a beat-up old dresser.

Pronouns

> **Traditional definition: A pronoun** is a word used in place of one or of more than one noun.

In this section we discuss four types of pronouns (the remaining two types, **interrogative** and **relative,** will be discussed in later sections). The four types are briefly introduced below, and then discussed in more detail.

Personal: *I, you, he, she, it, they, ...* Personal pronouns refer, obviously, to people.

Reflexive: *myself, himself, themselves, ...* Reflexive pronouns are personal pronouns that refer back to an antecedent. Reflexive pronouns always end in *-self* or *-selves.*

Indefinite: *anyone, all, few, somebody, ...* Indefinite pronouns refer to unspecified persons, things, or groups.

Demonstrative: *this, that, these, those.* Demonstrative pronouns refer to particular person(s) or thing(s).

Personal Pronouns

When people use the term *pronoun,* they are referring to personal pronouns, unless they specify otherwise. Personal pronouns are the most complex and important group of pronouns. Personal pronouns have many different forms depending on their **person, number,** and **form** (or **case**)

- Person: first person, second person, third person
  First person refers to the person(s) speaking (or writing).
  Second person refers to the person(s) being spoken (or written) to.
  Third person refers to the person(s) or thing(s) we are talking about.

  The third-person singular pronouns are further subdivided by **gender:**
  The **masculine** pronoun *he/him/his* refers to males.
  The **feminine** pronoun *she/her/hers* refers to females.
  The **neuter** pronoun *it/its* refers to objects or creatures of unknown gender.

- Number: singular, plural

- Form (or case): subject, object, possessive

  Subject pronouns are used as subjects of sentences. Here are some examples with various pronouns playing the role of subject:

  I know the answer.

  You know the answer.

  We know the answer.

  Object pronouns are used as objects of verbs and prepositions. Here are some examples with various pronouns playing the role of object of verbs:

  John saw *me.*

  John saw *us.*

  John saw *them.*

  Here are some examples of pronouns playing the role of objects of prepositions:

  John looked at *me.*

  John looked at *us.*

  John looked at *them.*

  Possessive pronouns occur in two different forms. One form is used as an adjective, the other is used by itself as a true pronoun. Here are some examples that illustrate the two different uses (adjectives underlined; pronouns in bold):

I got <u>my</u> book.	(*My* is an adjective that modifies the noun *book.*)
I got **mine.**	(*Mine* is a pronoun that stands for *my* book.)
<u>Their</u> books are gone.	(*Their* is an adjective that modifies *books.*)
Theirs are gone.	(*Theirs* is a pronoun that stands for *their* books.)
I found <u>your</u> book.	(*Your* is an adjective that modifies the noun *book.*)
I found **yours.**	(*Yours* is a pronoun that stands for *your* books.)

Pronoun Exercise #1: Use of Possessive Pronouns _____

In the following sentences, all the possessive pronouns have been underlined. Under each possessive pronoun, indicate whether it is being used as an adjective (Adj) or a pronoun (Pro). The first question is done as an example. (Answers to this exercise are on page 395.)

0. My dog is meaner than yours.

   Answer: My dog is meaner than yours.
          Adj   Pro

1. We left our car at home and took a taxi to their apartment.

2. His company is bigger than ours.

3. Our cat got its tail caught in the screen door.

4. Theirs is a highly unusual story.

5. Her house is about the same size as mine.

    The best way to represent the personal pronouns is in a chart organized around the three persons with form (case) on the left side of the chart and number across the top.

Personal Pronouns		
	Number	
Form (Case)	*Singular*	*Plural*
First-Person Pronouns		
Subject	I	we
Object	me	us
Possessive		
Used as adjective	my	our
Used as pronoun	mine	ours
Second-Person Pronouns		
Subject	you	you
Object	you	you
Possessive		
Used as adjective	your	your
Used as pronoun	yours	yours
Third-Person Pronouns		
Subject	he, she, it	they
Object	him, her, it	them
Possessive		
Used as adjective	his, her, its	their
Used as pronoun	his, hers, its	theirs

Pronoun Exercise #2: Identifying Personal Pronouns _____

In the following sentences, all the pronouns have been underlined. Under each pronoun, indicate its Person (1, 2, 3) Number (Sg, Pl), and Form (Sub, Obj, Pos). Assume that *you* is singular unless the context shows that it is plural. The first question is done as an example. (Answers to this exercise are on page 395.)

0. We saw them at the game.

Answer: We   saw them at the game.
      1-Pl-Sub   3-Pl-Obj

1. The high quality of the workshop surprised us.

2. Give me your address, will you? (Note: *your* is an adjective.)

3. We took the plants inside to keep them from freezing.

4. They gave it to him for his birthday.

5. I am a friend of hers.

6. We hope that you and your friends can join us this summer.

7. She took her roommate to see it last night.

8. Do you know where yours is?

9. It is up to you.

10. We only want what is ours.

Pronoun Exercise #3: Personal Pronoun Terminology _____

Fill in the correct missing pronouns. (1, 2, 3) indicates Person; (Sg, Pl) indicates Number, and (Sub, Obj, Pos) indicates Form. The gender of third-person pronouns is up to you. The first question is done as an example. (Answers to this exercise are on page 396.)

0. Didn't _____ meet _____ somewhere?
      1-Sg-Sub   3-Sg-Obj

Answer: Didn't ___I___ meet __her__ somewhere?
            1-Sg-Sub   3-Sg-Obj

1. Excuse _____ , that coat is _____ .
          1-Sg-Obj   1-Sg-Pos

2. _____ gave _____ the book back.
    3-Sg-Sub   3-Pl-Obj

3. _____ saw _____ at the movie last night.
    1-Pl-Sub   2-Sg-Obj

4. The cat left _____ on the porch.
                3-Sg-Obj

5. Give _____ to _____ .
        3-Pl-Obj   1-Sg-Obj

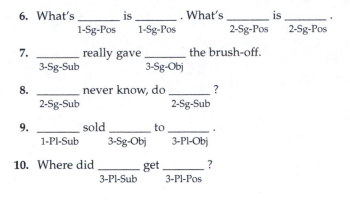

6. What's _____ is _____ . What's _____ is _____ .
      1-Sg-Pos   1-Sg-Pos   2-Sg-Pos   2-Sg-Pos

7. _____ really gave _____ the brush-off.
   3-Sg-Sub   3-Sg-Obj

8. _____ never know, do _____ ?
   2-Sg-Sub   2-Sg-Sub

9. _____ sold _____ to _____ .
   1-Pl-Sub   3-Sg-Obj   3-Pl-Obj

10. Where did _____ get _____ ?
                3-Pl-Sub   3-Pl-Pos

Choosing the right form of the personal pronoun can be tricky. For a detailed treatment, see "Pronoun Errors: *I/me; we/us; he/him; she/her; they/them*" in the Usage part.

Redefinition of Third-Person Pronouns.   The traditional definition of a pronoun as "a word used in place of one or of more than one noun" is misleading. Certainly, third-person pronouns CAN replace nouns, as in the following sentence, in which *she* replaces *Lois* and *him* replaces *Clark.*

> *Lois* saw *Clark* in a phone booth.
> *She*   *him*

The second part of the definition ("a word used in place of . . . more than one noun") refers to the fact that pronouns can replace **compound nouns** (two or more nouns joined by *and*). For example, in the following sentence, *they* replaces both *Lois* and *Clark:*

> *Lois and Clark* are both newspaper reporters on the *Daily Planet.*
> *They*

In many situations, however, a third-person pronoun does not actually replace a noun; it really replaces the noun *together with all of the noun's modifiers.* For example, consider the following sentence:

> The well-dressed young *woman* at the counter glanced into the mirror.

The third-person pronoun that replaces *woman* is *she.* If we took the traditional definition literally and replaced just the noun *woman* with *she,* we would create an ungrammatical sentence:

> *The well-dressed young *she* at the counter glanced into the mirror.

If we redefine third-person pronouns as replacing nouns *and all their modifiers*, then the result is grammatical:

> *The well-dressed young **woman** at the counter* glanced into the mirror.
> *She*

In this example, *she* replaces the noun *woman* and all its modifiers (*the well-dressed young* before the noun and *at the counter* after the noun)

We shall use the term **noun phrase** to refer to the noun and all its modifiers. In other words, third-person pronouns replace entire noun phrases. Within the noun phrase itself, the choice of number and gender of the third-person pronoun is dictated by the type of noun, as we can see in the following examples:

> *The well-dressed young **man** at the counter* glanced into the mirror.
> *He* (*He* is determined by *man*.)

> *The well-dressed young **woman** at the counter* glanced into the mirror.
> *She* (*She* is determined by *woman*.)

> *The well-dressed young **men** at the counter* glanced into the mirror.
> *They* (*They* is determined by *men*.)

> *The well-dressed young **women** at the counter* glanced into the mirrors.
> *They* (*They* is determined by *women*.)

> *The sleek new **car** in the driveway* belongs to my grandmother.
> *It* (*It* is determined by *car*.)

> *All the **cars** in the parking lot* need to be moved.
> *They* (*They* is determined by *cars*.)

As we mentioned briefly in the discussion of nouns in the previous section, pronoun substitution is the most reliable (albeit indirect) way to identify nouns. All nouns reside in noun phrases. All noun phrases can be identified by pronoun replacement. Thus, if a word (with or without modifiers) can be replaced by a pronoun, we have absolute proof that the word is a noun.

The pronoun replacement test for nouns. Whatever words are replaced by a third-person pronoun constitute a noun phrase. Whichever word WITHIN the noun phrase determines the form of the third-person pronoun is the noun.

The only problem with the noun replacement test is that it is not simple. What is replaced by the pronoun is not just the noun, it is the noun *together with all its modifiers.* Within the group of words that are replaced by the pronoun, we must also pick out which word is the noun, separating it from its modifiers. Fortunately, we are aided in this task by the fact that the choice of which third-person pronoun we use leads us directly to the noun that controls the pronoun. Here are some examples of the pronoun replacement test used to identify nouns.

In the following sentence, we can make these pronoun replacements:

> *The play* was *a big hit.*
>   It   it

The first *it* refers to *play* and the second *it* refers to *hit.* Therefore, *play* and *hit* are both nouns in this sentence.

In the following sentence, we can make these pronoun replacements:

> *The sober and hard-working students* answered *the professor's difficult question.*
>   They   it

The pronoun *they* replaces the entire noun phrase. Within the noun phrase, *they* can only refer to *students.* The pronoun *it* replaces the entire noun phrase. Within the noun phrase, *it* can only refer to *question.* Therefore, *students* and *question* are both nouns in this sentence.

Here is an example in which we attempt to apply the pronoun substitution test to a word that is not a noun:

> The students often *question* the professor.

In the previous example, *question* was a noun. How can we show that *question* is not a noun in this example? If *question* were a noun, the pronoun replacement test would have to be valid, but of course it is not:

> The students often *question* the professor.
>   *it

Since the pronoun replacement test fails, we know that *question* is not part of a noun phrase and thus cannot be a noun in this sentence.

Pronoun Exercise #4: Identifying Nouns by the Pronoun Replacement Test _____

Underline noun phrases once and nouns twice. Confirm your answer by the pronoun replacement test. The first question is done as an example. (Answers to this exercise are on page 396.)

0. The children were out flying big colorful kites.

    Answer: The <u>children</u> were out flying <u>big colorful</u> <u>kites</u>.

    Confirmation: They   them

1. The commander postponed the planned attack.

2. The obnoxious waiter finally brought our tepid dinners.

3. The French language is even more difficult to spell than English is.

4. The old bridges were badly in need of extensive repair.

5. The busy tugboats pushed the liner into its appointed berth.

6. The chill November rain never seemed to let up.

7. The overworked teacher couldn't correct any more student essays.

8. The day was turning out to be fine after all.

9. The driver took the passengers back to their hotel.

10. My hands and feet were absolutely frozen.

11. We had tuna sandwiches for our lunch.

12. The museum guards were in dark gray uniforms.

13. A 200% mark-up seemed excessive.

14. With any luck the meeting will be over soon.

15. The children had very bad sore throats.

16. The garage replaced the left front wheel.

17. The upper trail leads to some very nice lakes.

18. The hiring committee will be conducting several interviews.

19. Over the weekend, my parents stayed with my aunt and uncle.

20. According to my grandfather, nobody's property was safe while the legislature was in session.

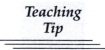

Teaching
Tip

The pronoun replacement test is one of the most important tests in the book. As we will see in later chapters, we can use the pronoun replacement test to identify some very complex constructions that would otherwise be very difficult to recognize as nouns.

Reflexive Pronouns

Reflexive pronouns are personal pronouns that refer back to an **antecedent,** which defines to whom or what the reflexive pronoun refers. In other words, reflexive pronouns do not have an independent meaning. They take their meaning from a noun or pronoun used earlier in the sentence. Usually (but not always) the antecedent is the subject. For example, compare the following two sentences:

John saw *him* in the mirror.

John saw *himself* in the mirror.

In the first sentence, *him* is a personal pronoun with its own meaning. *Him* cannot refer to *John;* it can only refer to someone else not named in this sentence. In the second sentence, *himself* is a reflexive pronoun that must refer back to and take its meaning from its antecedent, the subject *John* in this sentence.

Reflexive pronouns always end in *-self* (singular) or *-selves* (plural). The eight reflexive pronouns are:

First Person
    Singular: *myself*
    Plural: *ourselves*

Second Person
    Singular: *yourself*
    Plural: *yourselves*

Third Person
    Singular: *himself, herself, itself*
    Plural: *themselves*

Reflexive pronouns must always agree with their antecedent in number (singular/plural) and gender (masculine, feminine, or neuter). If reflexive pronouns do not agree with their antecedents, the results are outlandish:

*John cut *herself.*

*They bought *itself* a present.

*We found *themselves* in a difficult situation.

Pronoun Exercise #5: Using Reflexive Pronouns _____

In the following sentences, the subject(s) are in bold. Insert the proper reflexive pronoun in the space provided. The first question is done as an example. (Answers to this exercise are on page 397.)

0. The new **couple** introduced _____ .

    Answer: The new **couple** introduced __themselves__ .

1. Be careful, **you** will hurt _____ .

2. **We** entered _____ in a drawing.

3. The **propeller** tangled _____ in some weeds along the bank.

4. My **aunt and uncle** had _____ painted by a well-known local artist.

5. I talked _____ into taking a course in astrophysics.

The key to using reflexive pronouns correctly is to be sure that there are proper antecedents *in the same sentence*. Reflexive pronouns differ in this respect from third-person personal pronouns (*he, she, it, they*). Third-person pronouns can have antecedents in other sentences, but reflexive pronouns cannot. For example, compare the use of *she* and *herself* in the following sentences:

> Susan called the office. *She* was not feeling well.

> Susan called the office. **Herself* was not feeling well.

Herself is ungrammatical because its antecedent is in a different sentence.

There is no requirement that the antecedent be the subject of the sentence, though it usually is. Here is an example in which the antecedent is the object of a verb:

> Mary told John to help *himself* to some dessert.

Obviously, the antecedent of *himself* is *John*, not the subject *Mary*.

Pronoun Exercise #6: Identifying Reflexive Pronouns and Their Antecedents _____

Underline reflexive pronouns once and their antecedents twice. The first question is done as an example. (Answers to this exercise are on page 398.)

0. Dorothy told Toto to behave himself.

   Answer: Dorothy told Toto to behave himself.

1. The driveway curved back on itself.

2. Because of a potential conflict of interest, the judge excused herself.

3. Several skiers injured themselves badly on the icy slope.

4. Thelma told Louise to assert herself.

5. We didn't want to compete against ourselves.

6. Sam told Effie to address the letter to herself.

7. Stan and Ollie got themselves into another fine mess.

8. The constant racket forced us to keep repeating ourselves.

9. Miss Manners helped her improve herself.

10. The clerk told John to help himself.

11. TRICK QUESTION: What is the antecedent of *yourself/yourselves* in commands like the following?

    Behave yourself!

    Give yourselves up!

    Be true to yourself!

Reflexive Pronouns Used for Emphasis.   Normally we use reflexive pronouns as objects of verbs or as objects of prepositions:

> Object of verb: Fred cut *himself*.
> Object of Preposition: Fred was talking to *himself*.

Occasionally, however, we use reflexive pronouns in a very different way—for emphasis, as in the following sentences:

> I wouldn't kiss Miss Piggy *myself*.

> Miss Piggy *herself* will open the shopping mall.

This special use of reflexive pronouns for emphasis (called *emphatic* or *intensive* pronouns) is easy to recognize: since these pronouns are added only for emphasis, they can be deleted or moved around without affecting the grammaticality of the sentence, as in the following examples.

> Reflexive pronoun deleted:

> > I wouldn't kiss Miss Piggy ~~myself~~.

> > Miss Piggy ~~herself~~ will open the shopping mall.

> Reflexive pronoun moved:

> > I *myself* wouldn't kiss Miss Piggy.

> > Miss Piggy will open the shopping mall *herself*.

Naturally, when we try to delete or move a reflexive pronoun that is the object of a verb or preposition, the result will always be completely ungrammatical, because the resulting sentence will be missing an object:

> Reflexive pronoun deleted:

> > Object of verb: *Fred cut ~~himself~~.

> > Object of Preposition: *Fred was talking to ~~himself~~.

Reflexive pronoun moved:

Object of verb: *Fred himself cut.

Object of Preposition: *Fred himself was talking to.

Pronoun Exercise #7: Identifying Emphatic (Intensive) Reflexive Pronouns _____

Label the underlined emphatic reflexive pronouns by writing EMPH under them. Identify object reflexive pronouns by writing OBJ under them. Confirm your answers by trying to delete or move the reflexive pronouns. The first question is done as an example. (Answers to this exercise are on page 398.)

0. He wouldn't know the difference <u>himself</u>.

Answer: He wouldn't know the difference ~~himself.~~
                                       EMPH

Confirmation: He <u>himself</u> wouldn't know the difference.

1. The defeated rebels eventually turned on <u>themselves</u>.

2. The defeated rebels eventually acknowledged defeat <u>themselves</u>.

3. I saw <u>myself</u> in the play.

4. I <u>myself</u> know that I can make mistakes.

5. Finally, we can only depend on <u>ourselves</u>.

6. We finally talked <u>ourselves</u> into doing it.

7. You gave it to me <u>yourself</u>!

8. Dorothy <u>herself</u> did not believe in witches.

9. The vice president cast the deciding vote <u>himself</u>.

10. I locked <u>myself</u> out of my room.

Indefinite Pronouns

Indefinite pronouns refer to unspecified persons, things, or groups. Here are some common indefinite pronouns:

all	many	one
another	more	other
both	most	several
each	much	some
either	neither	such
few	none	

One group of indefinite pronouns are compounds of *any, every, no,* and *some* followed by *-body, -one,* and *-thing:*

	-body	-one	-thing
any	anybody	anyone	anything
every	everybody	everyone	everything
no	nobody	no one	nothing
some	somebody	someone	something

(Note the spelling of the compound *no one.* All of the other compound indefinite pronouns are written without a space between the words. In British spelling, the term is often hyphenated: *no-one.*)

Many of the words in the first group of indefinite pronouns (the non-compounded ones) can also be used as adjectives. For example, compare the use of *most* in the following sentences:

Most people find Watson slightly comical.

Most find Watson slightly comical.

In the first sentence, *most* is used as an adjective modifying the noun *people.* In the second sentence, *most* is used by itself as an indefinite pronoun.

Pronoun Exercise #8: Distinguishing Indefinite Pronouns from Adjectives

Underline adjectives and indefinite pronouns. Label adjectives ADJ and indefinite pronouns PRO. The first question is done as an example. (Answers to this exercise are on page 399.)

   0. <u>Many</u> people don't have <u>any</u>.

       Answer: <u>Many</u> people don't have <u>any</u>.
              ADJ   PRO

   1. All packages must be checked at the desk.

   2. Many are called, but few are chosen.

   3. Some people do not know how lucky they are.

   4. I wanted to get another box, but they didn't have one.

   5. Neither one was what I wanted.

   6. Please get me another.

   7. I don't get any respect.

   8. Few passenger trains stop here anymore.

9. Most are just freight trains.

10. All calls are routed to the secretary.

Demonstrative Pronouns

Demonstrative pronouns are a small, closed class consisting only of the following words: *this, that, these, those*. As with indefinite pronouns, the problem is distinguishing these same words used as adjectives. For example, compare the two uses of *that* in the following sentences:

> I wanted to buy *that* book.

> I wanted to buy *that*.

In the first sentence, *that is* an adjective modifying the noun *book*. In the second sentence, *that* is a demonstrative pronoun replacing the noun *book*.

Pronoun Exercise #9: Distinguishing Demonstrative Pronouns from Adjectives _____

This, that, these, and *those* are underlined. Label adjectives ADJ and demonstrative pronouns PRO. The first question is done as an example. (Answers to this exercise are on page 399.)

0. Those are the ones that I wanted.
   Answer: <u>Those</u> are the ones that I wanted.
        PRO

1. I didn't agree to do <u>that</u>.

2. <u>Those</u> cookies are getting stale.

3. I would like to buy <u>this</u> one.

4. Is <u>this</u> the face that launched a thousand ships?

5. <u>These</u> are the times that try men's souls.

6. Do you want <u>this</u> one or <u>that</u> one?

7. <u>These</u> pencils all need sharpening.

8. <u>That</u> is what you think!

9. <u>Those</u> questions were certainly hard.

10. Did you get answers to <u>these</u>?

We have now covered four classes of pronouns: personal, reflexive, indefinite, and demonstrative. By far the biggest problem in identifying pronouns

is distinguishing pronouns from the same words used as adjectives. Possessive personal pronouns, certain indefinite pronouns, and all demonstrative
pronouns can be distinguished from the same words used as adjectives by
paying attention to how they are used in the sentence. If the words stand alone
as subjects or objects, they are pronouns. If the same words are used to modify nouns (or occasionally indefinite pronouns), they are adjectives.

Pronoun Exercise #10: Identifying Pronouns _____

Underline all the pronouns in the following sentences. Identify the type of pronoun
above each one. Use PERS for personal pronouns, REFL for reflexive pronouns, INDEF
for indefinite pronouns, and DEMON for demonstrative pronouns. Be careful of the
same words used as adjectives. The first question is done as an example. (Answers
to this exercise are on page 400.)

0. Please, I would rather do it myself.

   Answer: Please, <u>I</u> would rather do <u>it</u> <u>myself</u>.
         PERS   PERS REFL

1. <u>He</u> asked about <u>that</u>.
    PERS   DEM
2. One for <u>all</u> and <u>all</u> for one.
3. Are <u>you</u> sure about <u>your</u> answers?
        P   POS
4. <u>Her</u> choice of words surprised <u>us</u>.
    POS   P
5. <u>I</u> wouldn't go to that movie if <u>it</u> were the last one on earth.
6. <u>Nobody</u> knows the trouble <u>I</u> have seen.
7. <u>That</u> contraption of <u>yours</u> will never get off the ground, Wilbur.
8. Can <u>we</u> get <u>you</u> <u>anything</u> at the store?
9. Another victory like <u>that</u> and <u>we</u> are done for.
10. Would <u>you</u> like another one?
11. <u>He</u> is a friend of her sister.
12. <u>They</u> are friends of <u>ours</u>.
13. <u>Someone</u> took <u>all</u> of the clean cups.
14. <u>All</u> the clean cups are over there.
15. <u>Your</u> logic is impeccable, but <u>it</u> is despicable.
16. No one knows that <u>they</u> did <u>it</u>.
17. <u>His</u> friends are not very realistic about those things.
18. <u>We</u> don't have much food left in that container.

19. I would like these to go, please.

20. Much of that egg is perfectly good.

Verbs

Traditional definition: A verb is a word used to express action or otherwise helps to make a statement.

The traditional definition identifies two classes of verbs: (1) verbs "used to express action" (**action verbs**), and (2) verbs that "otherwise help to make a statement" (**linking verbs**). There are only a relative handful of linking verbs (compared to the thousands of action verbs), but some of the linking verbs (such as *be*) are among the most frequent in English. Below are some short sentences that illustrate the two types of verbs.

Action Verbs	*Linking Verbs*
Fred *found* his folder.	Sam *is* silly.
Rudolph *wrote* a riddle.	The soup *smells* good.
Sally *scorched* her skirt.	Larry *looks* upset.

As you can see, the verbs in the Action column convey some action in which the subject was engaged: the subjects were variously finding, writing, and scorching things. The verbs in the Linking column, however, do not convey any activity on the part of the subject: Sam is not doing silly; the soup is not doing the smelling, and Larry is not doing the looking. Instead, all these verbs help DESCRIBE the subject—they help tell us something about Sam, the soup, and Larry.

In this chapter, however, we will ignore the difference between action and linking verbs. From the part-of-speech classification point of view, a verb is a verb is a verb. The tests we develop for recognizing verbs make no distinction between action and linking verbs. (When we get to Chapter 3, the distinction between the two classes of verbs will be very important.)

The defining characteristic of ALL verbs is that they must be capable of being used in the three verb **tenses: present, past,** and **future.** That is, every verb has three tense forms: a present tense form, a past tense form, and a future tense form. If a word cannot be used in these forms, it cannot be a verb. Here are two examples, one using the regular verb *answer,* and one using the irregular verb *tell.*

Present: Alfred *answers* the phone in the mornings.
              Terry always *tells* the truth.

Past:	Alfred *answered* the phone.
	Terry *told* the truth.
Future:	Alfred *will answer* the phone tomorrow.
	Terry *will tell* the truth.

We will now discuss each of the three tense forms in more detail. (The meanings of the various tenses will be discussed in Chapter 4.)

Present Tense

The present tense has a distinct *-(e)s* ending. However, this ending is used ONLY when the subject is one of the three third-person singular pronouns *he, she, it,* OR the subject is a noun that can be replaced by a third-person singular pronoun (which amounts to the same thing). For example:

John always **answers** every question
 He

John always **tells** the truth.
 He

Alice **answers** the phone in the afternoons.
 She

Alice **tells** us when it is time to go.
 She

The machine **answers** all calls.
     It

The gauge on the left **tells** the pressure.
          It

The form of the third-person singular verb is quite regular, with only the following exceptions:

Verb	*Irregular Third-Person Singular Form*
be	*is*
do	*does* (rhymes with *buzz,* not *booze* as one would expect)
have	*has*
say	*says* (rhymes with *fez,* not *phase* as one would expect)

When the subject is not a third-person singular pronoun (or a noun that can be replaced by a third-person singular pronoun), the present tense has no distinctive form—it is the same as the **base form** of the verb. The base form of a verb is also called the **dictionary form,** because that is the form under which it would be listed in the dictionary. For example, if you were to look up *went* in the dictionary, it would refer you to the base form *go.* Likewise, *be* is the base form of *am, is, are, was, were.*

Here are the remaining personal pronouns used with *answer* and *tell.* Note that the verbs are in the base form—they have no distinctive form or endings that can help us identify them as verbs.

First-person singular:	I **answer** the phone in the mornings. I always **tell** the truth.
Second-person singular:	You **answer** the phone in the mornings. You always **tell** the truth.
First-person plural:	We **answer** the phone in the mornings. We always **tell** the truth.
Second-person plural:	You **answer** the phone in the mornings. You always **tell** the truth.
Third-person plural:	They **answer** the phone in the mornings. They always **tell** the truth.

For historical reasons, the verb *be* is quite irregular in the present. It is the only verb whose base form is completely unrelated to the present-tense forms:

Base Form	*Present-Tense Forms*
be	I **am**
	you **are**
	he, she it **is**
	we **are**
	you (plural) **are**
	they **are**

Past Tense

There are two different types of past-tense forms: **regular** and **irregular.** The **regular** verbs form their past tense by adding *-(e)d* to the base form:

Base Form	*Past-Tense Form*
pass	passed
cough	coughed
dread	dreaded
roll	rolled
smile	smiled
turn	turned

Originally, all **irregular** verbs formed their past tenses by changing their vowels. A number of verbs still preserve this ancient way:

Base Form	Past-Tense Form
dig	dug
freeze	froze
ring	rang
run	ran
see	saw

At one time there were consistent patterns to the way the vowels shifted from present to past tense, but so many other changes have intervened that the vowel shifts are now a patchwork quilt of unpredictable changes.

Some verbs combine a vowel change with adding the regular ending *-d*:

Base Form	Past-Tense Form
flee	fled
hear	heard
say	said
sell	sold
tell	told

Some verbs have a vowel change and add a *-t*:

Base Form	Past-Tense Form
creep	crept
keep	kept
leave	left
sleep	slept
teach	taught
think	thought

Some one-syllable verbs that end in *-t* or *-d have* a past tense that is exactly the same as the present tense base form. For example, here is the verb *put* used first in the present tense and then in the past tense.

Present tense: I always *put* suntan lotion on when I go out.

Past tense: I *put* lotion on yesterday, but I still got burned.

Here are some more examples of verbs that follow this pattern:

Base Form	Past-Tense Form
bet	bet

cost	cost
rid	rid
shed	shed
shut	shut
wet	wet

The verb *have* adds *-d* in the past tense, but drops its final consonant: *have -had*.

There is even a verb whose past tense was actually taken from a completely unrelated word: *go—went*. (*Went* is related to *wander* and the now rare verb *wend*, as in *to wend one's way*.)

Be is the most irregular of all verbs in the past tense. It also has past-tense forms that are not related to the base form. In addition, it is the only verb that makes a singular/plural distinction in the past tense:

Base Form	*Past-Tense Forms*
be	I, you, he, she, it *was*
	we, you (plural), they *were*

Future Tense

Remarkably, the future tense is completely regular: it consists of the helping verb *will* plus the base form of the verb:

Base Form	*Future-Tense Form*
answer	will answer
bet	will bet
catch	will catch
do	will do
go	will go
see	will see
have	will have
be	will be

The fact that verbs and verbs alone have past and future tenses provides us with a simple and highly reliable test for verbs: change the tense of suspected words to the past or future. If the result is grammatical, we know that the words were indeed verbs. There is, of course, one catch: the sentence cannot otherwise change meaning. To see why this caveat is necessary, consider the word *chain* in the following sentences:

Noun: The *chain* is rusty.

Verb: We *chain* the dogs every night.

When we apply the tests to *chain* in the first sentence, the test radically changes the meaning, to the point of making the sentence ungrammatical:

Past tense:	*The *chained* is rusty.
Future tense:	*The *will chain* is rusty.

The reason, of course, is that *chain* in THIS sentence is not a verb.

When we apply the test to *chain* in the second sentence, the only change in the meaning is the predictable shift in the meaning of the tenses:

Past tense:	We *chained* the dogs every night.
Future tense:	We *will chain* the dogs every night.

These tests show that *chain* in this sentence is indeed a verb.

> **Tense-shift test for verbs:** Shift the word into either the past-tense or future-tense form. If the result is grammatical (and the meaning of the sentence has not been otherwise changed), then the word must be a verb.

The ability to recognize verbs is absolutely key to working out the grammar of sentences. The fact that only verbs can be shifted to the past or future tense provides an easy and completely reliable way to identify verbs. The importance of this test can hardly be overemphasized.

Verb Exercise #1: Identifying Verbs by Shifting Tense

Underline the verbs in the following sentences. Confirm your answer by shifting the verb to either past or future tense. The first question is done as an example. (Answers to this exercise are on page 401.)

0. The wheels slide into that groove.

   Answer: The wheels <u>slide</u> into that groove.

   Confirmation: Past: <u>slid</u>   Future: <u>will slide</u>

1. They score more points in the second half.   —d   will___

2. Critics characterize his plots as simplistic.   —d   will ___

3. The cookies have too much sugar in them.   had   will___

4. The rules generate a number of sentences.   -d   will___

5. South-bound trains usually depart from Platform 2.   -ed   will___

6. Red wines generally improve with age.   —d   will ___

7. Time and tide wait for no man.   *-ed*   *will* _____
8. They usually attain their goals on time.   *- ed*   *will*_____
9. The aches and pains persist for several days.   *-ed*   *will*_____
10. Crop rotation and good tilling habits reduce erosion.   *-d*   *will*_____
11. The rabbits need a lot of water and fresh food.   *- ed*   *will*_____
12. The sales people typically exaggerate about their successes.   *-ed*   *will* _____
13. The wines go well with the food.   *went*   *will* _____
14. Grammarians classify words by part of speech categories.   *-ied*   *will* __
15. Rolling stones gather no moss.   *-ed*   *will* _____

Adverbs

> **Traditional definition:** An *adverb* is a word used to modify a verb, an adjective, or another adverb.

The class of adverbs is large and very diverse. However, it is safe to say that if a word is a modifier but does not modify a noun (which only adjectives and other adjective structures can do), then it must be an adverb. In order of frequency, adverbs modify (1) verbs, (2) adjectives, and (3) other adverbs.

Adverbs That Modify Verbs

Adverbs that modify verbs have two distinctive features: (1) they answer **adverb questions**—questions beginning with *when, where, how, how often*, etc.; and (2) they are movable.

Adverbs that modify verbs tell us about the time, place, reason, manner, reason, frequency, etc., of the verb's action. A highly useful test for adverbs that modify verbs is to rephrase the sentence as a question that elicits the adverb as the answer.

> **The adverb question test:** If a word answers an adverb question (*when, where, how, how often*, etc.), then the word must be an adverb that modifies the verb.

Some examples of the different kinds of adverbs will make the technique clearer:

Time:	They unloaded the truck *yesterday*.
Adverb question:	**When** did they unload the truck?
Adverb answer:	*Yesterday*.

Since only adverbs of time can answer a *when* question, we know that *yesterday* must be an adverb of time.

Place:	They parked the truck *there*.
Adverb question:	**Where** did they park the truck?
Adverb answer:	*There.*

Since only adverbs of place can answer a *where* question, we know that *there* must be an adverb of place.

Manner:	They parked the truck *carefully*.
Adverb question:	**How** did they park the truck?
Adverb answer:	*Carefully.*

Adverbs of manner can answer *how* questions. (The *how* test is tricky because **predicate adjectives** can also answer *how* questions. For example, in the sentence *John is sick*, the word *sick* is a predicate adjective which also answers a question: *How is John? Answer: Sick.*)

Frequency:	They use the truck *occasionally*.
Adverb question:	**How often** do they use the truck?
Adverb answer:	*Occasionally.*

Because only adverbs of frequency can answer a *how often* question, we know that *occasionally* must be an adverb of frequency.

Adverb Exercise #1: Identifying Adverbs That Modify Verbs by the Adverb Question Test

Underline the adverbs that modify verbs in the following sentences. Confirm your answer by asking an adverb question to elicit the adverb as the answer. The first question is done as an example. (Answers to this exercise are on page 402.)

0. Watson hastily copied Holmes' secret message.
   Answer: Watson *hastily* copied Holmes' secret message.
   Adverb question: **How** did Watson copy Holmes' secret message?
   Adverb answer: Hastily.

1. The vet had examined the horse recently.

2. The ants were crawling everywhere.

3. He quickly unzipped the tent flap.

5. She answers all the questions correctly.

6. The operator will return your call soon.

7. They gradually became accustomed to the high altitude.

8. We rarely watch TV.

9. Leon invariably sleeps through his 8 o'clock class.

10. There will be a full moon tonight.

The second distinctive feature of adverbs that modify verbs is that these adverbs are movable. All other modifying words—all adjectives and all other types of adverbs—are locked in position next to the words they modify. The natural "home base" position for adverbs that modify verbs is at the end of the sentence. However, we can readily move most adverbs of this type to a position either in front of the verb or to the beginning of the sentence. Here are some examples:

Toto chased cats *frequently*.

Toto *frequently* chased cats.

Frequently, Toto chased cats.

Sam opened the door *cautiously*.

Sam *cautiously* opened the door.

Cautiously, Sam opened the door.

Alice opened the bottle *eagerly*.

Alice *eagerly* opened the bottle.

Eagerly, Alice opened the bottle.

A relatively easy test for adverbs that modify verbs is to see if the word in question can be moved to either of the other two adverb positions. Not all adverbs of this type can be moved, but if a word does move, we know for sure that it modifies the verb.

> **The adverb movement test:** If a word can be moved to a different position in the sentence, then the word must be an adverb that modifies the verb.

Note: not all adverb positions will sound equally good with all adverbs that modify the verb—some positions sound better than others. Accordingly, when you are testing an adverb for movement, try more than one possible position.

Adverb Exercise #2: Identifying Adverbs That Modify Verbs by the Adverb Movement Test _____

Underline the adverbs that modify verbs. Confirm your answer by moving the adverb to another position. The first question is done as an example. (Answers to this exercise are on page 403.)

   0. The waiter finally took our orders.

   Answer: The waiter <u>finally</u> took our orders.

   Confirmation: The waiter took our orders <u>finally</u>.

   <u>Finally</u>, the waiter took our orders.

   1. Toto is usually a good little dog.

   2. The teller carefully examined the signatures on the check.

   3. He reluctantly counted out the cash and gave it to me.

   4. They will twist in the wind slowly.

   5. The lawyer looked at the defendant knowingly.

   6. The bird repeatedly fluttered at his reflection in the window.

   7. We routinely check the files for errors.

   9. Magically the key opened the door.

   10. We will find out the truth ultimately.

*Teaching
Tip*

Neither of the tests for adverbs that modify verbs is perfect, but it would be a rare adverb that modifies a verb that completely failed both tests. So, if one adverb test does not give a clear answer, be sure to have students try the other one.

Adverbs That Modify Adjectives

Adjectives can only modify nouns; adjectives cannot modify other adjectives—only adverbs can do that. Here are some examples of adverbs (bold) modifying adjectives (underlined):

   a **completely** <u>false</u> idea
   a **very** <u>accurate</u> guess
   some **rather** <u>unusual</u> performances
   some **quite** <u>dangerous</u> weapons
   the **terribly** <u>hot</u> afternoon
   some **unusually** <u>good</u> results

As you can see from these examples, it is hard to tell adjectives and adverbs apart. Fortunately, there is a procedure that will distinguish them. Pair up each word in the noun phrase with the noun. Only adverbs will fail to match up with the noun.

> **The pair test for adverbs modifying adjectives:** If a word in a noun phrase CANNOT be paired up with the noun, then that word is an adverb modifying an adjective.

When we try to pair up an adverb with the noun, the results will always be ungrammatical. Here is an example:

It turned out to be a **completely** false idea.

Start with the noun *idea* and pair up each of the supposed modifiers, one by one, starting with the modifier nearest the noun.

> false idea
> *completely idea
> an idea (remember that the choice of *a* or *an* depends solely on whatever sound happens to begin the following word)

The pair test shows us that *false* and *a* are adjectives because they can directly and independently modify the noun *idea*. The pair test also shows us that *completely* cannot modify *idea* and thus cannot be an adjective. It is an adverb that must modify the adjective that follows it, *false* in this sentence. Adverbs that modify adjectives can never move away from the word they modify (unlike adverbs that modify verbs). Consequently, whatever adjective immediately follows the adverb is the only possible word that the adverb can modify.

Adverb Exercise #3: Identifying Adverbs That Modify Adjectives by the Pair Test

Underline all the modifying adjectives in the following sentences. Put ADV under any adverb that modifies an adjective. Confirm your answer by showing that the adverb cannot be paired up with the noun. The first question is done as an example. (Answers to this exercise are on page 403.)

0. Holmes offered Watson a crushingly logical explanation.

    Answer: Holmes offered Watson a **crushingly** logical explanation.
                                              ADV

Confirmation: *crushingly explanation

1. Their proposal brought a very swift response.

2. A day in the country was an extremely good plan.

3. They bought a quite beautiful old print.

4. Their first rafting trip had been a really terrifying experience.

5. The administration proposed a surprisingly bold diplomatic initiative.

6. I thought it was a very funny movie.

7. Donald memorized tediously long lists.

8. The perpetually damp British weather became depressing.

9. In an early story, an apparently naive young woman outwitted Holmes.

10. A good mystery writer makes us miss the obviously important facts.

Adverbs That Modify Other Adverbs

One of the most common situations in which one adverb modifies another is when an adverb modifying the verb is itself modified. Here is an example:

> They always answer their mail **very** <u>promptly</u>.

In this sentence, we can tell that the adverb *promptly* modifies the verb because it answers a *how* question: *How do they always answer their mail?* Answer: *Promptly.* The adverb *promptly* is in turn modified by the adverb *very*. Adverbs that modify other adverbs are locked into place. The only word they can modify is the word that immediately follows them. Thus, the only possible word that *very* can modify is the adverb *promptly*.

Adverb Exercise #4: Identifying Adverbs That Modify Other Adverbs

Underline all the adverbs in the following sentences. Put ADV under any adverb that modifies another adverb. The first question is done as an example. (Answers to this exercise are on page 404.)

0. We saw the movie rather recently.

   Answer: We saw the movie <u>rather</u> <u>recently</u>.
   ADV

1. We will be done pretty soon.

2. We played surprisingly well.

3. She talks so softly.

4. The changes have occurred somewhat irregularly.

5. Harvard fought rather fiercely.

Adverb Exercise #5: Identifying Adverbs _____

Underline all the adverbs in the following sentences. The first question is done as an example. (Answers to this exercise are on page 404.)

0. Tuesday, I went there early.

    Answer: Tuesday, I went there early.

1. The savagely stinging bugs nearly ruined our camping trip.

2. Unusually glib strangers naturally arouse our suspicions.

3. They nearly always come to see us afterwards.

4. Recently, we sent you our newly published report.

5. Nearly every reporter had filed a totally misleading story.

6. Too many cooks spoil the broth.

7. She smiled very sweetly.

8. Invariably Uncle Andrew makes a truly embarrassing speech.

9. The disgustingly dirty water eventually evaporated.

10. The unusually dry summer threatened many crops here.

11. The badly beaten army hastily withdrew from the field.

12. Unfortunately, I have to return there tonight.

13. The incredibly loud noise completely overwhelmed us.

14. Personally, I think she finally made a very good choice.

15. The unscheduled conference made us look foolish.

Prepositions

> **Traditional definition:** A **preposition** is a word that shows the relationship of a noun or a pronoun to some other word in the sentence.

Prepositions are "little words" such as *by, to, with, about, at, for,* etc. Prepositions occur only in larger structures called **prepositional phrases.** A prepositional phrase consists of a preposition plus its **object,** which must be a noun (and its modifiers, if any) or a pronoun. Here are some examples of prepositional phrases with the prepositions in bold and the preposition's object (either noun or pronoun) underlined:

> **in** the morning
> **after** class
> **by** Shakespeare
> **with** great difficulty
> **to** them

In traditional grammar, prepositional phrases are always modifiers. (In Chapter 7 we will see other uses of prepositional phrases in modern grammar.) If prepositional phrases modify nouns, they are called **adjective phrases.** If they modify verbs, adjectives, or other adverbs, they are called **adverb phrases.** Here are some examples of each type with the prepositional phrase underlined and the words they modify in bold.

Adjective phrase:	Please take the **cup** on the table.
	noun
Adverb phrase:	We will **see** each other in the morning.
	verb
	He is always **lucky** at cards.
	adjective
	We went to a movie **later** in the evening.
	adverb

In the traditional definition of prepositions given above, "a noun or a pronoun" refers to the object of the preposition. The "other word in the sentence" refers to the noun, verb, adjective, or adverb that the prepositional phrase modifies. For example, in the sentence

Please take the cup **on** the table.

the preposition *on* shows the relation between the noun *table* (the object of the preposition) and *cup,* the noun that the prepositional phrase modifies.

The reason the definition is so horribly convoluted is that the definition is trying to describe a phrase without using any of the terminology associated with phrases. From a teaching standpoint, it makes absolutely no sense to talk about prepositions at the single-word part-of-speech level because prepositions exist only as parts of prepositional PHRASES, and phrases are off-limits at the individual word-by-word, part-of-speech level. Either we need to interrupt teaching parts of speech and instead teach about phrases, or we need to explain briefly what prepositions are and then postpone further discussion until we get to the general discussion of what phrases are and how they work. The latter alternative makes much more sense pedagogically, and it is what we will do here. We will discuss prepositions as part of the discussion of prepositional phrases in Chapter 5, which focuses on phrases.

Conjunctions

Traditional definition: A **conjunction** joins words or groups of words.

There are two types of conjunctions: **coordinating conjunctions** and **subordinating conjunctions.** Coordinating conjunctions are words such as *and, but, or*, which join words and groups of words of EQUAL status. Subordinating conjunctions are used to join clauses of UNEQUAL status. Specifically, subordinating conjunctions join adverb subordinate clauses to main clauses. For example, in the sentence

I went to bed late **because** I had to study for a big test

because is a subordinating conjunction that joins the adverb subordinate clause *because I had to study for a big test* to the main clause *I went to bed late*. We will discuss subordinating conjunctions in Chapter 6, which discusses clauses.

There are seven coordinating conjunctions. A helpful acronym for remembering them is FANBOYS:

F for
A and
N nor
B but
O or
Y yet
S so

Six of the coordinating conjunctions can be used to join two sentences (or, more accurately, two **independent clauses**):

	for	
	and	
John loves Mary,	but	Fred loves Alicia.
	or	
	yet	
	so	

Nor can join sentences only if the first sentence is negative:

> <u>John does not love Mary,</u> **nor** <u>does Fred love Alicia.</u>

The conjunctions *and* and *or* are commonly used to join single words or groups of words that are less than a full sentence:

Words:
> <u>John</u> **and** <u>Mary</u> were asking about you.
> (two nouns)
> Gwendolyn <u>sings</u> **or** <u>dances.</u>
> (two verbs)
> The <u>boring</u> **and** <u>pointless</u> meeting lasted forever.
> (two adjectives)
> John terminated the interview <u>abruptly</u> **and** <u>rudely.</u>
> (two adverbs)

Groups of words:
> Melvin <u>read the book</u> **and** <u>saw the movie.</u>
> The reporters <u>took notes</u> **or** <u>made recordings.</u>

There is a subset of coordinating conjunctions called **correlative conjunctions.** Correlative conjunctions are two-part conjunctions. The most common correlative conjunctions used to join words and groups of words are *both . . . and; either . . . or; neither . . . nor;* and *not only . . . but also.* Here are some examples:

Words:
> John loves **both** <u>Mary</u> **and** <u>Alicia.</u>
> John loves **either** <u>Mary</u> **or** <u>Alicia.</u>
> John loves **neither** <u>Mary</u> **nor** <u>Alicia.</u>
> John loves **not only** <u>Mary</u> **but also** <u>Alicia.</u>

Groups of words:
> John turned on **both** <u>the TV</u> **and** <u>the radio.</u>
> The coach told me to **either** <u>practice harder</u> **or** <u>quit the team.</u>
> Without my car, I could **neither** <u>get to work</u> **nor** <u>go back home.</u>
> Marvin **not only** <u>missed the meeting</u> **but also** <u>the party later.</u>

Either . . . or and *not only . . . but also* can be used to join sentences:

> **Either** <u>I pay my rent,</u> **or** <u>I will have to find a new place.</u>
> **Not only** <u>was the movie stupid,</u> **but also** <u>it ran for three hours.</u>

Conjunction Exercise #1: Identifying Coordinating Conjunctions

Underline coordinating conjunctions twice; underline once the words, groups of words, or whole sentences that the conjunctions join. If there is a correlative conjunction, be sure to underline both elements twice. The first question is done as an example. (Answers to this exercise are on page 405.)

0. Ann's mother both planned the wedding and made up the guest list.

   Answer: Ann's mother <u>both</u> <u>planned the wedding</u> <u>and</u> <u>made up the guest list</u>.

1. We were tired, so we went home early.
2. This is either very good cheese or very bad meat.
3. I'm sure that he is OK, but I can't help worrying.
4. We got into the car and drove to the station.
5. Did you want coffee, tea, or milk?
6. Not only did Holmes fool Watson, but also he fooled Inspector Lestrade.
7. Thanks to careful planning and more than our share of good luck, we were successful.
8. John neither drinks nor watches daytime TV.
9. Either you give me my money back, or I will take you to court.
10. Unfortunately, I am neither rich nor famous.
11. They had better hurry, for the game is about to start.
12. He is either a fool or a knave.
13. Time and tide wait for no man.
14. It was getting late, so I decided to quit.
15. Either a Pepsi or a Coke is OK.

Review

Here is a summary of the six parts of speech covered in this chapter and some of the ways that we can recognize them.

Nouns

There are two types of nouns, common nouns and proper nouns. Proper nouns are the names of specific individuals and places. They are always capitalized. Some examples are *Uncle Charley* and *Rome*.

Common nouns are general names for categories of persons, places, things, or ideas. Some examples are *relative, city, applesauce, honesty.*

There are three tests for identifying common nouns.

The *Test.*   If a word can be modified by *the,* then that word must be a noun—for example, *the man, the idea, the flowers.* This test is highly reliable and quite easy to use, though there are a few abstract nouns that do not take *the: *the honesty, *the beauty.*

Plural *Test.*   If a word can be made plural, then that word must be a noun—for example, *cars, emergencies, repetitions.* This is an easy test to use, but it is not as helpful as the *the* test because many mass or noncount nouns cannot be used in the plural—for example: **airs, *milks, *thunders.*

Pronoun Replacement *Test.*   The pronoun replacement test is the definitive test for nouns. No noun can fail this test. The only catch is that the pronoun replaces the entire **noun phrase,** not just the noun. The noun phrase contains both the noun and all its modifiers. However, because the form of the pronoun (its number and gender) is determined solely by the noun, the noun is easy to identify within its noun phrase. For example:

Our first answer is often the best one.

>   *It* (*It* refers to *answer. Answer* must be a noun.)

Adjectives

Pair *Test.*   Modifying adjectives always precede the nouns they modify, so the simplest test is to pair up each adjective, one by one, with the noun it modifies. For example, in the phrase, *the suspicious old men,* each of the adjectives can be paired up with the noun *men: old men, suspicious men, the men.*

Very *Test.*   An additional test for descriptive adjectives (as opposed to determiners) is to see if the suspected adjective can be used with *very.* If it can be used with *very,* then it is probably a gradable adjective with comparative and superlative forms: v*ery old, older, oldest; very suspicious, more suspicious, most suspicious.*

Pronouns

Because pronouns are a closed class, we identify pronouns by simply knowing what words are members of the pronoun family. The biggest problem in identifying pronouns is confusing them with the same words used as modifying adjectives. Pronouns are not modifiers. Pronouns play the same role as nouns: they are subjects and objects of verbs or prepositions. Modifying adjectives always modify nouns. Here are some review sentences with the pronouns in bold and the same words used as modifying adjectives underlined:

John lost <u>his</u> book.
Jason found **his.**

<u>This</u> pencil belongs to Susan.
This belongs to Susan.

<u>Most</u> coats are in the hall closet.
Most are in the hall closet.

Verbs

Future-Tense Test.   Only verbs can occur in the future tense, so an easy and completely reliable test for verbs is to see if the word in question can be used in the future tense by adding the future-tense helping verb *will.* For example, we can prove that the word *question* in the following sentence is a verb by adding *will*:

The children question everything.

Test: The children *will* question everything.

Past-Tense Test.   The past-tense test is exactly like the future-tense test except that it shifts the word in question to the past tense rather than the future tense. The test works because only verbs have a past tense. This test may be hard to apply to a few highly irregular verbs such as *put,* whose past-tense form is identical to its present-tense form.

Of the two tests, the future-tense test is easier to use because we can add *will* without changing anything else in the sentence.

Adverbs

There are three different types of adverbs: (1) adverbs that modify verbs, (2) adverbs that modify adjectives, and (3) adverbs that modify other adverbs.

Adverbs That Modify Verbs
Adverb Question Test.   Adverbs that modify verbs answer *when, where, why,* and *how* questions. For example:

Jason went to Jasper *Wednesday.*

Adverb Question: **When** did Jason go to Jasper?
Adverb Answer: *Wednesday.*

Adverb Movement Test.   English is a fixed-word-order language. The only group of words that can be moved readily are adverbs that modify verbs. The fact that these adverbs can be shifted from one adverb position to another is a highly reliable test for this group—though not all adverbs sound equally good in all three positions. The three adverb positions are at the beginning of the sentence, before the verb, and at the end of the sentence—their normal "home base" position. For example, we can move the adverb *soon* from one adverb position to another readily:

> You will receive an offer *soon.*

> You will *soon* receive an offer.

> *Soon,* you will receive an offer.

Adverbs That Modify Adjectives
Pair Test.   Adverbs that modify adjectives are not movable and do not answer any adverb question except *how.* These adverbs are likely to be overlooked because they can occur in the middle of a string of adjectives that modify a noun. For this reason, it is very important to use the pair test in which each word is paired up with the noun. One of the great benefits of using this test is that it also helps identify adverbs that modify adjectives. Here is an example:

> It was *a remarkably unpleasant experience.*

When we pair up each word with the noun *experience,* we see that *remarkably* cannot modify *experience. Remarkably* is thus an adverb that modifies the adjective *unpleasant.*

Adverbs That Modify Other Adverbs.   Like adverbs that modify adjectives, adverbs that modify other adverbs are not movable and do not answer any adverb question except *how.* Because only adverbs can modify another adverb, these adverbs are not difficult to identify.

Conjunctions

The coordinating conjunctions are a closed class. An easy way to remember them is the FANBOYS acronym. The correlative conjunctions also need to be learned. The four most common ones are *both . . . and; either . . . or; neither . . . nor; not only . . . but also;.*

Review Exercise #1: Identifying Parts of Speech _____

Write the part of speech below each word. Use N for nouns, P for pronouns, Adj for adjectives, V for verbs, Adv for adverbs, C for conjunctions. The first question is done as an example. (Answers to this exercise are on page 405.)

0. The new mystery baffled both the local police and Scotland Yard.
   Answer: The new mystery baffled both the local police and <u>Scotland Yard</u>.
         Adj Adj   N   V   C   Adj Adj   N   C   N

1. Almost all professional writers keep a daily journal.

2. The FDA carefully evaluated the new drug.

3. They rebuilt the old gym and completely restored the chemistry lab.

4. Holmes finally located the missing gun and incriminating letters.

5. The plane circled the field and then landed smoothly.

6. The Constitution protects free speech.

7. Count Dracula appreciated her friendly attitude and unlocked windows.

8. A new conductor led the orchestra today.

9. Unfortunately, the tuba player had a bad cold and missed some notes.

10. I always have a good time there.

11. The waitress pocketed the tip and smiled politely.

12. John came home late last Thursday.

13. The cleaner nearly ruined my blue sweater.

14. The class passed the examination easily.

15. Fortunately, every dark cloud has a silver lining.

16. Our cat loves fresh fish or old catfood.

17. My mother loudly announced our engagement

18. Every graduate faces a frightening and thrilling new beginning.

19. Theirs was a very odd but happy marriage.

20. The black jacket is mine.

Review Exercise #2: Identifying Parts of Speech _____

Write the part of speech below each word. Use N for nouns; P for pronouns, Adj for adjectives, V for verbs, Adv for adverbs, C for conjunctions. The first question is done as an example. (Answers to this exercise are on page 406.)

0. I answered the first seven questions easily but missed the problem.
   Answer: I answered the first seven questions easily but missed the problem.
           P   V   Adj Adj Adj   N   Adv   C   V   Adj   N

1. The reporters interviewed the rookie cop and the witnesses.

2. Jason missed the bus again today.

3. The commission certainly expected a more favorable outcome.

4. Holmes always quizzed Watson and Inspector Lestrade unmercifully.

5. Godzilla ordered the poached fish and artichokes.

6. Sally sold Sarah and Susan some sardine sandwiches.

7. Both John and I completed the final project.

8. You left your coat.

9. Very few detectives resemble Sam Spade.

10. Only the brave deserve the fair.

11. The company hired too many consultants and outside experts.

12. I finally found my book, but Ralph lost his.

13. I caught the first ball, but missed the second.

14. He gave himself a truly awful haircut.

15. His carelessness nearly caused a serious accident.

16. Superman leapt pretty tall buildings.

17. The police finally arrested Bugsy.

18. They replaced the cracked and broken windows.

19. The basketball coach picked only the tallest players.

20. The outcome was amazing.

3

Basic Sentences and Their Diagrams

In Chapter 3 we will see how the parts of speech described in Chapter 2 are used together to form the basic sentence. We will then see how traditional diagramming can be used to draw a picture of how words fit together in a sentence.

Defining Sentence

what separates it from clauses

The traditional definition of sentence has two parts: (1) a sentence is a group of words expressing a complete thought, and (2) a sentence consists of a **subject** and a **predicate.** These two parts are complementary to each other because they focus on different aspects of what a sentence is. Part (1) defines sentence by its meaning, part (2) defines sentence by its structure. Part (2) is really incomplete without part (1). We will look at each part in turn.

1. A Sentence Is a Group of Words Expressing a Complete Thought.

The key to the first part of the definition is the term *complete.* **Complete** means that a sentence must be able to stand alone as a fully formed idea, not dependent on some previous context or understood sentence to fill significant missing pieces. For example,

> I would like a pizza with anchovies and pineapple.

is a complete sentence because it can stand alone as a complete idea. Compare that sentence with the following dialog:

> Waiter: What would you like?
> Customer: A pizza with anchovies and pineapple.

71

What the customer said is a **fragment.** A fragment is a piece of a sentence used or punctuated as though it were a complete sentence. The customer's answer is a complete thought in a way, but ONLY in the context of the waiter's question. It is a fragment because it cannot stand alone, without building on the waiter's question. The customer's answer is a typical fragment—a group of words that is meaningful only in reference to a previous context or understood sentence. (See **fragments** in the Usage part for a detailed discussion of the causes and treatment of fragments.)

All language is based on our ability to use and recognize sentences. In fact, our sense of "sentence-ness" is so strong that the biggest problem students have in identifying fragments is that they unconsciously provide some context or imaginary dialog to make the fragments into meaningful complete sentences. For example, a student might identify the fragment

   as soon as I can   .

as a complete sentence because she is supplying an understood question, such as

   When do you want to leave?

in order to make the fragment into a meaningful (and complete) sentence:

   (I want to leave) as soon as I can.

When students supply a context, they are using their intuitive knowledge of language to make communicative sense out of fragments. Their "mistake" is to do what all speakers of a language must do—supply a context to make sense of the language they encounter. Their "mistake" does not mean that they cannot tell fragments from complete sentences; their "mistake" means only that they do not understand the rules of the game for consciously distinguishing fragments and complete sentences. In the grammar game, for a group of words to be a complete sentence, the group of words cannot depend on some understood context or previous sentence to be meaningful. The group of words must be able to stand alone, in complete isolation.

Here is a particularly useful test for helping students isolate groups of words from understood contexts or previous sentences to see if they can really stand alone as complete sentences. To see if a group of words can really stand alone, put *I know that* in front of the words. For example, it is much easier to isolate

   as soon as I can

and see that it is a fragment when it is embedded inside a sentence following *I know that:*

   *I know that *as soon as I can.*

> **The *I know that* test for complete sentences.** If a group of words can be used correctly after *I know that* to make a new grammatical sentence, then that group of words must be a complete sentence.

Only complete sentences can be used correctly after *I know that.* However, to make the test work, students must be sure to use all three words, not just *I know.* As long as they are careful to include *that,* the test is easy to use and quite reliable. There are, of course, some catches. The test works only with statements. The test cannot be used with questions and commands. "Are you ready?" is a complete question, but because it is not a statement, it cannot be used with *I know that:* *"I know that are you ready?" Likewise, "Go away!" is a complete command, but because it is not a statement, it cannot be used with *I know that:* *"I know that go away!" Except for these two types of sentences, the *I know that* test is very reliable for statements.

Here are some examples of the *I know that* test. The first group of three are fragments, and the second group of three are all complete sentences.

- Fragments:
  Whatever you want
  OK by me
  When the Christmas rush is over
- Complete sentences:
  The party is over
  You left
  She knows the answer

Applying the *I know that* test:

   *I know that *whatever you want* (fragment)

   *I know that *OK by me* (fragment)

   *I know that *when the Christmas rush is over* (fragment)

   I know that *the party is over.* (complete sentence)

   I know that *you left.* (complete sentence)

   I know that *she knows the answer.* (complete sentence)

Sentence Exercise #1: Using the I know that Test to Distinguish Fragments and Complete Sentences _____

Determine which of the following groups of words are fragments and which are complete sentences by means of the *I know that* test. The first question is done as an example. (Answers to this exercise are on page 408.)

0. After the party
   Answer: Fragment
   I know that test: *I know that <u>after the party</u>.

1. Whatever you say

2. We were completely confused

3. On top of old smoky

4. More or less

5. Not a chance

6. I will go if you can

7. I couldn't believe it

8. Last evening when you called

9. He doesn't have a clue

10. At the office

2. A Sentence Contains a Subject and a Predicate.

The second half of the definition of a sentence is that a sentence consists of two parts: a **subject** and a **predicate**. This part of the definition is not based on meaning, as the first part was. The second part is based on the grammatical form that a group of words has to have in order to be a sentence. For a group of words to be a sentence, there must be both a subject and a predicate. For example, each of the following minimal sentences consists of just two words, a subject and a predicate:

> Fish swim.
>
> Birds fly.
>
> Teenagers sleep.

Obviously there is more to it than this. First we will discuss the subject and then turn to the much more complex topic of the predicate.

Subject

We must make a distinction between two meanings of the term *subject:* **simple subject** and **complete subject.** The distinction between the two meanings of *subject* is easy to make, as the following examples illustrate. The simple subjects are in bold, the complete subjects are underlined.

The **trucks** in the right lane slowed down.

The old **man** caught a big fish.

A rolling **stone** gathers no moss.

Recently, my **dog** went to the vet.

As you can see, **the simple subject is the subject noun (or pronoun),** and **the complete subject is the simple subject together with all its modifiers.**

Teaching
Tip

Be careful when using the term *subject*, because it is inherently ambiguous: it can refer to either the simple subject or the complete subject. Whenever you or your students are talking about subjects, be sure that it is clear which use of the term is meant.

You may have noticed that what we call a "complete subject" in Chapter 3 is what we called a "noun phrase" in Chapter 2. A noun phrase is a noun together with all its modifiers. A complete subject consists of a subject noun and all that noun's modifiers—exactly the same thing. Clearly, with the distinction between simple and complete subject, traditional grammar has developed the concept of a noun phrase, but strangely enough, it does not extend the concept beyond the subject. In traditional grammar, we do not talk about a simple and complete object, though the relationships are exactly the same.

You may recall from Chapter 2 that third-person pronouns replace nouns and all their modifiers. In fact, the best test for nouns depends on the fact that pronouns replace nouns (and their modifiers):

The pronoun replacement test for nouns. Whatever words are replaced by a third-person pronoun constitute a noun phrase. Whichever word WITHIN the noun phrase determines the form of the third-person pronoun is the noun.

Using the terminology of Chapter 3, we can say that third-person pronouns replace complete subjects:

The **trucks** in the right lane slowed down.
    They

The old **man** caught a big fish.
    He

A rolling **stone** gathers no moss.
                It

Recently, <u>my **dog**</u> went to the vet.
                    she

Note that in the last example, the pronoun *she* does not replace *recently* because *recently* is not actually part of the complete subject. It is an adverb that belongs to the predicate. This last example illustrates how useful the third-person pronoun is for identifying the complete subject: the complete subject is all of the words (and **ONLY** those words) that a third-person subject pronoun replaces.

The substitution of third-person pronouns also gives us another important piece of information. Recall from Chapter 2 that the actual form of the third-person pronoun (its number, gender, and case form) is determined by the noun it replaces. In the terminology of Chapter 3, the noun that determines the number and gender of the subject pronoun is the simple subject. In other words, the simple subject determines the form of the pronoun that replaces the complete subject. In the examples given above, *trucks* determines that we must use the plural pronoun *they*. *Man* determines that we must use the masculine singular pronoun *he*. *Stone* determines that we must use the neutral singular pronoun *it*. *Dog* determines that we must use a singular, gender-appropriate pronoun, which is *she* in the case of this particular dog.

Turning the argument around, we can help students find the simple subject by asking them to use a third-person pronoun in place of the complete subject. The pronoun that they intuitively select will help guide them to the simple subject. For example, when we replace the complete subject in the following sentence

The trucks in the right lane slowed down.
      They

the only pronoun that we can use is *they*, and *they* can only refer to *trucks*. Thus, *trucks* must be the simple subject.

The following test is a corollary of the pronoun replacement test tailored specifically for subject noun phrases:

Third-person pronoun test for subjects. The **complete subject** is the part of the sentence that is replaced by a third-person subject pronoun. The **simple subject** is the noun (or indefinite pronoun) inside the complete subject that controls the form of the third-person pronoun.

The substitution of a third-person pronoun for the subject gives us two pieces of information for the same price: the words replaced by the third-person pronoun define the exact boundaries of the complete subject—the complete subject is nothing more and nothing less than what the third-person pronoun replaces. The form of the third-person pronoun is controlled solely by the noun that is the simple subject. Thus the third-person pronoun that we would use intuitively gives us a powerful tool for identifying the simple subject.

Teaching
Tip

For students who have trouble with subject–verb agreement, the importance of the third-person pronoun test can hardly be overemphasized. (See "Subject–Verb Agreement" in the Usage part for a detailed discussion of the causes of subject–verb agreement error and for other techniques for helping students.)

Sentence Exercise #2: Third-Person Pronoun Test for Identifying Complete and Simple Subjects

Underline once the part of the sentence that is replaced by a third-person subject pronoun (the complete subject). Underline twice the noun (or indefinite pronoun) that determines the form of the third-person pronoun (the simple subject). The first question is done as an example. (Answers to this exercise are on page 408.)

   0. Naturally, the major sources for his story are a secret.

   Answer: Naturally, <u>the major <u>sources</u> for his story</u> are a secret.

   they

   1. A first-class education is worth its weight in rubies.

   2. The modern art world was shocked by Fred's use of bananas.

   3. The program has been canceled.

   4. The unions in that industry have always opposed open shops.

   5. A stitch in time saves a lot of extra stitches.

   6. The announcement will be made this week.

   7. The proposed new industry standards are likely to be controversial.

   8. The economic conditions of the country depend on the balance of trade.

   9. The opportunity for the launches is limited.

   10. The buildings near the river have become quite valuable.

   11. The treasurer made a sudden trip to Brazil.

12. The tax for purchases made after January 1 has been lowered.

13. As always, the list of suspects in her novel is overwhelming.

14. The new lamp in the den doesn't give enough light.

15. Increasingly, the internationalization of trade makes us an economic global village.

Predicate

The term **predicate** or **complete predicate** refers to everything in the sentence that is not part of the complete subject. (The term *complete predicate* is a bit confusing because it implies that there must be a part of the predicate that is not complete. In older terminology, the term *simple predicate* meant just the verb portion of the predicate. However, because the term *simple predicate* is rarely used anymore, the *predicate* and *complete predicate* have come to mean the same thing. They will be used interchangeably throughout the chapter.)

The sentence can thus be divided into two fundamentally different parts: the complete subject on the left and the (complete) predicate on the right. For example:

My cousin Alfred broke his leg while sunbathing.
   complete subject   complete predicate

My cousin Alfred is pretty clumsy.
   complete subject   complete predicate

My cousin Alfred will be in the hospital for a while.
   complete subject   complete predicate

As we have seen, every sentence in normal word order can be divided into two sections—the complete subject on the left and the predicate on the right. However, for emphasis or stylistic variation, we sometimes change the word order. A very common variation is to move an adverb or adverb phrase from its place at the end of the complete predicate to a position at the beginning of the sentence in front of the complete subject. Here is an example of a sentence with an adverb prepositional phrase (underlined) moved from its normal position in the predicate to the beginning of the sentence:

After school, the children can go shopping.

The purpose of this kind of inversion is to give the adverb phrase extra emphasis. Here is the same sentence back in its normal order:

The children can go shopping after school.

It is important to realize that sentences have a normal or basic form with the complete subject on the left and the complete predicate on the right. When we deviate from this normal order by moving a piece of the complete predicate to the beginning of the complete-subject half of the sentence, we call attention to the piece that is "out of order." Such variation from the norm is not bad as long as it is done deliberately for a particular purpose. Good writers, in fact, have a very strong sense of the reader's expectations for normal order and are thus able to deviate skillfully from these expectations to focus the reader's attention on important ideas.

Before we can begin to analyze the predicate portion of sentences, we must be sure that all the stray pieces of the predicate have been rounded up and put back in their proper half of the sentence. In other words, the first step in analyzing predicates is to normalize "out-of-order" sentences by moving adverbs and adverb phrases back to their normal place in the complete predicate.

Usually, these "out-of-order" or "inverted" adverbs and adverb prepositional phrases are easy to recognize. They are often, but not always, set off from the rest of the subject phrase by a comma. It is easy to confirm that an adverb or adverb prepositional phrase is out of order by applying the third-person pronoun test to identify the complete subject. Because these out-of-order expressions are not part of the complete subject, they will not be replaced by the third-person pronoun; for example,

> After school, <u>the children</u> can go shopping.
>   they

Sentence Exercise #3: Putting Sentences Back into Normal Order _____

Apply the third-person pronoun test to identify the complete subject. Then move any out-of-order adverbs and adverb prepositional phrases back to the predicate. The first question is done as an example. (Answers to this exercise are on page 409.)

  0. Nowadays an awful lot of coffee is grown in Brazil.

    Answer: Nowadays <u>an awful lot of coffee</u> is grown in Brazil.
                                   it

    Normal-order sentence: An awful lot of coffee is grown in Brazil nowadays.

  1. At first <u>the focus</u> is hard to adjust.

  2. By using a coat hook, <u>the young woman</u> managed to open the car.

  3. Later in the day, <u>the cashier</u> noticed the missing bills.

  4. This afternoon <u>the director</u> has several appointments.

  5. Today <u>Adam</u> bought some apples.

6. With surprising speed the little girl climbed into the canoe.

7. Recently a member of our sales staff contacted you.

8. With a flourish the detective pulled out his service revolver.

9. Somewhere the sun is shining.

10. Most of the time your answer would be right.

The second step in analyzing the predicate is to find the verb. The verb, as you may recall from Chapter 2, is unique in that only verbs can be used in past- and future-tense forms. Thus, the fact that only verbs are "tensed" makes them (relatively) easy to identify.

Another feature that makes the verb easy to find is that verbs are typically the first words in predicates. Unfortunately, there are exceptions to this generalization. The complete predicate can begin with an adverb that modifies the verb. In the following examples, verbs are in bold.

My cousin Alfred actually **broke** his leg while sunbathing.
complete predicate

My cousin Alfred really **is** pretty clumsy.
complete predicate

My cousin Alfred probably **will be** in the hospital for a while.
complete predicate

We can safely say the following about predicates:

- Predicates are not subjects and thus cannot be replaced by third-person pronouns.
- Every predicate must contain a verb that can be identified by its unique past tense or future tense form.
- Verbs occur at the beginning of predicates, sometimes preceded by adverbs.
- Everything that follows the verb must be part of the complete predicate.

Sentence Exercise #4: Identifying Verbs and Predicates _____

Underline the complete predicate once and the verb twice. Confirm your answer by shifting the tense of the verb to either the past (*-ed*) or the future (*will*) and by replacing the complete subject with the appropriate pronoun. The first question is done as an example. (Answers to this exercise are on page 410.)

0. The students had a surprise party for Donald's wife.

   Answer: The students had a surprise party for Donald's wife.

   Confirmation: They will have a surprise party for Donald's wife.

1. The students found the answer on the internet.

2. The cry of the hound of the Baskervilles echoed across the moor.

3. The garage normally has the car ready by noon.

4. The police usually rely only on verifiable information.

5. The TV was on at full volume.

6. The line at the restaurant stretched out the door.

7. The new car cost an arm and a leg.

8. Baseball games usually last about two and a half hours.

9. The state flower of Tennessee is the iris.

10. The operating system of my new computer really is a total mystery to me.

Verb Complements

In traditional grammar, a **complement** is a noun or adjective that is required by a verb to make a grammatical sentence. There is a complex vocabulary for describing different types of complements. Complements are divided into two main categories depending on whether the complement follows (1) an action verb or (2) a linking verb. Recall that the discussion of verbs in Chapter 2 began with these examples of action verbs and linking verbs:

Action Verbs	*Linking Verbs*
Fred *found* his folder.	Sam *is* silly.
Rudolph *wrote* a riddle.	The soup *smells* good.
Sally *scorched* her skirt.	Larry *looks* upset.

As the term **action** implies, the three example action verbs refer to some kind of physical action or activity that the subject is doing—the three subjects are variously finding, writing, and scorching things. In these examples the subjects are the "do-ers" of the action of the verb.

The term **linking** is not so obvious. The term actually refers to the way the verb connects or LINKS the complement to the subject. In the first example, the linking verb *is* connects the adjective *silly* to *Sam;* in the second example, *smells* connects the adjective *good* to *soup;* and in the third example, *looks* connects the adjective *upset* to *Larry.* In other words, linking verbs use their complements to DESCRIBE the subjects. In sentences with linking verbs, the subjects are not the "do-ers" of any action—the soup, for example, is not doing the smelling. Instead of being "do-ers," the subjects are "topics" that are described by the linking verb and its complement.

Thus as a first approximation, we may say that in sentences with action verbs, the subjects are the "do-ers" of the action of the verb. In sentences with linking verbs, the subjects are "topics" that the linking verbs and their complements describe.

The problem with this first approximation is in the definition of action verbs. Not all action verbs show action, and consequently, in these sentences, there is no action for the subject to perform. Many action verbs describe a "state" rather than convey an action. For example, compare the following sentences:

Ralph *bought* a new car. (action)

Ralph *has* a new car. (state)

Clearly, the verb *bought* refers to an action—Ralph engaged in the action of buying a new car. The verb *has*, however, is not really comparable. Ralph does not engage in the action of having a new car. Having a new car is a state, not an action. Does this mean that the verb *has* is a linking verb? No, because if it were a linking verb, it would describe Ralph. It would mean that Ralph IS a new car!

The bottom line is that the class of action verbs is so big and diverse (99 percent of all verbs are action verbs) that we can make no workable definition of action verbs except negatively. Action verbs share only one definable characteristic: **action verbs are not linking verbs.** This, then, is what we must do: define what linking verbs are, and any verb that does not meet the definition of a linking verb is thus classified as an action verb by default. Since linking verbs as a class are much smaller and much more cohesive than action verbs are, linking verbs are (relatively) easy to define. Accordingly, we will begin our discussion of complements with linking verbs.

Linking Verbs and Their Complements

Linking verbs share a number of features that help identify them: (1) the common linking verbs can be characterized and listed; (2) all linking verbs describe the subject; and (3) linking verbs have distinctive complements.

Common Linking Verbs

By far the most common linking verb is the verb *be*.

*Teaching
Tip*

Because *be* is the most irregular verb in English, students often do not realize that the term "the verb *be*" also includes *am, are, is, was,* and *were*. It is well worth the time to have students write out the various forms.

Following are the various tensed forms of *be*.

Forms of be		
	Present	
	Singular	**Plural**
1st person	I *am*	we *are*
2nd person	you *are*	you *are*
3rd person	he/she/it *is*	they *are*
	Past	
	Singular	**Plural**
1st person	I *was*	we *were*
2nd person	you *were*	you *were*
3rd person	he/she/it *was*	they *were*
	Future	
All persons and numbers		*will be*

Sentence Exercise #5: Recognizing Forms of the Linking Verb **be**

In the second space, put in the required form of the verb *be*. Then select the proper pronoun for the first space. 1st, 2nd, 3rd refer to person, Sg and Pl refer to number; and Pres, Past, and Future refer to tense. The gender of 3rd Sg is up to you. The first question is done as an example. (Answers to this exercise are on page 411.)

0. _____ _____ stuck up in the tree again.
       3rd-Sg-Past

Answer: ___It___ ___was___ stuck up in the tree again.
        3rd-Sg-Past

1. _____ _____ in very bad shape.
       3rd-Pl-Past

2. _____ _____ not your sweet baboo!
       1st-Sg-Pres

3. _____ _____ a menace to the general public.
       2nd-Sg-Future

4. _____ _____ such good friends.
       3rd-Pl-Past

5. _____ _____ an only child.
       1st-Sg-Pres

6. _____ _____ mistaken about that.
   3rd-Pl-Pres

7. _____ _____ such a big pain in the neck.
   2nd-Pl-Past

8. _____ _____ able to leap tall buildings at a single bound.
   3rd-Sg-Past

9. _____ _____ sixteen next month.
   2nd-Sg-Future

10. _____ _____ ready to go now.
    2nd-Pl-Pres

Many common linking verbs are verbs of appearance or sense perception, for example:

Sight:	Alice *appeared* angry about something.
	Luke *looked* a little lost.
	Sam *seemed* sad.
Sound:	The tenor *sounded* flat to me.
	The note *rang* true.
Smell:	The fruit *smelled* overripe.
Taste:	The bread *tasted* stale.

The remaining common linking verbs describe the nature or condition of the subject, for example:

The cook *got* angry.

They *grew* strong.

The patient *remained* weak.

The model *became* faint with hunger.

I *feel* terrific.

My face *turned* red with embarrassment.

All Linking Verbs Describe the Subject

All of the examples of sentences with linking verbs given above share one important feature: in all cases, the verb is not performing any action; rather, the verbs and their complements describe the nature of the subject.

Although all of the verbs listed above are indeed linking verbs, some of these same words can also be used as action verbs. However, when they are used as action verbs, they have a completely different meaning than when they are used as linking verbs. Here is an example using the verb *feel* that may help underline the uniquely descriptive function of linking verbs.

> Linking: The detective <u>felt</u> sick.
> Action: The detective <u>felt</u> the body for a gun.

In the first example, the linking verb *felt* describes the condition of the detective—the detective was not actively doing anything. In the second example, the action verb *felt* refers to the action in which the detective was engaged—the detective was feeling the body.

A number of jokes are based on the fact that some verbs can be interpreted as either linking verbs or action verbs, but with changes of meaning. Here is such a joke from *Monty Python's Flying Circus* that depends on the two different uses of the verb *smell:*

> A: My dog has no nose.
>
> B: How does he smell?
>
> A: He smells awful!

At the risk of being tedious about a joke, A's first line about the dog's having no nose sets us up to interpret B's question as referring to how A's dog engages in the act of smelling (i.e., we are led to think of *smell* as an action verb). In A's punch line, *smell* is used instead as a linking verb to describe the nature of the dog, not as an action verb describing the dog's engaging in the action of smelling.

Linking Verbs Have Distinctive Complements

From a purely grammatical standpoint, the most reliable way of distinguishing linking verbs from action verbs is by the differences in their complements. The complements of linking verbs are called collectively **subject complements.** There are two types of subject complements: **predicate adjectives** and **predicate nominatives.**

Predicate Adjectives.   Here are some examples of sentences with linking verbs followed by predicate adjectives (underlined):

> The day was <u>hot</u>.
>
> The cat is <u>scared</u>.
>
> Some of the children were <u>noisy</u>.
>
> The soup tasted <u>weird</u>.

The fence seemed <u>crooked</u>.

The author became <u>famous</u>.

I will get <u>rich</u>.

Predicate adjectives are **descriptive adjectives** used after linking verbs. Recall from the discussion of adjectives in Chapter 2 that descriptive adjectives have the distinctive characteristic of being **gradable.** (See page 29.) That is, descriptive adjectives have a **base form** that can be used with *very,* a **comparative form** in *-er* or *more,* and a **superlative form** in *-est* or *most.* The predicate adjectives in the examples above are all in their base form. The ability of predicate adjectives to be used in the comparative and superlative forms is proof that these words are indeed adjectives. Thus any complement that can be used with *very* or that can be used in the comparative or superlative forms is a predicate adjective. Here are two of the above sentences with the predicate adjectives in all three of their gradable forms:

Base:	The day was very <u>hot</u>.
Comparative:	The day was <u>hotter</u> than ever.
Superlative:	The day was the <u>hottest</u> of the year.

Base:	The fence seemed very <u>crooked</u>.
Comparative:	The fence seemed <u>more crooked</u> than it did last year.
Superlative:	The fence seemed the <u>most crooked</u> on the whole ranch.

Sentence Exercise #6: Using **very,** *the Comparative, and the Superlative to Identify Predicate Adjectives* _____

Underline the predicate adjectives. Confirm your answer by (a) using the predicate adjective with *very,* (b) putting it into the comparative form, and (c) putting it into the superlative form. The first question is done as an example. (Answers to this exercise are on page 411.)

   0. The patient was alert.

   Answer: The patient was <u>alert</u>.

   Confirmation: very alert

   more alert

   most alert

   1. Her entry was graceful.

   2. His sense of humor is strange.

   3. The investigation seemed thorough.

   4. Their gestures were often dramatic.

5. The approach to the problem seems practical.

6. The children got angry.

7. The society has been active for many years.

8. At that altitude, the air becomes thin.

9. The proposal seems interesting.

10. The person on the phone sounded upset to me.

Being able to identify predicate adjectives with confidence is the key to identifying linking verbs because only linking verbs can have predicate adjectives as their complements. The simplest way to show that a word is indeed a predicate adjective is to show that it can be used with *very*. The *very* test is especially useful because it helps students cope with one of the most difficult distinctions in grammar—telling predicate adjectives from verbs.

Here is the problem. Many adjectives are derived from verbs and retain their historical *-ing* or *-ed/-en* verb endings. These adjectives look just like verbs, and conversely, verbs that end in *-ing* or *-ed/-en* look just like predicate adjectives. The problem is most troublesome when verbs ending in *-ing* or *-ed/-en* follow some form of the verb *be* used as a **helping verb.** In this situation, *be* as a main verb + predicate adjective will look just like helping verb *be* + verb. Here are some examples of predicate adjective/verb lookalikes:

-ing

   The students were <u>sleeping</u>.

   The students were <u>interesting</u>.

-ed/-en

   The report was <u>rejected</u>.

   The report was <u>stolen</u>.

   The report was <u>confused</u>.

The *very* test clearly distinguishes between predicate adjectives and verbs because verbs can never be modified by *very*. Here is what happens when we use the *very* test on the example sentences:

-ing

   *The students were **very** <u>sleeping</u>. (*Sleeping* is a verb.)

   The students were **very** <u>interesting</u>. (*Interesting* is a predicate
                                                                  adjective.)

-ed/-en

    *The report was **very** <u>rejected</u>. (*Rejected* is a verb.)

    *The report was **very** <u>stolen</u>. (*Stolen* is a verb.)

    The report was **very** <u>confused</u>. (*Confused* is a predicate adjective.)

The *very* test for distinguishing predicate adjectives and verbs ending in *-ing* or *-ed/-en.* Most predicate adjectives can be used with *very*, but verbs can never be used with *very*.

Sentence Exercise #7: Using the **very** Test to Distinguish Predicate Adjectives from Verbs

Determine whether the underlined words are predicate adjectives or verbs by using the *very* test. The first question is done as an example. (Answers to this exercise are on page 412.)

  0. The students were *pleased* with their test results.

      Answer: The students were **very** *pleased* with their test results.
              Pleased is a predicate adjective.

  1. The children were <u>amusing</u>.

  2. The children were <u>sleeping</u>.

  3. The axle was <u>turning</u>.

  4. The play was <u>challenging</u>.

  5. Our car was <u>stolen</u>.

  6. The incident was <u>reported to the police</u>.

  7. The police were <u>involved</u> in the case.

  8. The lawyer's motion was <u>rejected</u>.

  9. The lawyer's motion was not <u>well presented</u>.

10. Unfortunately, the case was <u>thrown</u> out of court.

Teaching Tip

Students find that learning to use the *very* test to identify both modifying and predicate adjectives is one of the most important and useful tests in the book.

Despite the usefulness of the *very* test for identifying predicate adjectives, the *very* test does have one important limitation: it does not distinguish predicate adjectives from certain adverbs of manner that can also be used with *very*. For example, in the sentence

The children behaved *badly,*

badly is an adverb even though we can use *very* with it:

The children behaved very *badly.*

In most cases, predicate adjectives are easy to tell apart from adverbs because most adverbs of manner add *-ly* to a predicate adjective base form. For example:

Predicate Adjective	*Adverb of Manner*
quick	quickly
soft	softly
hungry	hungrily
greedy	greedily
regretful	regretfully
patient	patiently

However, not all adverbs of manner end in *-ly*. (And not all words that end in *-ly* are adverbs of manner. For example, in the sentence "He was *deadly,*" *deadly* is a predicate adjective.) If you are unsure if a word is a predicate adjective or adverb of manner, substitute some predicate adjective–adverb of manner pairs that are distinguished by the -ly. Then you can tell which one is grammatical, the predicate adjective or the adverb of manner. For example, in the sentence

He talks fast.

is *fast* a predicate adjective or an adverb of manner? Here are some substitutions for *fast:*

He talks rapid
       rapidly

He talks pleasant
       pleasantly

He talks convincing
       convincingly

He talks polite
> politely

He talks amusing
> amusingly

When you have a number of examples together, it is easy to see that while some of the adjective forms might be marginally OK, all of the adverb forms are correct. Therefore, despite the absence of *-ly, fast* is probably an adverb of manner.

Predicate Nominatives.   Linking verbs can also be followed by nouns or pronouns. These nouns and pronouns are called **predicate nominatives.** Predicate nominatives describe or rename the subject. Here are some examples with the predicate nominatives underlined:

Their child became an <u>actor</u>.

Frankenstein resembles a <u>zombie</u>.

Sally was a <u>seamstress</u>.

Dick was a <u>detective</u>.

Patricia looked the <u>part</u>.

Our first choice is <u>you</u>.

At first glance it might seem difficult for students to tell predicate nominatives from the objects of action verbs. However, once students know what to look for, the difference is obvious. Compare the following sentences:

Linking verb + predicate nominative: Harry was a lawyer.
Action verb + object: Harry hired a lawyer.

In the linking-verb sentence, *Harry* and the *lawyer* are the same person. In the action-verb sentence, *Harry* and the *lawyer* are two different people. In linking-verb sentences with predicate nominatives, the predicate nominative must always refer back to or identify the subject. Think of a linking verb as an equals sign. The subject and the predicate nominative must always refer to each other:

subject = predicate nominative

Here are the example sentences containing predicate nominatives with equals signs:

Their child became an <u>actor</u>.   child = actor
Frankenstein resembles a <u>zombie</u>.   Frankenstein = zombie

Sally was a <u>seamstress</u>.	Sally = seamstress
Dick was a <u>detective</u>.	Dick = detective
Patricia looked the <u>part</u>.	Patricia = part
Our first choice is <u>you</u>.	choice = you

Review of Linking Verbs and Their Complements

Let us now review the terminology of linking verbs.

Linking verb:	Verbs that describe the subject.
Subject complement:	The collective term for the complements of linking verbs. There are two types of subject complements: **predicate adjectives** and **predicate nominatives.**
Predicate adjective:	Descriptive adjectives that refer to the subject.
Predicate nominative:	Nouns or pronouns that identify or rename the subject.

Linking verbs are basically defined by the distinctive nature of their complements—adjectives and nouns that refer to or define the subjects. But are there linking verbs that do not have any complements at all? The answer to this question is that it depends on one's definition of "complement." Here is the problem. Some linking verbs can be followed by adverbs and adverb phrases of place that appear to function as complements. In the following examples, these adverb expressions are underlined:

My car is <u>here</u>.

The keys are <u>under the mat</u>.

In the first example, the adverb of place *here* describes where my car is. In the second example, the adverb phrase of place *under the mat* describes where the keys are. These adverb expressions are not optional modifiers, as adverbs and adverb phrases usually are. If we delete them, the resulting sentences are clearly incomplete and ungrammatical:

*My car is.

*The keys are.

However, the traditional definition of complements refers only to adjectives and nouns (or pronouns). So by the traditional definition, these adverbs cannot be counted as complements. Traditional grammar has painted itself into a corner by its overly restrictive definition of what a complement can be. In more modern grammars, the term *complement* is broadened to include ANY grammatical unit that is required by a verb to make a grammatical sentence. In Chapter 7 we will explore the modern approach. For now, however, we will simply ignore sentences in which linking verbs are followed by adverbs or adverb phrases of place "complements."

Sentence Exercise #8: Identifying Linking verbs and Subject Complements _____

Underline the linking verb once and the subject complements twice. Label the predicate nominatives as Pred Nom and the predicate adjectives as Pred Adj. The first question is done as an example. (Answers to this exercise are on page 412.)

  0. Thanks to his grammar teacher, Leon became a better person.

     Answer: Thanks to his grammar teacher, Leon <u>became</u> a better <u>person</u>.
                                                                    Pred Nom

  1. Throughout the ordeal, Holmes remained calm.

  2. The driver was drunk.

  3. Hearing the news, the general grew furious.

  4. Aunt Sally got angry at her car.

  5. Her car is a Ford.

  6. The cat goes crazy during thunderstorms.

  7. I am mad at myself for saying that.

  8. Rudolph remained a private for several more months.

  9. Later that year, Lady Windermere fell dangerously ill.

 10. In the *Hitchhiker's Guide to the Galaxy*, the answer to the meaning of life is 42.

 11. At first the idea sounded strange to me.

 12. After the blow-out, the tire resembled a pancake.

 13. Aunt Sally was upset.

 14. Louise looked angry.

 15. The dinner was a complete mess.

Action Verbs and Their Complements

Although many action verbs express an action, so many action verbs do not that we have no practical way of defining the group except negatively: action verbs are those verbs that are not linking verbs. Think of the class of linking verbs as being a small subgroup of verbs with special, unique characteristics. Once this special subgroup is removed from the class of verbs, everything left is an action verb. Linking verbs are the exception; action verbs are the norm.

The complements of action verbs are called **objects.** Action verbs that are used with objects are called **transitive verbs.** Objects are nouns or pronouns. (Recall that only linking verbs can have adjectives as complements.) An action verb followed by an object is the most common type of sentence in English (and probably all other languages as well). Here are some examples of transitive action verb sentences with their objects. The transitive verbs are in italic type, and their object nouns or pronouns are in bold:

Jack *met* a **stranger** at the fair.

Jack *sold* his **cow** to the stranger.

Jack *got* some **beans** in return.

Jack *planted* **them.**

The seeds *produced* giant **beanstalks.**

Some action verbs are used with no objects. Action verbs that are used without objects are called **intransitive verbs.** Here are some examples of sentences with intransitive verbs:

Sam *snores.*

Sally *sneezed.*

All of the flowers *wilted.*

The children *snickered.*

The old cow *died.*

Teaching
Tip

Students often have trouble remembering the terms "transitive" and "intransitive," or else reverse their meanings. It helps to remind students that the terms come from the Latin *trans,* which means "across." *Trans* also appears in the words *transportation* and *Rapid Transit System.* A transitive verb goes **across** to its object. An intransitive verb does not go across.

The term *intransitive* refers only to verbs that have no noun or pronoun objects; intransitive verbs can also be followed by adverbs and adverb phrases without losing their intransitive status. For example, we can add adverbs and adverb phases to the sentences above, and the verbs are still intransitive:

Sam *snores* all night long.

Sally *sneezed* loudly.

All of the flowers *wilted* in the heat.

The children *snickered* behind the teacher's back.

The old cow *died* yesterday.

Students are sometimes confused by adverb phrases that contain nouns, thinking that these nouns are objects of the verb. These adverb phrases are actually **adverb prepositional phrases,** which always consist of a preposition + a noun (with or without its modifiers) or a pronoun. To see the difference, compare the following two sentences:

Transitive: Leon bit the *dentist.*

Intransitive: Leon worried *about the **bill.***
                           Prepositional phrase

The nouns *dentist* and *bill* are both objects, but they are objects of different things. *Dentist* is the object of the verb *bit. Bill* is the object of the preposition *about.* In traditional grammar, objects of prepositions cannot be counted as objects of transitive verbs. (When we deal with modern grammar in Chapter 7, we will see that some verbs can be analyzed as verb + preposition compounds.)

The nouns that are objects of transitive verbs (together with their modifiers) can always be replaced by third-person pronouns. When this happens, the third-person pronoun will always be immediately next to the transitive verb, for example,

Transitive: Leon bit *the dentist.*
                        him

The third-person pronoun *him* and the verb *bit* are side by side, showing that *him* is the object of a transitive verb.

When we try the same substitution with a prepositional phrase, the preposition will always separate the third-person pronoun and the verb; for example,

Intransitive: Leon worried about *the bill.*
                            it

The third-person pronoun *it* and the verb *worried* are separated by the preposition *about,* showing that *bill* CANNOT be treated as the object of a transitive verb.

Sentence Exercise #9: Distinguishing Intransitive and Transitive Verbs _____

Underline the verbs and label intransitive verbs as Vi and transitive verbs as Vt. Confirm your answers by replacing the nouns (and their modifiers) following the verbs with third-person pronouns. The first question is done as an example. (Answers to this exercise are on page 413.)

0. The reporter looked into the allegation.

Answer: The reporter <u>looked</u> behind the door.
                              Vi

Confirmation: The reporter <u>looked</u>.
                                     Vi

1. I shot an arrow into the air.

2. Leon smiled at the dentist.

3. The judge suppressed the evidence.

4. The prosecution objected to the judge's action.

5. The infection damaged the crops in the area.

6. The planets revolve around the earth.

7. Adrian added chlorine to the pool.

8. The report will emphasize the need for better fiscal control.

9. The car slowly backed down the driveway.

10. That concludes the meeting.

A small but important group of verbs can have not one but TWO objects. For these verbs it is necessary to distinguish between an **indirect object** and a **direct object.** When there are two objects, the indirect object always comes before the direct object. Here are some examples. IO refers to indirect object, and DO refers to direct object.

Sally gave the *class* the *answer.*
                        IO   DO

Sally left *him* a *note.*
                    IO   DO

Indirect objects can usually be recognized by moving them after the direct object and adding *to* or *for:*

Sally gave the *class* the *answer.*
                        IO   DO

Sally gave the *answer* **to** the *class.*
                        DO

Sally left *him* a *note*.
      IO   DO

Sally left a *note* **for** *him*.
           DO

> ***To/for* paraphrase test for indirect objects.** An indirect object can
> be paraphrased by moving it after the direct object and adding *to*
> or *for*.

The term *direct object* is also used as a synonym for "object" with verbs
that have only a single object. Thus we can refer to *Mary* in the sentence

John saw *Mary*.

as either an object or a direct object. Put another way, the term *object* implies
"direct object" unless you say otherwise.

Sentence Exercise #10: Identifying Indirect Objects by the to/for Paraphrase Test

Underline the indirect objects twice and the direct objects once. Confirm your answer by applying the *to* or *for* paraphrase test to the indirect objects. Note: Not all
sentences contain indirect objects. The first question is done as an example. (Answers
to this exercise are on page 414.)

0. Alice gave Mary a present.
   Answer: Alice gave Mary a present.
   Confirmation: Alice gave a present **to** Mary.

1. Holmes finally told Watson the killer's name.

2. Paul fixed her an elegant dessert.

3. He saved us some.

4. Professor Fiditch taught the grateful students grammar.

5. Throw the dog a bone!

6. I ordered us some dinner.

7. The Fairy Godmother granted Cinderella three wishes.

8. Cinderella told the Prince her secret.

9. Marsha told John to leave her alone.

10. The restaurant reserved the couple a table by the window.

Although the *to/for* paraphrase work for most verbs with indirect objects, some verbs cannot be used with it. Here are some examples:

The health board fined little *Jack Horner $200.*
IO   DO

*The health board fined *$200* **to/for** little Jack Horner.
DO

Forgive *us* our *trespasses.*
IO   DO

*Forgive our trespasses **to/for** us.
DO

Scrooge allowed his *employees* only one *mistake.*
IO   DO

*Scrooge allowed only one *mistake* **to/for** his employees.
DO

Nevertheless, the *to/for* paraphrase does apply to nearly all indirect objects, and we can say with certainty that IF it does apply to a sentence, then the sentence must contain an indirect object.

Finally, few action verbs can have a direct object and an **object complement.** The object complement can be either a noun or a descriptive adjective. Object complements are highly restricted in meaning—they are tied to the direct object. In the case of the noun object complement, the object complement and the direct object must refer to the same person or thing. Here are some examples.

1. Noun as object complement:

    Sally considered John a <u>fool</u>. (fool = John)

    They elected her <u>president</u>. (president = her)

    The president appointed him <u>secretary</u>. (secretary = him)

2. Descriptive adjective as object complement:

    Keep your nose <u>clean</u>. (*clean* refers to *nose*)

    They painted the room <u>blue</u>. (*blue* refers to *room*)

    The jury believed him <u>innocent</u>. (*innocent* refers to *him*)

Nouns used as direct objects and object complements superficially resemble the more common indirect object and direct object combination. Nouns used as object complements have two distinctive features: (1) the object complement must refer to the direct object, and (2) the direct object + object complement combination will fail the *to/for* paraphrase test, since there is no indirect object:

> *to/for* paraphrase test:
>
> Sally considered John a fool.
> *Sally considered a fool **to/for** John.
>
> They elected her president.
> *They elected president **to/for** her.
>
> The president appointed him secretary.
> *The president appointed secretary **to/for** him.

Sentence Exercise #11: Identifying Object Complements ───────

Underline object complements (both noun and descriptive adjectives). In the case of nouns, confirm your answer by showing that the *to* or *for* paraphrase test fails. The first question is done as an example. (Answers to this exercise are on page 414.)

> **0.** Alice thought Linda a natural leader.
> Answer: Alice thought Linda a natural <u>leader</u>.
> Confirmation: *Alice thought a natural leader to/for Linda.

> **1.** Bill's idea made him rich.

> **2.** Bill's idea made him a billionaire.

> **3.** The Justice Department considered Bugsy a crook.

> **4.** Bugsy believed himself innocent.

> **5.** Judy painted the living room pink.

> **6.** The President appointed his bother Attorney General.

> **7.** She really made her mother angry.

> **8.** I told them the truth.

> **9.** They named the baby Theo.

> **10.** We chose the baby a present.

Review of Action Verbs and Their Complements

Let us now review the terminology of action verbs.

> **Action verb:**   Verbs that are not linking verbs.

Transitive verb:	Action verbs that have objects.
Intransitive verb:	Action verbs that do not have objects.
Object:	(a) The collective term for action verb complements. (b) The complement of action verbs that take only a single complement = **direct object.**
Direct object:	(a) The complement that follows an indirect object. (b) The complement of action verbs that take only a single complement.
Indirect object:	The first object for those verbs that take TWO objects as their complement. Most indirect objects can be paraphrased with *to* or *for.*
Object complement	Nouns or descriptive adjectives that follow direct objects and refer back to them.

Sentence Exercise #12: Identifying Action Verb Complements

Underline the action verb and label it Vt if it is transitive or Vi if it is intransitive. If the verb is transitive, underline and label the object(s). Use DO for direct objects, IO for indirect objects, and OC for object complements. The first question is done as an example. (Answers to this exercise are on page 415.)

0. We reserved my parents a room at the hotel.

   Answer: We <u>reserved</u> my <u>parents</u> a <u>room</u> at the hotel.
                Vt   IO   DO

1. The company employs ten workers.

2. I will arrange a meeting with them.

3. The green container will leak.

4. They refused the offer.

5. My brother sent me a package.

6. The little girl stared at the food on her plate.

7. Save me some.

8. The earthquake shook the house.

9. The movie made me sleepy.

10. The bank loaned the company two million dollars.

11. Time and tide wait for no man.

12. Holmes offered Watson some advice.

13. Joanne found the answer to her question on the Internet.

14. You gave me a scare.

15. I gave a contribution at the office.

16. Sleeping Beauty considered the dwarves idiots.

17. I finally got the answer.

18. Tell me a story.

19. The ghost accused Scrooge of being a miser.

20. We talked about your suggestion.

Summary

Let us now recapitulate the main points of this chapter in outline form:

1. A **sentence** consists of a **subject** and a **predicate.**

2. The term "subject" has two meanings:
   (a) The **simple subject** is the noun or pronoun with which the verb agrees.
   (b) The **complete subject** is the simple subject together with all its modifiers: the complete subject is everything that is not part of the complete predicate.

3. The predicate portion of the sentence consists of a verb together with its complements and modifiers (if any): the predicate (or complete predicate) is everything that is not part of the complete subject.

4. Verbs are divided into two groups depending on the type of **complements** they take:
   (a) **Linking verbs** take **subject complements.** There are two types of subject complements:
       (i) **Predicate adjectives**
       (ii) **Predicate nominatives**
   (b) **Action verbs** are further divided into two types:
       (i) **Intransitive verbs** do not take complements.
       (ii) **Transitive verbs** do take complements. The complements of transitive verbs are **objects,** and objects are noun or pronouns. There are three types of objects:
           (1) **direct objects**
           (2) **indirect objects,** which can appear only in front of direct objects.
           (3) **object complements,** which are nouns and descriptive adjectives that follow and refer to direct objects.

Teaching
Tip

Students need a lot of practice with the above terminology. They are likely to confuse the action verb/linking verb distinction with the transitive/intransitive verb distinction.

The complicated terminology of verb types and complements boils down to distinguishing six different combinations of verbs and complements: two with linking verbs, and four with action verbs. Here are the six types with some examples:

1. Linking verbs

   (a) Linking verb (LV) + predicate adjective (PA)

   Ralph *was rude.*
         LV   PA

   Tina *became angry.*
         LV   PA

   The movie *was* quite *different.*
         LV   PA

   (b) Linking verb (LV) + predicate nominative (PN)

   Ralph *was* a *waiter.*
         LV   PN

   Tina *became* a *movie-star.*
        LV   PN

   The movie *was* a complete *flop.*
         LV   PN

2. Action verbs:

   (a) Intransitive verb (Vi) (no noun or pronoun complement)

   Tim *smiled* bravely.
         Vi

   Your Honor, the defense *rests.*
                         Vi

   The judge *smiled* at the defendant.
            Vi

   (b) Transitive verb (Vt) + direct object (DO)

   Patricia *potted* her *petunias.*
         Vt   DO

Andrew *answered* the *phone* on the first ring.
      Vt   DO

He *took* a *message* for me.
   Vt   DO

(c) Transitive verb (Vt) + indirect object (IO) + direct object (DO)

The waiter *served Philip* his *dinner* at once.
            Vt   IO   DO

They *taught* old *dogs* new *tricks.*
     Vt   IO   DO

I *found them* a good used *car* at a terrific price.
  Vt   IO   DO

(d) Transitive verb (Vt) + direct object (DO) + object complement (OC)

John *considered Fred* a *fool.*
     Vt   DO   OC

John *made Fred angry.*
     Vt   DO   OC

Sentence Exercise #13: Identifying Verbs and Their Complements

Underline and identify all verbs and their complements. Use LV for linking verbs, Vt for transitive action verbs, and Vi for intransitive action verbs. Use PA for predicate adjectives and PN for predicate nominatives. Use DO for direct objects, IO for indirect objects, and OC for object complements. The first question is done as an example. (Answers to this exercise are on page 416.)

0. Finally, he found the ad in the paper.

Answer: Finally, he <u>found</u> the <u>ad</u> in the paper.
                    Vt   DO

1. The ship sank.

2. The torpedo sank the ship.

3. The teacher read the class a story.

4. William was a waiter.

5. William was weary.

6. These sentences are rich in complements.

7. We completed the first portion of the test.

8. The post office returned the package to Marty.

9. Cinderella grew fat in her old age.

10. Alice brought Fred a new dish towel for Father's Day.

11. The President appointed her Ambassador to the United Nations.

12. The cheese smells moldy.

13. The agent sold them a new house.

14. Today, Leon turned 30.

15. Aunt Sally fit the last piece into the puzzle.

Sentence Exercise #14: Identifying Verbs and Their Complements

Underline and identify all verbs and their complements. Use LV for linking verbs, Vt for transitive action verbs, and Vi for intransitive action verbs. Use PA for predicate adjectives and PN for predicate nominatives. Use DO for direct objects, IO for indirect objects, and OC for object complements. The first question is done as an example. (Answers to this exercise are on page 417.)

0. Santa Claus is allergic to fur.

   Answer: Santa Claus <u>is</u> <u>allergic</u> to fur.
                 LV   PA

1. Everyone likes chocolate.

2. No one noticed the incident in Lady Crumhorn's drawing room.

3. With deep regret, Charles declined a second helping.

4. Leon eventually became a famous and beloved grammarian.

5. The tenor sounded flat to me.

6. We walked to the end of the pier.

7. They offered us a lift back to town.

8. The play received great reviews.

9. They lied to us.

10. Marley gets upset easily.

11. With a flourish, the magician produced a tuba out of thin air.

12. They picked me first.

13. They were uninterested in my ideas.

14. The waiter slipped us the bill.

15. You look good.

Classifying Sentences by Purpose

There is one final bit of terminology we need to discuss before moving on to sentence diagramming: the four terms used to describe sentences by their purpose.

1. Declarative. Declarative sentences make a statement. **Declarative sentences are always punctuated with a period.**

This is a declarative sentence.

Declarative sentences can be positive or negative.

Declarative sentences cannot be punctuated with a question mark or an exclamation point.

2. Imperative. Imperative sentences are commands. Imperatives are defined not by punctuation, but by their unique grammar. **Imperative sentences MUST have an understood *you* as the subject.** They may be punctuated with either periods or exclamation points.

Go away.

Come here.

Stop it!

3. Interrogative. Interrogative sentences are questions. **Interrogative sentences MUST be punctuated with question marks.**

Did John leave?

Where are you?

What are interrogative sentences?

4. Exclamatory. **Exclamatory sentences are declarative sentences that are punctuated with exclamation points for emphasis.**

I can do it!

This really is an exclamatory sentence!

Sally has no cavities!

Declarative and interrogative are self-explanatory (as long as you remember that *interrogative* means question). However, students often confuse imperative and exclamatory sentences because both can use exclamation points. The key difference is in their grammar: imperative sentences MUST have an understood *you* as their subjects; exclamatory sentences can NEVER have an understood *you* as their subjects.

Sentence Exercise #15: Classifying Sentences by Purpose

Classify the following sentences by purpose as declarative, imperative, interrogative, or exclamatory. The first question is done as an example. (Answers to this exercise are on page 418.)

0. Get out of here!

   Answer: Imperative.

1. Well, what do you know about that?

2. It seems pretty simple to me!

3. That's what you think.

4. Holmes warned Watson to stay back.

5. To get the mean, total the data and divide by the number of observations.

6. Is everything OK here?

7. Return to headquarters at once!

8. You must be good while we're gone.

9. Blend in the cream cheese until smooth.

10. Publish or perish!

Diagramming the Basic Sentence

Diagramming is a visual representation of the grammatical relationships in a sentence. It provides students with a way to conceptualize abstract grammatical concepts in an easy-to-grasp way. For students who are primarily visual learners, it is really the only channel for understanding grammar. Finally, diagramming has a kind of gamelike nature that appeals to most students' puzzle-solving instincts. From a grammar-teaching standpoint, the main advantage of diagramming is that it helps students strip away the modifiers to reveal the basic structures of sentences.

The key point of reference in a sentence diagram is the **main sentence line.** On this line are the three basic elements of the sentence:

- The **simple subject**
- The **main verb** (preceded by helping verbs, if any)
- The **complement:** either the **direct object** if the main verb is an action verb, or the **subject complement** (a predicate nominative or predicate adjective) if the main verb is a linking verb.

There are two basic types of diagram, one for action verbs with direct objects and the other for linking verbs with subject complements. Notice the following about the main sentence line:

| Subject | Action Verb | Object |

| Subject | Linking Verb | Subject Complement |

- The subject part of the sentence is separated from the predicate part of the sentence by a long vertical line that extends above and below the main sentence line.
- Action verbs are separated from their direct objects by a short vertical line that does not extend below the main sentence line.
- Linking verbs are separated from their subject complements (either predicate nominatives or predicate adjectives—they are treated alike) by a line that slopes back to the left.

Teaching Tip

Students tend to forget whether the line for subject complements slopes back to the left or forward to the right. A helpful mnemonic trick is to extend the backward-sloping line so that it points to the subject. The idea is that subject complements always refer BACK to their subjects.

Here is an example illustrating the two different ways of representing complements using the sentences "Harry met Sally" (direct object) "and "Pop-eye is hungry" (subject complement).

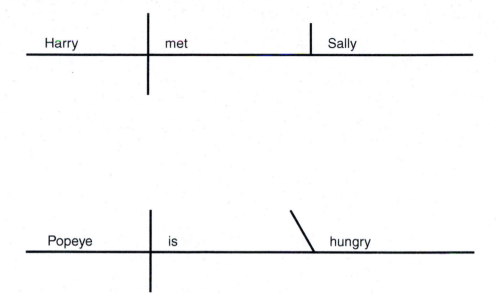

There is an unusual convention for representing **indirect objects.** Indirect objects are not drawn on the main sentence line (with the other complements), as one would expect. Instead, they are placed on a line drawn underneath and parallel to the main sentence line. The indirect object line is attached to the verb by a sloping line:

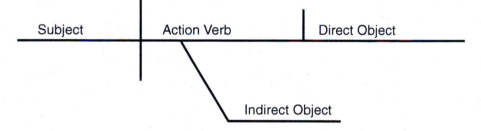

An actual sentence with an indirect object, "They told us stories," is diagrammed below:

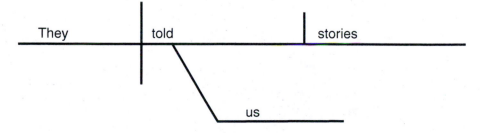

This representation of the indirect object makes the indirect object look like a prepositional phrase, and reflects another way of diagramming indirect objects as objects of prepositions. Recall that one of the main identifying characteristics of indirect objects is that they can be paraphrased with the preposition *to* or *for*. For example, we can paraphrase "They told us stories" as "They told stories to us," which is diagrammed with *to us* as a prepositional phrase:

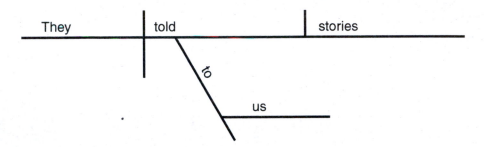

Object complements, whether nouns or descriptive adjectives, are put on the main sentence line following a backward-sloping line. Here are two examples, the first with a descriptive adjective as an object complement and the second with a noun.

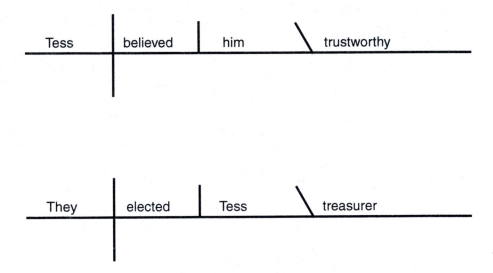

Sentence Exercise #16: Diagramming the Basic Sentence _____

Diagram the following sentences. (Answers to this exercise are on page 418.)

1. Fred heard Wilma.

2. Fred seems frantic.

3. Fred resembles Barney.

4. Barney coughed.

5. Fred gave Barney measles.

6. Wilma was angry.

7. Fred left.

8. Barney resented Fred.

9. Fred made Wilma angry.

10. Fred sold Barney Bedrock.

All **modifiers** are written on lines that slope down and to the right. (Remember, no modifier can appear on the main sentence line.) Modifiers are attached to the main sentence line underneath the words they modify. Thus, adjectives are attached to the nouns they modify, and adverbs are attached to the verbs or predicate adjectives on the main sentence line that they modify. Adverbs that modify modifying adjectives or adverbs are attached to the sides of the words they modify. Here is an example of all the various types of modifiers:

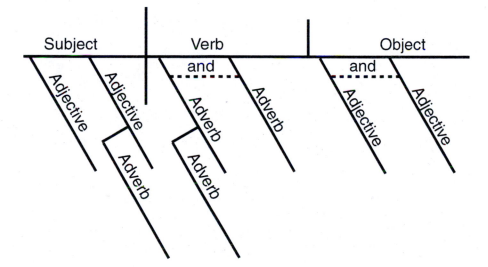

Note the compound adjectives modifying the object. The coordinating conjunction is put on a dashed line that connects the two adjectives.

Sentence Exercise #17: Diagramming the Basic Sentence _____

Diagram the following sentences. (Answers to this exercise are on page 419.)

1. They quickly lowered the last lifeboat.

2. Popeye nearly always split his infinitives.

3. The room was a complete mess.

4. The band played new and old songs.

5. The event became an urban legend.

6. The teacher appointed Marvin the room monitor.

7. The phones rang loudly and endlessly.

8. Dagwood made himself a huge sandwich.

9. The hiker was quite badly hurt.

10. That class always gives me a very bad headache.

There are also conventions for other types of sentences, some of which include the following.

Imperative sentences have an understood *you* as the subject. The convention for all understood words is to put them in parentheses. Here is how the sentence "Go away" is diagrammed.

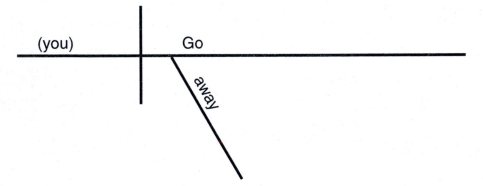

Interrogative sentences (questions) are diagrammed by rearranging the words so that they are in the same order as they would be in the corresponding declarative sentence (statement). Several examples are shown here:

Is John angry?

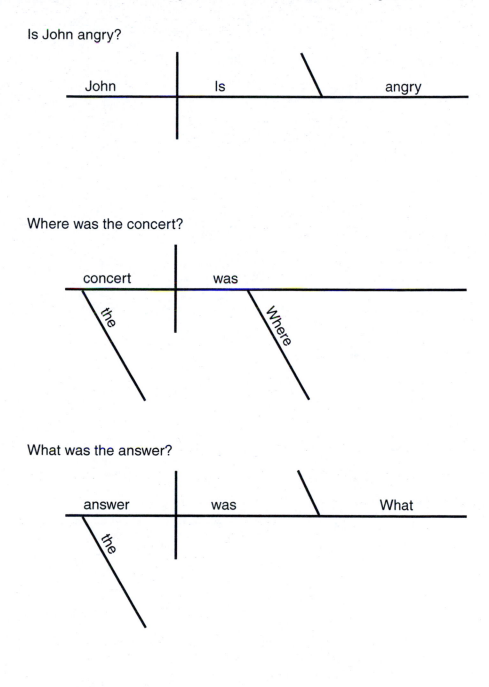

Where was the concert?

What was the answer?

The diagram for questions formed with the helping verb *do* (*do/does/did*) can lead to confusion with another use of *do*. For example, here is how we would diagram the question "Do you like anchovies?"

| you | Do like | anchovies |

Don't confuse the *do* in the diagram with the totally different *do* that is used to make emphatic statements, as in the following.

Normal statement: You like anchovies.
Emphatic statement: You **DO** like anchovies!

The following shows the conventions for diagramming **compound subjects, verbs,** and **complements.**

Compound Subjects

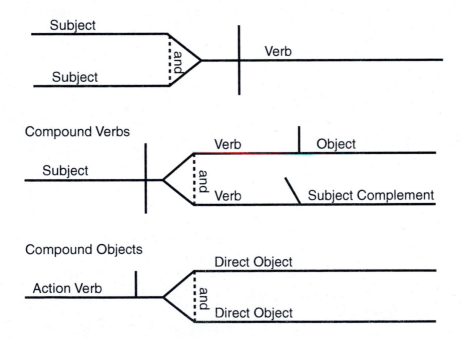

Compound Verbs

Compound Objects

Compound Subject Complements

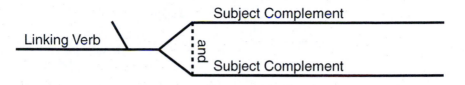

Finally, here are some helpful hints about diagramming:

- Always write the main sentence line first, and then fill in the modifiers.
- No sentence punctuation is used in diagramming—no periods, commas, question marks, or exclamation points. However, capital letters and apostrophes are kept.
- When two different adjectives or adverbs modify the same word on the main sentence line, put the adjectives or adverbs in the same left-to-right order in which they occur in the original sentence.
- *Not* is an adverb drawn underneath whatever word it modifies.
- Helping verbs are put in front of the main verb in their normal order.
- Multiple-word proper nouns—names and titles—are always kept together as though they were a single word.
- Hyphenated words are always kept together as a single word.

Sentence Exercise #18: Diagramming the Basic Sentence ———

Diagram the following sentences. (Answers to this exercise are on page 421.)

1. Most politicians kiss babies and shake hands.
2. Ralph's comment was not appropriate.
3. We went home and changed clothes.
4. Answer the phone.
5. He tapped his glass and cleared his throat loudly.
6. Joan and I sanded that old desk yesterday.
7. The residents were constantly complaining and whining.
8. It drove Ford crazy.
9. Are you coming?
10. Did you get my message?
11. When are we leaving?

12. The Count politely took a very small bite.

13. The plumber flooded the basement and the garage.

14. Lady Grenville greeted the humble peasants gracefully.

15. I must have been dreaming.

Sentence Exercise #19: Diagramming the Basic Sentence ⸺

Diagram the following sentences. (Answers to this exercise are on page 424.)

1. Did she find Anne an apartment?

2. A policeman's lot is not a happy one.

3. I had a really terrible cold recently.

4. Wasn't the rainy landscape gloomy and depressing?

5. They explored the constantly changing desert.

6. Tarzan and Jane loathe bananas.

7. Did you take your pills?

8. The mysterious red stain had appeared again.

9. The dog gave Holmes an idea.

10. I am getting tired.

11. What are you saying?

12. The office resembled a bad movie set.

13. What did you do then?

14. The press considered Senator Fogg a big windbag.

15. Naturally, he had wanted a full-time job and reasonable pay.

4

Verb Forms, "Tense," and Helping Verbs

This chapter discusses a number of topics related to verbs. The first part of the chapter describes all six verb forms—the **base**, the **present tense**, the **past tense**, the **infinitive**, the **present participle**, and the **past participle**. The second part discusses the many problems connected with the term "tense" in traditional grammar. This part of the chapter concludes with a redefinition of "tense" using concepts from modern grammar. The third part of the chapter pulls together the information from the first two parts to describe the four complex verb structures that are built with helping verbs: **modals**, the **perfect**, the **progressive**, and the **passive**.

Verb Forms

All verbs (with the exception of *be* and the **modal verbs** *can, may, must, shall,* and *will*) have six different forms. The six forms are listed below and illustrated by the regular verb *talk* and the irregular verb *sing*:

Verb Forms					
Base Form	*Present Tense*	*Past Tense*	*Infinitive*	*Present Participle*	*Past Participle*
talk	talk/talks	talked	to talk	talking	talked
sing	sing/sings	sang	to sing	singing	singing

We will now look at each of these six forms in more detail, seeing how each is formed.

Base Form

The **base form** is the dictionary-entry form of a word—the form of the word that appears in the dictionary. For example, if you look up the verb *sang* in the dictionary, the dictionary will refer you to *sing*. *Sing* is the dictionary-entry form (or base form) for that verb. The base form is used (1) in commands when the subject is an understood *you* (also known as imperative sentences), (2) after the modal verbs (*can, may, must, shall, will*), and (3) in a few other multiple-verb constructions.

At first glance, it may seem difficult to tell base forms from present tenses because in most cases they look identical. However, there is one verb whose base form is completely different from its present-tense forms: *be.*

> Base: <u>be</u>
> Present: I <u>am</u>,
>   you <u>are</u>,
>   he/she/it <u>is</u>,
>   we/you/they <u>are</u>.

We can use *be* to test whether a verb is being used in the present tense or in the base form. For example, here are a group of commands with understood *you:*

> *Go* away!
>
> *Stop* that!
>
> *Tell* me the truth!
>
> *Answer* the question.
>
> Oh, *behave*!

We can tell that commands require a base form when we use the verb *be* in the command:

> *Be* good!
>
> *Be* prepared!
>
> Please *be* on time.
>
> *Be* careful what you wish for.

If we use the present-tense form of *be* to agree with the understood *you*, the commands come out this way:

> **Are* good!
>
> **Are* careful!

*Please *are* on time.

*Are careful what you wish for.

These commands are all ungrammatical because we use the base form, not the present-tense form, in commands.

The other common use of base forms is with the five modal **helping verbs:** *can, may, must, shall,* and *will.* (Helping verbs are verbs that are used in front of a second verb and that control the form of the second verb.)

I can *talk.*	I can *sing.*
I may *talk.*	I may *sing.*
I must *talk.*	I must *sing.*
I shall *talk.*	I shall *sing.*
I will *talk.*	I will *sing.*

Again, we can tell that verbs following modal helping verbs are in the base form by using the verb *be:*

I can *be* ready at six.

We may *be* able to do that.

I must *be* mistaken.

We shall *be* prepared next time.

They will *be* upset.

If we try to use the present tense of the verb *be* to agree with the subject, the results are impossible:

**I can *am* ready at six.

**We may *are* able to do that.

**I must *am* mistaken.

**We shall *are* prepared next time.

**They will *are* upset.

The *be* replacement test. Replace any verb with the appropriate form of the verb *be.* If the appropriate form is the base form *be,* then that verb is a base form. If the appropriate replacement form is *am, are,* or *is,* then the verb is a present-tense form. Note: this test will often require you to change the verb's complement so that the substitution of *be* makes sense.

Here are several examples of the *be* replacement test applied to sentences with both base forms and present tenses.

<table>
<tr><td></td><td>We should *talk*.</td></tr>
<tr><td>*Be* replacement:</td><td>We should *be* good.</td></tr>
<tr><td></td><td>*We should *are* good.</td></tr>
</table>

(The successful substitution of *be* shows that *talk* is a base form.)

<table>
<tr><td></td><td>They *seem* upset about something.</td></tr>
<tr><td>*Be* replacement:</td><td>*They *be* upset about something.</td></tr>
<tr><td></td><td>They *are* upset about something.</td></tr>
</table>

(The successful substitution of *are*, a present-tense form, shows that *seem* is present tense, not base form, in that sentence.)

Verb Exercise #1: Identifying Base Forms by the be Replacement Test

Label the underlined verb forms as PRES or BASE. Confirm your answers by applying the *be* replacement test. The first question is done as an example. (Answers to this exercise are on page 426.)

0. The devil made me <u>do</u> it.

   Answer: The devil made me <u>do</u> it.

                                                 BASE

   Confirmation: The devil made me <u>be</u> unpleasant.

1. I can't <u>get</u> ready by then.

2. They never <u>become</u> very good players.

3. You wouldn't <u>want</u> that.

4. You shouldn't let it <u>upset</u> you.

5. The butler will <u>see</u> you out.

6. Sarah helped us <u>get</u> prepared.

7. It couldn't <u>come</u> at a worse time.

8. Have John <u>take</u> you home.

9. Sometimes, the easiest things <u>appear</u> the most difficult.

10. Let me <u>help</u> you.

Present Tense

The present-tense forms are all derived from the base form. In other words, if you know the base form of a verb (except for *be*, of course), you can predict all the present-tense forms. Let us again use as our example the regular verb *talk* and the irregular verb *sing*.

		Present-Tense Forms	
Base		*talk*	*sing*
1st-person singular:	I	talk	sing
2nd-person singular:	you	talk	sing
3rd-person singular:	he/she/it	talks	sings
1st-person plural:	we	talk	sing
2nd-person plural:	you	talk	sing
3rd-person plural:	they	talk	sing

As you can see, all persons and numbers are the same as the base form EXCEPT the 3rd-person singular, which adds *-(e)s* to the base form. The major exception to this pattern is the verb *be:*

Base		*be*
1st-person singular:	I	am
2nd-person singular:	you	are
3rd-person singular:	he/she/it	is
1st-person plural:	we	are
2nd-person plural:	you	are
3rd-person plural:	they	are

Another exception is the verb *have,* which uses *has* as its 3rd-person singular rather than the expected **haves.*

(The final group of exceptions is the modals. There are so many peculiar features about modals that we will postpone any further discussion of them until the third section of this chapter on helping verbs.)

Past Tense

For regular verbs, the past tense is also predictable from the base form, which is why regular verbs are called "regular." The past tense is the base form plus *-ed* (or *-d* if the base ends in *-e*), for example:

Base	*Past*
talk	talk*ed*
whisper	whisper*ed*
shout	shout*ed*
scream	scream*ed*
murmur	murmur*ed*
laugh	laugh*ed*
fade	fade*d*

However, for irregular verbs, the past tense form cannot be predicted from the base form. Each past tense must be learned separately. There is detailed discussion of the main types of irregular past tense verb forms in Chapter 2, beginning on page 51.

The verb *be* is unique in having two past tenses—*was* with singular subjects and *were* with plural subjects:

Singular: I *was* a student.
Plural: They *were* students.

Infinitive

The infinitive is also formed from the base form. It consists of *to* plus the base form of the verb. The infinitive is completely regular, for example,

Base	*Infinitive*
talk	*to* talk
sing	*to* sing
do	*to* do
have	*to* have
be	*to* be

(A note on terminology: Sometimes the term *infinitive* is also used for the base form. In this case, we distinguish between a "bare infinitive" without the *to* and a "marked infinitive" with the *to*.)

Present Participle

The present participle consists of the base form of the verb plus an *-ing* ending, for example,

Base	*Present Participle*
talk	talk*ing*
sing	sing*ing*
hop	hopp*ing*
hope	hop*ing*
have	hav*ing*
do	do*ing*
be	be*ing*

The present participle is also completely regular. Even the verb *be* is regular: *being*. Notice, however, that the rules of spelling will sometimes cause the present participle form to be SPELLED differently from the base form. For example, *hop* follows the doubled-consonant spelling rule when we add the

-ing, so *hop* becomes *hopping.* Words that end with a final silent *-e* predictably drop the *-e* when we add *-ing,* so *hope* becomes *hoping,* and *have* becomes *having.* These spelling changes are merely the normal result of adding a suffix beginning with a vowel (*-ing*) and have nothing to do with the grammar of how the present participle is formed.

Past Participle

Whereas the present participle is completely regular, the past participle is nothing but grief. The past participles of irregular verbs are hard to recognize because today there is no consistent identifiable form for the past participle. In Old English most past participles of irregular verbs ended in *-en.* Today, all we can say is that if a verb has an *-en* ending (or *-n* if the verb already ends in an *-e*), then it is a past participle, for example,

Base	*Past Participle*
fall	fall*en*
eat	eat*en*
see	see*n*
chose	chos*en*
freeze	froz*en*
rise	rise*n*
hide	hidd*en*
be	be*en*
do	do*ne*

(Note the irregularity of the pronunciation of *been* and *done. Been* rhymes with *sin* rather than *seen* (in American English, though not in British English). *Done* rhymes with *tun* rather than *tune.*)

The problem today is that the past participle of many irregular verbs does not end in *-en:*

Base	*Past Participle*
tell	told
sing	sung
have	had
bring	brought
sell	sold
hit	hit
put	put

The past-participle form of regular verbs poses a completely different problem. The past participle of regular verbs always ends in *-(e)d.* The problem is that the past tense also ends in *-(e)d,* so students easily confuse the past and past-participle forms of regular verbs.

Teaching Tip

When teaching the past-participle verb forms, whether regular or irregular, always use the helping verb *have* (*have/has/had*). The helping verb *have* MUST be followed by a past participle. This way, students can see the difference in usage between the past participle and the past tense. Here are some examples using the verb *talk:*

Past: They *talked* all night.

Past participle: They *have **talked*** all night.

                   They *had **talked*** all night.

Here are some regular verbs in the past participle form following *have:*

Base	**have + *Past Participle***
talk	have *talked*
whisper	have *whispered*
shout	have *shouted*
scream	have *screamed*
murmur	have *murmured*
laugh	have *laughed*

Verb Exercise #2: Identifying Verb Forms

Using the base form as your starting point, give the 3rd-person singular present, the past tense, the infinitive, the present participle, and the past participle forms. The first question is done as an example. (Answers to this exercise are on page 427.)

	Base	*3d Sg Pres*	*Past*	*Inf*	*Pres Part*	**have + *Past Part***
0.	sing	sings	sang	to sing	singing	have sung
1.	forget					
2.	choose					
3.	come					
4.	protest					
5.	fade					
6.	buy					
7.	go					
8.	run					

	Base	3d Sg Pres	Past	Inf	Pres Part	have + Past Part
9.	fulfill					
10.	substitute					
11.	dig					
12.	concede					
13.	dream					
14.	spend					
15.	inquire					
16.	do					
17.	sell					
18.	split					
19.	have					
20.	be					

The six verb forms can be divided into two categories, **tensed** and **nontensed**:

Tensed:	present tense (*talk/talks; sing/sings*)
	past tense (*talked; sang*)
Nontensed:	base (*talk; sing*)
	infinitive (*to talk; to sing*)
	present participle (*talking; singing*)
	past participle (*talked; sung*)

The tensed forms (present and past) can all stand by themselves without the aid of any helping verbs. With the exception of imperative sentences (commands with understood *you* as subject), which take base forms, **all sentences must contain a tensed verb.**

Tensed:	Present Tense:	She *is* happy.
	Past tense:	She *was* happy.

Nontensed verbs can never stand by themselves:

Nontensed:	Base:	*She *be* happy.
	Infinitive:	*She *to be* happy.
	Present Participle:	*She *being* happy.
	Past Participle:	*She *been* happy.

The nontensed forms of the verb are used in multiple-verb constructions. Here are some examples:

I *was*   *working*   on it.
  Past Present participle

He *has*   *reported*   the stolen car.
   Present   Past participle

The waiter *wanted* us *to order* something.
              Past   Infinitive

The teacher *made* the children *be* quiet.
               Past   Base

Notice that in multiple-verb constructions, the first verb (and only the first verb) is always a tensed verb, either present tense or past tense. This first, tensed verb is the only verb that requires subject–verb agreement. The nontensed forms never enter into subject–verb agreement relations with the subject.

Notice also that after the first, tensed verb, all subsequent verbs in multiple-verb constructions are nontensed: base, infinitive, present participle, or past participle.

Verb Exercise #3: Identifying Verb Forms _____

Label the underlined verb forms. Use Pres for present tense; Past for past tense; Base; Inf for infinitive; Pres Part for present participle; and Past Part for past participle. (Remember, only the first verb can be present or past tense.) The first question is done as an example. (Answers to this exercise are on page 427.)

0. I have been working on that.

Answer: I <u>have</u>   <u>been</u>   <u>working</u> on that.
        Pres   Past Part   Pres Part

1. I <u>have</u> already <u>read</u> that book.

2. They <u>criticized</u> the plot unmercifully.

3. He <u>was</u> <u>scratching</u> his head.

4. You <u>are</u> merely <u>prolonging</u> the situation.

5. The doctor <u>had</u> just <u>administered</u> the test.

6. We <u>have</u> <u>had</u> a very good time.

7. They <u>wanted</u> him <u>to come</u> back.

8. The bridge <u>was</u> slowly <u>collapsing</u> into the river.

9. The cars <u>merge</u> onto the freeway at a very high speed.

10. We <u>had</u> <u>been</u> <u>studying</u> for hours.

11. The instructor <u>made</u> us <u>try</u> it again.

12. I <u>wasn't</u> <u>going</u> <u>to do</u> anything.

13. The band <u>was</u> <u>featuring</u> the loudest amplifiers in the known universe.

14. The chair <u>demanded</u> that he <u>be</u> quiet.

15. We <u>wanted</u> you <u>to be</u> happy.

16. I <u>hate</u> them <u>interrupting</u> all the time.

17. The professor <u>let</u> her <u>give</u> the answer.

18. The children <u>have</u> <u>been</u> <u>watching</u> too much TV.

19. I <u>get</u> it.

20. We <u>heard</u> him <u>ringing</u> the doorbell.

"Tense"

The term "tense" is surprisingly confusing. At first glance, it may not seem to be an issue. Doesn't everybody know that "tense" means "time"—past, present, and future?

There are a number of problems in defining "tense" as time. For example, the "present tense" in English almost never means present time; the "future" isn't really a tense at all; and the "perfect tense" can refer to past, present, or future time equally well. Another problem is that the term "tense" excludes a number of important verb constructions as though they did not even exist. For example, there is literally no tense name to label the verbs in these sentences: I *can go;* It *is raining;* I *was sleeping.*

The source of the problem is historical: tense and the terminology we use for verbs was never originally intended for English. It is—lock, stock, and barrel—the terminology that evolved for describing the verb system of Latin. The origin of this bizarre situation is rooted in the first English grammar books and the traditions for teaching English that began in the renaissance and continued through the early part of the twentieth century.

One of the first, and by far the most important, schoolroom English grammar books was *Lyly's Grammar* by William Lyly (written around 1513). In 1542 King Henry VIII made it the standard text for all schools in England. It is undoubtedly the textbook that Shakespeare used in his schooling. Editions of this book continued to appear until 1858, a lifespan of over 300 years.

The purpose of the book was not to teach English grammar for its own sake. Instead, it was intended to introduce the terminology that students would need when they learned Latin. In other words, it introduced Latin grammar by using examples from English as a stepping-stone. Since the purpose of the book was to introduce Latin grammar, it is not surprising that just those features of English grammar that had counterparts in Latin grammar were taught. The many, many areas in which English differed from Latin were simply ignored as being irrelevant, which they were—from the standpoint of teaching the grammar of Latin. As a result of this book and the corresponding centuries-long teaching tradition built on this Latin foundation, we are stuck with a set of terms for describing English verbs that are (as we will see) at best misleading and at worst wrong.

All of this puts the English teacher in a difficult situation. We cannot simply abandon the conventional verb terminology, because there is no agreed-upon set of terms to replace it. The alternative that most textbooks follow to a greater or lesser degree is to use the conventional terms but to supplement them with more accurate descriptions. Junior and senior high school textbooks are relatively conservative in their use of conventional terms, but even in these books the teacher's edition often implicitly contradicts what the student's edition says. Grammar texts intended for non-native speakers tend to be much more descriptively accurate, for the obvious reason that the texts need to be much more specific about how the English verb system actually works because non-native speakers cannot fill in the gaps intuitively the way native speakers can.

The approach in this book is middle-of-the-road. It gives the conventional terminology, but supplements it quite extensively with a more modern analysis that will help both native and non-native speakers make sense out of the way English actually works.

Strangely enough, the terminology for verb tense that we use today is not ancient. It arose in the middle of the nineteenth century out of the then-current Latin grammar books being used in England. In this model there are three "simple" tenses, **present, past**, and **future;** and three **perfect tenses, present perfect, past perfect**, and **future perfect**.

Simple	*Perfect*
Present:	**Present Perfect:**
I *talk*	I *have talked*
I *sing*	I *have sung*
Past:	**Past Perfect:**
I *talked*	I *had talked*
I *sang*	I *had sung*
Future:	**Future Perfect:**
I *will talk*	I *will have talked*
I *will sing*	I *will have sung*

The reason we have these six tense names is that they are the translations of the six tensed verb forms in Latin. The term "tense" is much better defined in Latin than it is in English. In Latin, "tense" means the tensed forms of the verb. In other words, there are six tensed verb forms in Latin. The six forms given in the chart above are rough English translations of those six tensed forms.

The trouble with the traditional Latin-based terms for English is that they are not very accurate labels for the way English verbs really work. English and Latin are distantly related languages, but in terms of the verb, the two languages are not at all alike. What may work well for describing Latin verbs does not necessarily work very well for English verbs.

Starting from scratch, let's ask the same question of English that grammarians did of Latin: how many tensed verb forms are there? In other words, if we define "tense" strictly as the forms of the verb that can be used by themselves and that can enter into subject–verb agreement relations with the subject, how many tenses are there in English? The answer may come as a surprise: only two—the present tense and the past tense.

Present tense:	I *talk* a lot.
	I *sing* a lot.
Past tense:	I *talked* a lot.
	I *sang* a lot.

All of the other verb forms in English are multiple-verb constructions, and by the strict definition of tense as tensed verb forms that can stand alone, they are not tenses. The "future" doesn't count as a tense because it uses the helping verb *will*, and the "perfect tense" doesn't count because it uses the helping verb *have*.

Present and Past Tenses

Before we examine the four multiple-verb constructions that use helping verbs, let us look at the meaning and use of the present and past tenses in more detail.

Present Tense.   Contrary to what many people might think, we rarely use the present tense to refer to present time. The most common uses of the present tense are for (1) **statements of fact** or (2) **generalizations,** both of which are necessarily disconnected from the present moment of time.

Statements of Fact

> Two plus two *equals* four.

> Gold *dissolves* in mercury.

> I *hate* liver.

None of the above statements of fact refers to the present time. These statements are essentially "timeless." They range from mathematical truisms

("Two plus two equals four"), to laws of physics ("Gold dissolves in mercury"), to statements of fact that are true for the foreseeable future but that may not be true forever ("I hate liver"). Notice how strange it would be to tie these "timeless" statements of fact to the present moment:

> *Two plus two *equals* four now.

> *Gold *dissolves* in mercury now.

> *I *hate* liver now.

All three of these revised sentences imply that the statement is true ONLY for the present moment. For example, the first revised sentence implies that two plus two equals four is a recent development, and that it was not true in the past and may not continue to be true in the future.

Note that a statement of fact does not need to be true to be a statement of fact. A statement of fact is merely an assertion that something is factual, which may or may not be the case. By using the present tense, the writer is asserting that the statement should be accepted as factual.

Sometimes, statements of fact are used to describe some habitual action. For example, in the sentence

> I *shop* at Safeway.

the writer uses the present tense to state that it is his or her normal custom to shop at Safeway. It does not mean that the writer is in the process of shopping at Safeway at this very moment of present time. In fact, the sentence is still a valid statement of fact even if the writer has been out of town and has not shopped at Safeway in a month.

Generalizations

> Shakespeare *is* the most important playwright in English.

> The new Audi *is* the best-looking car on the road.

> Fast food restaurants *exploit* their employees.

Generalizations are assertions on matters of opinion—we can agree with the writer or not. Generalizations can be strongly or poorly supported, but they can never be reduced to a purely factual matter—if they could, they would become statements of fact. Since much of life is a matter of opinion, the use of the present tense to make generalizations is probably the most common use of the present tense. (Note that the previous sentence is a generalization made with the present tense.)

Verb Exercise #4: Identifying Uses of the Present Tense _____

Underline all of the present tense verbs and state whether they are statements of fact or generalizations. (Remember that a statement of fact does not need to be actually true.) The first question is done as an example. (Answers to this exercise are on page 429.)

  0. Everybody knows that Bismark is the capital of North Dakota.

     Answer: Everybody   <u>knows</u>   that Bismark <u>is</u> the capital of North Dakota.
                          Generalization   Fact

  1. Fortune cookies are unknown in China.

  2. There are 64 squares on a standard checker or chess board.

  3. The governor is soft on crime.

  4. Las Vegas, Nevada, is one of the fastest-growing cities in the country.

  5. The new drug reduces the risk of stroke by 50%.

  6. Everyone needs to take that drug.

  7. John Wayne's last movies are ridiculous because he is too old and fat for the roles.

  8. The reservoir holds 100 million gallons of water.

  9. A good supervisor knows when to ignore little problems.

 10. While pickup trucks are a lot cheaper than cars, they are less safe.

Past Tense. Mercifully, the past tense is straightforward. It refers to an action completed in the past, for example,

> Grampa finally *sold* the farm.

The past tense does not tell us whether selling the farm was a single, momentary event or a long-drawn-out, continuous process (which is what the past tense would mean in Latin). All it tells us is that the action of selling the farm was completed, over-and-done-with, sometime before the present moment.

    We use the past tense for talking about past events or for telling stories. Most novels, for example, are written in the past tense. The past tense and the present tense are complementary—we use the past tense for narratives and the present for statements of fact and generalizations. We shift constantly from one tense to the other as we shift back and forth from narration to generalization. For example, notice the shift from past-tense narrative to present-tense generalizations in the following quotation from an article by Robert D. Kaplan in the August 1998 issue of *The Atlantic Monthly:*

> As I *drove* through greater Los Angeles, the term "city-state" *was* foremost in my mind, not because L. A. *is* similar to ancient Athens or Sparta but because

of the very size and eye-popping variety of this thriving urban confederation. Santa Monica *has* the ambiance of a beach resort, East Los Angeles *is* like Mexico, Monterey Park *is* like Asia, and Cerritos *is* an Asian Levittown for the Nineties. (p. 43)

The first two verbs are in the past tense because the author is narrating a story drawn from his own experience. The remaining verbs are all in the present tense because the author shifts to making generalizations. The past tense is for events that are tied to a past moment; the present tense is for "timeless" generalizations.

Verb Exercise #5: Using Present and Past Tenses _____

Replace the underlined base-form verb with either a present tense or a past-tense verb as appropriate. The first question is done as an example. (Answers to this exercise are on page 429.)

   0. Shakespeare write Hamlet around 1600.

      Answer: Shakespeare write Hamlet around 1600.
                           wrote

   1. The play deal with extremely complex themes.

   2. Many critics think that Hamlet be Shakespeare's most difficult play.

   3. One problem be that apparently Shakespeare revise it a number of times.

   4. The modern text combine a number of different revisions.

   5. Until recent times, people believe that illness be caused by imbalances of humors in the blood.

   6. In the 1620s William Harvey, a British physician, discover the circulation of blood.

   7. Harvey's discovery destroy the basis for bloodletting, the main treatment for most illnesses.

   8. Nevertheless, the practice of bloodletting continue for a long time.

   9. In fact, George Washington be bled to death.

   10. It be amazing how conservative medical practices be even today.

Helping-Verb Constructions

Let us now turn to the four major multiple-verb constructions of English that use helping verbs: **modals**, the **perfect**, the **progressive**, and the **passive**. **Helping verbs** are verbs that come before a second verb and always control the form of that second verb. (Note: in this section we will reserve the term "tense" for just the present and past forms of the first verb, either a single main verb or the first verb in a multiple-verb construction.)

Modals

Why does English use the helping verb *will* for the future when Latin has a separate tensed form for the future? In other words, what happened to the future-tense form of the verb in English? The answer is that the future-tense form of the verb, which did exist at one time in the very distant past, disappeared from the Germanic ancestor language of English (and its other Germanic cousins—German, Dutch, and the Scandinavian languages) some 2,000+ years ago. One reason the future tense disappeared may be that it was driven into extinction by the growth of a set of helping verbs called **modal verbs** that was much better at describing future events than a single future-tense verb form was. In modern English there are five modal verbs:

	Modal Verbs	
Base	*Present*	*Past*
can	can	could
may	may	might
must	must	—
shall	shall	should
will	will	would

For complicated historical reasons, the modal verbs have very irregular forms. They do not have infinitive or participle forms. They are the only verbs in English that do not have a third-person singular -s. For example, we say *he **can** go*, not **he **cans** go; she **may** go*, but not **she **mays** go. Must* is the only verb in English that does not have a past-tense form. Even the terms "present" and "past" are misleading, because none of the modal forms really refers to time, present or past. When applied to modals, the terms "present" and "past" refer only to the historical form of the modals, NOT their meaning.

The most common use for the modals is to talk about the probability or necessity of something happening—which is why we often use them for talking about the future. Notice that we can use both "present" and "past" tense forms equally well to refer to the future.

Present modal:	I *can* go to Boston tomorrow.
Past modal:	I *could* go to Boston tomorrow.
Present modal:	I *may* go to Boston tomorrow.
Past modal:	I *might* go to Boston tomorrow.
Present modal:	I *must* go to Boston tomorrow.

Present modal:	I *shall* go to Boston tomorrow.
Past modal:	I *should* go to Boston tomorrow.
Present modal:	I *will* go to Boston tomorrow.
Past modal:	I *would* go to Boston tomorrow if I had the chance.

The nine different modal forms give us the ability to make very subtle distinctions about present and future events. None of the nine examples above means exactly the same thing, though we can generalize that the past-tense forms tend to imply doubt (*I **might** go to Boston tomorrow, but I probably won't*) or even that what is being said is not going to happen (*I **should** go to Boston tomorrow, but I'm not.*) The subtle differences in the meanings of modals is particularly difficult for non-native speakers because what a particular modal means is so dependent on context and even tone of voice.

Traditional grammar identified one of these forms, *will*, as the best translation of the future-tense form of the verb in Latin. Since there is nothing in Latin like the other eight modals, traditional grammars of English completely ignored them—as though they did not exist. Quite literally, there is no traditional name for any of the nine modal verbs above except for *will*. (Interestingly, Italian, the modern descendant of Latin, has developed two modals that correspond closely to *can* and *must*.)

Notice that in all of the modal verb examples above, the modal was followed by the base form of the verb *go*. This is a strict requirement. The modal helping verb MUST be followed immediately by a base-form verb. At this point we have a small terminological problem. The modal helping verb and the following base-form verb make a multiple-verb construction that has no conventional name because its existence was never recognized in traditional grammar. Let us adopt the following terminology. We will refer collectively to the multiple-verb construction as "modal" and to the actual helping verb itself as a "modal verb." We can think of the modal as having this formula:

Modal = Modal verb + Base verb

Verb Exercise #6: Modals and Base Forms _____

Add the indicated modal verb to the sentence. Change the main verb to its base form. The first question is done as an example. (Answers to this exercise are on page 430.)

0. I <u>am</u> ready to go anytime. **(can)**

   Answer: I <u>can be</u> ready to go anytime.

1. She <u>sings</u> in the church choir. **(can)**

2. I <u>answered</u> the question. **(could)**

3. The train <u>is</u> on time for a change. **(may)**

4. It <u>is</u> raining. **(might)**

5. Fred <u>did</u> the dishes for a change. **(must)**

6. General MacArthur is famous for saying, "I <u>return</u>." **(shall)**

7. We <u>are</u> leaving soon. **(should)**

8. I <u>am</u> seeing you. **(will)**

9. We thought that there <u>is</u> time for that later. **(would)**

10. You <u>took</u> an umbrella. **(should)**

Perfect

What is so perfect about the perfect? The answer is "nothing." The grammatical term "perfect" was coined in the nineteenth century to describe the three "nonsimple" tenses in Latin. The term "perfect" comes from the Latin phrase *per factus,* meaning "completely done." The three Latin tenses were called "perfect" because each of the three tenses dealt with two different times—an earlier time that was "completely done" or finished before the second, later time occurred. The **present perfect** meant a past action done (finished) before the present time. The **past perfect** meant a past action finished before a second, more recent past time. The **future perfect** meant an action to be done in the future before some even more distant time.

In English, the term "perfect" applies to a verb construction that uses the helping verb *have* in some form, followed by a verb in the past-participle form.

- If *have* is used in its present tense forms *have* or *has,* the construction is called the **present perfect.**
- If *have* is used in its past tense form *had,* the construction is called the **past perfect.**
- If *have* is preceded by the modal *will,* in what traditional grammar calls the future, the construction is called the **future perfect.**

Here is a brief discussion of the meaning of each of the three forms of the perfect, together with some examples that illustrate each of the meanings.

Present perfect = *have/has* + Past participle

We use the present perfect in two ways. The most common use is to describe actions that have occurred continuously or repeatedly from some past time right up to the present moment (sometimes with the implication that the actions will continue on into the future), for example:

Continuous action:

That line *has been* busy for half an hour.

The kids *have watched* TV all afternoon.

The garage *has had* my car for a week, and it still isn't finished.

Repeated action:

I *have talked* to them until I am blue in the face.

The choir *has sung* that hymn a hundred time.

It *has rained* all summer.

The difference between the present perfect and the past tense is that the present perfect emphasizes the continual or repeated nature of past events through a period of time lasting right up to the present, while the past tense describes a single past event that was over and done with in the past. Here is a pair of sentences that illustrates the difference:

Present perfect: Elliot *has lived* in Chicago for ten years.
Past tense: Elliot *lived* in Chicago for ten years.

In the first sentence, the use of the present perfect tells us (1) that Elliot has lived in Chicago for a period of ten continuous years, (2) that Elliot still lives in Chicago now, and (3) that Elliot will probably continue to live in Chicago for the foreseeable future. In the second sentence, the use of the past tense tells us that although Elliot used to live in Chicago, he doesn't live there anymore. Here is how we might represent these sentences on a timeline:

Present Perfect: Elliot **has lived** in Chicago for ten years.

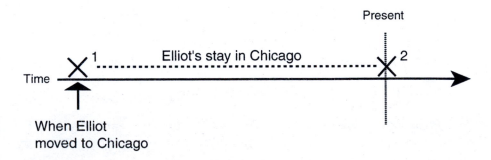

Past Tense: Elliot **lived** in Chicago for ten years.

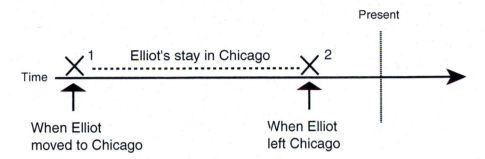

The second use of the present perfect is to describe a recent past event that still very much affects the present moment (as opposed to the over-and-done-with nature of the past tense), for example,

> I'm sorry, Mr. Smith *has stepped* away from his desk for a moment.
>
> Nothing for us thanks, we *have* already *eaten* dinner.
>
> I *have* just *figured* out the answer to the problem.

This use of the present perfect can be used to describe a single past event, but the event must be so recent that it directly and immediately impacts the present moment. Compare the following two sentences:

> Sam *has lost* his car keys.
>
> *Sam *has lost* his car keys yesterday.

The first sentence is grammatical because it implies that Sam is actively searching for his car keys even as we speak, and that it might be a good idea if we were to help him find them. The second sentence is ungrammatical because it too far in the past. How far something has to be in the past for the present perfect to be ungrammatical is somewhat arbitrary—to a geologist, a million years ago might seem like the immediate past.

Verb Exercise #7: Using the Present Perfect _____

Change the underlined past-tense verbs to the present perfect. The first question is done as an example. (Answers to this exercise are on page 430.)

0. John <u>watched</u> TV all afternoon.

Answer: John <u>has watched</u> TV all afternoon.

1. Freddy Fireball <u>was</u> a great pitcher.

2. Recently I <u>invested</u> a lot of money in mutual funds.

3. The reviewers <u>criticized</u> his recent movies.

4. You <u>hurt</u> their feelings.

5. The phone <u>was</u> out all afternoon.

6. We <u>were</u> here so long that I think our waiter must have gone home.

7. It <u>snowed</u> off and on all winter.

8. Your carelessness just <u>caused</u> an accident!

9. Thelma <u>read</u> every book that Louise ever wrote.

10. The mysterious hound <u>appeared</u> on the moor several times.

Past perfect = *had* + Past participle

We use the past perfect when we want to emphasize the fact that a particular event in the past was completed before a more recent event took place. Here are four numbered examples, each with a brief discussion:

(1) I *had* just *stepped* into the shower when the phone rang.

In example (1), there are two past-time events in this order: (a) first, my stepping into the shower, and then (b) the phone's ringing. If we were to use the past tense instead of the past perfect,

I just *stepped* into the shower when the phone rang,

it changes the meaning of the sentence. It sounds like the two events happened at the same time. The whole point of the past perfect is to emphasize the frustration of already being inside the shower BEFORE the phone started to ring. This is how we might represent this sentence on a timeline:

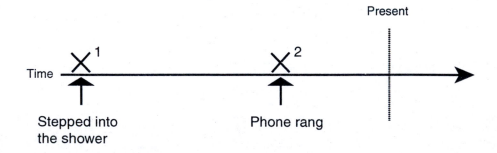

(2) When we bought the house last year, it *had been* empty for ten years.

In example (2), there are two statements about the house. The second part of the sentence uses the past perfect to show what had happened to the house in the ten-year period BEFORE the point in time last year when we bought the house. Here is how we might represent this sentence on a timeline:

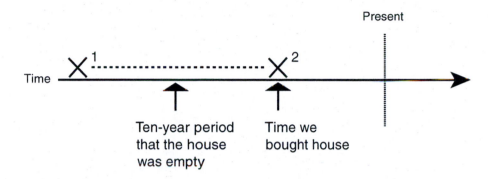

(3) When we got to the airport, we realized we *had left* our passports at home.

In example (3), the writer of this sentence wants to emphasize the relative order of the two events: (a) we got to the airport, and THEN (b) we realized that we had made a big mistake BEFORE we went to the airport. If the writer had remembered about their passports before they had left home, there would have been no problem. Shown below is how we might represent this sentence on a time line:

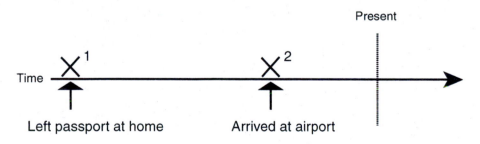

(4) They'*d had* a big fight just before they broke up.

In example (4) the writer of this sentence uses the past perfect to imply cause and effect. That is, the sentence leads us to believe that their having a big fight then caused them to break up as a result. Here is how we might represent this sentence on a time line:

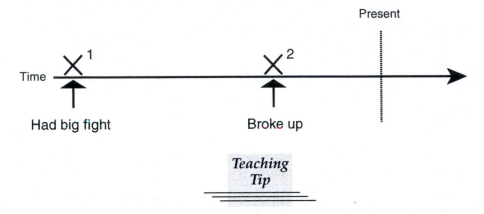

Teaching
Tip

Students typically do not have much feel for the past perfect (unlike the present perfect, which seems pretty normal to them). To help students become comfortable with the past perfect, have them draw timelines for a number of sentences with past perfects.

Notice that the part of the sentence that contains the past perfect can be either before the past-tense part, as in examples (1) and (4), or after the past-tense parts, as in examples (2) and (3). However, in the timeline, the past perfect always comes before the past tense, no matter what order they appear in the actual sentence.

Verb Exercise #8: Drawing Timelines for the Past Perfect _____

Underline the past-perfect verb form. Draw timelines to indicate the relative order of the two parts of the sentence. The first question is done as an example. (Answers to this exercise are on page 430.)

    0. Alice had called her parents three times before they finally answered.

        Answer: Alice <u>had called</u> her parents three times before they finally answered.

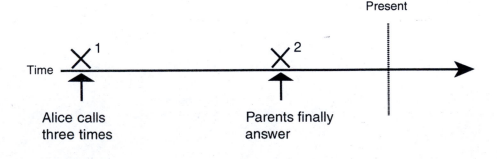

1. The curtain had gone up before the audience was seated.

2. The driver had suffered a heart attack before the accident happened.

3. I had read the book before I saw the movie.

4. The cruise ship returned to port after the captain had discovered a fuel leak.

5. I had fixed dinner before I picked them up at the hotel.

6. The concert was cancelled because the performers' plane had been grounded by bad weather.

7. Apparently Shakespeare had written his first play before he went to London.

8. The company recalled the product after there had been numerous complaints.

9. After Holmes had solved each case, Watson wrote it up in his memoirs.

10. The German tribes invaded Britain after the Legions had been recalled to Rome.

Future perfect = *will have* + Past participle

We use the future perfect when we want to emphasize the "no-later-than" time of completion of a future action. Compare the meaning of the following sentences, the first in the future, the second in the future perfect:

Future:	We *will finish* lunch around 1:00.
Future perfect:	We *will have finished* lunch by 1:00.

The first sentence uses the future tense to tell us the approximate time when lunch will be over. The second sentence uses the future perfect to put a "no-later-than" time limit on when lunch will be over. We could finish lunch at noon or even 11:00, but in any event, we will finish no later than 1:00. Here are some more examples of the future perfect:

The train *will have left* by the time we get to the station.

The paint *will have dried* by tonight.

The snowplows *will have cleared* the roads before we get there.

Verb Exercise #9: Identifying the Perfect _____

Underline the verbs that make up the perfect, and then name which form of the perfect it is. Use Pres Perf for the present perfect, Past Perf for the past perfect, and Fut Perf for the future perfect. The first question is done as an example. (Answers to this exercise are on page 432.)

0. I have revised my estimates based on the information you gave me.

 Answer: I <u>have revised</u> my estimates based on the information you gave me.
 Pres Perf

1. We soon learned that the rain had ruined our garden.
2. Hurry up! Dinner will have started already.
3. Fortunately, the ship had taken on provisions at its last port of call.
4. The cells have reproduced themselves in the laboratory.
5. The newspapers will have got the story by now.
6. Prompt action had minimized the damage.
7. The two companies have merged to form a new corporation.
8. The collision with the iceberg had punched a hole below the waterline.
9. He has always blamed himself for the incident.
10. By the time we get back, the flood water will already have reached the house.

The Progressive

The progressive doesn't get any respect. Traditional grammar books of English always describe the three forms of the progressive, but never call them tenses. They are quaintly described as "separate forms of the verb." They cannot be called tenses because that would mean that English has three more tenses than Latin has, and that, of course, would never do. (It is ironic that the best English translations of the three Latin "simple" tenses are the three forms of the progressive.)

The term "progressive" aptly describes the main characteristic of the progressive verb construction. The progressive is used to emphasize that the action of the verb is "in progress" or "ongoing" at a particular moment of time. The **present progressive** means that the action is "ongoing" at the present moment of time; the **past progressive** means that the action was "ongoing" at some past moment of time; and the **future progressive** means that the action will be "ongoing" at some future moment of time.

The progressive verb construction uses the helping verb *be* in some form, followed by a verb in the present-participle form, which in the case of the progressive is always the main verb. The present participle is particularly easy to recognize because it always ends in *-ing*.

- If *be* is used in its present-tense forms *am, are,* or *is,* the construction is called the **present progressive.**
- If *be* is used in its past-tense form *was* or *were,* the construction is called the **past progressive.**
- If *be* is preceded by the modal *will,* in what traditional grammar calls the future, the construction is called the **future progressive.**

Here are some examples:

Present progressive = *am/are/is* + Present participle

Can you call back later? I *am eating* dinner now.

The tide *is coming* in.

It must be windy. The flags *are* all *flapping* in the breeze.

I'*m* still *waiting* for your answer.

It'*s raining*.

Past progressive = *was/were* + Present participle

I couldn't sleep. Some cats *were fighting* under my window all night.

When I opened the door, the phone *was ringing*.

At that time, I *was working* in Chicago.

They *were talking* about the movie all during dinner.

My shoes *were pinching* me all afternoon.

Future progressive = *will be* + Present participle

I'*ll be seeing* you in all the old familiar places.

Johnson *will be pitching* this afternoon.

Tell me if they call since I *will be working* in the basement.

By tonight, she *will be feeling* better.

It *will be snowing* in the higher elevations after midnight.

Verb Exercise #10: Identifying the Progressive _____

Underline the verbs that make up the progressive, and then name which form of the progressive it is. Use Pres Prog for the present progressive, Past Prog for the past progressive, and Fut Prog for the future progressive. The first question is done as an example. (Answers to this exercise are on page 433.)

  0. I am working on it even as we speak.

  Answer: I <u>am working</u> on it even as we speak.
  Pres Prog

  1. The strike was crippling the plant's output.

  2. The electrician will be putting in the wires this afternoon.

  3. The wine stain was soaking into the tablecloth.

  4. Sorry, I can't make it. I'm working this evening.

5. The defense argued that the prosecutor was suppressing evidence.

6. Tomorrow I will be flying out to Seattle.

7. She is currently supervising six employees.

8. Dorothy made it clear that she was taking her little dog with her.

9. We will be spraying the park for beetles tomorrow.

10. I'm getting ready now.

We have now identified the following verb structures that use helping verbs:

1. Modal
   a. Modal verb + base form

   I *can eat* them in the rain.

   I *could eat* them in the rain.

2. Perfect
   a. Present perfect = *have / has* + past participle

   I *have eaten* them on a train.

   b. Past perfect = *had* + past participle

   I *had eaten* them on a train.

   c. Future perfect = *will have* + past participle

   I *will have eaten* them on a train.

3. Progressive
   a. Present progressive = *am/is/are* + present participle

   I *am eating* green eggs and ham, Sam-I-Am.

   b. Past progressive = *was/were* + present participle

   I *was eating* green eggs and ham, Sam-I-Am.

   c. Future progressive = *will be* + present participle

   I *will be eating* green eggs and ham, Sam-I-Am.

At first glance, the verb system looks overwhelming; however, there are two important regularities that make it much easier to grasp:

1. Tense marker. The first verb, and only the first verb, in every construction MUST be either present tense or past tense. The first verb must be

tensed, i.e., it must be in the past or present form. The tensed verb is the ONLY verb that can enter into subject–verb agreement with the subject. Logically, it makes no sense to single out the present-tense form of one modal (*will*) and give it the special name "future" when the eight remaining modal forms can all be used equally well for talking about the future. Either we should call all of them "futures" or none of them—preferably the latter. Logic, however, has little to do with verb terminology. In fact, the only reason we call *will* the "future" is that it was singled out from the other modals to translate the true future-tense form of the verb in Latin. The convention for using the term "future" is now so well established that it is pointless to whine about logical consistency. Accordingly, we will continue to use traditional terminology and refer to *will* + **base form** as a "future," but we will reserve the term "tense" just for the present tense and past tense. (In other words, we will call *will* + **base** the "future," but not the "future tense.")

    2. Main verb. The last verb, and only the last verb, in every construction MUST be the main verb. The main verb alone controls complements. Only the main verb can be an action verb or a linking verb. Only the main verb can be transitive or intransitive. The terms "action/linking," and "transitive/intransitive" cannot be applied to helping verbs.

    This rule has absolutely no exceptions—even when there is only a single verb. In that case, the single verb is both the first verb (the tensed verb), and the last verb (the main verb) because it is the ONLY verb.

Verb Exercise #11: Identifying Verb Constructions _____

Underline the verb constructions. Use the following abbreviations to label them: Pres for simple present tense; Past for simple past tense; Fut for future; Modal for modal verb + base; Pres Perf for the present perfect; Past Perf for the past perfect; Fut Perf for the future perfect; Pres Prog for the present progressive, Past Prog for the past progressive, and Fut Prog for the future progressive. The first question is done as an example. (Answers to this exercise are on page 433.)

    0. I can do it!

       Answer: I <u>can do</u> it!
               Modal

    1. Time and tide wait for no man.

    2. The president had resigned after the no-confidence vote.

    3. They will drive a very hard bargain.

    4. The machine smoothes the ice for the skaters.

    5. I burned myself.

    6. The electrician should finish this afternoon.

    7. The game will have ended by now.

8. We are now bidding for lot #127.

9. I will send it by overnight delivery.

10. The glare from the sun was really bothering me.

11. The engineers will be pumping water out for a week.

12. I had badly underestimated the costs of the damages.

13. I'm melting!

14. Steam was coming out of the pipes.

15. We will have played every team in the league.

16. You can be sure of that.

17. The phone is ringing.

18. I'm sorry about that.

19. Finally I had finished my homework.

20. Houston, we have a problem.

The Passive

In traditional grammar, verbs are said to have **voice**. There are two voices, **active** and **passive**. The active voice is the normal state of affairs. All the sentences we have examined in the book to this point have been in the active voice. In an active voice sentence, the subject is either the "do-er" of the action (action verb) or the "topic" of the sentence (linking verb). In a passive voice sentence, the subject is the "recipient" of the action of the verb. Compare the following sentences:

Active voice:	John *amused* Mary.
Passive voice:	Mary *was amused* (by John).

In the active sentence, *John* is doing the amusing. *Mary* is the recipient of the action—she is the one being amused. In the passive sentence, *Mary* is the nominal subject, but she is not doing the amusing; *John* still is. *Mary* is still the recipient of the action of the verb.

The purpose of the passive is to shift emphasis away from the "do-er" of the action and place it on the "recipient" of the action. In our example, the passive shifts emphasis away from what John did and instead focuses our attention on what happened to Mary. It does this by moving the object from its normal position after the verb to the much more prominent subject position

We form passive sentences by converting the object of a transitive verb in an active voice sentence to the "subject" of the corresponding passive voice sentence. That is why the underlying "do-er" and "recipient" relations are the same in both active and passive versions. *In other words, the passive shuffles the nouns around, but does not change their basic relationships.* The "subject" of a passive sentence is still functioning as the object of the verb. The original subject in the active sentence is converted into an "object" of the prepositional *by*, but it is still functioning as the subject—in our example, John is still the one doing the amusing.

The parentheses around the prepositional phrase *(by John)* indicates that often the original subject is not retained in the passive version. After all, the whole point of putting a sentence into the passive is to deemphasize the subject and emphasize the object. Sometimes we use the passive because we do not know (or care) who the subject is. For example, we would certainly prefer the passive

> My car was made in Japan.

to the corresponding active,

> Somebody made my car in Japan.

A few verbs are nearly always used in the passive, for example,

> I was born in Korea.

The corresponding active seems bizarre:

> My mother bore me in Korea.

By actual count, about 85 percent of the passive sentences in nonfiction books and articles do not retain the subject prepositional phrase.

If the prepositional phrase beginning with *by* is routinely deleted from passive sentences, how can we tell that a sentence is passive? The answer is that we recognize the passive the same way we do the other complex helping-verb constructions: they have unique combinations of a helping verb and a following verb. In the case of the passive, it is some form of the helping verb *be* followed by a past-participle verb form:

Passive = *be* (in some form) + Past participle

Here are a number of examples of sentences in the passive voice with the verbs in italics:

Passive: The announcement *is expected* at any moment.
Bugsy *was acquitted* by the jury.
The search *was suspended* at nightfall.
The yacht *is manned* by a novice crew.
The movie *was based* on a play.

As one would expect, we can convert these passive sentences to their active-voice counterparts. (If there is no prepositional phrase beginning with *by* to supply the subject, the subject is understood to be an indefinite "somebody/anybody/everybody.")

Passive:	The announcement *is expected* at any moment.
Active:	Everybody *expected* the announcement at any moment.
Passive:	Bugsy *was acquitted* by the jury.
Active:	The jury *acquitted* Bugsy.
Passive:	The search *was suspended* at nightfall.
Active:	Everybody *suspended* the search at nightfall.
Passive:	The yacht *is manned* by a novice crew.
Active:	A novice crew *mans* the yacht.
Passive:	The movie *was based* on a play.
Active:	Somebody *based* the movie on a play.

Notice that when we convert the passive into its active-voice counterpart, we turn the subject of the passive sentence into the object of verb in the active sentence, delete the verb *be*, and change the past participle into the tensed verb.

Verb Exercise #12: Identifying Passives

Underline the passive verb construction (*be* + past participle) and label it PASSIVE. Confirm your answer by turning the passive sentence into its active-voice counterpart. The first question is done as an example. (Answers to this exercise are on page 434.)

  0. The book was reviewed by the whole committee.

     Answer: The book <u>was reviewed</u> by the whole committee.
                        PASSIVE

     Confirmation: The whole committee reviewed the book.

  1. Attila the Hun was criticized by the social committee.

  2. The opening was concealed by a wooden screen.

  3. Bugsy's sentence was commuted by the Governor.

  4. Sleeping Beauty was sued by seven plaintiffs.

  5. Large debts were incurred by my client.

  6. The painting was greatly admired.

  7. The country was unified by the new President.

  8. The robot is programmed to use a Hula-Hoop.

  9. We were embarrassed by the regrettable incident.

 10. My resolve was weakened by the chocolate cheesecake.

To do the reverse, convert an active-voice sentence into its passive-voice counterpart, we must turn the object of the transitive verb in the active sentence into the subject of the passive sentence. We must also add *be* as a helping verb and change the tensed verb (either present or past tense) into a past participle. Here are some examples:

Active:	Everybody *missed* the first question.
Passive:	The first question *was missed* by everyone.
Active:	My sister *returned* the package to the post office.
Passive:	The package *was returned* to the post office by my sister.
Active:	Someone *left* the ladder against the garage wall.
Passive:	The ladder *was left* against the garage wall.

Verb Exercise #13: Converting Active-Voice Sentences into Passives

Convert the sentences into their passive counterparts and underline the passive verb construction. The first question is done as an example. (Answers to this exercise are on page 435.)

   0. Somebody stamped the date on the envelope.

   Answer: The date was stamped on the envelope.

   1. The movie really scared the children.

   2. A guard halted the trucks.

   3. The rookie pitched a good game.

   4. They confined him to his quarters.

   5. The exhibit rocked the art world.

   6. Everyone exploited the new tax loophole.

   7. The appeals court upheld the original decision.

   8. A rock shattered our windshield.

   9. They admired his sense of humor.

   10. We decorated the Christmas tree in record time.

Chaining Together Complex Verb Constructions

So far we have looked at the four complex verb constructions—modals, the perfect, the progressive, and the passive—in isolation from each other. In fact, we often chain two of them together, and occasionally three. It is much easier to identify such linked structures than you might think, because they can occur only in the following fixed order (ignoring the passive for the moment):

Modal + Perfect + Progressive

Modals always come before the perfect, the perfect always comes before the progressive, and the progressive always comes before the passive. There are really only four possible combinations (with examples).

1. Modal + Perfect

Thelma *may have gone* home.
      Modal   Perfect

You *should have been* ready.
    Modal   Perfect

I *will   have finished* by then.
   Modal   Perfect   (also called a "future" perfect)

2. Modal + Progressive

Thelma *might   be going* home soon.
        Modal Progressive

Louise *could be practicing* her backhand.
       Modal   Progressive

They *will   be worrying* about us.
      Modal   Progressive   (also called a "future" progressive)

3. Perfect + Progressive

Thelma *had been   going* home every weekend.
       Past perfect Progressive

Dr. Wong *has been   administering* the program.
          Present perfect   Progressive

We *will have been   working* on that for weeks now.
   Future perfect   Progressive

When the perfect and the progressive are combined, *been,* the middle of the three verbs, plays a role in both constructions: *have + been* forms the perfect, and *been + present participle* forms the progressive. *Been* is both the second verb in the perfect construction and the helping verb in the progressive.

The combination of present perfect and progressive is quite common. Both the present perfect and the progressive imply continuous action. So what is the difference between the present perfect, the present progressive, and the present perfect progressive? Let's compare an example of each of them:

Present perfect: I *have written* a paper.
Present progressive: I *am writing* a paper.
Present perfect progressive: I *have been writing* a paper.

Obviously, the differences are subtle:

- The present perfect I ***have written*** *a paper* implies that the speaker has recently completed the paper.
- The present progressive I ***am writing*** *a paper* implies that right now, at this moment, as we speak, the writer is in the process of composing the paper.
- The present perfect progressive I ***have been writing*** *a paper* implies that the paper is still in progress (but not necessarily at this moment). The speaker would also use the present perfect progressive to emphasize the duration of the process: it started some time in the past and has continued up to the present time.

4. Modal + Perfect + Progressive

I *will   have been   studying* Japanese for three years by then.
 Modal   Perfect   Progressive   (also called a "future" perfect progressive)

Thelma *must   have been   waiting* for hours.
        Modal   Perfect   Progressive

I *should   have been   diagramming* more sentences.
   Modal   Perfect   Progressive

Let us look at the last example in detail. The first verb is *should*, the past tense of the modal *shall*. Modals require that the following verb be in the base form. In this case, the base-form verb is *have*. Some form of *have* as a helping verb followed by a past participle means that the sentence contains a **perfect**. In this case, the past participle is *been*. Some form of *be* followed by a present participle (*diagramming*, in this case) means that the sentence also contains a **progressive**. The sentence thus contains **Modal + Perfect + Progressive.**

Verb Exercise #14: Identifying Complex Verb Constructions ____

Underline the verbs or verb constructions. Use the terms Present, Past, Modal, Perfect, and Progressive. (For *will*, use either Modal or Future.) The first question is done as an example. (Answers to this exercise are on page 435.)

0. We should have postponed the game.

   Answer: We <u>should have postponed</u> the game.
                   Modal Perfect

1. The senator's aides are denying the statement.

2. They will have finished by now.

3. I've been working on the railroad.

4. The doctor prescribed a non-aspirin pain reliever.

5. I will be very busy all afternoon.

6. The commercials always ruin movies on TV.

7. I had been thinking about it.

8. They will have invested a fortune in it.

9. He had nearly wrecked the stereo.

10. The children will have been sleeping all afternoon.

11. I should have known better.

12. There will be a small reception afterwards.

13. I've had it.

14. We must be going now.

15. Some rain might have been getting into the ceiling.

Combining Complex Verb Structures with the Passive

The passive always follows the other complex verb structures, so the full line-up of the four complex verb structures is this:

Modal + Perfect + Progressive + Passive

However, it is quite unusual to use the passive with more than one other complex verb structure. (Linguist James Sledd reports that he actually heard a university president use all four structures together in conversation in the following sentence: "I *will have been being told* that now all summer."

will	is a modal
have + been	is a perfect
been + being	is a progressive
being + told	is a passive

Here are more normal examples of the passive used with each one of the other complex verb structures.

Modal + Passive

The order *should be reversed.*
      Modal   Passive

Her diamonds   *will   be found.*
         Modal   Passive   (also called a "future" passive)

He *should be pleased* by his good fortune.
   Modal   Passive

Perfect + Passive

I *had been promised* a cash advance.
   Past Perfect Passive

The whole episode *has been made* up by the press.
       Present Perfect Passive

The company *had been squeezed* dry.
      Past Perfect Passive

Progressive + Passive

He *is being met* at noon.
 Present Progressive Passive

Bugsy *was being investigated* by the FBI.
     Past Progressive Passive

The companies *are being placed* in trusteeship.
     Pres Progressive Passive

Verb Exercise #15: Identifying Complex Verb Constructions with the Passive _____

Underline the verbs or verb constructions. Use the terms Present, Past, Modal, Perfect, Progressive, and Passive. (For *will,* use either Modal or Future.) The first question is done as an example. (Answers to this exercise are on page 436.)

  0. The cost had been estimated by the committee.

      Answer: The cost   <u>had</u>   <u>been estimated</u> by the committee.
                   Past Perfect   Passive

  1. The dog was being washed by the whole family.

  2. The writer has been threatened by his cruel editor.

  3. Children must be accompanied by an adult.

  4. The gun had been owned by a retired policeman.

  5. Corla's embarrassing slip will be noticed by everyone.

  6. The judge was being interviewed by a reporter.

  7. A serious accident had been prevented.

  8. The presentation was being recorded.

  9. The plan should be approved.

 10. The appointment will be announced tomorrow.

Review of Multiple Complex Verb Constructions

- The fixed sequence of multiple complex verb constructions is Modal + Perfect + Progressive + Passive.
- The first verb in the sequence is always the tensed verb—the ONLY tensed verb in the entire construction. Even the modal verbs are either present or past tense forms, though the terms "present" and "past" do not indicate much about their meanings.
- Helping verbs always control the form of the following verb, resulting in the following sequences:

Modal verb + Base form = **Modal**

have (in some form) + Past participle = **Perfect**

be (in some form) + Present participle = **Progressive**

be (in some form) + Past participle = **Passive**

- The modal *will* is called a "future" in traditional grammar because it is used to translate the true future tense in Latin.
- When the helping verbs *have* (perfect) or *be* (progressive) come first (i.e., when they are the tensed verbs), apply the terms "present," "past," to the perfect or progressive constructions.
- The last verb is always the main verb—the only verb that can take objects and subject complements.

Verb Exercise #16: Review Exercise _____

Underline the verbs or verb constructions. Use the terms Present, Past, Modal, Perfect, Progressive, and Passive. (For *will*, use either Modal or Future.) The first question is done as an example. (Answers to this exercise are on page 437.)

0. We should be doing our homework.

   Answer: We <u>should</u> <u>be doing</u> our homework.
             Modal Progressive

1. The students have been diagramming sentences.

2. The advertisement will attract a crowd.

3. The clutch engages the gears.

4. They have filed a motion.

5. The design must be approved.

6. He was a fool.

7. His claim is stretching the truth.

8. We should have warned them.

9. The Smiths would have been watching TV.

10. The children were frightened by Godzilla.

11. Holmes is checking Lord Bumfrey's story.

12. Bugsy had acquired a large fortune by devious means.

13. The combination may have been changed.

14. Lady Smithers could have taken the pearls.

15. Leon loves Lily.

16. Sir Desmond had had his answer.

17. The butler should have polished the silver.

18. The Legionnaires ordered clam juice.

19. The meeting was rudely interrupted.

20. I am tired now.

5

Phrases

According to a traditional definition, a **phrase** is a group of words used as a single part of speech. Phrases are "in-between" grammatical units that are larger than single words but smaller than sentences. Sentences, of course, do not act as single parts of speech and are built differently. Sentences have tensed verbs that agree with their subjects; phrases, on the other hand, never have tensed verbs and thus can never enter into true subject–verb agreement.

In this chapter we will look at six types of phrases: **noun phrases, prepositional phrases, appositive phrases, gerund phrases, participial phrases,** and **infinitive phrases.** Gerund, participial, and infinitive phrases are called **verbal phrases** because all three types are based on nontensed verb forms—participles and infinitives.

- **Noun phrases** consist of a noun together with its modifiers. Noun phrases always act as nouns.
- **Prepositional phrases** consist of a preposition together with its object noun or noun phrase. As a unit, a prepositional phrases function as a modifier—as an adjective or an adverb.
- **Appositive phrases** consist of an appositive together with its modifying adjectives. Appositive phrases act as noun phrases.
- **Verbal phrases** are phrases built around a nontensed verb. There are three types of verbal phrases.

  Gerund phrases: Gerunds are verbs in their present participle forms used as nouns. A gerund phrase consists of a gerund together with the verb's complement, modifiers, or subject. Gerund phrases act as noun phrases.

  Participial phrases: Participles are verbs in either their present or past participle forms used as modifying adjectives. A participial phrase consists of a participle together with the verb's complement, modifiers, or subject. Participial phrases act as modifying adjectives.

  Infinitive phrases: Infinitives consist of *to* + the base form of a verb and are used as nouns, adjectives, or adverbs. An infinitive phrase consists

TABLE 5.1   *Types of Phrases*

Type of Phrase	Part of Speech	Example
Noun phrase	Noun	*A sour-faced waiter* took *our order.*
Prepositional phrase	Adjective	The book *on the table* is mine.
	Adverb	I saw it *on the table.*
Appositive phrase	Noun	Hamlet, *Shakespeare's play,* is being performed tonight.
Gerund phrase	Noun	*Giving up now* would be a big mistake. *John's giving up now* would be a big mistake.
Participial phrase	Adjective	*Smiling broadly,* I waved back. (present participial phrase) *Beaten badly,* Senator Fogg retired. (past participial phrase)
Infinitive phrase	Noun	*To give up now* would be a big mistake. *For John to give up now* would be a big mistake.
	Adjective	That was the right decision *to make.* That was the right decision *for you to make.*
	Adverb	*To win now,* they would need a miracle. *For them to win now,* they would need a miracle.

of an infinitive together with the verb's complement, modifiers, or subject. Infinitive phrases act as nouns, modifying adjectives, or adverbs.

Table 5.1 summarizes the functions of the six types of phrases and gives examples of the use of each type.

Noun Phrases

Noun phrases were first introduced in Chapter 2. As you recall, a noun phrase is a noun together with its modifiers. The noun phrase acts as a single part of speech—a noun. The key to identifying noun phrases is the pronoun replacement test, discussed in Chapter 2 and repeated here:

> **The pronoun replacement test for nouns.** Whatever words are replaced by a third-person pronoun constitute a noun phrase. Whichever word WITHIN the noun phrase that determines the form of the third-person pronoun is the noun.

Here is an example of the pronoun replacement test:

*A sour-faced **waiter** took our **order.***
> He   it

The third-person pronouns *he* and *it* show that the sentence contains two noun phrases.

Noun phrases act in whatever ways the noun within them acts. In our example, the noun phrase *a sour-faced waiter* functions as the subject phrase (called a **complete subject** in traditional terms) because the noun *waiter* acts as the subject (called a **simple subject** in traditional terms). Likewise, the second noun phrase *our order* acts as the object phrase of the verb *took* because the noun *order* acts as the object of *took.*

Prepositional Phrases

Prepositional phrases consist of a preposition followed by its object, called **the object of the preposition.** The object of the preposition may be a single noun, a noun inside a noun phrase, or a pronoun. (Because pronouns can always be used in place of nouns and noun phrases, we will not always mention pronouns specifically when we are talking about nouns and noun phrases.)

In traditional grammar, prepositional phrases are always modifiers. If they modify nouns, they are called **adjective phrases.** If they modify verbs, predicate adjectives, or other adverbs, they are called **adverb phrases.** (In Chapter 7 we will see that modern grammar assigns additional roles to prepositional phrases.)

Prepositions are very individualistic—each has its own unique range of meanings. About the only generalization we can make about prepositions is that some of them can refer to some aspect of space or time:

Space:	*across* the lawn; *above* the window; *behind* the desk; *below* the stairs; *beneath* the floor; *between* the lines; *in* the building; *near* the river; *over* the mantel; *under* the roof
Time:	*after* class; *before* dinner; *during* the afternoon; *since* Tuesday; *till* Friday

Some prepositions can refer to either space or time—for example, the preposition *in:*

Space:	We met *in* the kitchen.
Time:	We met *in* the afternoon.

Most prepositions, however, have unique meanings and cannot be grouped semantically. For example, consider the diversity in the meanings of the prepositions in the following prepositional phrases:

for your friend; *by* your friend; *as* a friend; *concerning* your friend; *of* your friend; *except* your friend; *with* your friend; *from* your friend

Table 5.2 is a list of common single-word prepositions.

In addition to the single-word prepositions listed in Table 5.2, there are a large number of multiple-word prepositions called **compound prepositions.** Here are some examples:

as of today; *in addition to* the assignment ; *next to* Fred; *in spite of* your objections; *because of* the budget; *aside from* that; *in place of* Alice; *on account of* the bad weather; *in front of* the fireplace; *in case of* an accident; *on behalf of* the management

Teaching Tip

Even though the list of single-word prepositions is a closed class, it is probably too large to ask students to memorize. In addition, many of the words on the list of prepositions can also be used as other parts of speech, a fact that defeats the purpose of memorizing the list to begin with. For example, *but* is usually used as a coordinating conjunction, *since* is used as a subordinating conjunction, and many words on the list can also be used as adverbs—*after, along, around, before, behind, below, beside, down, in, inside, near, on, under.* Instead of telling them to memorize, we need to help students identify not just prepositions, but prepositional phrases.

TABLE 5.2   *Common Single-Word Prepositions*

aboard	beyond	out
about	but	over
above	by	past
across	concerning	since
after	down	through
against	during	throughout
along	except	till
among	for	to
around	from	toward
as	in	under
at	inside	underneath
before	into	until
behind	like	up
below	near	upon
beneath	of	with
beside	off	within
between	on	without

One way to help students identify prepositional phrases is to look at the noun inside the prepositional phrase. Nouns can play only three roles in a sentence: (1) subject, (2) complement of a verb (objects or predicate nominatives), or (3) object of a preposition. If a noun is neither the subject of a sentence nor the complement of a verb, then the noun MUST be the object of a preposition.

Phrase Exercise #1: Identifying Prepositional Phrases by Noun Roles

Underline all of the nouns (or pronouns) in the following sentences and label each according to the role it plays. Use Subj for subject; Verb-Comp for verb complement; and Obj-Prep for object of a preposition. Then put parentheses around the entire prepositional phrase. The first question is done as an example. (Answers to this exercise are on page 438.)

0. Mary Ann found her keys in the kitchen.

Answer: <u>Mary Ann</u> found her   <u>keys</u>   (in the <u>kitchen</u>).
         Subj   Verb-Comp   Obj-Prep

1. He answered the reporters' questions during the flight.

2. The computers in the library were replaced over Christmas.

3. We got curtains for the windows in the living room.

4. Except for the ending, I liked your ideas about your paper.

5. I haven't had a minute to myself since lunch.

6. The cars in the lot have already been washed.

7. A friend of mine received an award for her writing.

8. John's attitude toward the project is the main problem.

9. We got a good table near the window.

10. In the afternoon, we had a big thunderstorm.

Identifying prepositional phrases is not particularly difficult. It is a bit harder to determine the role they are playing, i.e., whether they are **adjective phrases** modifying nouns or **adverb phrases** modifying verbs, adjectives, or other adverbs. We will now discuss several tests that are very helpful in distinguishing adjective phrases from adverb phrases.

Adjective Phrases

The key to identifying adjective phrases is our old standby, the pronoun replacement test. As you know, the pronoun replacement test uses a pronoun to identify a noun and all its modifiers, INCLUDING prepositional phrases.

In other words, we can use the pronoun replacement test to tell us when a prepositional phrase is modifying a noun. If the pronoun replaces the prepositional phrase along with the noun, then that prepositional phrase must have been a modifier of the noun (or else the pronoun wouldn't have replaced it). For example:

> The **book** *on the shelf* should go back to the library.
> It

The fact that the pronoun *it* replaces the prepositional phrase *on the shelf* along with the other modifiers of *book* tells us that *on the shelf* modifies *book* and is thus an adjective phrase. Here is a corollary of the pronoun replacement test tailored for adjective phrases:

> **The pronoun replacement test for adjective phrases.** If a noun and a following prepositional phrase are BOTH replaced by a single third-person pronoun, then the prepositional phrase must be an adjective phrase modifying that noun.

The following is an example in which the prepositional phrase that follows a noun is NOT an adjective phrase. When we apply the pronoun replacement test, we see that the pronoun *it* does not replace the prepositional phrase *on the shelf*:

> I put *the book* on the shelf.
> it

In this case, the pronoun replacement test shows us that *on the shelf* is not an adjective phrase because it does not modify the noun *book*.

Phrase Exercise #2: Identifying Adjective Phrases by the Pronoun Replacement Test ___

Underline the adjective phrases in the following sentences. Confirm your answer by applying the pronoun replacement test. The first question is done as an example. (Answers to this exercise are on page 438.)

0. The time before dawn is always the darkest.

   Answer: The time <u>before dawn</u> is always the darkest.

   Confirmation: <u>The time before dawn</u> is always the darkest.
   It

1. Tickets to Seattle cost $338 round-trip.

2. The apartment in the basement was all that I could afford.

3. A book by Toni Morrison was required.

4. The lamp next to my desk isn't working.

5. Two hours between classes doesn't give me much time.

6. We should eat the apples in the refrigerator first.

7. Several pictures at that gallery caught our eye.

8. Some instructors in white lab coats asked what we wanted.

9. I needed to find a book about Sicily.

10. The first of the month will be here soon.

Another characteristic of adjective phrases is that they usually answer *which* questions about the nouns they modify. For example, in the sentence

We used the path *along the river.*

the prepositional phrase *along the river* tells us WHICH path we used—the one along the river.

> **The *which* test for adjective phrases.** If a prepositional phrase gives information about which noun we are talking about, then the prepositional phrase is an adjective phrase.

Predictably, the *which* test fails when a prepositional phrase is not an adjective phrase. For example, in the sentence

They found the car *behind the barn.*

the prepositional phrase *behind the barn* does not tell WHICH car they found— it tells us WHERE they found the car. Compare the above sentence with the following:

The car *behind the barn* belongs to Sam.

In this sentence, *behind the barn* does tell which car we are talking about. It is the car behind the barn as opposed to all the other cars that are not behind the barn. Thus, *behind the barn* is an adjective phrase in this sentence.

Phrase Exercise #3: Identifying Adjective Prepositional Phrases by the Which Test _____

Underline the adjective prepositional phrases in the following sentences. Confirm your answer by applying the *which* test. The first question is done as an example. (Answers to this exercise are on page 439.)

0. The present for Jerry will be a surprise.

   Answer: The present <u>for Jerry</u> will be a surprise.

   Confirmation: Which present? The one <u>for Jerry</u>.

1. The meeting at the hotel lasted only a few minutes.

2. The computers in the library were updated recently.

3. All prepositional phrases in these sentences should be underlined.

4. The award for her writing was a pleasant surprise.

5. I framed the picture of my parents.

6. The meeting about class schedules has been postponed.

7. I found several books by our teacher in the library.

8. The new computers at work are much faster than the old ones.

9. I never got used to the winters in the Midwest.

10. The class in advanced Spanish was canceled.

Adverb Phrases

Adverb phrases that modify (1) verbs, (2) predicate adjectives, and (3) other adverbs behave much like ordinary, single-word adverbs. Nearly everything that we said about single-word adverbs also applies to adverb phrases.

Adverb Phrases That Modify Verbs.   The same tests that we used in Chapter 2 to identify adverbs that modify verbs work quite well for identifying adverb phrases that modify verbs: adverb phrases answer adverb questions and adverb phrases can be moved.

The adverb question test for adverb phrases that modify verbs.
If a prepositional phrase answers an adverb question, then that prepositional phrase is an adverb phrase modifying the verb.

To see if a prepositional phrase modifies the verb, ask an adverb question that will give back the prepositional phrase as the answer. The common adverb questions are *where, when, why,* and *how.* Here are some examples that show the various adverb questions used to produce adverb phrases as answers.

Where:	They had classes in astronomy *at my high school.*
Adverb question:	*Where* did they have classes in astronomy?
Answer:	*At my high school.*
When:	They unloaded the truck *after dinner.*
Adverb question:	*When* did they unload the truck?
Answer:	*After dinner.*

Why:	They left early *because of the heat.*
Adverb question:	*Why* did they leave early?
Answer:	*Because of the heat.*
How:	We cleaned the tools *by hand.*
Adverb question:	*How* did we clean the tools?
Answer:	*By hand.*
How long:	I have worked there *for ages.*
Adverb question:	*How long* have I worked there?
Answer:	*For ages.*

Phrase Exercise #4: Identifying Adverb Prepositional Phrases by the Adverb Question Test

Underline the adverb prepositional phrases in the following sentences. Confirm your answer by applying the adverb question test. The first question is done as an example. (Answers to this exercise are on page 440.)

0. I took a nap before dinner.

Answer: I took a nap <u>before dinner</u>.

Confirmation: When did I take a nap? <u>Before dinner</u>.

1. I took algebra in community college.

2. We painted the kitchen ceiling with a roller.

3. She finished her paper after class.

4. The freeway goes by the airport.

5. I stood there like a fool.

6. It must have rained during the night.

7. Our doors always stick in wet weather.

8. I got a ticket for parking there.

9. We ate breakfast at McDonald's this morning.

10. I scheduled all my classes in the afternoon.

The second test is based on the fact that the only type of prepositional phrase that can be moved is one that modifies a verb. This is probably the simplest and easiest test to use, but it has the disadvantage that one type of adverb phrase cannot be moved without sounding odd.

> **The adverb phrase movement test.** If a prepositional phrase can be moved to the front of the sentence, it must be an adverb phrase that modifies the verb.

For most types of adverb phrases, the adverb movement test works well:

They had classes in astronomy *at my high school.*

At my high school, they had classes in astronomy.

They unloaded the truck *after dinner.*

After dinner, they unloaded the truck.

They left early *because of the heat.*

Because of the heat, they left early.

When the adverb movement test is applied to adverb phrases that answer *how* questions, however, the resulting sentences often sound odd:

We cleaned the tools *by hand.*

?By hand, we cleaned the tools.

I did it *by myself.*

?By myself, I did it.

Phrase Exercise #5: Identifying Adverb Prepositional Phrases by the Adverb Phrase Movement Test _____

Underline the adverb prepositional phrases in the following sentences. Confirm your answer by applying the adverb phrase movement test. The first question is done as an example. (Answers to this exercise are on page 440.)

0. There is a phone booth by the front door.
   Answer: There is a phone booth <u>by the front door</u>.
   Confirmation: <u>By the front door</u>, there is a phone booth.

1. We are going to watch a program at eight.

2. I need to get home after class.

3. I nearly fell asleep during the lecture.

4. There was a small grocery store behind the post office.

5. We will begin the presentation in just a minute.

6. We discussed the problem before lunch.

7. John found the missing letter in a desk drawer.

8. The wind began to rise toward dawn.

9. The lawyer addressed the jury with barely concealed outrage.

10. The streets had become completely empty but for a few delivery trucks.

Adverb Phrases that Modify Predicate Adjectives. Predicate adjectives are often modified by adverb phrases. Here are some examples with the adjective in bold and the adverb phrase in italics:

He is **lucky** *at cards.*

I am **happy** *with my job.*

We are **ready** *for dinner.*

They were **wise** *beyond their years.*

Predictably, adverb phrases that modify predicate adjectives fail both tests for adverb phrases that modify verbs. Adverb phrases that modify predicate adjectives do not answer adverb questions:

Adverb Phrase Question Test:
*How is he lucky? *At cards
*How am I happy? *With my job
*How are we ready? *For dinner
*How were they wise? *Beyond their years

Adverb phrases that modify predicate adjectives can be moved, but the resulting sentence (if it is grammatical at all) has a different meaning—a kind of ironic emphasis that is grammatical only if it is said with unusual stress:

Adverb Phrase Movement Test:
?*At cards,* he is lucky.
?*With my job,* I am happy.
?*For dinner,* we are ready.
?*Beyond their years,* they were wise.

There is no positive test that can be used to identify adverb phrases that modify predicate adjectives. However, once we have established that these adverb phrases do not modify the verb, the only thing they can modify is the predicate adjective.

Adverb Phrases That Modify Other Adverbs. Although this use of adverb phrases does exist, it is not very common. Here are two examples with the adverb in bold and the adverb phrase in italics:

We went there **later** *in the morning.*

Our team had scored a touchdown **earlier** *in the game.*

Again, adverb phrases that modify other adverbs fail both adverb phrase tests for adverbs that modify verbs. Here the tests produce odd, off-the-wall sentences that no one would ever actually say.

Adverb Phrase Question Test:
*When did we go there later? **In the morning*.
*When had our team scored a touchdown earlier? *In the game*.

Adverb Phrase Movement Test:
**In the morning*, we went there later.
**In the game*, our team had scored a touchdown earlier.

As was the case with adverb phrases that modify predicates, adverbs that modify other adverbs are rather easy to identify by default (negative results from the two tests that identify adverbs that modify verbs are nearly as helpful as positive tests):

- They cannot be adjective phrases because there is no noun for them to modify.
- They cannot modify the verb because they fail verb modifier tests.
- Because they cannot move, they must modify the adverb they follow.

Phrase Exercise #6: Identifying Adverb Phrases _____

Underline the adverb phrases once and the words they modify twice. Identify the part of speech of the words being modified. Confirm your answer by applying either the adverb phrase question or the adverb phase movement test. The first question is done as an example. (Answers to this exercise are on page 441.)

  0. The count was sympathetic to Igor.

     Answer: The count was <u>sympathetic to Igor</u>.
                            Adjective

     Confirmation: *How was the count sympathetic? *To Igor.
                ?To Igor, the count was sympathetic.

  1. They are very efficient at their jobs.

  2. The soldiers paraded across the field.

  3. She returned our call late in the evening.

  4. I felt guilty at our behavior.

  5. Everybody was upset about the accident.

  6. The judge supported the defense in the Brown case.

  7. The ruling seemed favorable to the prosecution.

  8. We left early in the morning.

9. We were ready for any problem.

10. The offer seemed comparable with the previous offer.

Review of Prepositional Phrases

Prepositional phrases consist of a preposition and its object. The object of a preposition can be a single noun, a noun phrase, or a pronoun. Prepositional phrases function as adjectives modifying nouns or as adverbs modifying verbs, predicate adjectives, or other adverbs. The most common problem is deciding whether a prepositional phrase modifies a noun or is an adverb phrase modifying a verb.

There are two different sets of tests for each type of prepositional phrase. Although the tests are quite reliable, sometimes one test will work better than the other. For that reason, it is important to keep both tests for each type of prepositional phrase in mind when you are deciding on the function of prepositional phrases. Here is a brief summary of the tests.

Adjective Phrases

Pronoun replacement test for adjective phrases. Pronouns replace nouns and all their modifiers, including adjective phrases, for example,

> *The book on the desk* is yours.
>   It

Since *it* replaces the prepositional phrase *on the desk,* we know that it is an adjective phrase modifying *book.*

Which test. An adjective phrase identifies which noun we are talking about, for example,

> The book *on the desk* is yours.

Since *on the desk* identifies WHICH book we are talking about, *on the desk* is an adjective phrase modifying *book.*

Adverb Phrases

Adverb phrase question test. Adverb phrases that modify verbs answer where, when, why, and *how* questions, for example,

> We went shopping *after lunch.*

Since *after lunch* answers the adverb question *When did we go shopping,* we know it is an adverb phrase.

Adverb phrase movement test. Most adverb phrases that modify verbs can be moved to the front of the sentence, for example,

After lunch, we went shopping.

Adverb phrases can also modify predicate adjectives and other adverbs. In both cases, these adverb phrases fail the adverb phrase question and adverb phrase movement tests. Both types of adverb phrase must modify the word to their immediate left, whether that word is a predicate adjective or an adverb.

Phrase Exercise #7: Identifying Adjective and Adverb Prepositional Phrases _____

Underline prepositional phrases in the following sentences and identify their function by writing Adj under adjective phrases and Adv under adverb phrases. Identify which word the adverb phrase modifies. Confirm your answer by applying an appropriate test. The first question is done as an example. (Answers to this exercise are on page 442.)

  0. The answers in the book always seem so easy.

     Answer: The answers <u>in the book</u> always seem so easy.
                                 Adj

     Confirmation: <u>The answers in the book</u> always seem so easy.
                             They   (pronoun replacement test)

  1. I liked your paper about the Civil War.

  2. They crossed the road during the night.

  3. The proposal for a new bridge has become quite controversial.

  4. I liked your paper except for the ending.

  5. The governor issued a statement concerning the trial.

  6. We washed the plants with great care.

  7. The building behind ours has become vacant.

  8. I was very upset at the time.

  9. The rebellion in 1845 caused many Germans to immigrate.

10. The meeting on Tuesday has been canceled.

11. I couldn't understand his attitude toward the play.

12. We might have some rain during the game.

13. The relentless inflation after WWI destroyed Germany's economy.

14. Holmes examined the cloak with great care.

15. Holmes examined the cloak with the torn fringe.

16. The decision was favorable to the opposition.

17. I returned the car early in the morning.

18. We grew angry at the unnecessary delay.

19. I searched the Web for an answer.

20. Washing dishes is hard on your hands.

Diagramming Prepositional Phrases

Since prepositional phrases are modifiers, they are drawn underneath the main sentence line and are attached to the word they modify. Adjective phrases are attached to the nouns they modify; adverb phrases are attached to the verb, predicate adjective, or adverb they modify. The noun or pronoun object of the preposition is put on a horizontal line. All modifiers of the object noun are attached to it as they would be to any noun. Here are some examples:

We swam at the pool in the hotel.

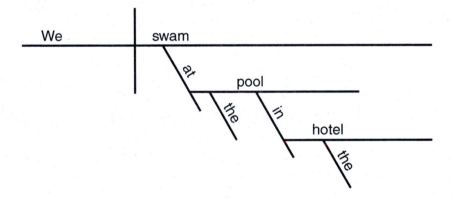

Note that there are two prepositional phrases in the sentence above. The adjective phrase *in the hotel* modifies the noun *pool*, the object of the preposition *at*. The adverb phrase *at the pool* modifies the verb *swam*. This kind of nesting of one prepositional phrase inside another is quite common. This sentence illustrates one of the great advantages of diagramming: We can show at a glance how prepositional phrases are related to one another, something that is sometimes hard to explain verbally.

Note also the convention of the little tail on the slanted prepositional line that extends beyond the horizontal line on which the object of the preposition is placed.

We swam at the pool in the afternoon.

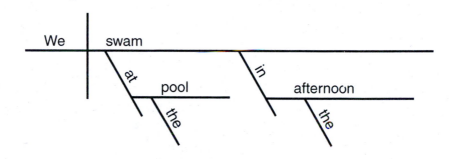

There are also two prepositional phrases in the above sentence, but now they are both adverb phrases that modify the same verb. The diagram shows that the two prepositions do not interact with each other, as they did in the previous example.

The diagram below shows how to diagram an adverb phrase that modifies a predicate adjective.

She is lucky at cards.

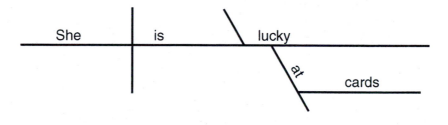

The diagram below shows how to diagram an adverb phrase that modifies another adverb.

We arrived late in the evening.

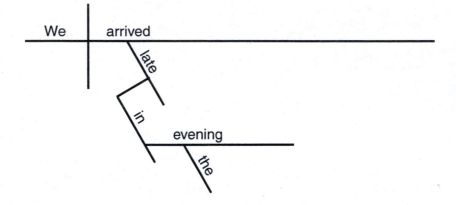

Phrase Exercise #8: Diagramming Prepositional Phrases _____

Diagram the following sentences. The first question is done as an example. (Answers to this exercise are on page 444.)

0. Toto found him behind the curtain.

Answer:

Toto found him behind the curtain.

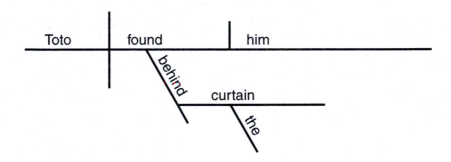

1. I knew all the people at the party.

2. The house on the corner is vacant.

3. The carrier delivered a package to our new address.

4. We went to the library.

5. After breakfast, we ran some errands at the mall.

6. Naturally, Watson was misled by the clue.

7. With great relish, he discussed the causes of the problem.

8. They issued a retraction of their previous press release at the next meeting.

9. The European Union boycotted the importation of beef from the United States.

10. After dinner, we watched some TV at a friend's house.

11. My cousin was active in politics after graduation.

12. I suggested some revisions to the plans for the new office.

13. The count was polite to everyone in the vault.

14. It had rained earlier in the day.

15. I saw the movie about the killer tomatoes.

Appositive Phrases

According to the traditional definition, an **appositive** is a noun that follows another noun or pronoun to identify or explain it. An appositive phrase consists of an appositive and its modifiers. In other words, an appositive phrase is a noun phrase that renames or identifies another noun. Appositives and appositive phrases are normally set off with commas. Here are examples of sentences with the appositive noun in bold and the appositive phrase in italics:

> Emma, *the only* **child** *in class to have no cavities,* smiled proudly.
>
> Dr. Goldhord, *a* **member** *of the Chicago School,* urged restraint.
>
> The Wicked Witch of the West, *Dorothy's old* **enemy,** attacked the scarecrow.

In each of the examples, the appositive phrase identifies or gives new information about the noun it follows. Since the appositive noun must be identical in meaning to the noun it follows, that noun and the appositive are redundant. That is, we can delete either one of them and still have a grammatical sentence (though obviously we will lose the specific information that was contained in the one we delete).

The appositive deletion test. If either of two side-by-side nouns or noun phrases can be deleted without making the sentence ungrammatical, then the second noun or noun phrase is an appositive to the first.

For example, we can delete either the appositive phrase or the noun phrase from the above examples and still have grammatical sentences:

Emma, *the only child in class to have no cavities,* smiled proudly.

Emma smiled proudly.

The only child in class to have no cavities smiled proudly.

Dr. Goldhord, *a member of the Chicago School,* urged restraint.

Dr. Goldhord urged restraint.

A member of the Chicago School urged restraint.

The Wicked Witch of the West, *Dorothy's old enemy,* attacked the scarecrow.

The Wicked Witch of the West attacked the scarecrow.

Dorothy's old enemy attacked the scarecrow.

Phrase Exercise #9: Identifying Appositive Phrases by the Appositive Deletion Test _____

Underline the appositive phrases in the following sentences. Confirm your answer by applying the appositive deletion test. The first question is done as an example. (Answers to this exercise are on page 447.)

0. Lady Montcrief, the heir to Abington Hall, stood aghast.
   Answer: Lady Montcrief, <u>the heir to Abington Hall</u>, stood aghast.
   Confirmation: Lady Montcrief stood aghast.
                    <u>The heir to Abington Hall</u> stood aghast.

1. He gave his daughter a new toy, a stuffed teddy bear.

2. PDQ Bach, an imaginary son of JS Bach, composed *The Stoned Guest.*

3. Atolls, small coral islands, cover tropical waters.

4. Watson, a slightly comic figure, is the perfect foil for Holmes.

5. Calvin Coolidge, the 30th President, was known as "Silent Cal."

6. The theater, one of the old movie palaces, was undergoing renovation.

7. Mr. Brown, a friend of my grandfather's, refused to use electric lights.

8. The test, a multiple-choice philosophy exam, proved to be easy.

9. The police found his last address, an old hotel in Denver.

10. The first talking motion picture, *The Jazz Singer,* appeared in 1927.

Sometimes the appositive phrase is inverted; that is, the appositive phrase is moved in front of the noun it explains. The most common inversion is when the appositive phrase explains a subject pronoun. For example, in the following sentence, the appositive *a hopeless romantic* has been inverted:

A hopeless romantic, I always want movies with happy endings.

When an appositive phrase follows a pronoun, even though that is the normal position for appositives, it sounds stagy and artificial:

?I, a hopeless romantic, always want movies with happy endings.

There is a second, less common use of appositives in which the appositive or appositive phrase is not redundant. Here is an example:

Shakespeare's play *Hamlet* is one of his longest.

If we delete the appositive *Hamlet,* we do not know which of Shakespeare's many plays the sentence is about. This type of appositive is called an **essential appositive** because the appositive or appositive phrase cannot be deleted without destroying the meaning of the sentence. Essential appositives are generally proper nouns or at least common nouns that contain much more specific information than the nouns they rename.

Note that essential appositives and appositive phrases are never set off with commas as are the more common redundant appositives and appositive phrases.

Phrase Exercise #10: Distinguishing Redundant and Essential Appositive Phrases _____

Underline the appositive phrases in the following sentences. If the appositive phrase is redundant, set it off by commas. Confirm your answer by deleting the phrase. If the appositive phrase is essential, label it **Essential**. The first question is done as an example. (Answers to this exercise are on page 448.)

  0. Homer the Greek poet was blind.
     Answer: Homer, the Greek poet, was blind.
     Confirmation: Homer was blind.

  1. The Greek poet Homer was blind.

  2. Children love tortillas a type of cornmeal pancake.

  3. Mr. Smith a teacher at our school greatly admires appositives.

  4. My friend Amy wants to become a dentist.

  5. Noel Coward wrote *Private Lives* his best-known play in 1930.

1. The novel *Pride and Prejudice* is required for the course.

7. They moved to Olympia the capital of Washington State.

8. The novelist William Faulkner became a successful film writer.

9. She is going out with Richard a guy in her geology class.

10. A small start-up company Apexx made the headlines.

Diagramming Appositive Phrases

Appositives are diagrammed by putting the appositive in parentheses and placing it immediately after the noun or pronoun it modifies. For example, the sentence "My English teacher, Mr. Smith, loves gerunds," is diagrammed in this manner:

My English teacher, Mr. Smith, loves gerunds.

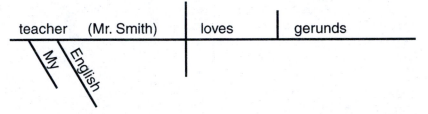

Appositive phrases are diagrammed like any other noun phrases. The appositive noun is put in parentheses after the noun it renames and all the modifiers of the appositive noun are placed below, attached on slanted lines. They are nothing more than adjectives modifying a noun. Here is an example with an inverted appositive phrase.

A man in a hurry, Senator Smithers flies his own jet.

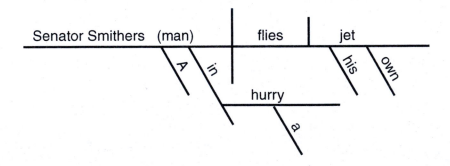

Notice that the appositive phrase, *a man in a hurry*, has been moved behind the noun it renames. Inverted appositives and appositive phrases are always diagrammed as following the noun they rename. This follows the general practice of diagramming in which sentences are diagrammed in a normal sentence order. For example, inverted adverbs are diagrammed under the verb, and questions are diagrammed in statement word order.

Essential appositives and appositive phrases are diagrammed exactly the same way as the more common redundant ones.

Phrase Exercise #11: Diagramming Appositives and Appositive Phrases

Diagram the following sentences. The first question is done as an example. (Answers to this exercise are on page 449.)

0. Dorothy's dog Toto is a major part of the plot.

   Answer:

   Dorothy's dog Toto is a major part of the plot.

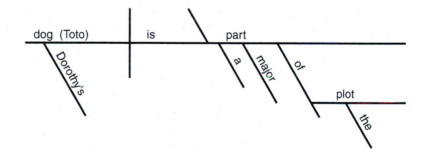

1. Cereal, an American invention, is now a universal breakfast.

2. His apartment, a dingy little room in Manhattan, cost a fortune.

3. Mrs. McCormick, the first foreign-affairs reporter, wrote only about Europe.

4. We got new dishes, some beautiful pottery from Mexico.

5. The driver, a new arrival, couldn't find the address.

6. The plane, an old DC-3, was waiting at the airstrip.

7. I contacted the salesman at his e-mail address, greed.com.

8. Please bring that briefcase, the one with a red tag.

9. Have you met my friend Sarah?
10. She asked Mrs. Brown, our English teacher, a hard grammar question.

Verbal Phrases

The term **verbal phrase** does not mean a phrase that is cleverly worded. A verbal phrase is built around a nontensed verb form used as a different part of speech (i.e., not as a verb). Before doing anything else, we need to distinguish between a **verb phrase** and a **verbal phrase.**

- A **verb phrase** MUST contain a tensed verb. A tensed verb, you recall, is a verb in the present or past tense form.
- A **verbal phrase** is just the opposite: it NEVER contains a tensed verb. Verbal phrases contain nontensed verbs used as nouns, adjectives, or adverbs.

There are three types of verbal phrases, called **gerunds, participles, and infinitives.** Table 5.3 shows for each type of verbal phrase the nontensed verb form it uses and the part-of-speech roles those forms play.

Gerund Phrases

According to the traditional definition, a **gerund** is the present participle form of a verb used as a noun. The present participle form of the verb is easy to

TABLE 5.3   *Types of Verbal Phrases*

Type of Verbal Phrase	Nontensed Verb Form	Part of Speech	Example
Gerund	Present participle	Noun	*Eating ice cream* makes me cold.
Participle	Present participle	Adjective	The child *eating ice cream* is my daughter.
	Past participle	Adjective	Ice cream *eaten too quickly* can give you a headache.
Infinitive	Infinitive	Noun	I love *to eat ice cream.*
	Infinitive	Adjective	Harry's is the place *to get good ice cream.*
	Infinitive	Adverb	We went to Harry's *to get some ice cream.*

recognize because it always ends in *-ing*. For once, even the verb *be* is completely regular: its present participle form is *being*. Here are some examples of the gerund *swimming* playing different noun roles:

Subject:	*Swimming* is an excellent form of exercise.
Object:	I hate *swimming*.
Predicate nominative:	His favorite sport is *swimming*.
Object of preposition:	The pool is used for *swimming*.

The difference between a gerund and a gerund phrase is that a gerund is just the verb (in its present participle form) by itself, whereas a gerund phrase is the verb together with its "subject" (explained below), complement, or modifiers. For example, here are various gerund phrases with the gerund in bold and the entire gerund phrase in italics:

Swimming *in a race* requires extensive preparation.

Swimming *twenty laps a day* is great exercise.

Ted's **swimming** *the butterfly stroke* was the highlight of the race.

In the last example, *Ted's* is called **the subject of the gerund** for the obvious reason that it was Ted who was doing the swimming. The subject of the gerund must always be in possessive form. (Think of it this way: underneath the gerund *swimming* is an actual tensed verb with its subject—*Ted swam*. If this underlying subject is retained, it must be converted into a nonsubject form—a possessive—because the gerund is a nontensed form of the verb that cannot be used with a true subject. No tensed verb, no true subject.) Here are some more examples of gerund phrases with subjects of the gerund:

John's returning the tools so promptly was greatly appreciated.

My making the coffee turned into a near disaster.

Their laughing at my paper was not very nice.

Gerunds and gerund phrases have an important characteristic that makes them relatively easy to identify: they are always singular and abstract, and can thus be replaced by the pronoun *it*.

The *it* test for gerunds and gerund phrases. If a present participle (*-ing* form) of a verb can be replaced by *it*, then the present participle is a gerund. Whatever words the *it* replaces in addition to the gerund make up the complete gerund phrase.

Notice that the *it* test is particularly helpful in identifying the boundaries of the entire gerund phrase. Whatever the *it* replaces is the complete gerund phrase—no more, no less.

Here are some examples of the *it* test applied to gerunds (in bold) and gerund phrases playing various noun roles:

> **Worrying** won't help anything.
>   It (subject)

> **Finding** *a parking place* can be very time consuming.
>   It (subject)

> We appreciated *your **helping** us out.*
>   it (object of verb)

> We were worried about *our **getting** back on time.*
>   it (object of preposition)

Gerunds and gerund phrases used as predicate nominatives after the verb *be* are very easy to miss because they look like so much like progressives. For example, compare the following sentences:

> (a) John's idea of a good time *is watching* reruns on TV.

> (b) John *is watching* reruns on TV.

At first glance, both sentences look like *is watching* is a present progressive verb sequence. In fact, in sentence (a) *is* actually is the main verb and *watching* is a gerund in a gerund phrase, as we can see when we use the *it* test:

> (a2) John's idea of a good time is ***watching*** *reruns on TV.*
>   it

It is a meaningful replacement of *watching reruns on TV.* It tells us what John's idea of a good time is—watching reruns on TV.

However, when we apply the *it* test to sentence (b), the result is meaningless:

> (b2) John is *watching reruns on TV.*
>   *it

It does not equal *watching reruns on TV.*

Another way to see the difference between the two sentences is to eliminate the supposed helping verb *is* and make *watching* into the simple past tense *watched:*

(a3) *John's idea of a good time *watched* reruns on TV.

(b3) John *watched* reruns on TV.

Clearly, *John's idea of a good time* didn't watch reruns on TV, *John* did. This verb paraphrase shows us that we can change the present participle verb *watching* to the past tense verb *watch,* but we cannot change the gerund *watching* to the tensed verb *watch.* The reason is simple: the gerund *watching* is no longer being used as a verb, it is being used as a noun.

Phrase Exercise #12: Identifying Gerunds and Gerund Phrases by the It Test

Underline the gerunds and whole gerund phrases in the following sentences. Confirm your answer by applying the *it* test. The first question is done as an example. (Answers to this exercise are on page 451.)

0. Fixing a flat tire can be hard work.

    Answer: <u>Fixing a flat tire</u> can be hard work.
    　　　　　　　　It

1. Their main job is protecting the President.

2. We talked about our going out for something to eat.

3. Seeing is believing.

4. His always being late gets him into unnecessary trouble.

5. I usually avoid working after dinner.

6. They are always complaining about their having to do the dishes.

7. Getting stuck in traffic was a real pain.

8. My goal is studying classical Greek in Athens.

9. Alicia learned English by listening to the radio.

10. My adjusting the antenna did not help the reception.

Another way to recognize gerunds (and, by extension, gerund phrases, because gerund phrases must contain a gerund) is to see if you can add a possessive noun or pronoun to serve as the subject of the gerund. Only gerunds can be preceded by such possessive words; the other uses of present participles do not permit possessive subjects because they are not nouns.

The possessive subject test for gerunds. If you can add a possessive noun or pronoun to serve as the subject of a word ending in *-ing* (a present participle), then that word is a gerund.

Using our earlier examples, we can add the possessive pronoun *his* to the gerund (a), but not to the verb (b):

(a) John's idea of a good time is **his** *watching reruns on TV.*

(b) *John is **his** watching reruns on TV.

Phrase Exercise #13: Identifying Gerunds by the Possessive Subject Test _____

Underline the gerunds in the following sentences. Confirm your answer by applying the possessive subject test. The first question is done as an example. (Answers to this exercise are on page 452.)

0. We thought about going to a movie.

    Answer: We thought about <u>going</u> to a movie.

    Confirmation: We thought about our <u>going</u> to a movie.

1. Playing tennis helps keep me in shape.

2. I didn't like missing so many classes.

3. They insisted on telling us the plot of the entire movie.

4. Leaving for summer vacation requires a lot of preparation.

5. She had a good reason for not going to class yesterday.

6. Producing a good dinner is a major undertaking.

7. The company was worried about expanding so quickly.

8. We enjoyed participating in the festivities.

9. Appointing the committee proved surprisingly difficult.

10. I liked getting there early.

Review of Gerunds and Gerund Phrases.   Gerunds are present participle verb forms (forms that always end in *-ing*) used as nouns. A gerund phrase is a gerund together with any of the following: the subject of the gerund (a noun or pronoun in a possessive form), the verb's complement, or its modifiers.

The It *Test.*   Both single-word gerunds and entire multiword gerund phrases can be replaced by *it*. The *it* test is particularly helpful in identifying the exact boundaries of a gerund phrase, for example,

> *Redesigning the program* proved to be very costly.
> It

The Possessive Subject Test.   Only when present participles are used as gerunds can possessive subjects be added to them, for example,

Their *redesigning the program* proved to be very costly.

Diagramming Gerunds and Gerund Phrases.   Gerunds (and gerund phrases) are diagrammed in a manner that reflects their noun function. The convention for diagramming gerunds is to put them on a stand according to the noun role that the gerund plays. Here are examples of gerunds and gerund phrases playing the major noun roles of subject, object of a verb, predicate nominative, and object of a preposition.

Subjects: **Parking** their cars is a problem for them.

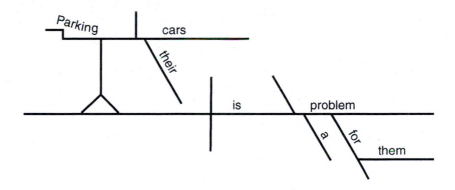

Object of verb: I hate **doing** the dishes.

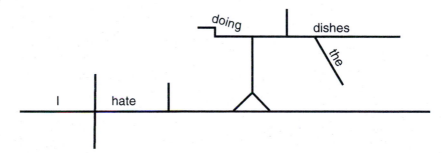

Predicate nominative: His idea of a good time is **watching** reruns on TV.

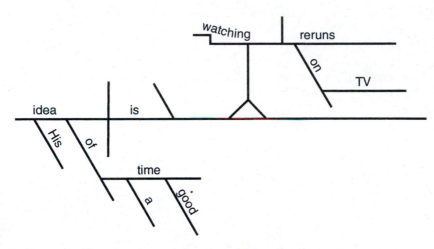

Object of a preposition: It was an excuse for **taking** a break.

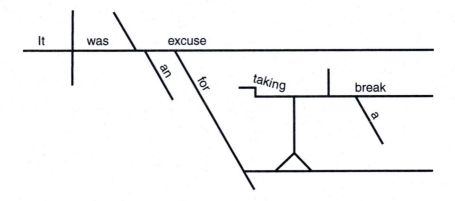

Phrase Exercise #14: Diagramming Gerunds and Gerund Phrases

Diagram the following sentences. The first question is done as an example. (Answers to this exercise are on page 452.)

0. Their finishing the job was important.

   Answer:

   Their **finishing** the job was important.

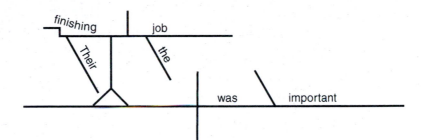

1. Answering the phone takes all morning.
2. I worried about finishing my paper on time.
3. Making an outline is always the first step in writing a paper.
4. The prosecutor's accusing Bugsy of perjury caused a mistrial.
5. I appreciated his getting good information.
6. Getting their cooperation in this matter was not easy.
7. Leon often regretted his picking a fight with all those Marines.
8. Don't bother about washing the dishes now.
9. He muttered something about finding the Maltese Falcon.
10. Lowering the interest rate usually spurs consumers' spending.
11. Their winning the big race capped a successful season.
12. Playing second fiddle is never much fun.
13. They had anticipated their getting a bonus.
14. I hate meeting tight deadlines.
15. We laughed at Leon's retelling of the incident.

Participles and Participial Phrases

According to the traditional definition, a **participle** is a verb in either its present or past participle form used as an adjective. Participles are normally used in front of the nouns they modify, for example,

Present Participial	***Past Participial***
winning coaches	*sanded* floors
blushing maidens	*understood* subject

participating schools	*reported* incident
disgusting mess	*injured* party
trusting students	*trusted* students

As the last example indicates, the same verb can be used in either its present-participle adjective form (***trusting*** *students*) or its past-participle adjective form (***trusted*** *students*), but with substantial differences in meaning. In the present participial expression *trusting students,* the students are doing the trusting. In the past participial expression *trusted students,* the students are being trusted by somebody else. The distinction between present and past participles used as adjectives is a considerable problem for non-native speakers. (See "Participles Used as Adjectives" in the Usage part for ways of helping non-native students.)

Even though participles function as ordinary adjectives modifying the nouns they precede, most participles fail the *very* test because the participles carry over a strong sense of their origin as verbs (and verbs can never be used with *very*), for example,

Present Participial	**Past Participial**
*very *winning* coaches	*very *sanded* floors
*very *blushing* maidens	*very *understood* subject
*very *participating* schools	*very *reported* incident
?very *disgusting* mess	?very *injured* party
?very *trusting* students	*very *trusted* students

The difference between a participle and a participial phrase (besides the annoying difference in spelling) is that a participle is just the verb (in either its present or past participle form) by itself, while a participial phrase is the verb together with its complement and/or modifiers. In the following examples, the participle is in bold and the entire participial phrase is in italics:

Present Participial Phrases

The reporters ***covering*** *the accident* interviewed the chief of police.

The clouds ***blanketing*** *the mountains* lifted in the afternoon.

The man ***wearing*** *a hat* is my uncle.

The incident amused the people ***waiting*** *in line with me.*

Past Participial Phrases

Several of the statements ***made*** *by defendants* were disallowed.

The houses ***situated*** *in the flood plain* all suffered extensive damage.

One book ***required*** *for the course* was out of print.

The quote is from a play ***written*** *by Shakespeare.*

As you can see, single-word participles go in front of the nouns they modify, and participial phrases follow the nouns they modify. Note that past participial phrases contain a past participle verb, often followed by a prepositional phrase beginning with *by,* as in the last example above:

The quote is from a play ***written*** *by Shakespeare.*

You may recall from Chapter 4 that sentences in the passive voice also have past participles followed by prepositional phrases beginning with *by.* This similarity is not accidental: all past participial phrases are derived from passive sentences. Thus, corresponding to the past participle phrase

. . . a play *written by Shakespeare*

is the underlying active-voice sentence

Shakespeare wrote a play.

The prepositional phrases beginning with *by* that occur in passive sentences and past participial phrases are unique. These prepositional phrases carry the underlying subject of the sentence. They are diagrammed as adverb phrases.

Since participial phrases are noun modifiers, a good way to identify them is to apply the pronoun replacement test, here modified for participles and participial phrases:

The pronoun replacement test for participles and participial phrases. If a noun and a following present or past participle verb form and its attached words are BOTH replaced by a single pronoun, then the verb form and any attached words is a participle or participial phrase modifying that noun.

Here is the pronoun replacement test applied to the examples of participial phrases given above, with the participial phrase in bold.

Present Participial Phrases
*The reporters **covering the accident*** interviewed the chief of police.
   They

*The clouds **blanketing the mountains*** lifted in the afternoon.
   They

*The man **wearing a hat*** is my uncle.
   He

The incident amused *the people **waiting in line with me.***
                   them

Past Participial Phrases

Several of *the statements* **made by defendants** were disallowed.
        them

The houses **situated in the flood plain** all suffered damage.
   They

One book **required for the course** was out of print.
  It

The quote was from *a play* **written by Shakespeare**.
             it

Phrase Exercise #15: Identifying Participial Phrases by the Pronoun Replacement Test

Underline the participial phrases in the following sentences. Confirm your answer by applying the pronoun replacement test. The first question is done as an example. (Answers to this exercise are on page 456.)

0. The view overlooking the bay was wonderful.

   Answer: The view <u>overlooking the bay</u> was wonderful.

   Confirmation: <u>The view overlooking the bay</u> was wonderful.
                           It

1. The place was a gloomy old brick factory built in the nineteenth century.

2. The document summarizing the proposal was finally finished.

3. Several trees weakened by the relentless storm came down during the night.

4. The room adjoining ours was much larger.

5. The workers terminated after the strike sued the employer.

6. We disconnected the cables leading to the power source.

7. The council adopted the proposal submitted by the subcommittee.

8. The peasants found the accents cultivated by the local aristocracy to be laughable.

9. The runners competing in the first event were called to the announcer's booth.

10. We collected the paper cups discarded by the runners.

All of the examples of participial phrases that we have examined so far have been **restrictive;** that is, the participial phrases limited or defined the meaning of the nouns they modified. For example, in the sentence

A dog *resting in the shade of a parked car* looked at us warily.

the participial phrase *resting in the shade of a parked car* defines WHICH dog looked at us. Restrictive modifiers are never set off by commas from the nouns they modify.

Participial phrases, however, can also be used as **nonrestrictive** modifiers. Nonrestrictive modifiers do not restrict or change the meaning of the nouns they modify; they merely give additional information. In function, nonrestrictive participles are very much like appositives. And like appositives, they are always set off with commas. For example, in the sentence

Senator Fogg, *discouraged by the small crowd*, cut his remarks short.

the participial phrase *discouraged by the small crowd* is nonrestrictive because there is only one Senator Fogg, whether he was discouraged by the small crowd or not. (The distinction between restrictive and nonrestrictive modifiers will be treated in much greater detail when we discuss adjective clauses in the next chapter.)

For our purposes now, though, we will merely define nonrestrictive participial phrases as the ones set off with commas. Nonrestrictive participial phrases have a highly unusual characteristic: they can be moved away from their normal position following the nouns they modify. For example, in the following sentences, the nonrestrictive participial phrase *muttering under his breath* can be moved to the beginning of the sentence or even to the end:

Scrooge, *muttering under his breath,* returned to his work.

Muttering under his breath, Scrooge returned to his work.

Scrooge returned to his work, *muttering under his breath.*

Because nonrestrictive participial phrases can be separated from the nouns they modify, we need to be able to tell with certainty which noun they modify. Fortunately, there is a highly reliable way to do this.

The understood-subject test for participial phrases. The noun that the participial phrase modifies is the understood subject of the participle.

Using the above example about Scrooge, we can ask, "**Who** was muttering under his breath?" Clearly, Scrooge was. Therefore, the participial phrase must modify Scrooge. The test works equally well for both restrictive and nonrestrictive ones, but restrictive ones do not pose such a problem because they can never be moved away from the nouns they modify. Here are some more examples with nonrestrictive participial phrases.

Pitching into the task, we quickly got the job done.

Who was pitching into the task? We were. Thus, *pitching into the task* modifies *we*.

The children quickly fell asleep, *warmed by the fireplace.*

Who was warmed by the fireplace? The children were. Thus, *warmed by the fireplace* modifies *children*.

Phrase Exercise #16: Identifying Participial Phrases by the Understood-Subject Test _____

Underline the participial phrases in the following sentences. Underline twice the noun that the participial phrase modifies. Confirm your answer by applying the understood subject test. The first question is done as an example. (Answers to this exercise are on page 457.)

    0. Rejected by the voters, Senator Fogg burned his bumper stickers.

       Answer: <u>Rejected by the voters</u>, <u>Senator Fogg</u> burned his bumper stickers.

       Confirmation: Who was rejected by the voters? Senator Fogg was.

    1. Picking their spot carefully, the hikers set up camp.

    2. The professor made his point, gesturing at the figures on the blackboard.

    3. Worried about his grades, Chadwick decided he had better get to work.

    4. The runner slid into second base, easily ducking under the tag.

    5. Giving me a dirty look, she concluded her prepared remarks.

    6. I remembered the strange sound occurring in the night.

    7. Closing his book, the teacher signaled the end of class.

    8. How could he have paid the fine, being completely broke?

    9. Scrooge took a deep breath, realizing that he shouldn't get upset over small matters.

   10. The events scheduled for the afternoon were postponed.

Sometimes nonrestrictive participle phrases are misused. This error is called a **dangling participle.** Here is an example:

    *Having hiked all day, my backpack was killing me.

Even though the writer did not mean it this way, it sounds as though the backpack had been hiking all day. For a detailed discussion of dangling participles, see "Dangling Modifiers" in the Usage part.

Review of Participles and Participial Phrases.   Participials are the present or past participle forms of verbs used as adjectives. Single-word participles are used in front of the nouns they modify. Participial phrases consist of participles together with complements or the modifiers of the verb underlying the participle. Participial phrases normally follow the nouns they modify. However, if the participial is nonrestrictive, it may be moved away from the noun it modifies.

There are two tests for recognizing participial phrases:

The pronoun replacement test. Since participles and participial phrases are noun modifiers, they will be replaced along with the nouns they modify by pronouns. For example, in the following sentence the pronoun replacement test shows that *blocking the driveway* is a participial phrase modifying *car:*

*The car **blocking the driveway** belongs to one of the guests.*
        It

The understood-subject test. The understood subject of a participial phrase is ALWAYS the noun in the sentence that the participial phrase modifies. For example, in the following sentence, we can tell that the participial phrase *ignoring the reporters' shouts* modifies Senator Fogg because Senator Fogg is the understood subject of *ignoring.*

Senator Fogg stalked out of the room, *ignoring the reporters' shouts.*

Diagramming Participles and Participial Phrases. Because single-word participles function as adjectives preceding the nouns they modify, they can be diagrammed as ordinary adjectives—on slanted lines attached to the nouns they modify. Participial phrases have a special convention. The participle is drawn on a slanted line that is attached to a horizontal line on which any noun complements of the participle may be drawn. The participle itself is elegantly draped between the slanted and horizontal lines as follows:

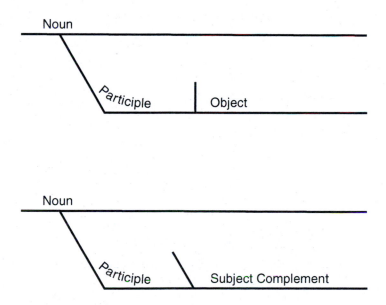

As you can see, complements are drawn as though they were following a finite verb. Modifiers are attached in the normal manner. Here is an example of a sentence containing a present participial phrase:

Swallowing his disappointment, Tom accepted defeat gracefully.

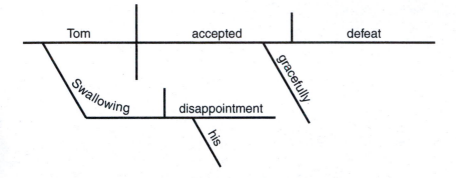

Here is an example of a sentence containing a past participial phrase. Notice that the *by* phrase is attached to the participle.

Rejected by the voters, Tom burned all his bumper stickers.

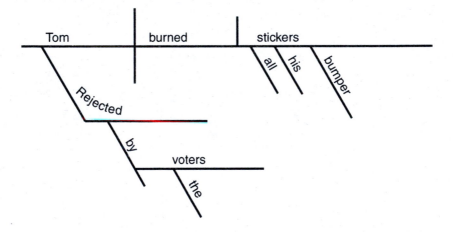

Phrase Exercise #17: Diagramming Participial Phrases _____

Diagram the following sentences. The first question is done as an example. (Answers to this exercise are on page 458.)

0. The rookie teacher took the chalk, wiping his sweaty palms.

Answer:

The rookie teacher took the chalk, wiping his sweaty palms.

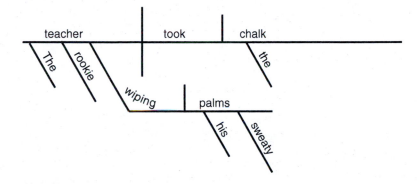

1. The student answering the first question did a good job.

2. Upset by their carelessness, the director reprimanded the actors sharply.

3. The actors took their places, grumbling under their breath.

4. The children, experiencing really cold weather for the first time, huddled together.

5. Inspector Lestrade, completely misled by Holmes's suggestions, made absurd accusations.

6. I opened the refrigerator, looking for a quick snack.

7. Confusing enthusiasm with talent, Leon quit his day job.

8. Disturbed by her weight, Sleeping Beauty began an exercise program.

9. They were studying Italian, motivated by their planned trip to Italy.

10. Underscoring his concern, Senator Fogg commissioned a survey.

11. Scrooge, frightened by his strange dreams, slept very badly.

12. Tiny Tim skipped through the town, strumming his ukulele.

13. Batting her eyes flirtatiously, Miss Piggy answered the reporters' questions.

14. We talked to the children playing in the park.

15. I asked the woman standing next to me a question.

Distinguishing Present Participles from Gerunds. Present participles and gerunds are easily confused because they are both formed from the *-ing* present participle verb form. Although their forms are indeed identical, their functions are quite different: participles are adjectives and gerunds are nouns.

The easiest way to tell them apart is to see if you can delete them. Gerunds and gerund phrases play essential noun roles—subjects and objects—and can never be deleted. Participials and participial phrases, on the other hand, are always modifiers, and modifiers can always be deleted without affecting the basic grammar of the remaining sentence.

The deletion test for distinguishing participles and gerunds. If a present-participle verb form used as another part of speech can be deleted, then it is being used as an adjective—a participle or participial phrase. If it cannot be deleted, then it is being used as a noun—a gerund or gerund phrase.

Here are some examples of the deletion test:

Present participle:	*Laughing,* Alice answered the question.
	~~*Laughing,*~~ Alice answered the question.
Gerund:	*Laughing* gives Alice a side ache.
	*~~Laughing~~ gives Alice a side ache.
Present participial phrase:	*Parking his car,* Fred ran into the store.
	~~*Parking his car,*~~ Fred ran into the store.
Gerund phrase:	*Parking his car* is a real problem for Fred.
	*~~Parking his car~~ is a real problem for Fred.

Phrase Exercise #18: Distinguishing Participles and Participial Phrases from Gerunds and Gerund Phrases by the Deletion Test _____

Underline and label the participles, participial phrases, gerunds, and gerund phrases in the following sentences. Confirm your answer by applying the deletion test. The first question is done as an example. (Answers to this exercise are on page 462.)

0. Handing in my exam, I left the room confidently.

 Answer: <u>Handing in my exam,</u> I left the room confidently.
           Participial phrase

 Confirmation: ~~Handing in my exam,~~ I left the room confidently.

1. Handing in my exam was the easy part of the test.

2. Keeping an eye on the time, I wrote as fast as I could.

3. Keeping an eye on the time is a good idea.

4. Thinking about the problem gave me a headache.

5. Thinking about the problem, I came up with a possible solution.

6. Asking the question is not the same as an answer.

7. Asking the question, he looked around for someone to answer.

8. I learned a lot, writing the paper.

9. I learned about writing the paper.

10. They left the room complaining about the test.

Infinitive Phrases

According to the traditional definition, an **infinitive** is a verb form preceded by *to* and used as a noun, adjective, or adverb. An infinitive phrase consists of an infinitive together with the verb's "subject" (explained below), complement, and/or modifiers. The good news is that because of their distinctive form, infinitives and infinitive phrases are very easy to recognize. The bad news is that infinitives are the only verbals that can be used as more than one part of speech. Infinitives can be used as (1) nouns, (2) adjectives, or (3) adverbs.

Infinitives and Infinitive Phrases Used as Nouns. Here are some examples of the infinitive *to work* playing three different noun roles:

Subject:	*To work* is something that we all must do.
Object:	I hate *to work*.
Predicate nominative:	His least favorite activity is *to work*.

(Infinitives and infinitive phrases cannot be used in the fourth noun role—object of preposition.)

Here are examples of infinitive phrases used as nouns. The infinitive is in bold and the entire infinitive phrase is in italics:

***To learn** Italian* requires a lot of effort.

I wanted ***to learn** the truth about the accident.*

Bugsy's plan was ***to grab** the loot and run like crazy.*

*For Ted **to learn** his part overnight* required a lot of commitment.

In the last example, *Ted* is called the **subject of the infinitive** for the obvious reason that it was Ted who was doing the learning. The subject of the infinitive must always be the object of the preposition *for*. (Notice the parallel with gerunds: The subject of a gerund must always be in the possessive case form. The two "subjects" of nontensed verb forms are in non-subject case forms: possessive case with gerunds and object case with infinitives.) Here are some more examples of infinitive phrases with subjects of the infinitive.

For John **to return** *the tools so promptly* was a pleasant surprise.

For me **to make** *the coffee* was a sign of how desperate they were.

For them **to laugh** *at my paper* was not very nice.

Infinitives and infinitive phrases used as nouns have an important characteristic that makes them relatively easy to identify: they are always singular, and can thus be replaced by the pronoun *it*.

The *it* test for infinitives and infinitive phrases used as nouns.
If an infinitive can be replaced by *it*, then the infinitive is being used as a noun. Whatever words the *it* replaces in addition to the infinitive comprise the entire infinitive phrase.

The *it* test is particularly helpful in identifying the boundaries of the entire infinitive phrase. Whatever the *it* replaces is the complete infinitive phrase, no more, no less.

Here are some examples of the *it* test applied to infinitives and infinitive phrases.

To worry won't help anything.
    It

To find *a parking place* can be very time consuming.
    It

The plan was *for you* **to do** *the dishes.*
                   it

For him **to forget** *his homework* was completely out of character.
    It

Phrase Exercise #19: Identifying Infinitives and Infinitive Phrases Used as Nouns by the It Test _____

Underline the infinitives and infinitive phrases used as nouns. Confirm your answer by applying the *it* test. The first question is done as an example. (Answers to this exercise are on page 463.)

0. I needed to fix that flat tire.

Answer: I needed <u>to fix that flat tire</u>.

Confirmation: I needed <u>to fix that flat tire</u>.
                                      it.

1. Their main job is to protect the President.

2. For her to win so easily encouraged the whole team.

3. We expected to be done by now.

4. The best opportunity was for them to lead hearts.

5. To keep on smoking now seemed foolish.

6. He claimed to be a friend of hers.

7. I like to eat French fries with mustard.

8. For us to take such an early flight meant we left before dawn.

9. To do the right thing is important.

10. To miss an inch is to miss a mile.

As you have probably noticed, infinitives and infinitive phrases are used in much the same way as gerunds and gerund phrases. Often, in fact, they are interchangeable with no obvious difference in meaning, for example:

Infinitive:	*To win* is everything.
Gerund:	*Winning* is everything.
Infinitive phrase:	I like *to eat* pizza.
Gerund phrase:	I like *eating* pizza.

Even phrases with subjects seem to be interchangeable:

Infinitive phrase:	*For Popeye **to turn** down spinach* was a bit surprising.
Gerund phrase:	*Popeye's **turning** down spinach* was a bit surprising.

There are, however, three differences between the two types of phrases.

- Infinitives and infinitive phrases cannot be used as objects of prepositions, but gerunds and gerund phrases can:

Infinitive phrase:	*We talked about **to go** to the movies.
Gerund phrase:	We talked about *going to the movies*.

- While infinitive phrases used as subjects are grammatical, we often prefer to replace them with a dummy *it* and move the infinitive phrase to the end of the sentence. For example, we would probably prefer to change

*For Popeye **to turn** down spinach* was a bit surprising

to

It was a bit surprising *for Popeye **to turn** down spinach.*

However, we do not feel the need to use the same dummy *it* paraphrase with gerund phrases used as subjects; indeed, the resulting sentences usually sound somewhat odd:

> ? It was a bit surprising, *Popeye's **turning** down spinach.*

- Some verbs will allow infinitives and infinitive phrases as objects but the same verbs will not allow gerunds and gerund phrases. For example, infinitives and infinitive phrases can be used as objects of *want*, but not gerunds or gerund phrases:

Infinitive phrase: I want *to eat* pizza.
Gerund phrase: *I want *eating* pizza.

Other verbs are just the opposite—permitting gerunds and gerund phrases as objects but not infinitives and infinitive phrases, for example, the verb *enjoy:*

Infinitive phrase: *I enjoy *to eat* pizza.
Gerund phrase: I enjoy *eating* pizza.

There is no obvious pattern to which verbs will permit which type of phrase as objects. The unpredictability of which type of phrase to use is a considerable problem for non-native speakers.

Teaching Tip

Naturally enough, non-native speakers want grammar "rules" that will help guide them in when to use infinitives and when to use gerunds. Unfortunately, no such rules exist. The only way to learn which verbs take gerunds, which take infinitives, and which take both is through extensive reading. There are no short cuts.

Infinitives and Infinitive Phrases Used as Adjectives. Infinitives and infinitive phrases (with or without subjects) can be used to modify nouns. Here are some examples with the infinitive in bold and the infinitive phrase in italics:

Infinitives:
The need *to sleep* was almost unbearable.
He was the last guest *to leave.*
They picked some songs *to sing.*

Infinitive Phrases:
That is the attitude *for them **to encourage.***
We marked the items *to be put on sale.*
The best route *for you **to take** to Detroit* is the freeway.

Since infinitives and infinitive phrases are noun modifiers locked into place following the nouns they modify, they are easily identified by the pronoun replacement test, here tailored for infinitives and infinitive phrases:

The pronoun replacement test for infinitives and infinitive phrases used as adjectives. If a noun and a following infinitive or infinitive phrase are BOTH replaced by a single pronoun, then the infinitive or infinitive phrase must modify that noun.

Here is the pronoun replacement test applied to the above examples of infinitives and infinitive phrases (the entire infinitive phrase is in bold)

Infinitives:
The need **to sleep** was almost unbearable.
          It

He was *the last guest* **to leave.**
                         it

They picked *some songs* **to sing.**
                       them

Infinitive Phrases:
That is *the attitude* **for them to encourage.**
                    it

We marked *the items* **to be put on sale.**
                    them

The best route **for you to take to Detroit** is the freeway.
          It

Phrase Exercise #20: Identifying Infinitives and Infinitive Phrases Used as Adjectives by the Pronoun Replacement Test

Underline the infinitives and infinitive phrases used as adjectives. Confirm your answer by applying the pronoun replacement test. The first question is done as an example. (Answers to this exercise are on page 464.)

0. The man for you to see will be back at noon.

   Answer: The man <u>for you to see</u> will be back at noon.

   Confirmation: <u>The man for you to see</u> will be back at noon.
                              He

1. The schedule for us to go on field trips is posted on the door.

2. Here is a list of the drugs to avoid during pregnancy.

3. I got the books to read for class.

4. The plot to overthrow the king was discovered.

5. I bought a gift for us to take to the housewarming.

6. That is the edition to get.

7. I set a goal for myself to reach.

8. They had quite a story to tell us.

9. We had the good fortune to be in just the right place.

10. She was the first woman to serve as governor.

Infinitives and Infinitive Phrases Used as Adverbs.   Infinitives and infinitive phrases (with or without subjects) can also be used as adverbs to modify (1) verbs and (2) predicate adjectives.

Using Infinitives and Infinitive Phrases to Modify Verbs.   Here are some examples of infinitives modifying verbs with the infinitive in bold and the infinitive phrase in italics:

> *Infinitives:*
> You must practice hard **to win.**
> I stayed up all night **to finish.**
> We came here **to relax.**

> *Infinitive Phrases:*
> They went to the post office *for Sally **to get** some stamps.*
> I went to the registrar's office **to drop** *a course.*
> I need a doctor's note *for the druggist **to fill** my prescription.*

These infinitives and infinitive phrases are adverbs, and like other adverbs that modify verbs, they answer adverb questions, and they can be moved.

Infinitives and infinitives phrases that modify the verb act as adverbs of reason and always answer a *why* question.

The *why* test for infinitives and infinitive phrases that modify verbs. If an infinitive or infinitive phrase answers a *why* question, then that infinitive or infinitive phrase modifies the verb.

Here are examples of the *why* test applied to the examples of infinitives and infinitive phrases given above.

> *Infinitives:*
> You must practice hard **to win.**
> **Why** must you practice hard? **To win.**

I stayed up all night *to finish.*
Why did I stay up all night? *To finish.*

We came here *to relax.*
Why did we come here? *To relax.*

Infinitive Phrases:
They went to the post office *for Sally **to get** some stamps.*
Why did they go to the post office? *For Sally **to get** some stamps.*

I went to the registrar's office *to drop a course.*
Why did I go to the registrar's office? *To drop a course.*

I need a doctor's note *for the druggist **to fill** my prescription.*
Why do I need a doctor's note? *For the druggist **to fill** my prescription.*

Infinitives and infinitive phrases that modify verbs can usually (but not always) be moved to the beginning of the sentence.

The adverb movement test for infinitives and infinitive phrases that modify verbs. If an infinitive or infinitive phrase can be moved to the beginning of the sentence, then that infinitive or infinitive phrase modifies the verb.

Here are some examples of the adverb movement test applied to infinitives and infinitive phrases.

Infinitives:
To win, you must practice hard.
To finish, I stayed up all night.
**To relax,* we came here.

Infinitive Phrases:
*For Sally **to get** some stamps,* they went to the post office.
To drop a course, I went to the registrar's office.
*For the druggist **to fill** my prescription,* I need a doctor's note.

*Teaching
Tip*

As you can see from the last example of the infinitives, **To relax, we came here,* the movement test sometimes fails. This reinforces the importance of having students routinely use more than one test.

Phrase Exercise #21: Identifying Infinitives and Infinitive Phrases that Modify Verbs by the Why Test and the Adverb Movement Test _____

Underline the infinitives and infinitive phrases that modify verbs. Confirm your answers by applying the *why* test and the adverb movement test. The first question is done as an example. (Answers to this exercise are on page 465.)

0. The president called a meeting to discuss the proposal.

   Answer: The president called a meeting <u>to discuss the proposal</u>.

   Why test: **Why** did the president call a meeting? To discuss the proposal.

   Adverb movement test: To discuss the proposal, the president called a meeting.

1. He brought up the issue to provoke an argument.

2. The new drug shrinks the blood vessels to deprive the cancer cell of oxygen.

3. There had to be a consensus for them to reach an agreement.

4. We took the kids to the harbor for them to see the sailboats.

5. I turned off the water to fix a leak in a pipe.

6. We added some extra time for them to comply with the new regulations.

7. Congress raised salaries in the military to help retain more officers.

8. She is staying off her foot to give it a chance to heal.

9. We got a video camera for them to see what they were doing.

10. The judge delayed the trial for the defendant to get a new lawyer.

In addition to the above two tests that you would expect to be able to apply to any type of adverb that modifies the verb, there is a reliable test specifically for infinitives and infinitive phrases that modify verbs: the *in order* paraphrase.

The *in order* test for infinitive and infinitive phrases that modify verbs. If you can add *in order* to the beginning of an infinitive or infinitive phrase, then that infinitive or infinitive phrase modifies the verb.

Here are examples of the *in order* paraphrase test applied to the same examples of infinitives and infinitive phrases:

Infinitives:
You must practice hard *in order* to win.
I stayed up all night *in order* to finish.
We came here *in order* to relax.

Infinitive Phrases:
They went to the post office *in order* for Sally to get some stamps.
I went to the registrar's office *in order* to drop a course.
I need a doctor's note *in order* for the druggist to fill my prescription.

*Teaching
Tip*

The *in order* test is the first test students should use in identifying infinitives and infinitive phrases that modify verbs. The test is highly reliable and easy to use, because it does not require any manipulation of the sentence beyond adding two words.

Phrase Exercise #22: Identifying Infinitives and Infinitive Phrases that Modify Verbs by the in order Test _____

Underline the infinitives and infinitive phrases that modify verbs. Confirm your answer by applying the *in order* test. The first question is done as an example. (Answers to this exercise are on page 466.)

0. I left work early to do some shopping.

    Answer: I left work early <u>to do some shopping</u>.

    Confirmation: I left work early **in order** <u>to do some shopping</u>.

1. France fought England to protect her colonies in America.

2. We sprayed the fruit trees to prevent rust and scale.

3. The committee called a recess for the negotiators to consult with their embassies.

4. Senator Fogg attacked his opponent to cloud the issues.

5. They needed a pump for them to drain the pool.

6. We closed the blinds for the children to fall asleep.

7. Wash them in cool water to prevent them from shrinking.

8. There was a fee for us to enroll in the program.

9. The plans were revised to make more space in the living room.

10. I sold the bonds to invest in a new mutual fund.

Using Infinitives and Infinitive Phrases to Modify Predicate Adjectives. Infinitives and infinitive phrases often modify predicate adjectives. Here are some examples with the infinitive in bold and the infinitive phrase in italics:

Infinitives
I am ready *to go.*
They were glad *to leave.*
I am prepared *to begin.*

Infinitive Phrases
They were happy *to see* us again.
We were anxious *to start* packing.
It was silly *to get* so upset about nothing.

These adverb infinitives and infinitive phrases do not modify the verb, so they fail the adverb movement test, and the *in order* test gives results that are either ungrammatical or completely change the meaning of the original sentence. (The *why* test is marginal and thus not very helpful.) Quite literally, there is nothing these infinitives and infinitive phrases can modify except the predicate adjective. In order to confirm that these adverbs do modify the predicate adjective, you should apply the adverb movement test and the *in order* test for adverbs that modify the verb in order to rule out that analysis.

- **Adverb movement test.** When we apply the adverb movement test to infinitives and infinitive phrases that modify predicate adjectives, the result is a kind of odd, unworldly English that sounds like Yoda in *Star Wars*:

  *To go, I am ready.

  *To leave, they were glad.

  *To begin, I am prepared.

  *To see us again, they were happy.

  *To start packing, we were anxious.

  *To get so upset about nothing, it was silly.

- ***In order* test.** Sometimes the *in order* test will produce quasi-grammatical results, but the new sentences have completely different meanings from the original sentences. Here is the *in order* test applied to the first example:

  I am ready **in order to go.*

  If the sentence means anything at all, it has the odd meaning that the speaker got ready so that, as a result of being ready, the speaker could go. The sentence has lost its original meaning of being prepared to go. Here are the remaining examples:

  They were glad **in order to leave.*

  I am prepared **in order to begin.*

  They were happy **in order to see us again.*

  We were anxious **in order to start packing.*

  It was silly **in order to get so upset about nothing.*

Phrase Exercise #23: Identifying Infinitives and Infinitive Phrases Used as Adverbs

Underline the infinitives and infinitive phrases. Label whether the infinitive or infinitive phrase modifies the **Verb** or a **Pred Adj**. Confirm your answer by applying the adverb movement or *in order* test. The first question is done as an example. (Answers to this exercise are on page 467.)

0. I was happy to take a break.

   Answer: I was happy <u>to take a break</u>.
   Pred Adj

   Confirmation: Adverb movement test: *To take a break, I was happy.
   In order test: *I was happy **in order** <u>to take a break</u>.

1. They are ready for us to leave.

2. They took a trip to use up their frequent flyer miles.

3. I was not able to finish my paper on time.

4. The rules were put in place to ensure fair competition.

5. Nonsense, I am happy to do it.

6. We need a key to unlock the garage door.

7. It is rude for the hostess to call her guests bad names.

8. They retired early to take advantage of the buy-out.

9. I am pleased to make the following announcement.

10. It was nice to see them again.

Review of Infinitives. Infinitives and infinitive phrases are unlike the other two types of verbal phrases in that infinitive and infinitive phrases can be used as more than one part of speech. Gerunds and gerund phrases, you recall, are always nouns, and participles and participial phrases are always adjectives. With infinitives and infinitive phrases, we always need to determine whether they are being used as nouns, adjectives, or adverbs. Fortunately, the three uses of infinitives and infinitive phrases are so distinct that we can easily tell the three uses apart by the following tests.

1. Infinitives and infinitive phrases used as nouns
   (a) *It* test
      Example: I wanted *to have dinner.*
      it

2. Infinitives and infinitive phrases used as adjectives
   (a) Pronoun replacement test
      Example: We marked *the items to be put on sale.*
      them.

3. Infinitives and infinitive phrases used as adverbs modifying verbs
   (a) *Why* test
       Example: We left early *to have dinner.* **Why** did we leave early? *To have dinner.*
   (b) Adverb movement test
       Example: We left early *to get dinner ready.* **To get dinner ready,** we left early.
   (c) *In order* test
       Example: We left early *to get dinner ready.* We left early **in order** *to get dinner ready.*

4. Infinitives and infinitives phrases used as adverbs modifying predicate adjectives: There are no positive tests; however, infinitives and infinitive phrases following predicate adjectives that fail the adverb movement test and the *in order* test must modify the predicate adjectives, because there is nothing else for them to modify.

Phrase Exercise #24: Identifying Infinitives and Infinitive Phrases _____

Underline the infinitives and infinitive phrases in the following sentences. Label them Noun, Adj, or Adv. If the infinitive or infinitive phrase is an adverb, specify what it modifies. Confirm your answer by applying one or more tests. The first question is done as an example. (Answers to this exercise are on page 468.)

0. Senator Fogg decided to run for re-election.

   Answer: Senator Fogg decided <u>to run for re-election.</u>
                                   Noun

   Confirmation: Senator Fogg decided <u>to run for re-election.</u>
                                        it.

1. The plan is for you to leave your car at the station.

2. They bought some tape to mail the box.

3. Leon planned for them to have a romantic dinner.

4. Napoleon hung a few generals occasionally to encourage the others.

5. Aunt Sally is in the mood to play Monopoly.

6. Toto ran behind the curtain to expose the wizard.

7. John was eager to take the test.

8. They waited there politely for us to introduce the stranger.

9. To admire the book is to admire the author.

10. We got a new external drive to run the new programs.

11. I got a notice to pay my library fines.

12. For me to explain the situation, I will need a pencil and some paper.

13. We tried to correct Leon's weak backhand.

14. The effect of the ruling is to increase property taxes.

15. Check the label to find the directions.

16. We received the approval to start our project on Monday.

17. It was very upsetting to be so late.

18. I took piano lessons to please my mother.

19. To forgive is divine.

20. For them to refuse the offer was a big mistake.

Diagramming Infinitives and Infinitive Phrases.   Infinitives and infinitive phrases are diagrammed according to whether they are functioning as nouns or modifiers.

Infinitives and Infinitive Phrases Used as Nouns.   When infinitives and infinitive phrases are used as nouns, they are diagrammed much like gerunds and gerund phrases. Both types of verbs are put up on little stands above horizontal lines. Both can have subjects attached as modifiers. The only difference is that with infinitives and infinitive phrases, the infinitive marker *to* is put on a slanted line and the subject of the infinitive is treated as a prepositional phrase, like this:

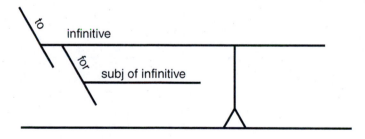

Infinitive phrases are drawn much like gerund phrases. Complements are drawn on the main sentence line after the verbal. Here are examples of infinitive phrases used in the three noun functions of subject, object, and predicate nominative. (Recall that infinitives and infinitive phrases cannot be used as the objects of prepositions.)

Subject: **To write** the great American novel became my great dream.

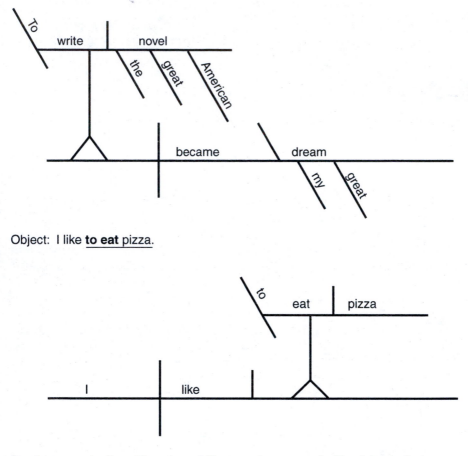

Object: I like **to eat** pizza.

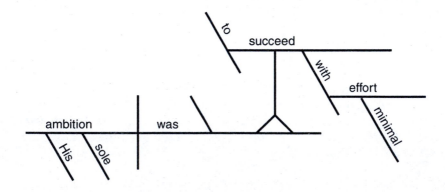

Predicate nominative: His sole ambition was **to succeed** with minimal effort.

Phrase Exercise #25: Diagramming Infinitives and Infinitive Phrases Used as Nouns

Diagram the following sentences. The first question is done as an example. (Answers to this exercise are on page 470.)

 0. Jack Sprat wanted to have some lean meat.

    Answer:

Jack Sprat wanted to have some lean meat.

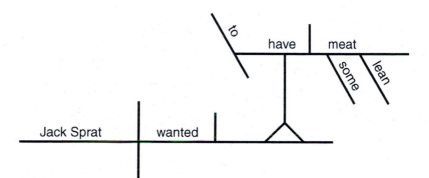

 1. I needed to update my calendar.

 2. To start over was my last choice.

 3. For them to make a fuss about it seemed unfair.

 4. I like to swim.

 5. The answer to our problem was to be very creative.

 6. I hated to yell at them.

 7. Their mission was to boldly explore space.

 8. For me to finish on time was a real stretch.

 9. We need to increase our sales.

10. To stay still was difficult.

Infinitives and Infinitive Phrases Used as Modifiers.   When infinitives and infinitive phrases are used as adjectives to modify nouns or adverbs to modify verbs or predicate adjectives, the infinitive is drawn under the word it modifies. The *to* is placed on the slanted line much like a preposition would be. Here are three examples: an infinitive phrase used as an adjective to modify a noun, an infinitive phrase used as an adverb to modify a verb, and an infinitive phrase used as an adverb to modify a predicate adjective.

Modify a noun: The time **to fix** the roof is before winter.

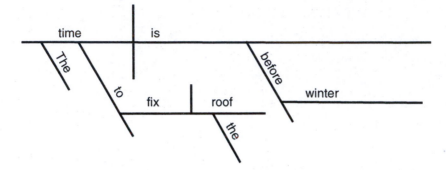

Modify a verb: You must practice constantly **to win** at basketball.

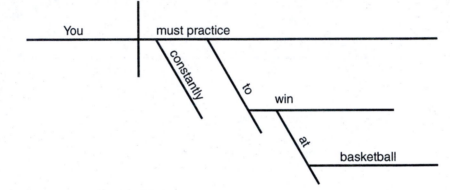

Modify a predicate adjective: I am ready **to finish** my paper now.

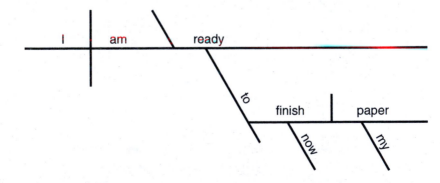

(Note: *Now* is ambiguous; *now* could also modify *am*.)

Phrase Exercise #26: Diagramming Infinitives and Infinitive Phrases Used as Modifiers

Diagram the following sentences. The first question is done as an example. (Answers to this exercise are on page 472.)

   0. The decision to audit the course was a good one.

   Answer:

The decision to audit the course was a good one.

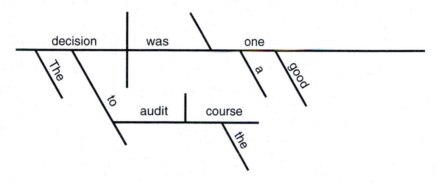

   1. It was crazy to even try it.

   2. I went to the airport to meet a friend.

   3. Congress passes a lot of bad bills in the rush to adjourn.

   4. I bought a new computer to run the new software.

   5. The general was wise to delay the attack.

   6. The general's decision to delay the attack was wise.

   7. The general moved slowly to delay the attack.

   8. The desire to modernize seems irreversible.

   9. The country modernized to create more jobs.

   10. It is usually desirable to modernize.

Chapter Review

A phrase is a group of words that acts as a single part of speech. There are six types of phrases: noun phrases, prepositional phrases, appositive phrases, and the three verbal phrases: gerund, participial, and infinitive.

1. **Noun phrases.** Noun phrases consist of a noun together with the noun's modifiers. Noun phrases are easily identified by the pronoun replacement test.
   Pronoun replacement test. All noun phrases can be replaced by third-person pronouns. The noun within the noun phrase determines the form of the third-person pronoun, for example,

   > *The **children** at the zoo* were all watching the monkeys.
   >   They

2. **Prepositional phrases.** Prepositional phrases are either adjective phrases that modify nouns or adverb phrases that modify verbs, adjectives, or other adverbs. Here are the tests that tell us which role prepositional phrases are playing.
   (a) Adjective phrases
       (i) **Pronoun replacement test.** Pronouns replace nouns and all their modifiers, including adjective phrases, for example,

   > *The book **on the desk*** is yours.
   >   It

       Because *it* replaces the prepositional phrase *on the desk*, we know that it is an adjective phrase modifying *book*.
       (ii) ***Which* test.** Adjective phrases identify WHICH noun we are talking about, for example,

   > The book *on the desk* is yours.

       Because *on the desk* identifies which book we are talking about, *on the desk* is an adjective phrase modifying book.
   (b) Adverb phrases that modify verbs
       (i) **Adverb question test.** Adverb phrases that modify verbs answer *where, when, why,* and *how* questions, for example,

   > We went shopping *after lunch.*

       Because *after lunch* answers the adverb question, **When** *did we go shopping*, we know it is an adverb phrase.
       (ii) **Adverb movement test.** Most adverb phrases that modify verbs can be moved to the front of the sentence, for example,

   > *After lunch,* we went shopping.

   (c) Adverb phrases that modify predicate adjective and other adverbs
       These adverb phrases fail both the tests for adverbs that modify verbs: they do not answer adverb questions nor do they move. These adverb phrases modify whatever adjective or adverb is on their left.

3. **Appositive phrases.** Appositives are nouns that rename or identify a preceding noun. Appositive phrases consist of an appositive and its mod-

ifying adjectives. Appositives and appositive phrases are normally grammatically redundant. That is, they can be deleted without affecting the grammar or the basic meaning of the sentence. These appositives and appositive phrases are always set off with commas. The main test for redundant appositives and appositive phrases is the appositive deletion test.

(a) Appositive deletion test. The fact that we can delete the noun phrase *an aging skyscraper* from the following sentence tell us that the deleted noun phrase is an appositive.

The Empire State Building, ~~an aging skyscraper,~~ is the symbol of New York.

Essential appositives are those appositives and appositive phrases whose deletion would make their sentence meaningless. For example, if we deleted the appositive *Star Wars* from the following sentence, we would have no idea what the sentence was talking about.

The film *Star Wars* was a huge commercial success.

Note that essential appositives and appositive phrases are not set off with commas.

4. **Verbal Phrases**. There are three types of verbal phrases: gerunds, participial, and infinitive.

(a) Gerund phrases. A gerund phrase consists of a gerund (an -*ing* present participle verb form used as a noun) together with that verb's subject, complement, and/or modifiers. There are two tests for identifying gerunds and gerund phrases.

(i) **The *it* test.** Both single-word gerunds and multiple word gerund phrases can be replaced by *it*. The *it* test is particularly helpful in identifying the exact boundaries of a gerund phrase, for example,

Unfortunately *redesigning the program* proved to be very costly.
                    it

(ii) **Possessive subject test.** Only when present participles are used as gerunds can possessive subjects be added to them, for example,

Unfortunately ***their*** *redesigning the program* proved to be very costly.

(b) Participial phrases. A participial phrase consists of a participial (a present or past participle verb form used as an adjective) together with that verb's complement or modifiers. There are two tests for recognizing participles and participial phrases.

(i) **The pronoun replacement test.** Because participles and participial phrases are noun modifiers, they will be replaced along with the nouns they modify by pronouns. For example, in the following sentence the pronoun replacement test shows that *blocking the driveway* is a participial phrase modifying *car*:

The car **blocking the driveway** belongs to one of the guests.
         It

(ii) **The understood-subject test.** The understood subject of a participial phrase is always the noun in the sentence that the participial phrase modifies. For example, in the following sentence, we can tell that the participial phrase *ignoring the reporters' shouts* modifies *Senator Fogg* because *Senator Fogg* is the understood subject of *ignoring*.

Senator Fogg stalked out of the room, *ignoring the reporters' shouts.*

(iii) **Deletion test.** Participles and gerunds are both formed with *-ing*, so a good way to tell them apart is by the deletion test. Because participles and participial phrases are modifiers, they can always be deleted from the sentence. However, because gerunds and gerund phrases are nouns that play the role of subjects or objects, they can never be deleted.

(c) Infinitive phrases. An infinitive phrase consists of an infinitive (*to* + the base form of a verb) together with that verb's subject, complement, and/or modifiers. Infinitives and infinitive phrases are used in three ways: as nouns, as adjectives, or as adverbs that modify verbs or adjectives.

(i) Infinitives and infinitive phrases used as nouns
   (1) **The *it* test.** The pronoun *it* replaces infinitives and infinitive phrases, for example,

   For him to forget his homework was completely out of character.
              It

(ii) Infinitives and infinitive phrases used as adjectives
   (1) **Pronoun replacement test.** Infinitives and infinitive phrases used as adjectives are replaced by pronouns along with the nouns they modify, for example,

   We marked *the items to be put on sale.*
                  them.

(iii) Infinitives and infinitive phrases used as adverbs modifying verbs. There are three tests that can help identify this use of infinitives and infinitive phrases.
   (1) **The *why* test.** Infinitives and infinitive phrases that modify verbs answer *why* questions, for example,

We left early *to have dinner*. **Why** did we leave early? *To have dinner*.

(2) **The adverb movement test.** Infinitives and infinitive phrases that modify verbs tend to be moveable, for example,

We left early *to have dinner*. *To have dinner*, we left early.

(3) **The *in order* test.** An especially effective test for infinitives and infinitive phrases that modify verbs is to add *in order* in front of the phrase, for example,

I went home early *to feed the cat*. I went home early **in order** *to feed the cat*.

(iv) Infinitives and infinitive phrases used as adverbs modifying predicate adjectives. Like prepositional phrases modifying predicates, there are no positive tests for identifying this use of infinitives and infinitive phrases. The key to identifying them is the fact that they fail both the *why* and *in order* tests.

Phrase Exercise #27: Review of Verbals _____

Underline and label all verbals: gerunds and gerund phrases; participles and participial phrases; infinitives and infinitive phrases. Briefly indicate the role the underlined words play. The first question is done as an example. (Answers to this exercise are on page 474.)

   0. Jason was glad to finish the dishes.

   Answer: Jason was glad <u>to finish the dishes</u>.
   Infinitive phrase—adjective modifying predicate
   adjective *glad*

   1. To further delay our plans would be a big mistake.

   2. The farmers burned all the trees infected by the insects.

   3. A man fingering his sword welcomed them aboard.

   4. Organizing his work is never easy.

   5. It is very difficult for me to do that.

   6. I began to warm up, humming under my breath.

   7. We bought an insecticide intended for commercial use.

   8. She came early to finish her project.

   9. Salting your food excessively can be unhealthy.

   10. The official abruptly terminated the conference, ignoring the reporters' questions.

   11. He was the first person to eat raw snails.

12. Shaking his burned fingers, Rollo dropped the hot pan.

13. It is a little late to worry about that.

14. For you to take the blame was very honorable.

15. The building was ready to be occupied.

Phrase Exercise #28: Review of Verbals _____

Underline and label all verbals: gerunds and gerund phrases; participles and participial phrases; infinitives and infinitive phrases. Briefly indicate the role the underlined words play. The first question is done as an example. (Answers to this exercise are on page 475.)

0. The head office appreciated getting the report.

   Answer: The head office appreciated <u>getting the report</u>.

   Gerund phrase—noun playing role
of object of verb

1. Selecting his club carefully, the golfer approached the tee.

2. Mr. Wilson gave a lecture about investing in international bonds.

3. We bought a new computer for Hugh to use.

4. She is certain to take the job offer.

5. It began raining heavily.

6. We got some pizza to take to the party.

7. They heard a car leaving the garage.

8. Touched by their plight, Scrooge gave them some good advice.

9. The movie playing at the local theater was a real hit.

10. I welcomed their ideas about solving the problem.

11. It was the first restaurant to receive three stars.

12. It seemed petty to raise the issue.

13. I regret bringing you some bad news.

14. Avoiding every possible issue, Senator Fogg concluded his lengthy talk.

15. Taking a shortcut can be very dangerous.

6

Clauses

According to the traditional definition, a clause is a group of words that contains a subject and verb. Implicit in the traditional definition is the fact that the verb is a **tensed verb;** that is, a present- or past-tense verb that enters into a subject–verb relationship with the subject. Clauses differ from verbal phrases (gerund, participial, and infinitive phrases) in that clauses have tensed verbs whereas verbal phrases have only nontensed verb forms—present participles, past participles, and infinitives. Consequently, verbal phrases never have true subject–verb relationships.

There are two kinds of clauses: **independent (main) clauses** and **dependent (subordinate) clauses.** Since the terms "independent" and "main" are interchangeable, as are "dependent" and "subordinate", for the sake of simplicity we will use only "independent" and "dependent" from this point on.

Independent Clauses

Independent clauses express complete thoughts and can stand by themselves, for example,

> I hate Mondays.
>
> Can you read this?
>
> Stop!
>
> This is an independent clause.

All sentences must contain at least one independent clause.

Dependent Clauses

Dependent clauses do not express complete thoughts and cannot stand by themselves. Dependent clauses act as a single part of speech—an adjective, adverb, or noun. Since dependent clauses cannot stand alone, they must always be attached to an independent clause. If a dependent clause is used without being attached to an independent clause, it is considered a **sentence fragment.** (See "Fragments" in the Usage part for a detailed discussion of sentence fragments.)

Dependent clauses typically begin with a special word that flags the fact that the clause is dependent. These flag words are shown in bold in the following examples of dependent clauses:

before the party is over

when you called

if I were you

what you said

because I was finished with my homework

that we might be late

how you feel

which is on your left

Dependent clauses are classified according to the part-of-speech role that they play: (1) as **adjective clauses,** (2) as **adverb clauses,** or (3) as **noun clauses.** In this chapter we will discuss each of these three types of dependent clauses in turn. We will end the chapter with the terminology used for classifying sentences by their clause structure.

Adjective (Relative) Clauses

An adjective clause is a dependent clause used as an adjective to modify a noun or (less commonly) a pronoun. Adjective clauses normally begin with **relative pronouns,** which is why adjective clauses are often called "relative" clauses. Here are some examples of relative clauses (in italics), with the relative pronouns printed in bold:

The weatherman *who is on Channel 7* is always wrong.

She married a man *whom she met at school.*

They called the person *whose turn was next.*

The radio, ***which** I had left on,* woke me up.

She found it in the book ***that** you lent her.*

I know a place ***where** we can get a quick lunch.*

These pronouns are called "relative" pronouns because they "relate" to the noun on their immediate left. In other words, relative pronouns have no meaning of their own—they take their meaning from the nouns to which they refer. These nouns are called the pronoun's **antecedent.** The antecedents of the relative pronouns *who, whom,* and *whose* are people. In the examples above, *who* refers to *weatherman; whom* refers to *man;* and *whose* refers to *person.* The antecedents of *which* and *that* are objects or ideas. In the examples above, *which* refers to *radio* and *that* refers to *book.*

Where is something of an anomaly since, technically speaking, it is not a pronoun at all: it is actually an adverb. We use it as a kind of honorary relative pronoun (sometimes called a **pronominal adverb**) to refer to nouns of location. In the last example above, *where* refers to the noun *place.*

Adjective clauses are relatively easy to identify (just a little grammar joke). Actually, adjective clauses really are easy to identify for two reasons: (1) they always follow the nouns they modify and thus can be identified by the **pronoun replacement test,** and (2) they usually begin with a relative pronoun (or pronominal adverb).

Here is the pronoun replacement test tailored for adjective clauses:

Pronoun replacement test. If a clause following a noun is also replaced by a third-person pronoun, then that clause is an adjective clause modifying the noun.

Here are some examples of the pronoun replacement test applied to relative clauses:

I read *the book* ***that you told me about.***
                    it

It replaces *book* and its modifying adjective clause *that you told me about.*

*The children **whose names were called*** should be on the bus.
                    They

They replaces *children* and its modifying adjective clause *whose names were called.*

Clause Exercise #1: Using the Pronoun Replacement Test to Identify Adjective Clauses _____

Underline the adjective clauses in sentences once and the nouns they modify twice. Confirm your answer by applying the pronoun substitution test. The first question is done as an example. (Answers to this exercise are on page 476.)

0. I lost the letter that the IRS sent me.

Answer: I lost the <u>letter that the IRS sent me</u>.

Confirmation: I lost <u>the letter that the IRS sent me</u>.
                                    it

1. The scientists discussed the issues that the conference had raised.

2. Senator Fogg, who was up for re-election, was for the bill.

3. The company rejected the parts whose design was defective.

4. I rented a movie that we had already seen.

5. We found the bird whose wing had been damaged.

6. It was in an old trunk that had belonged to my parents.

7. The children whom you asked about live next door.

8. The desserts that they serve are really good.

9. He passed the exam that he was studying for.

10. The neighborhood where I live is changing a lot.

Relative pronouns play their own roles INSIDE the adjective clause. We can see the differences in roles most clearly in the *who–whom–whose* family of relative pronouns.

who = the subject of the adjective clause

whom = the object of a verb or preposition in the adjective clause

whose = a possessive pronoun modifying the following noun

Returning to the example sentences above, we see the following roles that the relative pronouns play:

The weatherman *who is on Channel 7* is always wrong.
            who is the subject of *is*

She married a man *whom she met at school.*
            whom is the object of the verb *met*

They called the person *whose turn was next.*
            whose is a possessive pronoun modifying *turn*

The grammar of adjective clauses requires that the relative pronoun must appear at the beginning of the clause. When the relative pronoun is the subject of the sentence, there is no problem because the relative pronoun is already in the first position. However, when the relative pronoun is an object, the pronoun must be moved out of its normal object position and moved to the front of the dependent clause For example, in the sentence

She married a man ***whom*** *she met at school,*

we know that the relative pronoun *whom* is actually the object of *met:*

she met **(whom)** at school

We can confirm that *whom* is an object by replacing *whom* with its antecedent *man.*

She met **a man** at school.

(When we come to diagramming adjective clauses, we will always move object relative pronouns back to their normal object positions.)

The fact that adjective clauses that refer to people can begin with either the subject or object form of the relative pronouns causes confusion about whether we should use *who* or *whom.*

Teaching Tip

When helping students decide between *who* and *whom,* remind them that the *m* in who**m** is the same *m* that appears in the object form of the personal pronouns hi**m** and the**m.** In other words, the *m* is an object marker in pronouns.

In informal spoken English, we tend to avoid the choice between *who* and *whom.* Either we duck the issue entirely and use *that* to refer to people, for example,

*She married a man **that** she met at school.

or we use *who* for both subjects and objects, for example,

*She married a man ***who*** *she met at school.*

The key to choosing between *who* and *whom* is to determine the role of the relative pronoun in its clause. If the relative pronoun is the subject, use *who;* if it is the object, use *whom.* (See "Pronoun Error: *Who* and *Whom,*" in the Usage part for ways to help students choose between *who* and *whom.)*

The rules for adjective clauses allow several options.

- Object of a preposition. If the relative pronoun is the object of a preposition, then we have the option of either moving just the pronoun to the beginning of the dependent clause or moving both the preposition and its pronoun object to the beginning:

Pronoun alone: I know the woman *whom you were speaking* **to.**
Pronoun + preposition: I know the woman **to whom** *you were speaking.*

Either choice is grammatical, but there is a difference in formality. Moving the pronoun alone is less formal than moving both the preposition and the pronoun. That is, in formal writing, some people prefer to use

I know the woman **to whom** you were speaking

rather than

I know the woman **whom** you were speaking **to.**

- Deletion of object relative pronouns. If the relative pronoun is an object of a verb or the object of a preposition, it may be deleted from the sentence:

Object of verb: It was a decision ***that*** *we all regretted.*
Object deleted: It was a decision *we all regretted.*
Object of preposition: She was a person *whom we looked up to.*
Object deleted: She was a person *we looked up to.*

Obviously, when the flag word that signals the beginning of an adjective clause is deleted, it makes the adjective clause somewhat more difficult to spot. (When we diagram adjective clauses, we put the understood relative pronoun back into the sentence.)

Clause Exercise #2: Identifying Adjective Clauses with Deleted Relative Pronouns _____

Underline the adjective clauses in the following sentences. Confirm your answer by supplying the missing relative pronoun. The first question is done as an example. (Answers to this exercise are on page 477.)

0. I lost the letter the IRS sent me.

   Answer: I lost the letter *the IRS sent me.*

   Confirmation: I lost the letter <u>that the IRS sent me.</u>

1. The doctor is treating the pain I get in my knees.

2. We put the pictures the children draw on the bulletin board.

3. It is not the city I used to know.

4. The students he selected did very well.

5. They all appreciated the dinner we served them.

6. The books I put on reserve have all been checked out.

7. We saw the movie you told us about.

8. We got the response we expected.

9. It is a name you can count on.

10. The teacher I had in the 6th grade married my uncle.

Restrictive and Nonrestrictive Adjective Clauses.   Adjective clauses pose a special problem of punctuation. Some adjective clauses, called **nonrestrictive clauses,** are set off from the rest of the sentence with commas, while other adjective clauses, called **restrictive clauses,** are not set off with commas.

Restrictive clauses do just what their name suggests: they restrict or limit the meaning of the noun they modify to one specific thing or person. In other words, a restrictive clause defines WHICH particular thing/person a noun refers to. Here is an example:

Students *who miss the final* will fail the course.

Who will fail the course? All students, or just the ones who miss the final? Obviously it is the latter. The adjective clause *who miss the final* defines WHICH students the sentence is talking about. Thus *who miss the final* is a clause that restricts the meaning of the noun *students.* Here is another example of a restrictive clause:

I can't find the book *that I got from the library.*

The clause *that I got from the library* tells us WHICH book the speaker is talking about and is therefore restrictive.

Commas are never used with restrictive clauses. Think of the restrictive clause as being attached to the noun it modifies because the restrictive clause significantly changes the meaning of that noun.

What happens when the noun being modified is not a general reference noun such as *students* or *book,* but is already a specific thing or person? In this case, the adjective clause is said to be **nonrestrictive** because it does not limit or restrict the noun it modifies. Rather, the nonrestrictive modifier gives additional information about the noun. Here is an example of a nonrestrictive adjective clause:

The moon, *which was nearly full,* lit the room.

There is only one moon. Giving us the information that it was nearly full does not define WHICH moon of several moons the sentence is about. In this sense, nonrestrictive adjective clauses are like appositives—they give further information about an already identified topic. Nonrestrictive adjective clauses are always set off with commas, just as appositives are.

A common way to teach the difference between restrictive and nonrestrictive clauses is that restrictive clauses give essential information and nonrestrictive clauses give nonessential information. Although this explanation is true up to a point, it runs into problems with proper nouns. Proper nouns, as you recall, are the names of particular persons, places, and things. Here is an example of the problem:

Mr. Smith, *who lives next door,* complained about the dog again.

There are a million Smiths in the world. The adjective clause *who lives next door* gives us essential information: it tells us WHICH Smith the sentence is talking about. Doesn't that mean that *who lives next door* is a restrictive clause? Logically, yes, but it doesn't work that way. Proper nouns are simply a special case. BY DEFINITION a proper noun is already a specific, individual entity and thus cannot be further restricted by an adjective clause. Accordingly, proper nouns can only be modified by nonrestrictive adjective clauses.

Is the following sentence an exception to the generalization that proper nouns are modified only by nonrestrictive clauses?

The Mr. Smith *that I know* lives next door.

Not really. The use of the definite article *the* tells us that we are now using *Mr. Smith* as a COMMON noun, and common nouns can be modified by restrictive adjective clauses. We simply need to set aside proper nouns as a special case. They are always used with nonrestrictive adjectives (commas). End of story.

Teaching Tip

Even if students understand the difference between restrictive and nonrestrictive clauses, they tend to get the terms backwards. Somehow they (and the rest of us) tend to associate the *non* in the term *nonrestrictive* with the phrase "no commas." Students need to be reminded frequently what the term *restrictive* really means—a restrictive clause "restricts" (i.e., narrows or limits) the meaning of the noun it modifies. A nonrestrictive clause does NOT restrict the noun it modifies.

Any time we use an adjective clause to modify a common noun, we need to decide how that clause affects the meaning of the noun. If the modifier significantly changes the meaning of the noun, it is restrictive (no commas). If it does not change the noun, it is nonrestrictive and thus is set off with commas like an appositive.

The way that the adjective clause affects the noun it modifies is a real-world information question, not a grammatical one. For example, is the adjective clause in the following sentence restrictive or nonrestrictive?

Sally's cousin *who lives in Florida* is visiting her.

The answer, of course, depends entirely on how many cousins Sally has—information we cannot get from a grammar book. If she has only one cousin, the clause is nonrestrictive. If she only has one cousin, the fact that her cousin lives in Florida does not distinguish one cousin from another because there is only one cousin to begin with. On the other hand, if she has more than one cousin, the clause is restrictive because it tells us WHICH one of Sally's many cousins is visiting—the one from Florida.

| One cousin: | Sally's cousin, who lives in Florida, is visiting her. |
| Many cousins: | Sally's cousin who lives in Florida is visiting her. |

The question we always need to answer is, "Does the adjective clause significantly change the meaning of the common noun it modifies?" If the answer is "yes," then it is restrictive. If the answer is "no," then it is nonrestrictive and is set off with commas. The following test is one way to help decide whether a clause is restrictive or nonrestrictive.

> **Deletion test for restrictive/nonrestrictive clauses.** If an adjective clause modifying a common noun can be deleted without changing WHICH noun we are talking about, then it is nonrestrictive and requires commas. If deleting the clause changes the meaning of the noun, then the modifier is part of the meaning of the noun and cannot be separated from it by commas.

Here is an example of the deletion test:

I bumped into my boss *who was also doing some shopping.*

When we delete the clause, we are left with

I bumped into my boss.

On the reasonable assumption that there is only one person that I can call "my boss," deleting the adjective clause does not change the meaning of boss. My boss is my boss whether I bumped into him or not. Therefore the clause is nonrestrictive and requires commas:

I bumped into my boss, *who was also doing some shopping.*

Here is another adjective clause to test:

The people *who were at the party* are old classmates.

When we delete the clause, we are left with

The people are old classmates.

In this case, the meaning of the word *people* seems too vague. We don't know what people the sentence is talking about. The clause tells us WHICH people are old classmates—the ones who were at the party. The clause cannot be deleted without affecting the meaning of the noun it modifies. Therefore, the clause is restrictive and cannot be set off with commas:

The people *who were at the party* are old classmates.

Clause Exercise #3: Using the Deletion Test to Distinguish Restrictive and Nonrestrictive Clauses _____

Underline the adjective clauses in the following sentences. Use the deletion test to decide whether the clause is restrictive or nonrestrictive. Punctuate accordingly. The first question is done as an example. (Answers to this exercise are on page 477.)

0. I found a pen that you gave me.
    Answer: I found a pen <u>that you gave me</u>.
    Test applied: I found a pen.
    Restrictive because the meaning changes: we do not know which pen was found.
    Punctuation: (no commas) I found a pen that you gave me.

1. Napoleon who was actually from Corsica became a French patriot.

2. They identified the person who won the lottery.

3. The first Sherlock Holmes story which was set in America made the author famous.

4. People who live in glass houses shouldn't throw stones.

5. The first question which was a math problem was the hardest.

6. Anybody who likes jazz will love this CD.

7. I found a place where we could talk quietly.

8. The milk that is in the refrigerator is getting too old.

9. My new computer which I bought through the university is a Mac.

10. The woman who sat in front of me forgot her umbrella.

The distinction between restrictive and nonrestrictive clauses has some bearing on the choice of *that* and *which*. Most people strongly prefer to use *which* rather than *that* in nonrestrictive clauses. For example, we would write

We went to Fred's apartment, **which** *is over on Elm Street.*

rather than

*We went to Fred's apartment, **that** *is over on Elm Street.*

In restrictive clauses, *that* and *which* seem to most people to be interchangeable:

The car **that** *is parked in our driveway* belongs to my roommate.

The car **which** *is parked in our driveway* belongs to my roommate.

However, some people do prefer *that* in restrictive clauses. For example, the writers of some technical writing manuals, who apparently like the world to be a more orderly place than it may actually be, insist on a clear-cut distinction between *that* and *which*: *that* in restrictive clauses, *which* in nonrestrictive ones. (Research studies show that most established writers use both *that* and *which* in restrictive clauses. See, for example, Quirk's *A Comprehensive Grammar of the English Language,* section 6.33.)

Diagramming Adjective Clauses.   Here are the main conventions for diagramming adjective clauses:

- Adjective clauses are put on their own sentence line underneath and parallel to the main sentence line.
- Relative pronouns and pronominal adverbs are placed within the diagram according to their grammatical function. For example, relative pronouns that function as objects are moved from their position at the beginning of the adjective clause back to their normal position following the verb. Relative pronouns that function as objects of prepositions are put back inside their prepositional phrase.

- If a relative pronoun has been deleted from the adjective clause, an appropriate "understood" relative pronoun (in parentheses) is added to the adjective clause in the proper place.
- Relative pronouns are then connected by dotted lines to the nouns on the main sentence line that they modify.
- There are no differences between the ways restrictive and nonrestrictive clauses are diagrammed.

Here are examples of adjective clauses (underlined) with relative pronouns (in bold) playing different roles.

Subject: I met a man **who** knows four languages.

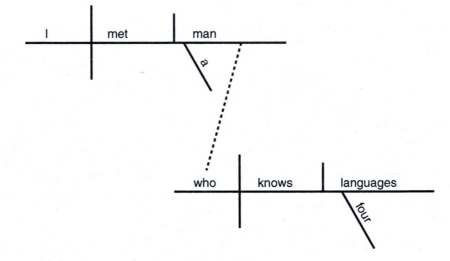

Object: I met a man **whom** you would like.

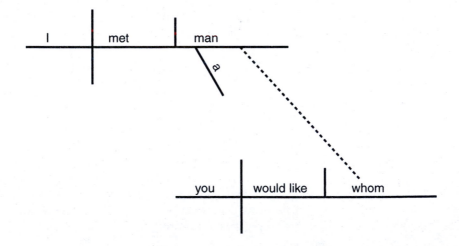

Possessive noun: I met a man **whose** wife knows four languages.

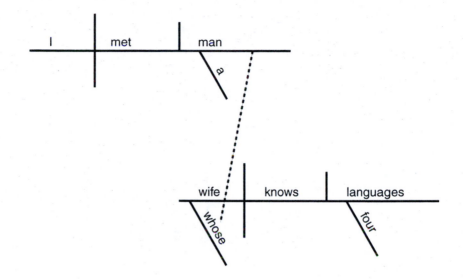

Object of preposition: I met a man about **whom** I had read.
I met a man **whom I had read about**.
(Note: The same diagram is used for both sentences.)

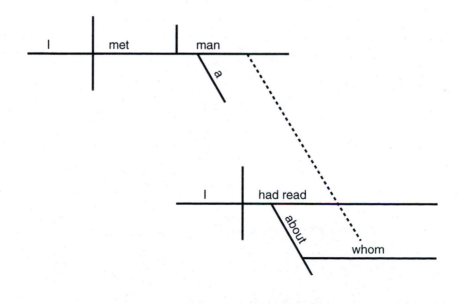

Understood relative: The teacher asked a question <u>I couldn't answer</u>.

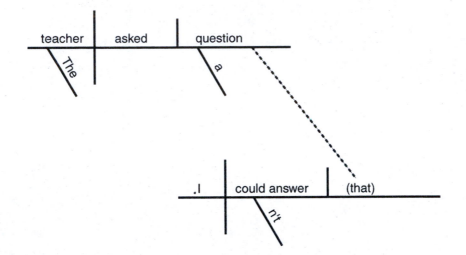

Pronominal adverb: I know a place **where** you can get good coffee.

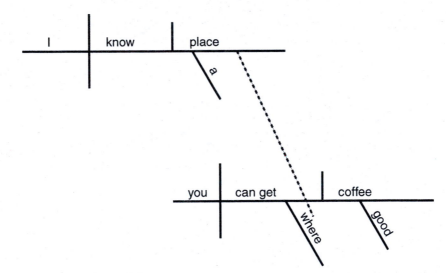

Clause Exercise #4: Diagramming Adjective Clauses _____

Diagram the following sentences. The first question is done as an example. (Answers to this exercise are on page 479.)

0. The passages we omitted were not very important.

Answer:

The passages we omitted were not very important.

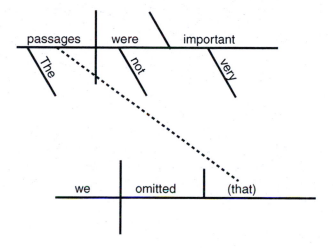

Note: *Not* could also modify *very*:

1. The person who entered the tomb would die.

2. The cat that we found in the woods had kittens yesterday.

3. I like restaurants where the service is not rushed.

4. Adrian, whose parents were from Milan, speaks Italian.

5. An article we featured in our last issue has won an award.

6. Watson found the revolver that Holmes had been looking for.

7. The barges that we had discussed earlier are now available.

8. They rejected the suggestions we had offered.

9. The union whose offer we accepted contacted their members.

10. I finally found a doctor I like.

11. My parents thanked the students whose rooms they had used.

12. We really missed the things we had left behind.

13. The Council, which meets on Tuesdays, will review your request.

14. The campers checked the supplies that they had ordered.

15. The coach took the names of the players who had missed practice.

16. Everyone whose paper is finished may leave now.

17. They listed the topics about which we might write.

18. The employers we approached liked our ideas.

19. That was the place where we had planned to meet.

20. Give the man I told you about the package.

Adverb Clauses

Adverb clauses modify verbs, adjectives, or other adverbs. Adverb clauses begin with a **subordinating conjunction.** Here are some examples of adverb clauses (in italics) that modify adjectives, adverbs, and verbs, with the subordinating conjunctions in bold.

- Modifying adjectives:

  I am sorry *that* *you are not able to come.*

  She was worried *that* *we would not finish in time.*

  The movie was better *than* *I had expected it to be.*

- Modifying other adverbs:

  I answered more sharply *than* *I had intended to do.*

  The team played more aggressively *than* *they had at practice.*

  The professor talks faster *than* *I can take notes.*

- Modifying verbs:

  I ordered a whole pizza *because* *I had missed lunch.*

  We went into the lab *after* *the classroom presentation.*

  Give me a call *if* *I can help you.*

As you can see from the examples, adverb clauses consist of a subordinating conjunction followed by a complete underlying sentence. (Here the term "underlying sentence" means a sentence that can never stand alone because it is encased inside a dependent clause.) For example, in the sentence

Give me a call *if* *I can help you.*

the subordinating conjunction *if* plays no role in the underlying sentence *I can help you.* All adverb clauses have this same two-part structure:

Adverb clause

Subordinating conjunction + Underlying sentence

Adverb clauses are built quite differently from adjective clauses. In adjective clauses the flag word that begins the clause, the relative pronoun, is an essential part of the underlying sentence: it is a subject, object, or possessive pronoun inside that underlying sentence. For example, in the sentence

He is a person ***whom*** *we can count on.*

the relative pronoun *whom* is actually the object of the preposition *on.* In contrast, subordinating conjunctions are introductory words that stand outside the complete sentence that follows them. In that sense, subordinating conjunctions are more like "bridge words."

We will now examine each of the three different uses of adverb clauses: (1) to modify verbs, (2) to modify adjectives, and (3) to modify other adverbs.

Adverb Clauses That Modify Verbs. Adverb clauses that modify verbs are by far the most common type of adverb clause. A relatively large number of subordinating conjunctions are used with this type of adverb clause. Since adverb clauses that modify verbs behave like single-word adverbs, their subordinating conjunctions can be classified by adverb function. Here is a list of the more common ones classified by adverb function:

Time:	after, as, as soon as, before, even after, even before, just after, just before, since (meaning "when"), until, when, whenever, while
Place:	every place, everywhere, where, wherever
Manner:	as, as if, as though
Cause:	as, because, inasmuch as, since, so that
Condition:	if, on condition that, provided that, unless
Concession:	although, even though, though

Following are some examples of adverb clauses illustrating the different categories of subordinating conjunctions:

Time:	I had finished my popcorn ***before*** *the movie started.* The theater gets quiet ***when*** *the movie starts.*
Place:	We found broken glass ***where*** *the accident had happened.* They had a good time ***everywhere*** *they went.*

Manner:	Marian looked *as though* she would die laughing. They went ahead *as if* we were not there.
Cause:	I decided not to go *since* I was not feeling well. They got up early *so that* they could get a good start.
Condition:	I would not do that *if* I were you. We had a great time *even though* it rained a lot.
Concession:	We ordered pizza, *even though* I wasn't very hungry. The kids went for a walk *although* it was getting late.

Notice that with one exception, the adverb clauses are not set off with commas. Adverb clauses are just like single-word adverbs. When adverb clauses are in the normal adverb position at the end of the independent clause, they are not set off with commas. The one exception to this rule is when the adverb clause has the meaning of **concession,** that is, when the adverb clause begins with *although, even though,* or *though.* A comma is used with adverb clauses of concession to indicate that they are "contrary to expectations."

Most adverb clauses that modify verbs behave very much like single-word adverbs that modify verbs in two important respects: they both answer adverb questions and they both move.

> **Adverb clause question test.** If a dependent clause can answer an adverb question (*when, where, how, why*), then that clause is an adverb clause modifying the verb.

Several categories of adverbs (time, place, manner, cause) that modify verbs answer adverb questions. The answer to the adverb question will be the adverb clause. Here are some examples:

Time:	I'll give you a call *after I am finished.*
Adverb Q:	**When** will I give you a call?
Answer:	*After I am finished.*
Place:	Fred parks *wherever he can find an open space.*
Adverb Q:	**Where** does Fred park?
Answer:	*Wherever he can find an open space.*
Manner:	John always acts *as if he has a chip on his shoulder.*
Adverb Q:	**How** does John always act?
Answer:	*As if he has a chip on his shoulder.*
Cause:	Sue needs the key *because she has to lock up.*
Adverb Q:	**Why** does Sue need the key?
Answer:	*Because she has to lock up.*

Clause Exercise #5: Identifying Adverb Clauses That Modify Verbs by the Adverb Clause Question Test _____

Underline the adverb clauses that modify verbs. Confirm your answer by asking the appropriate adverb question. The first question is done as an example. (Answers to this exercise are on page 485.)

0. Ralph answered the phone since he was nearest to it.

    Answer: Ralph answered the phone <u>since he was nearest to it</u>.

    Confirmation: **Why** did Ralph answer the phone?
    <u>Since he was nearest to it</u>.

1. We completed the test after we had lunch.

2. The bank will finance the development after they approve the site.

3. We lost the game because our quarterback got injured.

4. He described the book as though he had written it.

5. They complained just because we got a little lost.

6. I'll get the paper before you start breakfast.

7. The restaurant held the reservation since they weren't very busy.

8. The roof leaks every time it rains.

9. They dropped the issue as if it had been a hot potato.

10. I'll tell you since you asked.

The second way that adverb clauses resemble single-word adverbs that modify verbs is that they both can be moved to the front of the sentence.

> **Adverb clause movement test.** If a dependent clause can be moved to the front of the sentence, then it is an adverb clause that modifies the verb.

Here is the adverb clause movement test applied to the same example sentences:

Time:	*Before the movie started*, I had finished my popcorn. *When the movie starts*, the theater gets quiet.
Place:	*Where the accident had happened*, we found broken glass. *Everywhere they went*, they had a good time.
Cause:	*Since I was not feeling well*, I decided not to go. *So that they could get a good start*, they got up early.

Condition: ***If** I were you,* I would not do that.
                 ***Even though** it rained a lot,* we had a great time.

Concession: ***Even though** I wasn't very hungry,* we ordered pizza.
                 ***Although** it was getting late,* the kids went for a walk.

Notice that whenever an adverb clause is moved to the beginning of the sentence (i.e., in front of the independent clause), the adverb clause MUST be set off with a comma. The comma tells the reader where the introductory adverb clause ends and the independent clause begins. (For details on commas with introductory elements, see "Commas and Introductory Elements" in the Usage part.)

Teaching Tip

Students are usually quite interested to learn that leaving off the comma from introductory adverb clauses is the single most common error in the writing of college students.

Notice also that there was one group of adverb clauses that was omitted from the above list: **adverb clauses of manner.** This type of clause can never be moved:

Manner: **As though** *she would die laughing,* Marian looked.
              As if *we were not there,* they went ahead.

Teaching Tip

The fact that the two main tests for adverb clauses that modify verbs do not work equally well for all categories of adverb clauses means that students need to be encouraged always to use both tests. When one test fails, the other will work.

Clause Exercise #6: Identifying Adverb Clauses That Modify Verbs by the Adverb Clause Movement Test _____

Underline the adverb clauses that modify verbs. Confirm your answer by moving the adverb clause to the front of the sentence. (Be sure to put in a comma after a relocated adverb clause.) The first question is done as an example. (Answers to this exercise are on page 486.)

0. The phone rang as I was getting into the shower.

Answer: The phone rang <u>as I was getting into the shower.</u>

Confirmation: <u>As I was getting into the shower,</u> the phone rang.

1. We will cut off your phone unless you pay your bill.

2. I am still gaining weight, although I eat only carrot sticks.

3. I bought my roommate a new ribbon because I use her printer.

4. I couldn't finish my paper until I got all the references.

5. His dog followed him wherever he went.

6. I looked at the menu before you came.

7. She liked the movie after all, though she won't admit it.

8. Fill these orders as they come in.

9. I have spent a lot of time on the net since I got my new computer.

10. Watson tried to act normally, although he was wearing a wig.

Adverb Clauses That Modify Adjectives.   Adverbs can only modify predicate adjectives, not modifying adjectives. There are two slightly different patterns of adverb clauses, depending on the nature of the predicate adjective: (1) adverb clauses that modify predicate adjectives in their base form, and (2) adverb clauses that modify predicate adjectives in their comparative form.

Adverb Clauses That Modify Base-Form Predicate Adjectives.   The only subordinating conjunction used in this pattern is *that.* A unique feature of this pattern is that the subordinating conjunction *that* may be omitted—it is the one instance in which an adverb clause of any type can occur WITHOUT an overt subordinating conjunction. Here are some examples of this pattern:

Base-form predicate adjective + (*that*) + underlying sentence

We were *glad* (that) you could come.

John is *afraid* (that) it will rain.

I am *sure* (that) I am right.

I was *convinced* (that) we would win.

I am *disappointed* (that) we couldn't meet.

Adverb Clauses That Modify Comparative Predicate Adjectives.   The only subordinating conjunction used in this pattern is *than.* Remember that comparative adjectives can take two forms: *-er* in one-syllable adjectives and many two-syllable adjectives, and *more* with most multiple-syllable adjectives. Here are some examples of this pattern:

Comparative predicate adjective + *than* + underlying sentence

It is *later* than you think it is.

The party was *more formal* than I had expected.

Sally is *stronger* than she was before.

The sequel was *more frightening* than the original was.

Adverb Clauses That Modify Adverbs.   There is only one pattern for adverb clauses that modify other adverbs. In this pattern, which is quite similar to the pattern immediately above, adverb clauses modify comparative adverbs. (Comparative adverbs, like comparative adjectives, are formed with either -*er* or *more.*) Also as in the previous pattern, the only subordinating conjunction that can be used is *than.* Here are some examples of this pattern:

Comparative adverb + *than* + underlying sentence

I answered *more sharply* than I had intended.

She will finish *quicker* than you can.

Their ships went *faster* than any had gone before.

The fire spread *more rapidly* than we had expected

Adverb clauses that modify adverbs and predicate adjectives are not difficult to recognize because they occur in such rigid patterns: adverb clauses can only modify base-form predicate adjectives and comparative adjectives and adverbs. Also, the subordinating conjunctions are severely limited: *that* with base-form predicate adjectives and *than* with comparative adjectives and adverbs. The only tricky part is identifying adverb clauses that modify base-form predicate adjectives when the flag word *that* has been omitted.

Clause Exercise #7: Identifying Adverb Clauses That Modify Adjectives and Adverbs _____

Underline the adverb clauses in the following sentences once and the words they modify twice. Identify whether the word being modified is an adjective (Adj) or an adverb (Adv). If *that* has been deleted from an adverb clause modifying a base-form predicate adjective, restore it in parentheses. The first question is done as an example. (Answers to this exercise are on page 486.)

   0. I am sad they will miss the party.

Answer: I am <u>sad (that) they will miss the party</u>.
          Adj

1. Aluminum bats can hit a ball farther than wood bats can.

2. Airplane accidents are rarer than the public believes.

3. The coach was surprised the goal counted.

4. The machine scans much more accurately than the old one did.

5. Yellow objects are more visible than red objects are.

6. My dog is bigger than your dog is.

7. Buses during the day are more frequent than buses are at night.

8. We are confident you can do it.

9. Twins often talk sooner than single children do.

10. The first dress was more attractive than the second one was.

Subordinating Conjunctions and Conjunctive Adverbs.   Subordinating conjunctions are easily confused with **conjunctive adverbs.** Conjunctive adverbs show how the ideas in one independent clause relate to the ideas in another independent clause. The confusion is not merely academic, since the two types of linking words trigger completely different punctuation. Here is an example:

Sub Conj: John was in an accident *after* he took driver's education.
Conj Adv: John was in an accident; *however*, he was not hurt.

After is a subordinating conjunction that introduces an adverb dependent clause. The adverb clause is not separated from the independent clause by any punctuation.

However is a conjunctive adverb. A clause introduced by a conjunctive adverb is still an independent clause. The second independent clause must still be separated from the first independent clause by either a period or a semicolon. Here is a list of the more common conjunctive adverbs roughly grouped by meaning:

in addition	*as a result*	*on the other hand*
again	accordingly	however
also	consequently	nevertheless
besides	hence	nonetheless
further	then	otherwise
furthermore	therefore	still
likewise	thus	
moreover		
similarly		

*Teaching
Tip*

One of the biggest problems is not distinguishing subordinating conjunctions from conjunctive adverbs, it is trying to remember which term is which. The trick is to remind students of the second part of the terms. Subordinating conjunctions are CONJUNCTIONS, and conjunctions join clauses together. Conjunctive adverbs are ADVERBS, and adverbs have no power to join clauses together.

Short of tediously memorizing long lists of words, how can we tell subordinating conjunctions from conjunctive adverbs? Fortunately, there are two tests that quite reliably distinguish the two types of words.

The first test we have already encountered: the adverb clause movement test.

> **Adverb clause movement test.** If a dependent clause can be
> moved to the front of the sentence, then it is an adverb clause
> that modifies the verb.

Adverb clauses move, but independent clauses introduced by conjunctive adverbs do not. Here is the adverb clause movement test applied to our example sentences:

Sub Conj: John was in an accident **after** he took driver's education.
Test: *After he took drivers education,* John was in an accident.

When we attempt to apply the same test to an independent clause beginning with a conjunctive adverb, the result is completely ungrammatical:

Conj Adv: John was in an accident; **however,** he was not hurt.
Test: **However, he was not hurt,* John was in an accident.

The first test, the adverb movement test, gives us a positive test for subordinating conjunctions. The second way of telling subordinating conjunctions and conjunctive adverbs apart is a positive test for conjunctive adverbs. This test exploits the fact that conjunctive adverbs behave like normal adverbs—they can be moved around INSIDE THEIR OWN CLAUSES.

> **Conjunctive adverb movement test.** Conjunctive adverbs (but
> not subordinating conjunctions) can be moved around INSIDE
> their clause. If it can be moved inside its own clause, then it is
> a conjunctive adverb.

On the other hand, subordinating conjunctions, like all flag words that introduce dependent clauses, have a fixed position at the beginning of the independent clause. The whole adverb clause can move, but not the subordinating conjunction by itself.

Here is an example of the conjunctive adverb movement test applied to a conjunctive adverb:

> I stayed up for the late show; **however,** it was worth it.
>
> Test: I stayed up for the late show; it was, **however,** worth it.
>
> I stayed up for the late show; it was worth it, **however.**

(Note the punctuation of the conjunctive adverb. It is ALWAYS set off from the rest of its clause by a comma.)

When we attempt to apply the same conjunctive adverb movement test to a subordinating conjunction, the result is completely ungrammatical:

> I stayed up for the late show **because** a favorite film was on.
>
> Test: *I stayed up for the late show; a favorite film was, **because,** on.
>
> *I stayed up for the late show; a favorite film was on, **because.**

Clause Exercise #8: Distinguishing Subordinating Conjunctions from Conjunctive Adverbs _____

Underline the subordinating conjunctions and conjunctive adverbs. Label them Sub Conj and Conj Adv, respectively, and supply the correct punctuation. Confirm your answer by applying the positive test: the adverb clause movement test in the case of subordinating conjunctions and the conjunctive adverb movement test in the case of conjunctive adverbs. The first question is done as an example. (Answers to this exercise are on page 487.)

0. Ralph missed the bus nevertheless he got to work on time.

    Answer: Ralph missed the bus; <u>nevertheless,</u> he got to work on time.
    Conj Adv

    Confirmation: Ralph missed the bus; he got to work on time, <u>nevertheless</u>.

    (Note the corrected punctuation: a semicolon between the two independent clauses and the conjunctive adverb set off with a comma.)

1. I was upset however there was nothing I could do about it.

2. I was upset because I had damaged the VCR.

3. We are ready to leave unless there is anything else to do.

4. We are ready to leave otherwise we will miss the bus.

5. Aunt Sally has been depressed because she lost at Monopoly.

6. Aunt Sally has been depressed moreover she lost at Monopoly.

7. The accident ruined the experiment thus we had to start all over.

8. The accident ruined the experiment while it was still in process.

9. The doctor testified inasmuch as she had taken the X-rays.

10. The doctor testified after she had taken the X-rays.

Summary of Adverb Clauses.   Like single-word adverbs, adverb clauses modify verbs, adjectives, and other adverbs. By far the most common use of adverb clauses is to modify verbs. Adverb clauses that modify verbs are easily identified because adverb clauses behave like single-word adverbs: they both answer adverb questions and move:

> **Adverb clause question test**
> > Aunt Sally gets upset *whenever she loses at Monopoly.*
> Test: **When** does Aunt Sally get upset? *Whenever she loses at Monopoly.*

> **Adverb clause movement test**
> > Aunt Sally gets upset *whenever she loses at Monopoly.*
> Test: *Whenever she loses at Monopoly,* Aunt Sally gets upset.

(Note that when an adverb clause is moved to the front of the sentence, it MUST be set off from the independent clause by a comma.)

Adverb clauses begin with **subordinating conjunctions,** a flag word that is not part of the underlying sentence that makes up the rest of the dependent clause. Subordinating conjunctions are easily confused with **conjunctive adverbs.** Clauses that begin with conjunctive adverbs are independent clauses that must be set off from the preceding independent clause by either a period or a semicolon.

There are two tests for telling them apart. **The adverb clause movement test** applies only to clauses that begin with subordinating conjunctions. Clauses that begin with conjunctive adverbs are not movable and thus fail the adverb clause movement test.

The other test is the **conjunctive adverb movement test.** Conjunctive adverbs are adverbs and therefore can be moved around inside their clause—something that subordinating conjunctions can never do.

> **Conjunctive adverb movement test**
> > Aunt Sally hates to lose; **however,** she doesn't pout afterwards.
> Test: Aunt Sally hates to lose; she doesn't pout afterwards, **however.**

The other two uses of adverb clauses, to modify adjectives and adverbs, are restricted to the following fixed patterns:

> **Base-form predicate adjective + (*that*) + underlying sentence**
> Example: We were **glad** (*that*) *you could come.*

Comparative predicate adjective + *than* **+ underlying sentence**

Example: It is **later** *than you think it is.*

Comparative adverb + *than* **+ underlying sentence**

Example: I answered **more sharply** *than I had intended.*

Clause Exercise #9: Identifying Adverb Clauses _____

Underline adverb clauses once. Underline twice the words that the clauses modify, and then identify their part of speech. The first question is done as an example. (Answers to this exercise are on page 488.)

0. The test was harder than I thought it would be.
    Answer: The test was <u>harder</u> <u>than I thought it would be</u>.
    Adjective

1. I returned the book as soon as I was done with it.

2. The movie lasted much longer than we had expected.

3. I get a headache whenever I am under a lot of stress.

4. I am afraid that we must leave now.

5. Since we would be late, we called them.

6. The kids began to party after their parents left for the weekend.

7. We finished poorer than we had started.

8. John took a taxi to the airport so he wouldn't miss his flight.

9. After the party was over, we began cleaning the apartment.

10. The movie was funnier than the book was.

11. If you had led spades, we could have set them.

12. I want to finish my paper before it is due.

13. We were afraid that we would stick in the wet snow.

14. I have learned a lot since I began going to classes regularly.

15. Although they won the battle, they have not won the war.

16. I answered more calmly than I thought I could.

17. The church is much older than it appears on the outside.

18. If you look to your right, you will see the river.

19. Aunt Sally was glad that you wanted to play Monopoly with her.

20. The test was hard; however, I had reviewed all the material.

Diagramming Adverb Clauses.   As with adjective clauses, adverb clauses are diagrammed as complete sentences on a sentence line drawn underneath and parallel to the main sentence line. Adverb clauses are connected by dotted lines to whatever words they modify on the main sentence line: predicate adjectives, the main verbs, or other adverbs.

As you might expect, adverb clauses that have been moved in front of the main clause are diagrammed the same way as adverb clauses that have not been moved. An understood *that* in adverb clauses that modify predicate adjectives is put back on the dotted line in parentheses.

What is different about diagramming adverb clauses is the placement of the subordinating conjunction. Subordinating conjunctions are placed on the dotted line because subordinating conjunctions are "bridge words" that are not really part of the sentence underlying the adverb clause. Subordinating conjunctions belong outside the adverb clause.

In this respect the diagrams of adverb clauses are quite different from the diagrams of adjective clauses. Adjective clauses begin with relative pronouns, but unlike subordinating conjunctions, relative pronouns belong inside the adjective clauses—relative pronouns are subjects or objects within the adjective clauses. Relative pronouns belong inside the adjective clause.

Teaching
Tip

Students who had diagrammed adjective clauses without any problems will start diagramming them with the relative pronouns placed incorrectly on the dotted lines after they have learned how to diagram adverb clauses. Students need to be reminded of the difference in function between relative pronouns in adjective clauses and subordinating conjunctions in adverb clauses.

Here are some examples of diagrams for the various types of adverb clauses.

Adverb clause modifying verb: **Unless** you stop that, I will leave.

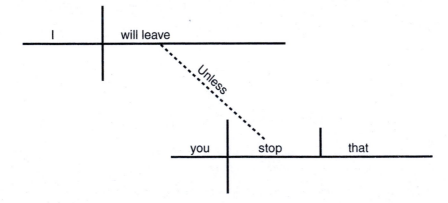

Adverb clause modifying predicate adjective (with understood *that*):
I am glad you can come.

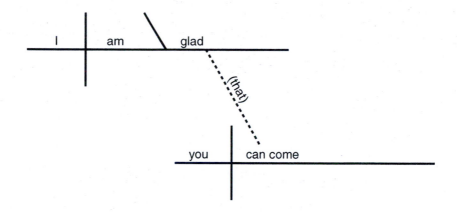

Adverb clause modifying adverb: Their ships went farther **than** any had before.

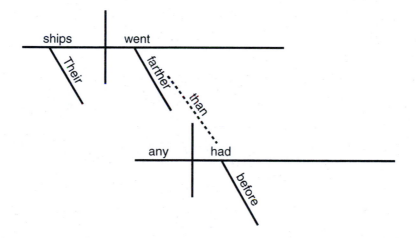

Clause Exercise #10: Diagramming Adverb Clauses _____

Diagram the following sentences. The first question is done as an example. (Answers to this exercise are on page 489.)

   0. I spoke more harshly than I had intended.

Answer:
I spoke more harshly than I had intended.

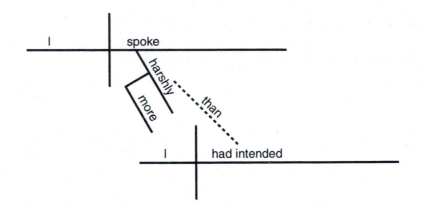

[Note the convention for diagramming comparative adjectives and adverbs that use *more*.]

1. I am sorry that we must leave now.
2. Since we would be late, we called them.
3. When their parents left, the kids ordered pizza.
4. We finished worse than we had started.
5. So that he would not miss his flight, John took a taxi to the airport.
6. We began the job as soon as we got the order.
7. The movie was funnier than we had expected.
8. If you had led spades, we could have set them.
9. Since the undercoat was not dry, the finish was always sticky.
10. I finished my paper before it was due.
11. I was glad that it was finished.
12. He was more upset than he should have been.
13. Although we won the battle, we have not won the war.
14. He is very snide whenever he discusses other people's work.
15. The church is older than it looks.

Noun Clauses

According to the traditional definition, a **noun clause** is a dependent clause used as a noun. Here are some examples of noun clauses (in italics) used in the various noun functions:

Subject:	*What he knows about art* is a mystery.
Object of verb:	They know *who we are.*
Object of preposition:	I sell them for *whatever I can get for them.*
Predicate nominative:	The decision was *that we go ahead as planned.*

Noun clauses are always singular, even when the nouns within the clause are plural. For example, in the following sentence, notice that while both the subject and the object within the noun clause are plural, the noun clause as a whole is the subject of the singular verb *pleases:*

*That **they** usually win all their **games*** pleases the coach.

Since noun clauses always function as nouns and are always singular, noun clauses (like gerund phrases and infinitive phrases used as nouns) can be readily identified by the *it* test, here tailored for noun clauses:

The *it* test for noun clauses. If a dependent clause can be replaced by *it*, then that clause is a noun clause.

Subject:	*What he knows about art* is a mystery.
	It
Object of verb:	They know *who we are.*
	it
Object of preposition:	I sell them for *whatever I can get for them.*
	it
Predicate nominative:	The decision was *that we go ahead as planned.*
	it

Noun clauses are constructed in two different ways, depending on the nature of the flag word that begins the noun clause. The first kind begins with *that, if,* or *whether (or not).* Since *that* is by far the most common word in this group, this kind is called the ***that*-type noun clause.**

In the second kind of noun clause, most flag words begin with the letters *wh-* (for example, *who, what, where, whatever*). For this reason the second kind of noun clause is called the ***wh-* type noun clause.**

As we will see, the difference between the two types is more than just the choice of the introductory flag word. The two types of noun clauses are built quite differently.

The that-Type Noun Clause. The *that*-type noun clause is built like an adverb clause in the sense that both consist of a flag word followed by a complete underlying sentence in which the flag word plays no role. (The term "underlying sentence" means an independent clause that can never stand alone because it is encased inside a dependent clause.) All *that*-type noun clauses have the following structure:

> *that*-type noun clause
> _____
> flag word + underlying sentence

Here is an example:

> I know **that** *I am in trouble.*

In the noun clause **that** *I am in trouble,* the flag word *that* plays no role in the following underlying sentence, *I am in trouble.* Here are some examples of this type of noun clause:

Flag word	*Underlying sentence*
that	I had a good time
if	Leon calls
whether	it might rain
whether or not	you are ready

Here are further examples of *that*-type noun clauses in the three noun roles that they can play:

Subject:	**Whether or not** *you are right* remains to be seen.
Object of verb:	I don't know **if** *I can come.*
Predicate nominative:	Our expectation is **that** *you will win.*

A *that*-type noun clause cannot be used as the object of a preposition:

> *They debated about **that** *they should go.*

All *that*-type noun clauses beginning with *that* (but not *if, whether,* or *whether or not*) have one peculiarity: If the noun clause is the object of the verb, then the *that* may be deleted—for example,

> I know **that** *you are right.*

> I know *you are right.*

Obviously, when the flag word *that* has been deleted, noun clauses are somewhat more difficult to recognize. However, the *it* test still applies equally well:

> I know *you are right.*
>   it

(As you have probably already guessed, when we diagram *that*-type noun clauses, we will restore the missing *that* in parentheses.)

Clause Exercise #11: Identifying that-*Type* Noun Clauses by the It Test _____

Underline the *that*-type noun clauses. Confirm your answer by applying the *it* test. If *that* has been deleted, restore it. The first question is done as an example. (Answers to this exercise are on page 493.)

0. Lady Smyth-Bumpford suspected something was afoot.

Answer: Lady Smyth-Bumpford suspected **that** **something was afoot**.

Confirmation: Lady Smyth-Bumpford suspected **it.**

1. I don't think they believe you.

2. That the plan was already approved squelched the opposition.

3. The idea was that we would get up early.

4. They argued about whether Dorothy should take her slippers.

5. That he was no friend of mine was apparent to everyone.

6. They should tell us if they are coming.

7. The question is whether or not they can be trusted.

8. That he could diagram those sentences strained credulity.

9. I don't know whether I can go.

10. That you are here shows that you are interested.

A *that*-type noun clause beginning with *if* can be mistaken for the much more common adverb clause beginning with *if*. Compare the following sentences:

Noun clause:	I don't know *if I can come.*
Adverb clause:	I will meet you there *if I can come.*

Actually, the two types of clauses are easy to tell apart by using the appropriate tests. The *it* test works for the noun clause but fails with the adverb clause:

Noun clause: I don't know *if I can come.*
                              it

Adverb clause: I will meet you there *if I can come.*
                                    *it

Conversely, the adverb clause movement test works for the adverb clause but not for the noun clause:

Noun clause:	**If I can come,* I don't know.
Adverb clause:	*If I can come,* I will meet you there.

Another problem is telling *that* beginning adjective clauses from *that* beginning noun clauses. For example, compare the following:

Noun clause:	I know **that** *we can all accept the plan.*
Adjective clause:	I know a plan **that** *we can all accept.*

If we apply the *it* test directly to the two clauses, we can see that *it* will replace the noun clause, but not the adjective clause:

Noun clause:	I know **that** *we can all accept the plan.*
	it
Adjective clause:	I know a plan **that** *we can all accept.*
	*it

Teaching Tip

Pop quiz: What is wrong with the following use of the *it* test?

> I know *a plan that we can all accept.*
>   it

Doesn't this use of the *it* test prove that *that we can all accept* is a noun clause, not an adjective clause as we said above?

While the *it* test works well, there is an even simpler way to tell the two different uses of *that* apart.

The *which* test for distinguishing *that* in noun clauses and adjective clauses. If you can replace *that* at the beginning of a dependent clause with *which*, then *that* is a relative pronoun beginning an adjective clause. However, if you cannot replace *that* with *which*, then *that* begins a *that*-type noun clause.

Here is an example of the *which* test:

Noun clause:	I know **that** *we can all accept the plan.*
Which test:	*I know **which** *we can all accept the plan.*
Adjective clause:	I know a plan **that** *we can all accept.*
Which test:	I know a plan **which** *we can all accept.*

Teaching
Tip

Students get the various uses of *that* very confused. The *which* test is so easy to use that it will get them out of a lot of trouble.

Clause Exercise #12: Distinguishing Adjective and Noun Clauses by the Which Test

Underline and label the adjective and noun clauses beginning with *that*. Confirm your answer by applying the *which* test. The first question is done as an example. (Answers to this exercise are on page 493.)

0. The paper that I get only comes out once a week.

   Answer: The paper **that I get** only comes out once a week.
   Adjective clause

   Confirmation: The paper **which I get** only comes out once a week.

1. I bet that you can't diagram this sentence.

2. Did you fill out the questionnaire that I gave you?

3. Bugsy denied that he had fired the fatal shot.

4. I will personally guarantee that there will be no problem.

5. Bugsy made him an offer that he couldn't refuse.

6. I hated that I had become addicted to tic-tac-toe.

7. I understood the hatred that they felt.

8. Romeo murmured that he hated to leave.

9. I regret that I have only one life to give to my country.

10. The regret that I feel can only be imagined.

Diagramming that-*Type Noun Clauses.*   The *that*-type noun clause shares one major feature with the *wh-* type noun clause: both are set on stands on the main sentence line and on horizontal lines when they are used as the objects of prepositions, in much the same manner as gerunds and infinitive phrases used as nouns.

However, since the two types of noun clauses have quite different internal structures, we will need to diagram them differently. The internal structure of *that*-type noun clauses is like the internal structure of adverb clauses in one key respect: both begin with an introductory "bridge word." In the case of *that*-type clauses, the introductory bridge words are *that, if, whether,* and *whether or not* (treated as a single unit). The bridge words are placed above the horizontal line on which the noun clause is drawn. The understood *that* is restored in parentheses.

Here are examples of *that*-type noun clauses in the three different noun roles they can play.

Subject: **Whether or not** they can come makes no difference.

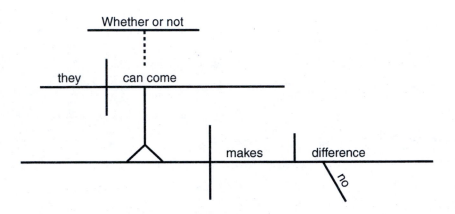

Object: I know you are right.   (Note: understood *that*)

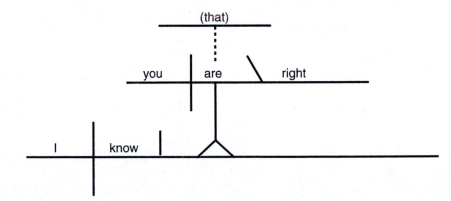

Predicate nominative: It seemed **that** they would succeed.

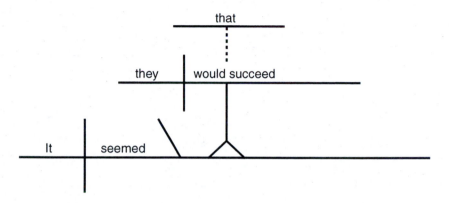

Clause Exercise #13: Diagramming **that**-*Type Noun Clauses* ___

Diagram the following sentences. The first question is done as an example. (Answers to this exercise are on page 494.)

0. I wondered if you were free on Friday.

Answer:

I wondered if you were free on Friday.

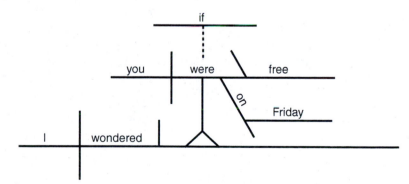

1. Whether we would succeed was a big question.

2. I believed that I was ready.

3. We didn't know if it would rain.

4. That the new program worked better was not a surprise.

5. I knew we were in big trouble.

6. Whether or not you fail is your decision.

7. That the sun shines every day is true.

8. I couldn't decide if I should go.

9. I wish we could quit now.

10. We thought it was time to quit.

The **wh-***Type Noun Clause.*   The *wh*-type noun clause begins with (guess what?) a *wh*- word. The *wh*- words are like relative pronouns in that both can play different roles inside the noun. However, *wh*- words are even more diverse: they can be nouns, adjectives, or adverbs.

Here are the most common *wh*- words that begin noun clauses, classified by their parts of speech:

Nouns:	what	whatever
	who	whoever
	whom	whomever
Adjectives:	whose	
	which	whichever
Adverbs:	when	whenever
	where	wherever
	why	
	how	however

Notice that the last two words on the list (*how, however*) do not actually begin with *wh*. However, we will treat them as honorary members of the *wh*- family.

The following is a set of examples of *wh*-type noun clauses in the four noun roles in the independent clause. (Remember, we are talking about the role of the entire noun clause in the larger sentence, not about the internal construction of the noun clause itself.)

Subject:	**Whatever** *you want* is OK with me.
	Whom *I talk to* is none of your business.
Object of verb:	I don't know **how** *I should do it.*
	I saw **who** *shot Bugsy.*
Object of preposition:	We debated about **where** *we should go.*
	We looked at **what** *everyone was wearing.*
Predicate nominative:	Zen is **whatever** *you want it to be.*
	The situation is **what** *we expected.*

In discussing *wh*-type noun clauses, we must be very careful to distinguish the OUTSIDE role of the entire noun clause from the role of the *wh*- word

INSIDE the noun clause. The entire noun clause always functions as a noun within the independent clause (as in the examples above).

INSIDE the noun clause, however, the *wh-* word can play any number of different roles—noun, adjective, or adverb. The only requirement is that the *wh-* word must be moved to the first position in the dependent clause (like relative pronouns in adjective clauses). Here are some examples.

In the sentence

I believe ***what*** *you tell me.*

the *wh-* word *what* is actually the direct object of the verb *tell*. Wh- words, like relative pronouns in adjective clauses, are moved to the beginning of the dependent clause.

In the sentence

I know ***where*** *he put the key.*

the *wh-* word *where* is an adverb that has been moved forward from its normal position at the end of the sentence (*He put the key **somewhere***).

Following are examples of *wh-* words playing a variety of roles INSIDE the noun clause.

Role of **wh-** *word* inside noun clause	*Example*
Subject:	***Whoever*** *calls first* will win the prize.
Object of verb:	***Whomever*** *we pick* will win the prize.
Object of preposition:	***Whatever*** *we talk about* will be interesting.
Predicate nominative:	***What*** *you will be* is anybody's guess.
Adjective:	***Whichever*** *CD you pick* will be OK with me.
Adverb of time:	***When*** *you returned* was a surprise.
Adverb of place:	***Where*** *you live* is very important.
Adverb of manner:	***How*** *you respond* tells a lot about you.
Adverb of reason:	***Why*** *he said that* is a complete mystery.

Clause Exercise #14: Identifying the Role of Noun Clauses and the Role of **wh-**Words Inside the Noun Clause _____

The *wh-*type noun clauses in the following sentences have been underlined. (1) Label the role of the entire noun clause (use Subj; Verb Obj; Prep Obj; Pred Nom), and (2) label the role of the *wh-* word inside its clause (use the terms from the list above). The first question is done as an example. (Answers to this exercise are on page 496.)

0. I am worried about **where** I should park the car.

   Answer: (1) I am worried about **where** I should park the car.

   Prep Obj

   (2) **Where** is an adverb of place

1. **What** we did wrong is obvious to us now.

2. I know **why** we should floss our teeth.

3. I was worried about **which** computer would be best.

4. The problem was **what** we should wear.

5. I was surprised at **how** they had behaved.

6. **What** they talked about was a big secret.

7. Everyone asked **where** you were.

8. He would not tell me **who** he was.

9. I asked **why** the lights were left on.

10. **What** you see is **what** you get.

The distinction between the function of the noun clause as a whole and the function of the *wh-* word inside the noun clause requires careful analysis. For example, in the following sentences, which is correct, *whoever* or *whomever*?

We will sell it to ***whoever*** bids the highest.

We will sell it to ***whomever*** bids the highest.

The correct answer is *whoever*, not *whomever*, because the object of the preposition *to* is not just the *wh-* word *whomever*; it is the WHOLE noun clause, *whoever bids the highest*. The *wh-* word itself takes its form from its function inside the noun clause. In this case, the *wh-* word is the subject of the verb *bids*; therefore, it must be in the subject form *whoever*.

A *wh-*type noun clause, like a *that-*type noun clause, can almost always be identified by the *it* test. (With a few verbs that take *wh-*type noun clauses as objects, the *it* test is not very convincing, even though it is clear that the dependent clause must be a noun clause. Here is an example of such a verb:

We wondered	***what*** *we should do.*
	why *they weren't there.*
	who *they were.*
It test:	?We wondered **it**.)

Except for the occasional unusual verb like *wonder*, the *it* test is a highly reliable way of identifying *wh-type noun clauses.*

Clause Exercise #15: Identifying wh-Type Noun Clauses by *the* it Substitution Test _____

Underline the *wh-*type noun clauses and label the function of the *wh-* word inside its clause. Confirm your answer by the *it* substitution test. The first question is done as an example. (Answers to this exercise are on page 497.)

0. Save whatever you can salvage.

    Answer: Save **whatever** you can salvage.

    Confirmation: Save **whatever** you can salvage.
                                      it

whatever is the object of the verb *salvage.*

1. We did what was necessary.

2. What Bugsy said aroused the police's suspicion.

3. They relied on what they had been told.

4. What they were serving for lunch was fine with us.

5. Which shoes you take matters a lot on a long hike.

6. Our limited time restricted where we could go for lunch.

7. What you say may be used in evidence against you.

8. We were surprised at how Margie reacted to the news.

9. I understood why they felt that way.

10. Where Fred took his date made a lasting impression.

Diagramming wh-*Type Noun Clauses.*   The main difference between *wh*-type noun clauses and *that*-type noun clauses is the function of the *wh-* word. *Wh-* words are part of the internal structure of *wh*-type noun clauses. When we diagram *wh*-type noun clauses, we must put the *wh-* word into the diagram in whatever function it plays. For example, if it is an object, we put it on the main sentence line after the verb. If it is an adverb, it goes under the main verb.

    Here are examples of *wh*-type noun clauses playing the four noun functions.

Subject: **Whatever** you want is OK.

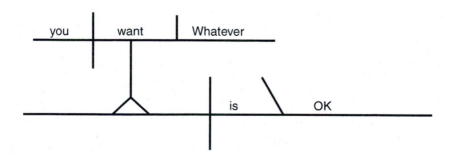

Object: I know **why** they left.

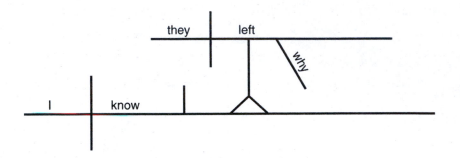

Predicate nominative: The pizza is **what** you ordered.

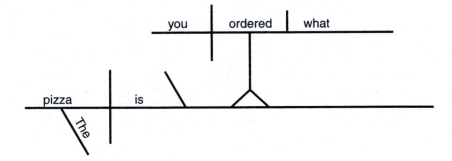

Object of preposition: Tell me about **where** he went.

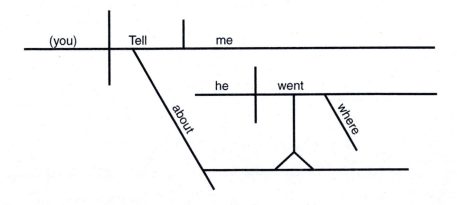

Clause Exercise #16: Diagramming wh-*Type Noun Clauses*

Diagram the following sentences. The first question is done as an example. (Answers to this exercise are on page 498.)

0. I don't know what I should do.

    Answer:

    I don't know what I should do.

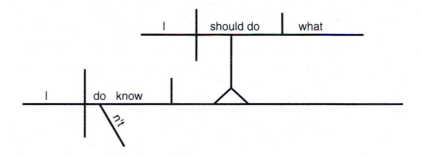

1. They depend on what you give them.

2. I know where you are.

3. What they said really surprised us.

4. I'll have whatever you are having.

5. What they did is none of your business.

6. I sympathize with what they were feeling.

7. I gave them whatever they wanted.

8. They had answers for whatever questions we asked.

9. What you say may be used against you.

10. The answer was what you said it was.

Infinitives with wh- *Words.*   Often we can reduce a *wh*-type noun clause to a *wh*- infinitive by deleting the subject of the noun clause and changing the main verb to an infinitive (often deleting a **modal** [the helping verbs *can, may, must,* *shall,* and *will* in their present- or past-tense forms] in the process). Here are some examples of *wh-* noun clauses reduced to *wh-* infinitives:

I know ***what*** I should do.

I know ***what*** to do.

I learned ***how*** *I should behave in that situation.*

I learned ***how*** *to behave in that situation.*

We talked about ***where*** *we could get the parts.*

We talked about ***where*** *to get the parts.*

What *one wears to a formal party* is always a problem.

What *to wear to a formal party* is always a problem.

The biggest problem was ***whom*** *we should invite.*

The biggest problem was ***whom*** *to invite.*

Clause Exercise #17: Changing wh-*Type Noun Clauses* into wh-*Infinitives* _____

Underline *wh-*type noun clauses and then change them into *wh-* infinitives. The first question is done as an example. (Answers to this exercise are on page 500.)

   0. The map will show you where you should go.

      Answer: The map will show you <u>where you should go</u>.

      wh- infinitive: where to go

   1. I was concerned about what I should tell Sally.

   2. They told us where we should park our cars.

   3. I figured out how I could solve the problem.

   4. What we should do about the accident was a major concern.

   5. The staff talked about whom we should hire.

   6. We were confused about when we should leave.

   7. They showed us how we should use chopsticks.

   8. What we should say in this situation is always a problem.

   9. I don't understand what I should do.

  10. Our training taught us how we should react to a crisis.

Review of Noun Clauses.   Since noun clauses always play the role of a noun inside the independent clause, they are easily identified by the *it* substitution test (nearly always). The most difficult aspect of noun clauses is the fact that they are built in two quite different ways.

A *that*-type noun clause begins with a flag word that is not part of the following underling sentence. For example, in the sentence

> I believe **that** *you are mistaken.*

The flag word *that* plays no role in the underlying sentence, *you are mistaken.*

A *wh*-type noun clause begins with a *wh*- word that is a component of the underlying sentence. For example, in the sentence

> I believe **what** *you tell me.*

the *wh*- word *what* is actually the direct object of the verb *tell*. *wh*- words, like relative pronouns in adjective clauses, are moved to the beginning of the dependent clause.

Some *wh*-type noun clauses can be reduced to *wh*- infinitive phrases by deleting the subject and changing the main verb to an infinitive, for example,

> *wh*- noun clause: I know **where** *I should go*
> *wh*- infinitive phrase: I know **where** *to go*.

Clause Exercise #18: Identifying Noun Clauses and wh-Infinitives _____

Underline noun clauses and *wh*- infinitives. Identify their function (subject, object, predicate nominative, object of preposition) within the independent clause. The first question is done as an example. (Answers to this exercise are on page 501.)

 0. Senator Fogg will talk to whoever will listen to him.

Answer: Senator Fogg will talk to <u>whoever will listen to him</u>.
Object of the preposition *to*

 1. I know who you are.

 2. Aunt Sally has decided that we should play Scrabble.

 3. Whomever you elect will have a hard time.

 4. We learn how to behave.

 5. You will know if you have a problem.

 6. We argued about whether we should get travelers' checks.

 7. Their position was that they would accept any valid offer.

8. How she manages to stay thin is a miracle.

9. They took advantage of whatever opportunity they found.

10. The slowest line is whichever one I pick.

11. We hear what we want to hear.

12. What they said seemed pretty unbelievable.

13. I do not know if I can get ready by then.

14. Nobody told me where I should go.

15. They were angry about how the clerk had treated them.

16. Whoever finishes the coffee must make the next pot.

17. Do you understand how to do it?

18. Whether or not he is right is quite debatable.

19. I heard what you said about where the test was.

20. I believe that what you said is correct.

Sentences Classified According to Structure

There are four kinds of clause structures in sentences: **simple, compound, complex,** and **compound-complex.**

Simple Sentences

Simple sentences contain a single independent clause and no dependent clauses. Simple sentences can be statements, questions, commands, or exclamations—as long as they do not contain a dependent clause. A simple sentence can also have compound subjects or compound verbs, but only a single set of subject–verb relations. Here are some examples of simple sentences:

This is a simple sentence.

It contains only a single independent clause.

Is this a simple sentence?

Sure it is!

Sam and Sally save soda straws.   (compound subject)

The birds fluttered and squawked in the trees.   (compound verb)

Compound Sentences

Compound sentence have two (or more) independent clauses but no dependent clauses. In the following examples, the independent clauses are italicized.

Jack went to the fair, and *he bought some beans.*

The beans were magic; they made Jack rich and famous.

In the first example, the two independent clauses are joined by a coordinating conjunction. In the second example, the two independent clauses are joined by a semicolon.

Diagramming Compound Sentences. Compound sentences that are joined by coordinating conjunctions are diagramed in the following manner:

Compound sentences

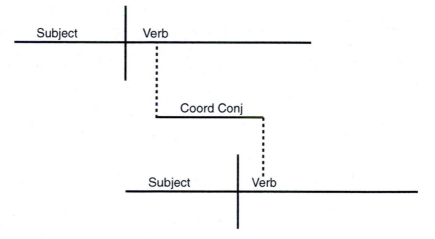

For example, here is how the compound sentence, *We had dinner, and then I went home* would be diagramed:

We had dinner, and then I went home.

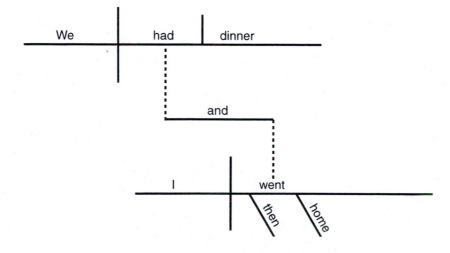

Compound sentences that are joined by semicolons are diagramed in the following manner:

Compound sentences: Two independent clauses joined by a semicolon.

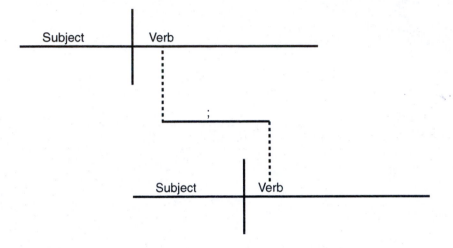

For example, here is how the compound sentence, *Jack ate the beans; he stayed poor* would be diagramed:

Jack ate the beans; he stayed poor.

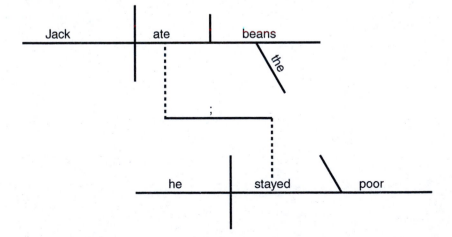

Complex Sentences

Complex sentences have a single independent clause but at least one dependent clause, which may be of any type (adjective, adverb, or noun). Here are some examples with the dependent clauses italicized:

The sentence *that you are reading* contains a dependent clause.

This is a complex sentence *because it contains a dependent clause.*

Whatever sentence contains an independent clause and a dependent clause is a complex sentence.

Teaching Tip

The terms "compound" and "complex" are easily confused. Remind students that the term "compound" in grammar means two of the same thing—a compound subject is two subjects; a compound predicate is two predicates. Thus, a compound sentence is two sentences, i.e., two independent clauses.

Compound-Complex Sentences

As the name suggests, a compound-complex sentence combines together two independent clauses with at least one dependent clause. Here is an example:

Since he was here, *he helped me roll up the rug,* and *then we took it upstairs.*
dependent clause   independent clause #1   independent clause #2

Chapter Review

This chapter has dealt with **dependent** (or subordinate) clauses. Dependent clauses cannot stand alone; they are grammatical only if they are attached to or included in an independent clause. There are three types of dependent clauses, each playing a single part-of-speech role: **adjective clauses, adverb clauses,** and **noun clauses.** Most of the tests for identifying single-word adjectives, adverbs, and nouns can also be used for identifying the dependent clauses that play the same part-of-speech roles.

Adjective Clauses

Adjective clauses always follow the nouns they modify. A good test for identifying adjective clauses is the **pronoun replacement test.** The test replaces nouns together with their adjective clause modifiers. For example, in the sentence,

The book **that you loaned me** is overdue at the library.
     It

the pronoun *it* replaces the noun *book* and the adjective clause *that you loaned me.*

If an adjective clause significantly changes the meaning of the noun it modifies by narrowing or limiting it to some individual or smaller group within a larger class to which the the noun refers, then the adjective clause is said to be **restrictive.** Restrictive clauses are never set off with commas. However, if the adjective clause merely renames or gives additional, nonlimiting information about the noun it modifies, and can be deleted without changing the meaning of the noun being modified, it is said to be **nonrestrictive.** Nonrestrictive clauses are always set off with commas.

Adverb Clauses

Adverb clauses modify verbs, adjectives, and other adverbs. Adverb clauses that modify verbs answer adverb questions and move.

> *Adverb Clause Question Test*
> We will go for a walk *after it stops raining.*
> Test: **When** will we go for a walk?
> *After it stops raining.*

> *Adverb Clause Movement Test*
> We will go for a walk *after it stops raining.*
> Test: *After it stops raining,* we will go for a walk.

Adverb clauses that modify predicate adjectives and adverbs have very restricted patterns:

Base-form predicate adjective + (*that*) + underlying sentence

Example: We were **glad** (*that*) *you could come.*

Comparative predicative adjective + *than* + underlying sentence

Example: It is **later** *than you think it is.*

Comparative adverb + *than* + underlying sentence

Example: I answered **more sharply** *than I had intended.*

Noun Clauses

Noun clauses play the role of noun in the independent clause they are part of: the noun clauses are subjects, objects of verbs, objects of prepositions, or predicate nominatives. Since noun clauses are noun phrases, they can nearly always be identified by the *it* test:

Subject:	*What he said* really upset me.
	It
Object of verb:	I know *that you are very worried.*
	it
Object of preposition:	We learned about *what we should do.*
	it
Predicate nominative:	The answer was *what we had expected.*
	it

Sentences Classified According to Structure

There are four kinds of clause structures in sentences: **simple, compound, complex,** and **compound-complex.** Simple sentences contain only a single independent clause. Compound sentences contain at least two independent clauses. Complex sentences contain a single independent clause and at least one dependent clause. Compound-complex sentences contain at least two independent clauses and at least one dependent clause.

Clause Exercise #19: Identifying Dependent Clauses _____

Underline all dependent clauses and label them by type: Adj, Adv, or Noun. The first question is done as an example. (Answers to this exercise are on page 502.)

  0. What they said upset me when I thought about it later.

      Answer: <u>What they said</u> upset me <u>when I thought about it later.</u>
               Noun   Adv

  1. I didn't like the program that we were watching.

  2. When I was your age, I had never been outside River City.

  3. Scratch it where it itches.

  4. If you think that you can do that, you are mistaken.

  5. He was bitter that Senator Fogg had defeated him.

  6. The kingdom became richer than it ever had before.

  7. Since you asked about what I know, I will tell you.

  8. What you said surprised everyone who was there.

  9. After we ate, I charged what we had spent on my credit card.

10. We saw the ad everyone had been talking about.

11. While you were out, Matthew called again.

12. Tell me when you will be ready to leave.

13. The salesman talked faster than I could follow.

14. The press viewed the story with suspicion that verged on disbelief.

15. I wrote about the French who invaded England in 1066.

16. What we found was hardly worth looking for.

17. I was a little disappointed considering all the work we had done.

18. We repeated what we had heard over the radio.

19. I gave a list of what I needed.

20. As I was going to St. Ives, I met a man who had seven wives.

7

Redefining Verb Complements

In this chapter we will borrow from modern grammar an expanded definition of verb complement that will greatly increase our ability to analyze sentences.

In traditional grammar, the **complement** is a noun/pronoun or predicate adjective that is required by a **main verb** to make a grammatical sentence. (Recall that helping verbs do not control complements.) For example, in the sentence

Farmer Brown planted	*alfalfa*	*in his field*	*this spring.*
	Complement	Modifier	Modifier

the verb *plant* requires a noun/pronoun as a complement. In other words, when you plant, you have to plant SOMETHING (*alfalfa*, in this case). However, the other two components in the predicate are optional modifiers, not complements. *In his field* and *this spring* tell us where and when Farmer Brown planted alfalfa, but the verb *plant* does not require this information to make a grammatical sentence. The sentence is still fully grammatical without them:

Farmer Brown planted alfalfa.

If a complement is deleted from a sentence, the sentence is either no longer grammatical or the sentence is grammatical only with a different meaning. When we delete a complement from a verb that normally requires the complement, the verb usually shifts meaning in a predictable way to mean "engage in the act of the verb." For example, if we delete the complement *alfalfa* from the above sentence, we get the marginally grammatical sentence

?Farmer Brown planted.

which, if it is grammatical at all, could only mean that Farmer Brown engaged in the act of planting—as opposed to other things that farmers do, such as weeding or harvesting.

In modern grammar, the definition of complement has been broadened to include **any grammatical structure** that is required by a main verb to make a grammatical sentence. In other words, complements are not restricted to being just nouns/pronouns or predicate adjectives. Complements can also be various kinds of adverbs, prepositional phrases, and other structures, in addition to the nouns/pronouns and predicate adjectives we have seen in traditional grammar.

Below are three examples of main verbs that take adverbs and prepositions as complements. We will see that when adverbs and prepositions are complements, they do not behave at all like normal adverb modifiers. After discussing these examples by way of introduction, we will then do a systematic survey of all the major verb complement types.

Examples of Main Verbs That Take Adverbs and Prepositions as Complements

Adverb

John gave *up*.

Many verbs take a particular adverb as a complement, creating a kind of compound structure. In the example sentence, *give up* is such a compound. The phrasal verb *give up* has the special meaning of "surrender" that is not predictable from the meanings of the two words *give* and *up* taken separately. If we delete the adverb complement *up*, we get a different sentence with a completely different meaning:

John gave.   (engaged in the act of giving)

Up is an adverb, but it is not a modifier. We cannot ask an adverb question the way we can with a modifying adverb:

Adverb question: ***Where** did John give?
Adverb answer: *Up.*

We cannot move *up* the way we can a modifying adverb:

Adverb movement test: *Up* John gave.

The reason these tests fail is that *up* is not a modifying adverb: it is a complement required by the verb.

Adverbial of Place

>John is *at school.*   (adverb prepositional phrase of place)
>He was *nearby.*   (single-word adverb of place)

In these sentences, the adverbials of place are required by the verb *be* as complements. The proof of this is simple: if we delete the adverbials, the sentences become ungrammatical:

>*John is.

>*He was.

When adverbials of place are used as complements, they will answer an adverb question because they are still adverbs:

>Adverb question test: **Where** is John?
>Answer: *At school.*
>Adverb question test: **Where** was he?
>Answer: *Nearby.*

However, adverbials of place used as complements will fail the adverb movement test because that test applies only to adverb modifiers:

>Adverb movement test: **At school* John is.
>   **Nearby* was he.

Particular Prepositions

>We depended **on** *them.*

>I skimmed **through** *my notes.*

Many verbs require prepositional phrases beginning with particular prepositions as their complements. If we delete the prepositions and their objects, the sentences are either ungrammatical or are grammatical with a completely different meaning:

>*We depended.

>?I skimmed.   (engaged in the act of skimming)

There is a very tight bond between particular verbs and particular prepositions. Speakers of English just have to know that *depend* requires the preposition *on* and *skim* requires the preposition *through*. For example, we cannot reverse the prepositions in these two examples without making them ungrammatical:

> *We depended **through** *them.*

> *I skimmed **on** *my notes.*

Since these prepositional phrases are not adverb phrases but are part of the complement, they will fail the adverb movement test:

> Adverb movement test: We depended **on** *them.*
> *On* *them* we depended.

> Adverb movement test: I skimmed **through** *my notes.*
> ***Through** my notes* I skimmed.

This concludes our brief introduction to the ways in which adverb and preposition complements differ from adverbs and prepositions used as normal modifiers. We will now turn to a survey of the many different types of complements that English uses. A major task facing every learner of a language is mastering the scores of different complements and sorting out which particular verbs go with which particular complements. The task is even more challenging than it first appears, because most verbs can be used with many different complement types, each combination having its own meaning.

Survey of Verb Complements

The complement types listed below are broken into three groups: complements of verbs with no more than one complement, complements of verbs with multiple complements, and complements of a special group of verbs called **phrasal verbs** that form a kind of compound with adverb or preposition complements.

For the sake of easy reference, we will number the complement types. The order in which the complement types are listed is largely arbitrary, but the order does move from the simpler and more familiar complements to the more complex and exotic.

(A) Complements of Verbs with No More than a Single Complement

(1) No Complement.   Some verbs can be used with no complement at all.

John *sneezed.*

The old cow finally *died.*

My knee *hurts.*

These verbs are often used with adverbs, but the adverbs are optional modifiers that are not required to make the verb grammatical. They are not part of the complement of these verbs.

John *sneezed* loudly.

The old cow finally *died* last night.

My knee *hurts* all the time.

(2) Noun Phrase.   In modern grammar, the term "noun phrase" is broader than it is in traditional grammar. In modern grammar a "noun phrase" is a collective term that includes single-word nouns, nouns with modifiers (the meaning we used for "noun phrase" in Chapter 2), and pronouns. Noun phrase complements are probably the single most common type of complement.

John answered *questions.*	(single noun)
John answered *the phone in the office.*	(noun plus modifiers)
John answered *it.*	(pronoun)

One of the characteristics of noun phrase complements is that they can be made into the subjects of the corresponding **passive** sentence:

Active:	John answered *questions.*
Passive:	*Questions* were answered by John.
Active:	John answered *the phone in the office.*
Passive:	*The phone in the office* was answered by John.
Active:	John answered *it.*
Passive:	*It* was answered by John.

(3) Predicate Nominative.   Predicate nominatives are noun phrases that have a special characteristic: they must always refer back to their subjects. In other words, the subject and the predicate nominative must refer to the same person or thing.

Tarzan became *a vegetarian.*   *(vegetarian = Tarzan)*

His prize was *a brand-new bicycle.*   *(bicycle = prize)*

Their new house resembled *a meatloaf.*   *(meatloaf = house)*

Predicate nominatives differ from ordinary noun phrase object complements in two respects:

(a) Predicate nominatives must refer back to the subjects of their sentences, but noun phrase complements do not. For example, in the following sentence even personal pronouns used as noun phrases cannot refer back to the subject:

John saw *him* in the mirror.

The noun phrase *him* cannot refer to *John*.

(b) One of the formal ways of telling predicate nominative complements from noun phrase complements is that predicate nominatives (unlike noun phrases) cannot be made into the subjects of passive sentences:

Active:	Tarzan became *a vegetarian.*
Passive:	**A vegetarian* was become by Tarzan.
Active:	His prize was *a brand-new bicycle.*
Passive:	**A brand-new bicycle* was been by his prize.
Active:	Their new house resembled *a meatloaf.*
Passive:	**A meatloaf* was resembled by their new house.

Complement Exercise #1: Using the Passive to Identify Predicate Nominatives

Underline the predicate nominatives and the subjects they refer to. Confirm your answer by showing that the predicate nominative CANNOT become the subject of the corresponding passive sentence. The first question is done as an example. (Answers to this exercise are on page 503.)

0. Cinderella became a bartender.

   Answer: <u>Cinderella</u> became a <u>bartender</u>.

   Confirmation: *A bartender was become by Cinderella.

1. Moby Dick was a white whale.

2. Moby Dick is also the name of a rock group.

3. Jason seemed a nice young man.

4. Humpty Dumpty was a good egg.

5. Alice remains a close friend of mine.

6. Scrooge became a better person.

7. The proposal seemed a good idea at the time.

8. He is such an alarmist.

9. I felt a complete fool.

10. It was the best of times.

(4) Predicate Adjective. Predicate adjectives are typically **gradable** (see p. 29).

Dinner seemed *better* tonight.

That tasted *terrific*.

George was *green* with jealousy.

(5) Adverbial of Place. This group was discussed in the introductory section. Adverbials of place can be either single-word adverbs or prepositional phrases. Here are more examples of each type:

Single-word adverb:

John lives *there*.

They are staying *here*.

They parked *here*.

Prepositional phrase:

Aunt Bea is *in the hospital*.

They stayed *at home*.

He is *in the building*.

Recall that if adverbial of place complements are deleted, the resulting sentence becomes either ungrammatical or grammatical with a completely different meaning. For example, compare the following sentences:

John lives *there*.

John lives.

In the first sentence, in which *there* is a complement, the verb *lives* means "resides." In the second sentence, in which *lives* is used without a complement, the verb has now shifted to the meaning of "remains alive."

Adverbial of place complements also differ from adverb of place modifiers in that adverbial of place complements cannot be moved, but adverb of place modifiers can:

Adverbial of place complements:

They parked *here*.

*Here they parked.

Aunt Bea is *in the hospital.*

*In the hospital Aunt Bea is.

Adverb of place modifiers:

They met each other *here.*

Here they met each other.

You can get some lunch *in the hospital.*

In the hospital you can get some lunch.

Complement Exercise #2: Identifying Adverbial of Place Complements _____

Underline the adverbial of place complements. Confirm your answer by showing that the adverbial complement fails the adverb movement test. The first question is done as an example. (Answers to this exercise are on page 503.)

0. The kittens were on the back porch.
   Answer: The kittens were on the back porch.
   Confirmation: *On the back porch the kittens were.

1. The men remained in the dining room.

2. The boat is staying at the dock.

3. We parked in their driveway.

4. They live next door.

5. The cereal is above the refrigerator.

6. I have always lived in Georgia.

7. The next delivery is close by.

8. Ralph stayed behind.

9. We all sat on the couch.

10. The suspect last resided in Miami.

Review of Complements of Verbs That Require No More than a Single Complement.   We have identified the following five complement types:

(1) No complement

John sneezed.

(2) Noun phrase

John answered *the phone.*

(3) Predicate nominative

Tarzan became *a vegetarian.*

(4) Predicate adjective

That tasted *terrible.*

(5) Adverbial of place

He is *in the building.*

Complement Exercise #3: Review of Verbs with No More Than One Complement

Underline the complements. Identify the complement type using the names given above. The first question is done as an example. (Answers to this exercise are on page 504.)

0. I should have stayed in bed.

    Answer: I should have stayed <u>in bed</u>.
    Adverbial of place

1. The earthquake nearly destroyed the building.

2. They are very good workers.

3. I have lived here for several years now.

4. The audience laughed loudly.

5. We rebuilt the carburetor.

6. They are such good friends.

7. Sticks and stones will break my bones.

8. They stayed at a motel near the freeway.

9. I am really upset.

10. We discussed the problem.

11. The problem seemed insurmountable.

12. The car hung over the guardrail.

13. Several of my teachers have retired recently.

14. We postponed any decision.

15. They really seem strange.

16. That carburetor is missing again.

17. At the time of the crime, Bugsy was on a plane to Vegas.

18. Please begin any time.

19. Tarzan became a grammarian.

20. The train left the station.

(B) Verbs with More than One Complement

(6) *Noun phrase + Noun Phrase.* Some verbs take two noun phrases (NP1 + NP2) as their complements. (This complement type is identified in traditional grammar as taking an indirect object + a direct object.) Even though the number of verbs that take this complement type is small (about fifty verbs), the verbs are relatively high-frequency.

> John gave *Mary   a present.*
>   NP1   NP2
>
> They were telling *us   the truth.*
>   NP1   NP2
>
> We found *our friends   a house-warming gift.*
>   NP1   NP2

A distinguishing characteristic of this complement type is a paraphrase in which the two noun phrases can be reversed and the original first noun phrase used with a preposition, usually *to* or *for.* We will call this the ***to/for* paraphrase:**

> John gave a *present* **to** *Mary.*
>   NP2   NP1
>
> They were telling *the truth* **to** *us.*
>   NP2   NP1
>
> We found a *house-warming gift* **for** *our friends.*
>   NP2   NP1

Complement Exercise #4: Identifying NP1 + NP2 Complements _____

Underline and label the NP1 + NP2 complements. Confirm your answer by applying the *to/for* paraphrase. The first question is done as an example. (Answers to this exercise are on page 505.)

0. Show me the money.

> Answer: Show me the money.
>   NP1   NP2
>
> Confirmation: Show the money **to** me.

1. Save me some dessert.

2. The wizard granted the knight his wish.

3. Hand me a towel.

4. Bugsy made them a non-negotiable offer.

5. You can't teach an old dog new tricks.

6. Throw the dog a bone.

7. Don't do me any favors.

8. They sent us a bill.

9. Order me a tuna sandwich.

10. "Friends, Romans, countrymen, lend me your ears."

(7) Noun Phrase + Object Complement. Some verbs also take two noun phrases as complements, but with the added restriction that the second of the two noun phrases, the object complement (OC), must refer to the first noun phrase (the object). In other words,

> Noun phrase object = Object complement

For example, in the sentence

> Alice considered *Lord Bumpfry*   *a fool.*
>   NP   OC

the object complement *a fool* must refer to *Lord Bumpfry.* Here are some more examples of this complement type:

> I consider *myself*   *a reasonable person.*
>   NP   OC

> The chair appointed *John*   *the permanent secretary.*
>   NP   OC

> We found *them*   *an odd couple.*
>   NP   OC

The NP + OC complement type looks a lot like the NP1 + NP2 complement type. One way to tell the two complement types apart is by the *to/for* paraphrase. Sentences with an object complement will always fail this test with *to*:

> NP + OC: Captain Hook kept *Wendy*   *a prisoner.*
>   NP   OC
> *to* paraphrase: *Captain Hook kept *a prisoner* **to** *Wendy.*
>   OC   NP

Sometimes the *for* test will appear to work, but only because the *for* phrase changes meaning completely:

for paraphrase: *Captain Hook kept *a prisoner* **for** Wendy.

The new sentence is grammatical in the completely unrelated sense that Captain Hook kept a prisoner for Wendy's benefit or at Wendy's request. The new sentence is ungrammatical as a paraphrase of the original sentence, where *prisoner* and *Wendy* are one and the same persons.

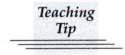

Teaching Tip

Have students explain the grammar of this classic Marx Brothers gag:

Stooge: Call me a taxi!

Groucho: OK, you're a taxi.

Complement Exercise #5: Identifying NP + OC Complements

Underline and label the NP + OC complements. Confirm your answer by showing that the object noun phrase and the object complement refer to the same person. The first question is done as an example. (Answers to this exercise are on page 506.)

0. She considered him a prince.

Answer: She considered <u>him</u> <u>a prince</u>.
                          NP   OC

Confirmation: him = a prince

1. The committee rated her the best applicant.

2. Holmes proved the butler an imposter.

3. The stock market made them millionaires.

4. We elected Marsha class president.

5. The jury believed him the guilty party.

6. I pronounce you man and wife.

7. They named their first child Philip.

8. His decision proved him an outstanding general.

9. I consider myself a decent person.

10. She thought him an older man.

(8) Noun Phrase + Predicate Adjective. A similar group of verbs takes a noun phrase and a kind of predicate adjective (Pred Adj) as complement. This kind of predicate adjective must refer to the object noun phrase, not the subject.

> Object = Pred Adj

For example, in the sentence

> Mary considered *John   foolish.*
> NP   Pred Adj

the predicate adjective *foolish* refers to the object *John,* not the subject *Mary.* Here are more examples of this complement type:

> Keep *your powder   dry.*
> NP   Pred Adj

> The report made *him   angry.*
> NP   Pred Adj

> The court declared *the defendant   sane.*
> NP   Pred Adj

(9) Noun Phrase + Adverbial of Place. Some verbs can be used with a noun phrase + adverbial of place complement. The adverbial of place (ADVplace) can be either a single-word adverb or an adverbial prepositional phrase. Here is an example:

> Felix put *the milk   in the refrigerator.*
> NP   ADVplace

There are two arguments that *in the refrigerator* is a complement and not an optional modifier: (1) if we delete the adverbial of place, the sentence becomes ungrammatical (not true, of course, for adverb modifiers):

> *Felix put the milk.

(2) If *in the refrigerator* were an adverb modifier, it should pass the adverb movement test, which it does not:

> Adverb movement test: *In the refrigerator* Felix put the milk.

Here are more examples:

> I keep *the keys   in the desk drawer.*
> NP   ADVplace

Leave *the cards*   *on the table.*
        NP   ADVplace

I stuck *my keys*   *there.*
         NP   ADVplace

Complement Exercise #6: Identifying NP + Pred Adj and NP + ADVplace Complements _____

Underline and label the NP + Pred Adj and the NP + ADVplace complements. Confirm the NP + ADVplace answer by showing that the adverb movement test fails. The first question is done as an example. (Answers to this exercise are on page 506.)

  0. I set the coffee cup on the table.

     Answer: I set <u>the coffee cup</u> <u>on the table.</u>
                     NP   ADVplace

     Confirmation: *On the table I set the coffee cup.

  1. Jason left the fleece on the boat.

  2. I like my coffee really hot.

  3. The cold snap turned the leaves red.

  4. I put the money in the bank.

  5. Get it ready.

  6. She placed the vase on the mantle.

  7. It really made me angry.

  8. They put me on hold.

  9. The Thermos keeps the milk cold.

 10. The bank robbers left the stolen vehicle at the airport.

     The next two complement types share the common feature of having a **nontensed verb phrase** as the second complement element. A nontensed verb phrase is a verb in a nontensed form together with that verb's complements and/or modifiers. The two nontensed verb forms that are commonly used as complements are the **present participle** and the **infinitive**. A quick review of verb form terminology may be in order.

- The **present participle** is the base form plus *-ing*, for example, *going, singing, walking, being.*
- The **infinitive** is *to* + the base form, for example, *to go, to sing, to walk, to be.*

(10) *Noun Phrase + Present Participle Verb Phrase.* Some verbs can take a noun phrase and a present participle verb phrase (VPpres part) as their complement. Here is an example:

> We heard *Tarzan   singing in the shower.*
>   NP   VPpres part

At first glance, *singing in the shower* looks like a gerund or a participial phrase used as an adjective. The best test for gerunds is the *it* test. Since gerunds are always singular noun phrases, they can always be replaced by *it*. When we apply the *it* test to a verb complement, the test fails:

> We heard Tarzan ***singing*** *in the shower.*
>   *it

Here is a somewhat comparable sentence with a true gerund:

> We heard *Tarzan's* ***singing*** *in the shower.*
>   it

Notice that the subject of the gerund, *Tarzan's,* must be in the possessive form.

The proper use of the pronoun replacement test clearly shows that *singing in the shower* is not a participial phrase used as an adjective since the pronoun does not replace the participial (which it would if it were a noun modifier):

> We heard *Tarzan* singing in the shower.
>   him

Here are some more examples of this present participle verb phrase complement type:

> I found *myself*   ***watching*** *daytime television.*
>   NP   VPpres part
>
> We watched *the planes*   ***taking*** *off.*
>   NP   VPpres part
>
> I smell *something*   ***cooking*** *in the oven.*
>   NP   VPpres part

Complement Exercise #7: Identifying NP + VPpres Part Complements

Underline and label the NP + VPpres part complements. Confirm your answers by showing that the pronoun replacement test applies only to the noun, not to the present participial phrase (VPpres part). The first question is done as an example. (Answers to this exercise are on page 507.)

0. We heard the band rehearsing for the concert.

   Answer: We heard <u>the band</u> <u>rehearsing for the concert.</u>
                            NP   VPpres part

   Confirmation: We heard <u>the band</u> <u>rehearsing for the concert.</u>
                                      them

1. We left John studying for his test.

2. The contractor had his crew tearing off the old shingles.

3. The coach caught some players reading a book.

4. I felt the walls shaking.

5. We really got them thinking about it.

6. Snow White overheard the dwarves planning to go on strike.

7. The kids were watching the kittens chasing each other.

8. I left the water running.

9. Did you notice the guy eating at the counter?

10. The whole office heard the boss chewing me out.

(11) *Noun Phrase + Infinitive Verb Phrase.* Some verbs can take a noun phrase plus an infinitive verb phrase (VPinf) as their complement. Here is an example:

We finally got *him*   *to ask* for a raise.
                    NP   VPinf

At first glance, the infinitive verb phrase *to ask for a raise* might look like either an infinitive phrase used as a noun or an infinitive phrase used as an adverb. If *to ask for a raise* were a noun, we could replace the infinitive phrase with *it*. However, the *it* test fails in this case because *to ask for a raise* is a verb complement:

We finally got him ***to ask*** for a raise.
                                     *it

If *to ask for a raise* were an adverb phrase, then we should be able to move it to the beginning of the sentence using the adverb movement test, but we can't:

*****To ask*** for a raise, we finally got him.

Here are some more examples of infinitive verb phrases as verb complements:

We dared *him*   *to do* *it again.*
       NP   VPinf

The police believed *Bugsy*   *to be* *telling the truth.*
             NP   VPinf

They expected *us*   *to be there around six.*
        NP   VPinf

Complement Exercise #8: Identifying Noun Phrase + VPinf Complements

Underline and label the NP + VPinf complements. Confirm your answers by showing that both the *it* test and the adverb movement test fail when applied to the VPinf. The first question is done as an example. (Answers to this exercise are on page 508.)

0. Senator Fogg declared his intention to run for re-election.

Answer: Senator Fogg declared <u>his intention</u> <u>to run for reelection</u>.
                            NP   VPinf

Confirmation:

it test: *Senator Fogg declared his intention <u>it</u>.

Adv movement: *<u>To run for re-election</u>, Senator Fogg declared his intention.

1. Darth Vader forced Luke to get a haircut.

2. Allow me to introduce a friend.

3. I found them to be very helpful.

4. Senator Fogg told the reporters to mind their own business.

5. Cinderella got the mice to help her.

6. The password enabled me to run the program.

7. The students wanted their papers to be perfect.

8. The book really helped me to understand the conflict.

9. We encouraged them to start over.

10. The IRS requires tax payers to file every year.

Review of Verbs with Multiple Complements.   We have identified the following complement types:

(6) Noun phrase + noun phrase

We gave *Mary*   *the prize.*
       NP1   NP2

(7) Noun phrase + object complement

They considered *him*   *a fool.*
          NP   OC

(8) Noun phrase + predicate adjective

They considered *him   crazy.*
                    NP   Pred Adj

(9) Noun phrase + adverbial of place

Felix put *the milk   in the refrigerator.*
            NP   ADVplace

(10) Noun phrase + present participle verb phrase

We heard *Tarzan   singing in the shower.*
            NP   VPpres part

(11) Noun phrase + infinitive verb phrase

We got *him   to ask for a raise.*
       NP   VPinf

Complement Exercise #9: Review of Verbs with Multiple Complements

Underline the complements. Identify the complement type using the names given above. The first question is done as an example. (Answers to this exercise are on page 509.)

0. The jury found them innocent.

    Answer: The jury found <u>them</u> <u>innocent.</u>
                                NP   Pred Adj

1. The jury found them to be innocent.

2. I found the kids playing in the back yard.

3. We found the kittens a good home.

4. She put the umbrella under her seat.

5. Kit caught William stealing his lines.

6. We wanted them to be more careful.

7. They sold them their old car.

8. Bugsy placed a gun on the table.

9. We heard them arriving during the night.

10. The company named him the new president.

11. The company named him to succeed the old president.

12. I hate John doing that.

13. Events proved me wrong.

14. Stan made Ollie the chairman of the board.

15. Tell me the truth.

16. The Archbishop placed the crown on his head.

17. We expected you to do better.

18. The coach thought the team ready.

19. I found myself falling asleep in class.

20. Keep them in their seats.

(C) Complements of Phrasal Verbs.

Phrasal verbs are verbs that form idiomatic compounds with particular adverbs or prepositions. Compounding verbs with adverbs or prepositions is the major way that English creates new verbs. The best student reference book for phrasal verbs, the *Longman Dictionary of Phrasal Verbs,* has over 12,000 entries.

In the following presentation, phrasal verbs are divided into four categories based on the type of complement. The four types are listed here with an example. Each type is then discussed in greater detail.

(12) Adverb

John gave *up*   (*give up* = "surrender")
       Adv

(13) Adverb + noun phrase

John turned *down*   *the offer.*   (*turn down* = "reject")
      Adv   NP

(14) Preposition + noun phrase

The class went *over*   *the notes*   (*go over* = "review")
      Prep   NP

(15) Noun phrase + prep + noun phrase

They talked *us*   *into*   *the plan.*   (*talk someone into* = "persuade
      NP Prep   NP   someone to accept something")

(12) Adverb.   As discussed in the introductory section, a number of phrasal verbs are used with particular adverbs to form verb–adverb compounds, each combination having its own, often unpredictable, meaning. Here is another example that illustrates some of the characteristics of this complement type:

The patient pulled *through.*

The verb–adverb combination *pull through* creates the new meaning of "survive," which is somewhat different from the meanings of *pull* and *through* by themselves. Through also fails both standard tests of adverbs used as modifiers because although *through* is an adverb, it is a complement, not a modifier:

Adverb question test:	***How (when, where, why)** did the patient pull?
Adverb answer:	**Through*
Adverb movement test:	**Through* the patient pulled.

This complement type is very productive. There are many hundreds of combinations of different verbs and adverbs. Table 7.1 lists some examples that illustrate the different adverbs that can be used as adverb complements of intransitive verbs.

Complement Exercise #10: Identifying Adverb Complements

Underline the adverbs that are complements of verbs. Confirm your answer by showing that the adverb complement fails the adverb movement test. (Answers to this exercise are on page 510.)

   0. The children eventually calmed down.

   Answer: The children eventually calmed <u>down</u>.

   Confirmation: Adverb movement test: *Down the children eventually calmed.

   1. Snow White and Prince Charming broke up.

TABLE 7.1   *Adverbs That Can Be Used as Adverb Complements*

Verb	Adverb	Meaning	Example
grow	apart	"become estranged"	Sometimes couples *grow apart*.
fool	around	"act silly"	They are always *fooling around*.
run	away	"flee"	The animals *ran away*.
strike	back	"retaliate"	Eventually the Empire *struck back*.
break	down	"fail"	The old truck finally *broke down*.
drop	by	"visit"	Some old friends *dropped by*.
chip	in	"contribute"	They needed help, so we *chipped in*.
show	off	"exhibit oneself"	Fred is always *showing off*.
catch	on	"understand"	Finally, the students *caught on*.
pass	out	"faint"	Macho Man *passed out*.
turn	over	"flip"	The pages kept *turning over*.
keep	together	"stay in a group"	The sheep *kept together*.
shut	up	"stop talking"	Bugsy finally *shut up*.

2. They were always butting in.

3. I am going to have to drop out.

4. Bugsy and his gang got away.

5. Eventually, Snow White and Prince Charming made up.

6. Everybody pitched in.

7. I really screwed up.

8. The old plant finally shut down.

9. We had to start over.

10. The batter struck out.

(13) Adverb + Noun Phrase. These phrasal verbs are also compounds of verbs with particular adverb complements, but now the phrasal verbs are followed by noun phrase objects. Here is an example with the adverb complement in bold:

John turned *down* the offer.

At first glance, the sentence looks like it has the following structure:

John *turned*   *down the offer.*
   intransitive verb   adverb preposition phase

However, when we attempt to apply the two standard adverb tests to the supposed prepositional phrase **down** *the offer,* they both fail:

Adverb question test: ***Where** did John turn?
Adverb answer: ****Down** the offer.*
Adverb movement test: ****Down** the offer* John turned.

The reason that the two tests fail is that **down** *the offer* is not an adverb preposition phrase used as a modifier; it is not even a prepositional phrase at all.

Now let us do a comparable analysis on a sentence that really does contain an intransitive verb and adverb prepositional phrase:

The truck   *turned*   *down the road.*
    intransitive verb   adverb prepositional phrase

When we apply the two adverb tests to *down the road,* the results are predictably positive:

Adverb questions test: **Where** did the truck turn?
Adverb answer: ***Down** the road.*
Adverb movement test: ***Down** the road* the truck turned.

Let us now return to our original example of a transitive phrasal verb:

John turned *down* the offer.

If *turn down* is a phrasal verb compound, what does that make *the offer?* It makes *the offer* an object of the compound verb *turn down:*

John *turned down the offer.*
          transitive verb   object

The confirmation that *offer* is an object following a transitive verb comes from the passive. As you may recall, to change an active sentence into a passive sentence, we turn the object of the active sentence into the subject of the corresponding passive sentence, for example,

Active: John saw *Mary.*
Passive: *Mary* was seen by John.

If *offer* is the object of the compound verb *turned down,* then there must be a corresponding passive, as indeed there is, one that sounds completely normal:

Active: John turned down *the offer.*
Passive: *The offer* was turned down by John.

Transitive phrasal verbs have an absolutely unique feature that sets them off from all other complement structures. The adverb part of the compound can break away from the verb and move to a position after the object noun phrase:

John turned *down* the offer.
John turned the offer *down.*

There seems to be no difference at all in meaning between the two versions of the sentence. Even more remarkable, the movement of the adverb is OBLIG-ATORY if the object noun phrase is a pronoun. For example, if we replace *the offer* with the pronoun *it,* the original word order is ungrammatical:

*John turned *down* it.

We must now move the adverb after the pronoun:

John turned it *down.*

This obligatory movement of the adverb to a position after an object pronoun is the defining feature of this type of transitive phrasal verbs.

> **Phrasal adverb movement test.** If an adverb used with a main verb must move after the object when the object is replaced by a pronoun, then the adverb is part of a transitive phrasal verb construction.

Here is a negative example. When we apply the phrasal adverb movement test to a sentence with a genuine prepositional phrase, the result is ungrammatical because the test moves the preposition away from its object:

Preposition phrase:	The truck turned *down* the road.
Phrasal adverb movement test:	*The truck turned it **down**.

If *turned down* were a transitive phrasal verb, the above sentence would have to be grammatical.

Complement Exercise #11: Identifying Adverb + NP Complements by the Phrasal Adverb Movement Test _____

Underline and label the adverbs and noun phrases that make up transitive phrasal verb compounds. Confirm your answer by applying the phrasal adverb movement test to the adverb. (Answers to this exercise are on page 511.)

  0. The coaches called off the game.
  Answer: The coaches called <u>off</u> <u>the game</u>.
                                   Adv   NP
  Confirmation: The coaches called the game off.

  1. Philip called up his girl friend.

  2. We brought back some pictures of our trip.

  3. I finally cleaned out the attic.

  4. Susan dropped off some of your books.

  5. Stan and Ollie figured out the problem.

  6. They wandered up the path.

  7. The children made up a new game.

  8. The teacher pointed out their mistake.

  9. The company laid off the temporary workers.

  10. I sent back the defective part.

This particular complement type is very common. Table 7.2 gives a number of examples of phrasal verbs using different adverbs. Note especially how

TABLE 7.2   *Phrasal Adverbs*

Verb	Adverb	Meaning	Example
throw	away	"discard"	John *threw away* his notes. John *threw* them *away*.
put	back	"return"	John *put back* the book. John *put* it *back*.
turn	down	"reject"	John *turned down* the offer. John *turned* it *down*.
turn	in	"submit"	John *turned in* his paper. John *turned* it *in*.
call	off	"cancel"	John *called off* the meeting. John *called* it *off*.
turn	on	"activate"	John *turned on* the TV. John *turned* it *on*.
find	out	"discover"	John *found out* the answer. John *found* it *out*.
talk	over	"discuss"	We *talked over* the problem. We *talked* it *over*.
string	together	"link"	John *strung together* the beads. John *strung* them *together*.
hang	up	"disconnect by returning phone to cradle"	John *hung up* the phone. John *hung* it *up*.

unpredictable the meanings of the compound are. You can well imagine how difficult this kind of phrasal verb is for non-native speakers of English.

(14) *Preposition + Noun Phrase.* This complement type was also discussed in the introduction. To recap briefly: many verbs require as their complement a prepositional phrase beginning with a specific preposition. To take another pair of examples,

> They asked *for* you.

> She knows *about* the meeting.

These are not ordinary adverb prepositional phrases that modify the verb; these prepositional phrases are complements. They fail the normal adverb tests. There is no adverb question that will produce these prepositional phrases as answers:

> Adverb question test: ***When (where, why, how)** did they ask?
> Adverb answer: ***For** *you.*

Adverb question test: ***When (where, why, how)** does she know?*
Adverb answer: ****About** the meeting.*

The adverb movement test also fails:

Adverb movement test: ****For** you they asked.*
Adverb movement test: ****About** the meeting she knows.*

This complement type is a common type of phrasal verb compound with hundreds of different combinations of verbs with particular prepositions. Table 7.3 gives some more examples that illustrate the different prepositions that can be used as complements of verbs.

Since both this complement type and the adverbial of place complement type can begin with prepositions, how can we tell them apart? Simple. If a prepositional phrase answers an adverb of place question, it belongs to the adverbial of place complement type. Here is an example:

I stayed with some friends.

In this sentence, is *stay with* a phrasal verb compound with a particular preposition, or does *stay* take an adverbial of place complement? When we apply the adverb of place question, the answer is clear—the latter:

Adverb of place question: **Where** did I stay?
Adverb answer: *With some friends.*

TABLE 7.3   *Prepositions That Can Be Used as Complements of Verbs*

Verb	Preposition	Example
know	about	She *knows about* the meeting.
look	after	I will *look after* the kids.
guard	against	Fred must *guard against* overconfidence.
hint	at	They only *hinted at* the problem.
stand	by	She will *stand by* her man.
ask	for	They *asked for* you.
abstain	from	One should *abstain from* vigorous exercise.
bump	into	We *bumped into* Sally at the store.
repent	of	He *repented of* all his past actions.
bet	on	You can *bet on* it.
puzzle	over	We *puzzled over* the mystery.
riffle	through	The thief *riffled through* all our suitcases.
talk	to	They *talked to* the president of the company.
tinker	with	We *tinkered with* the engine.

Another test is to see if you can replace the prepositional phrase with the single-word adverb *there*. If this substitution is valid, then the complement is an adverbial of place:

> I stayed *with some friends.*
>   there

Complement Exercise #12: Identifying Preposition Complements _____

Underline the preposition complements twice and their objects once. Confirm your answer by showing that these prepositional phrases fail the adverb movement test. (Answers to this exercise are on page 511.)

0. We went over the instructions.

   Answer: We went over the instructions.

   Confirmation: *Over the instructions we went.

1. We jumped at the chance.

2. The students wondered about the assignment.

3. The whole class participated in the experiment.

4. The drama students posed as their favorite movie stars.

5. She was searching for exactly the right dress.

6. The firm specializes in solid-waste disposal.

7. The kitten stared at the barking dogs.

8. I'm studying for a big test.

9. They take after their mother.

10. People are always messing with my stuff.

The preposition + noun phrase complement type has another characteristic that distinguishes it from verbs followed by adverb prepositional phrases. In many ways, the preposition in the preposition + noun phrase complement is compounded with the verb to form a transitive verb. The noun phrase part of the complement then becomes a direct object of the verb compound. Here is an example:

> The whole company relied *on   Mary's advice.*
>   Prep   NP

Suppose now that we reanalyze this sentence and attach the preposition *on* to the verb *rely* to form the verb compound *rely on:*

The whole company *relied on Mary's advice.*
$\qquad\qquad\qquad\quad$ Verb $\qquad\qquad$ NP

If *Mary's advice* actually is the object of a transitive verb, there should be a valid passive sentence in which *Mary's advice* is the subject, as there is:

Passive: *Mary's advice* was relied on by the whole company.

In a large number of cases, the function of the preposition in this complement type is to change an intransitive verb into a transitive one. Here is an example using the verb *lie,* "to tell a falsehood." When the verb *lie* is used by itself, it is always intransitive:

Senator Fogg is lying.

However, we can change *lie* into a transitive verb by compounding it with a prepositions *about* or *to* and turning the object of the preposition into the object of the verb compounds *lie about* and *lie to.* The proof of this analysis is the fact that the noun phrase that follows the compound verb can be made into the subject of the corresponding passive sentence:

Active: Senator Fogg lied about *the appropriation.*
Passive: *The appropriation* was lied about by Senator Fogg.

Active: Senator Fogg lied to *the committee.*
Passive: *The committee* was lied to by Senator Fogg.

Complement Exercise #13: Identifying Prep + NP complements ⸻

Underline and label the Prep + NP complements. Confirm your answer by turning the sentence into the corresponding passive. Sometimes the answer will sound better if you leave the *by* phrase off. (Answers to this exercise are on page 512.)

  0. They argued against the proposal.

     Answer: They argued <u>against</u> <u>the proposal</u>.
                        Prep   NP

     Confirmation: The proposal was argued against (by them).

  1. We disagreed with their answer.

  2. You can count on me.

  3. He looked for the answer.

  4. Sue hinted at the problem.

5. The mechanic checked on the battery.

6. The accountant went over the books.

7. Sam looked at the proposal.

8. Everyone knew about the problems.

9. The receiver locked onto the transmitter.

10. Our investigators will look into the situation.

"Separable" and "Inseparable" Phrasal Verbs.   Books about teaching English as a second or foreign language often use the terms "separable" and "inseparable" to describe adverb + NP complements and preposition + NP complements, respectively. These two complement types are very similar: (1) they are both verb compounds with unpredictable meanings, and (2) both verb compounds create what amount to transitive verbs followed by objects. For example, compare the following sentences:

Adverb + NP:	The prince turned *down* *the king.*
turned down	Adv NP
= "rejected"	

Prep + NP:	The prince turned *against* *the king.*
turned against	Prep NP
= "became an enemy of"	

Both sentences have passive counterparts, showing that *king* is an object of a transitive verb in both sentences, since only the objects of transitive verbs can become the subjects of passive sentences:

Adverb + NP:	The *king* was turned down by the prince.
Prep + NP:	The *king* was turned against by the prince.

Up to this point, the two complement types seem completely alike. However, there is one key difference: the adverb can be moved after the object, but the preposition cannot:

"separable" Adverb + NP:	The prince turned the king *down.*
"inseparable" Prep + NP:	*The prince turned the king *against.*

The problem that non-native speakers of English face is that they have no simple way of telling which phrasal verb compounds are "separable" and which are "inseparable." This is not a trivial matter, since there are many hundreds of each of these compounds.

The solution (such as it is) to telling the two structures apart lies not in the verb part of the compound, because many verbs (like *turn*) can form both separable compounds with adverbs and inseparable compounds with prepositions. Instead, the difference between the two types is in the second part of the compound—the words that are used as adverbs or prepositions.

It turns out that there are only twelve words that are commonly used as adverbs in "separable" compounds. Ten of these words are normally used ONLY as adverbs. That is, the following ten words are predictably used as "separable" adverbs:

Ten "Separable" Adverbs

apart	off
around	out
away	over
back	together
down	up

One solution, then, is simply to memorize this list. If a verb forms a compound with one of these words, the compound is almost certainly "separable."

The remaining two adverbs that form "separable" compounds have corresponding preposition forms: *in* and *on*. These two words can be used as adverbs in "separable" compounds and prepositions in "inseparable" compounds:

"separable"

John *turned in* his paper.

John *turned* his paper *in*.

We *turned on* the TV.

We *turned* the TV *on*.

"inseparable"

They *engaged in* conversation.

*They *engaged* conversation *in*.

We *called on* some friends.

*We *called* some friends *on*.

Complement Exercise #14: Distinguishing "Separable" and "Inseparable" Phrasal Verbs _____

Underline and label the phrasal verb compounds as "separable" and "inseparable," using the list of ten "separable" adverbs as your guide. Confirm your answer by moving the second element in the compound. The first question is done as an example. (Answers to this exercise are on page 513.)

0. The coach stalled for time.

Answer: The coach <u>stalled for</u> time.
         inseparable

Confirmation: *The coach stalled time for.

1. The coach used up all their time-outs.

2. I defer to your opinion.

3. Portia just got by the bar exam.

4. All the king's men put together Humpty Dumpty again.

5. Naturally, we jumped at the offer.

6. Keep up the good work.

7. I think that they lied about the accident.

8. They are living beyond their means.

9. Can I make up the test?

10. I was looking for my keys.

(15) Noun Phrase + Prep + Noun Phrase.   Some phrasal verbs have a three-part complement: a noun phrase object + a particular preposition + the object of that preposition. Here are two examples:

We talked *Ralph* *into* *it.*
          NP   prep NP

We talked *Ralph* *out of* *it.*
          NP   prep   NP

Talk can be used as an intransitive verb (*We talked all night*), but it cannot be used as an ordinary transitive verb without adding an additional prepositional phrase beginning with either *into* or *out of.*

Table 7.4 gives some examples that illustrate the variety of specific prepositional phrases that can be used in this three-part complement type.

The evidence that the prepositional phrase is part of the complement and not an optional adverb is that it fails both the adverb question test and the adverb movement test:

Adverb question: ***Where (when, how, why)** did we talk Ralph?
Adverb answer: **Into it.*
Adverb movement: **Into it* we talked Ralph.

TABLE 7.4 *Noun Phrase + Prep + Noun Phrase Examples*

Verb	NP	Prep	NP	Example
ask	NP	about	NP	We asked *the clerk about our order.* NP Prep NP
stack	NP	against	NP	They stacked *the odds against us.* NP Prep NP
thank	NP	for	NP	We thanked *them for their support.* NP Prep NP
take	NP	from	NP	He removed *the dishes from the table.* NP Prep NP
engage	NP	in	NP	We engaged *them in a lengthy debate.* NP Prep NP
talk	NP	into	NP	They talked *us into the plan.* NP Prep NP
deprive	NP	of	NP	The robbery deprived *us of our livelihood.* NP Prep NP
blame	NP	on	NP	You always blame *it on me.* NP Prep NP
leak	NP	to	NP	We leaked *the information to the press.* NP Prep NP
provide	NP	with	NP	Our garden provides *us with plenty of lettuce.* NP Prep NP

Complement Exercise #15: Identifying NP + Prep + NP Complements

Underline and label the NP + Prep + NP complements. Confirm your answer by showing that the adverb movement test fails with the prepositional phrase. (Answers to this exercise are on page 513.)

0. The police asked John about the accident.

    Answer: The police asked <u>John</u> <u>about</u> <u>the accident</u>.
                               NP   Prep   NP

    Confirmation: *About the accident, the police asked John.

1. John lodged a complaint against his noisy neighbors.

2. The play portrayed Elizabeth as a tough-minded politician.

3. Ralph got himself into a lot of trouble.

4. We talked them out of their original plan.

5. His help got me out of a bad situation.

6. Holmes took Watson as a bit of a simpleton.

7. The librarian supplied us with the necessary information.

8. The fairy godmother turned the pumpkin into a coach.

9. He asked me for a favor.

10. The recipe substituted yogurt for sour cream.

Review of Complements of Phrasal Verbs.   We have identified the following complements:

(12) Adverb

John gave *up*   (*give up* = "surrender")
                   Adv

(13) Adverb + noun phrase (separable phrasal verb)

John turned *down*   *the offer.*   (*turn down* = "reject")
               Adv   NP

(14) Preposition + noun phrase (inseparable phrasal verb)

The class went *over*   *the notes*   (*go over* = "review")
                  Prep   NP

(15) Noun phrase + preposition + noun phrase

They talked *us*   *into*   *the plan.*   (*talk someone into* = "persuade
              NP   prep   NP   someone to accept something")

Complement Exercise #16: Review of Complements of Phrasal Verbs _____

Underline the complements of phrasal. Identify the complement type using the names given above. (Answers to this exercise are on page 514.)

0. Bugsy took over the business.

   Answer: Bugsy took <u>over the business</u>.
                        Adv   NP

1. Talk to me!

2. The plane took off.

3. Ruth takes after her mother's side of the family.

4. I have thought over your proposal.

5. The police have closed the highway to traffic.

6. The store is out of computer ribbons.

7. The hounds ran down the fox.

8. The wizard turned the prince into a frog.

   9. They ran down the opposition.

  10. The knight was searching for the princess.

  11. They set aside their differences.

  12. Senator Fogg was working against the bill.

  13. She put across her ideas very effectively.

  14. We participated in the review session.

  15. The senate limited debate to five hours.

  16. We were living beyond our means.

  17. Put up your hands!

  18. We went over the problem.

  19. We just dropped by.

  20. Brush up your Shakespeare!

Chapter Review

In this chapter we have identified and discussed fifteen types of verb complements. The list of complements is much larger than in traditional grammar
because we have used a broader definition of what counts as a complement.
In traditional grammar, only nouns/pronouns and predicate adjectives are considered to be complements. In modern grammar, adverbs and prepositional
phrases can be complements too, as long as they meet the definition of a complement: **whatever is required by the verb to make a complete sentence.**
   The main evidence in support of treating adverbs and prepositional
phrases as complements is the following:

   • Positive evidence: If these adverbs or prepositional phrases are
deleted from the sentence, the sentence becomes ungrammatical in its original meaning—exactly what one would expect with complements.

   • Negative evidence: If the adverbs and prepositional phrases were not
complements, then they would be adverb modifiers and should thus meet the
standard tests for adverb modifiers—the adverb question test and the adverb movement test. However, these adverbs and prepositional phrases fail
the tests, showing that they are not modifying adverbs.

We have divided the complements into three categories: verbs that have no
more than one complement, verbs that have multiple complements, and
phrasal verbs. The last category, phrasal verbs, is worthy of special notice both
because they are very numerous and because they were largely ignored by
traditional grammar.

Here is a summary of the fifteen complement types with an example of each:

Verbs with No More Than One Complement

(1) No complement

John sneezed.

(2) Noun phrase

John answered *the phone*.

(3) Predicate nominative

Tarzan became *a vegetarian*.

(4) Predicate adjective

That tasted *terrible*.

(5) Adverbial of place

He is *in the building*.

Verbs with Multiple Complements

(6) Noun phrase + noun phrase

We gave *Mary   the prize*.
           NP1   NP2

(7) Noun phrase + object complement

They considered *him   a fool*.
             NP   OC

(8) Noun phrase + predicate adjective

They considered *him   crazy*.
             NP   Pred Adj

(9) Noun phrase + adverbial of place

Felix put *the milk   in the refrigerator*.
         NP   ADVplace

(10) Noun phrase + present participle verb phrase

We heard *Tarzan   singing in the shower*.
        NP   VPpres part

(11) Noun phrase + infinitive verb phrase

We got *him   to ask for a raise*.
    NP   VPinf

Complements of Phrasal Verbs

(12) Adverb

John gave *up*   (*give up* = "surrender")
        Adv

(13) Adverb + noun phrase (separable phrasal verb)

John turned *down*   *the offer.*   (*turn down* = "reject")
          Adv   NP

(14) Preposition + noun phrase (inseparable phrasal verb)

The class went *over*   *the notes*   (*go over* = "review")
            Prep   NP

(15) Noun phrase + preposition + noun phrase

They talked *us*   *into*   *the plan.*   (*talk someone into* = "persuade
          NP   Prep   NP   someone to accept something")

Complement Exercise #17: Review of All Complement Types

Underline all the complements. Identify the complement type using the number and names given above. (Answers to this exercise are on page 515.)

0. I parked my car in Harvard Yard.
    Answer: I parked <u>my car</u> <u>in Harvard Yard</u>.
             #9   NP   ADVplace

1. The movie really grossed out the kids.
2. The pop star dedicated the song to his agent.
3. The remote control is on the coffee table.
4. Henry VII essentially proclaimed himself king.
5. We prayed for rain.
6. Ralph hurt himself playing soccer.
7. We wanted them to apologize.
8. Sally broke off their engagement.
9. She told him about Harry.
10. The wedding seemed very tasteful.
11. I told the children to leave.
12. The Wicked Queen looked into the mirror.
13. The thieves got completely away.
14. The law limits hunters to three ducks.

15. They lied about the situation.

16. We were living beyond our means.

17. I rushed off to pick up the kids.

18. We put aside our differences.

19. Senator Fogg seemed the perfect candidate.

20. His boss exerted real pressure on him.

Complement Exercise #18: Review of All Complement Types

Underline all the complements. Identify the complement type using the number and names given above. (Answers to this exercise are on page 516.)

0. I parked my car in Harvard Yard.

    Answer: I parked <u>my car</u> in <u>Harvard Yard</u>.
         #9   NP   ADVplace

1. The missing test never turned up.

2. Carefully, she put the full coffee cup on the counter.

3. Everybody thought the Wright brothers foolhardy.

4. Everyone responded to the news.

5. Please convey our sympathies to your friend.

6. We felt the building shaking in the wind.

7. Tell him to stop.

8. Senator Fogg withdrew from the race.

9. They never caught on.

10. I cleaned out the refrigerator.

11. I want you to quit now.

12. The union reacted against the company's proposal.

13. It crossed my mind.

14. He is still living at home.

15. She put the baby in the crib.

16. Prince Charming noticed Cinderella looking at her watch.

17. Igor threw up his hands.

18. The jury found Bugsy innocent.

19. The teacher got the students some new books.

20. It rained all night.

II

Usage

Guide to Usage Topics

The following index is an alphabetical listing of usage topics covered in this part. Included in this listing are cross-references to grammar-based discussions of usage topics in the grammar part. Under most topics is a listing of important subtopics. These subtopics are included to enable you to see at a glance what issues are covered under each heading. Topics marked (ESL) are of special importance to students of English as a second or foreign language.

Index of Usage Topics

Apostrophes
    Causes of apostrophe error
    Contraction
    Possession
        Teaching the possessive apostrophe
        Subjects of gerunds
        It's and *its*
        "Possessive" apostrophes for time expressions

Articles (ESL)
    Articles with mass and count nouns
    Indefinite articles with new information
    Definite articles with already known information
    Generalizations with no articles

Comma Splices
   See Run-on sentences

Commas and Appositives
   Commas with appositives
   Essential appositives without commas

Commas and Adjective Clauses
   See Chapter 6, page 221

Commas and Coordinate Adjectives
   Five classes of descriptive adjectives

Commas and Coordinating Conjunctions
   FANBOYS
   Commas with two independent clauses
   No commas with parallel predicates or complements

Commas and Introductory Elements
   Commas with introductory elements
   No commas with inverted sentences

Conjunctive Adverbs
   See Chapter 6, page 237

Dangling Modifiers
   Dangling participial phrases
   Dangling reduced adverb clauses

Fragments
   Causes of fragments

Fused Sentences
   See Run-on sentences

Participles Used as Adjectives (ESL)
   Present participles
   Past participles

Progressive Usage (ESL)
   Stative verbs

Pronoun Errors: **I/me; we/us; he/him; she/her; they/them**
   Pronoun errors in noun compounds

Pronoun Errors: **who** *and* **whom**
  Who and *whom* for people
  Who for subjects
  Whom for objects

Run-On Sentences
  Causes of run-on sentences

Subject–Verb Agreement
  Causes of subject–verb agreement errors
  Wrong subject number
  Misidentified subjects
  Subject–verb agreement errors in existential sentences

Usage Topics

Apostrophes

Two common uses of the apostrophe are likely to result in errors:

- Contractions
- Possession (including the confusion of *it's* and *its,* and possessives used as the subjects of gerunds)

Contractions.   We use apostrophes in contractions to imitate shortened pronunciations of words. For this reason, contractions convey a somewhat informal tone to writing. Many beginning writers overuse contractions because they are more comfortable with the sound of spoken language than they are with the look of formal written language.

In written language, missing letters in a contraction are signaled by an apostrophe, a convention that goes back to sign painting in the Middle Ages. The most common error in using contractions is omitting the apostrophe, for example,

  *cant   *lets   *doesnt   *wont

A less common error is putting the apostrophe in the wrong place, for example,

  *do'nt   *did'nt.

Notice that in these typical examples of misplaced apostrophes, the apostrophe has been placed between the verb and the negative suffix. It is as though the writer is using the apostrophe to separate word elements—the verb from the suffix. A possible explanation for this error may be based on the writer's misanalysis of the contraction *can't,* which looks superficially as though the apostrophe is separating *can* from the negative suffix.

The best way to see if an apostrophe is needed in a contraction is to expand the contraction.

The expansion test. If you can expand a contracted word to a full word by adding one or more letters, then an apostrophe can be used to indicate where the missing letters came from.

Here is the expansion test applied to the first three examples of contractions with omitted apostrophes:

	*cant
Test:	can *not* = can't
	*lets
Test:	let *us* = let's
	*doesnt
Test:	does *not* = doesn't

The one contraction the expansion test cannot be used with is *won't.* The test fails for historical reasons: the positive *will* came from one dialect in Middle English and the negative *won't* is from a different dialect, so the two forms are not directly related to each other.

Here is the expansion test applied to the two examples of contractions with misplaced apostrophes:

	*do'nt
Test:	do *not*
	*did'nt
Test:	did *not*

The apostrophes do not mark the place of the missing letters, so the apostrophes are placed incorrectly.

Apostrophe Exercise #1: Placing Apostrophes in Contractions

Underline all of the contracted words and insert the missing apostrophes. Confirm your answers by applying the expansion test. The first question is done as an example. (Answers to this exercise are on page 517.)

0. That isnt my idea of a good time.

    Answer: That isn't my idea of a good time

    Confirmation: isn't = is not

1. I wouldnt do that if I were you.

2. Didnt you get my message?

3. Lets do it!

4. Havent we met before?

5. I cant imagine why.

6. Dont do it unless you have to.

7. Im not able to go.

8. Arent you ready yet?

9. I wasnt watching.

10. They werent any friends of ours.

Possession.   The use of the apostrophe to indicate possession is a historical quirk. In the seventeenth century the possessive *s* in a phrase like

> Johns book

was thought to be a contraction of *his,* so that the full phrase was believed to be

> John, his book

Accordingly, the apostrophe was used to show the contraction of *his:*

> John's book = John *hi*s book

In fact, this is completely wrong. Historically, the possessive *s* has absolutely nothing to do with the contraction of *his.*

The use of an apostrophe after the *s* to indicate the possessive of a plural noun as in *the actors' costumes* came about much later—in fact, it was not fully standard until the early 1900s.

*Teaching
Tip*

Don't teach *s'* as the "plural possessive" because students will spell the plural possessive of irregular nouns such as *man* and *child* as **mens'* and *childrens'* rather than the correct *men's* and *children's.*

Teaching the Possessive Apostrophe.   The best way to teach the possessive apostrophe is by the following table showing the three different uses of the s inflectional suffix (or, equivalently, the use of three different inflections, all of which happen to be s):

's	"possessive"
s	"plural"
s'	"both plural AND possessive"

Here is this table applied to regular nouns:

Singular	Sg poss	Plural	Pl poss
dog	dog's	dogs	dogs'
cat	cat's	cats	cats'
horse	horse's	horses	horses'
girl	girl's	girls	girls'
boy	boy's	boys	boys'
spy	spy's	spies	spies'

In the last column, the s' signals that the noun is both possessive AND plural. (By the way, notice that in the last example of *spy*, the use of apostrophes is completely regular despite the spelling convention of changing y to i and adding *es*.)

Teaching Tip

A good way to teach s' is to have students think of it as representing two s's: the possessive s and the plural s written together.

The real advantage of the table is with irregular nouns that form their plural by means of a vowel change, for example:

Singular	Sg poss	Plural	Pl poss
man	man's	men	men's
woman	woman's	women	women's
child	child's	children	children's

In the final column, the 's signals that the word it attaches to is possessive. What makes the noun plural is the vowel change, not the added s, which has ONLY the function of showing that the noun is possessive.

Apostrophe Exercise #2: Possessives and Plurals _____

Fill out the missing forms in the following table. The first question is done as an example. (Answers to this exercise are on page 518.)

	Singular	Sg poss	Plural	Pl poss
0.	senator	senator's	senators	senators'
1.	cow			
2.	girl			
3.	mouse			
4.	wife			
5.	farmer			
6.	niece			
7.	nephew			
8.	goose			
9.	aunt			
10.	ox			

The real problem with using the possessive apostrophe is knowing when a word is possessive. There are two quite reliable tests for identifying possessive nouns: substituting a possessive personal pronoun and asking a *whose* question.

The possessive pronoun test. If you can replace a noun (and its modifiers) with any of the possessive personal pronouns *his, her, its, their,* then that noun is possessive and requires the appropriate possessive apostrophe.

Here are some examples of the possessive pronoun test:

	The childrens school gets out early today.
Test:	Their
Correction:	*The children's* school gets out early today.
	My best friends sister is going to West Point.
Test:	His/Her
Correction:	*My best friend's* sister is going to West Point.
	The council reviewed *the partys* position.
Test:	its
Correction:	The council reviewed *the party's* position.

Apostrophe Exercise #3: Identifying Possessives by the Possessive Pronoun Test

Underline the possessive nouns and insert the missing possessive apostrophes. (Assume that the possessive nouns are singular unless the context clearly indicates that they are plural.) Confirm your answers by applying the possessive pronoun test. The first question is done as an example. (Answers to this exercise are on page 518.)

0. The ball bounced off a defenders head.

   Answer: The ball bounced off a <u>defender's</u> head.

   Confirmation: <u>a defender's</u> head
                 his/her

1. The children played the queens helpers.

2. It's something that happens in every childs life.

3. The coach measured each players height and weight.

4. They appealed the judges ruling.

5. We had to memorize the bodys major muscles.

6. The program calculated all the planets orbits.

7. The candidates press release ignored the issue.

8. The exam covered the entire courses content.

9. I found them in my grandmothers basement.

10. The ships anchor began to drag in the heavy wind.

The second test takes advantage of the fact that only a possessive noun or pronoun can answer a question beginning with *whose*.

The *whose* test. Any noun that answers a *whose* question is possessive and requires a possessive apostrophe.

Here are some examples of the *whose* test:

	The childrens school gets out early today.
Test:	WHOSE school gets out early today?
Correction:	*The children's* school.
	My best friends sister is going to West Point.
Test:	WHOSE sister is going to West Point?
Correction:	*My best friend's* sister.
	The council reviewed *the partys* position.
Test:	The council reviewed WHOSE position?
Correction:	*The party's* position.

Apostrophe Exercise #4: Identifying Possessives by the **whose** Test _____

Underline the possessive nouns and insert the missing possessive apostrophes. (Assume that the possessive nouns are singular unless the context clearly indicates that they are plural.) Confirm your answers by applying the *whose* test. The first question is done as an example. (Answers to this exercise are on page 519.)

0. We decided that it was Johns turn.

   Answer: We decided that it was John's turn.

   Confirmation: Whose turn? John's turn.

1. The court ordered the suspects release.

2. The babys blanket is in the dryer.

3. The teams goal was the first for the season.

4. I hated being called the teachers pet.

5. Newarks airport is now the busiest in the New York area.

6. We picked up Philips toys.

7. I ignored the tooth fairys warning.

8. They doubted the economists dire predictions.

9. The referees whistle stopped the action.

10. A plumbers snake is a flexible metal tool.

One of the limitations of the *whose* test is that sometimes it seems awkward to use *whose* in reference to inanimate objects, for example:

	The cars trunk wouldn't close.
whose test:	?WHOSE trunk wouldn't close?
	The car's trunk.

With inanimate objects, the possessive pronoun test gives better results.

Subjects of Gerunds.   A **gerund** is the *-ing* form of a verb (the present participle) used as a noun. If the verb retains its underlying noun or pronoun subject, that subject must be in its possessive form. (See the discussions of gerunds and subjects of gerunds beginning on page 177.) Here are two examples of subjects of gerunds with the subject in bold and the gerund in italics:

Fred's *getting* upset made us uncomfortable.

We were delayed by my **uncle's** *having* a flat tire.

Despite the complexity of this construction, the gerund acts like a normal noun and the subject of the gerund like a normal possessive modifier. Thus we can use the possessive pronoun and *whose* tests:

	Fred's *getting* upset made us uncomfortable.
Poss test:	*His* getting upset made us uncomfortable.
whose test:	WHOSE getting upset made us uncomfortable? Fred's getting upset.

	We were delayed by my **uncle's** *having* a flat tire.
Poss test:	We were delayed by *his* having a flat tire.
whose test:	We were delayed by WHOSE having a flat tire? My uncle's having a flat tire.

Apostrophe Exercise #5: Identifying Subjects of Gerunds _____

Underline the subjects of gerunds and insert the missing possessive apostrophes. (Assume that the possessive nouns are singular unless the context clearly indicates that they are plural.) Confirm your answers by applying either the possessive pronoun or *whose* test. The first question is done as an example. (Answers to this exercise are on page 520.)

0. Wilbur hated Orvilles flying all those kites.

   Answer: Wilbur hated <u>Orville's</u> flying all those kites.

   Confirmation: Wilbur hated <u>his</u> flying all those kites.

1. The schools offering soccer is something new.

2. The parrots knowing classical Greek was a surprise.

3. We hadn't expected the companys agreeing to the offer.

4. The lights coming through the open window woke us up.

5. We never got used to the restaurants being open so late.

6. Lincolns walking miles to return two pennies is probably a myth.

7. The brokers recommending the stock made a difference.

8. We encouraged the childrens participating in sports.

9. Aunt Beas selling her car turned out to be a mistake.

10. The councils approving the motion was a foregone conclusion.

It's and Its. Undoubtedly the single most common error involving apostrophes is the confusion of *it's* (the contraction of *it is*) and *its* (the possessive form of *it*). Not only do the two constructions sound exactly alike, the apostrophe in the *it's* contraction is easily confused with a possessive because an apostrophe with a noun signals possession. Of course, *it* is a personal pronoun, and like all personal pronouns, there is no apostrophe in the possessive form:

Subject	Object	Possessive
I	me	my
you	you	your
he	him	his
it	it	**its**
she	her	her
we	us	our
they	them	their

*Teaching
Tip*

Remind students that the *s* in the possessive pronoun *its* is not set off with an apostrophe, just as the *s* in *his book* is not set off with an apostrophe: **hi's book.*

The best test for distinguishing *it's* and *its* is to apply the expansion test. The test will work with the contraction *it's* and fail with the possessive *its.* If the expansion test succeeds, then *it's* is correct. If the expansion test fails, then *its* is correct.

	Its raining.
Test:	*It is* raining. *It is* is grammatical.
Correction:	It's raining.
	The dog knew it's name.
Test:	*The dog knew *it is* name. *It is* is not grammatical.
Correction:	The dog knew its name.

Apostrophe Exercise #6: Distinguishing it's and its by the Expansion Test

Underline all uses of *it's* and *its* and make the necessary corrections. Confirm your answers by applying the expansion test. The first question is done as an example. (Answers to this exercise are on page 520.)

0. The country gets most of it's energy from oil.

   Answer: The country gets most of its energy from oil.

   Confirmation: *The country gets most of it is energy from oil.

1. I think its up to you.

2. The bank closed its drive-in window.

3. I think its too cold to eat outside.

4. The movie had its moments.

5. We planted a tree, and now its blooming.

6. The ice cream is so cold that its giving me a headache.

7. Its about dinner time.

8. A store's reputation is only as good as its employees.

9. The cat refused to eat its food.

10. Its an ill wind that blows no good.

"Possessive" Apostrophes for Time Expressions.   One might think that "possessive" apostrophes are always used to show possession. Actually, there is another common use of the so-called possessive apostrophe—in expressions of time. The reason for this confusing state of affairs is historical. In Old English, the *s* inflectional suffix had two basic uses: (1) to show possession, and (2) to express time. Both of these uses survive in Modern English. We have seen many examples of the inflectional *s* used to show possession. Here are some examples using *s* to express time:

> *Today's* world is very demanding.
>
> It cost *two weeks'* wages.

These words with apostrophes are not possessive: *today* does not own or possess the *world*, and *two weeks* do not own or possess *wages*. Since they are not possessive, they tend to fail the possessive pronoun test and the *whose* test:

	Today's world is very demanding.
Possessive pronoun:	**Its* world is very demanding.
Whose question:	Whose world is very demanding?
	*Today's world.

	It cost *two weeks'* wages
Possessive pronoun:	**It cost their* wages.
Whose test:	It cost WHOSE wages?
	*Two weeks' wages.

Fortunately, there is another test that works with these expressions of time.

> **The *of* paraphrase test.** Any time expression that can be paraphrased using *of* requires an apostrophe.

Here are some examples of the *of* paraphrase test:

	Todays world is very demanding.
Test:	*The world of today is very demanding.*
Correction:	Today's world is very demanding.

	It cost two *weeks* wages.
Test:	It cost *the wages of two weeks.*
Correction:	It cost two *weeks'* wages.

Apostrophe Exercise #7: Identifying Time Expressions Requiring Apostrophes by the of *Paraphrase* _____

Underline time expressions requiring apostrophes and make corrections. Confirm your answers by applying the *of* paraphrase test. The first question is done as an example. (Answers to this exercise are on page 521.)

0. I got todays newspaper.

Answer: I got today's newspaper.

Confirmation: I got the newspaper of today.

1. It is a problem in todays fast-paced society.

2. I've got ten days vacation coming to me.

3. They are debating this years budget.

4. That's tomorrows problem.

5. That's a whole weeks work.

6. A days wages back then was only about a dollar.

7. I can't do it on a minutes notice.

8. I got the minutes of last weeks board meeting.

9. Todays lesson is from St. Paul.

10. It is this centurys first major crisis.

The *of* paraphrase test can be used with purely possessive apostrophes with somewhat mixed success. Sometimes it works very well, for example,

	She is my sister's best friend.
of test:	She is *the best friend of* my sister.

Sometimes, however, the *of* paraphrase sounds like a bad translation from an elementary French grammar book:

	That is my aunt's pen.
of test:	That is *the pen of* my aunt.

Fred's book is on the desk.

of test: *The book **of** Fred is on the desk.*

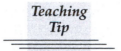

*Teaching
Tip*

There is a kind of hierarchy to apostrophe errors. Typically, the first apostrophe that beginning writers learn to use correctly is the apostrophe for contraction. Then they learn to use possessive apostrophes correctly. Finally, writers gain control of apostrophes used with time expressions.

Review of Apostrophies.
Contractions.   The most common contraction error is omitting the apostrophe with contractions.

> **Expansion test.** Expand a contraction to the full, uncontracted form. Use an apostrophe to mark the place where the letters were added.

> Example: I dont know the answer.
> Expansion test: I *do not* know the answer. do not = don't.

Possessive.   In teaching the forms of the possessive apostrophe, use the following table:

> 's   "possessive"
> s   "plural"
> s'   "both plural AND possessive"

The key is to teach *s'* as being both plural AND possessive. Teaching *s'* this way avoids problems with the plural possessive of irregular nouns.

The biggest problem writers have with possessive apostrophes is not recognizing when nouns are possessive. Here are two tests that will help them.

> **Possessive pronoun test.** If a noun can be replaced by a possessive pronoun, then that noun requires a possessive apostrophe.

> Example: *The books* index is very helpful.
> Possessive pronoun: *Its* index is very helpful.
> Correction: *The book's* index is very helpful.

> **Whose test.** Only a possessive noun can answer a *whose* question.

Example: *The dollars* value was increasing.
whose test: WHOSE value was increasing?
Correction: *The dollar's* value.

Both the possessive pronoun test and the *whose* test help identify the subjects of gerunds.

Example: We appreciated *Freds* returning the car.
Possessive pronoun: We appreciated **his** returning the car.
Correction: We appreciated *Fred's* returning the car.

Example: *The tooth fairys* leaving an IOU was bad news.
whose test: WHOSE leaving an IOU was bad news?
Correction: *The tooth fairy's* leaving an IOU.

Confusing It's and Its.   The expansion test is a good way to tell *it's* (the contraction of *it is*) and the possessive pronoun *its* apart. If the expansion test is grammatical, use *it's*; if the expansion test is ungrammatical, use *its*.

Example: *Its* OK with me.
Expansion: *It is* OK with me.
Correction: *It's* OK with me.

Example: The building changed *its* address.
Expansion: *The building changed *it is* address.
Correction: The building changed *its* address.

"Possessive" Apostrophe for Time Expressions.   Apostrophes are also used with time expressions. The possessive pronoun and *whose* tests do not work very well for time expressions, since they are not possessive.

The *of* paraphrase test. If a time expression can be paraphrased using *of*, the expression requires an apostrophe.

Example: Everybody is so busy in *todays* society.
of paraphrase: Everybody is so busy in *the society of* today.
Correction: Everybody is so busy in *today's* society.

The *of* paraphrase often can be used to identify possessive apostrophes.

Apostrophe Exercise #8: Review _____

Underline and correct all apostrophe errors. Confirm your answers by applying an appropriate test. The first question is done as an example. (Answers to this exercise are on page 521.)

0. Everyone admires Miss Piggys sunny disposition.
    Answer: Everyone admires <u>Miss Piggy's</u> sunny disposition.
    Confirmation: Everyone admires <u>her</u> sunny disposition.

1. Its a valuable Swiss watch.

2. Did you get todays menu?

3. He doesnt understand the question.

4. The computers keyboard needed cleaning.

5. Dracula replaced the coffins lid.

6. I appreciated the clerks returning my call so quickly.

7. Somebodys car was stuck in the ditch.

8. The hawk returned to it's roost.

9. We could hear the churches bells.

10. I didnt catch what she said.

11. The stores specials were not very impressive.

12. Obviously, the bird had lost it's way in the fog.

13. I was worried about the childrens getting too much sun.

14. After an hours delay, the umpire postponed the game.

15. Youre missing the point.

16. We ordered the chefs special for dinner.

17. The voters rejecting the bond issue was a disappointment.

18. Its always fair weather when good fellows get together.

19. A years delay will cost the company a fortune.

20. We had to postpone the authors reception.

Articles (ESL)

One of the most difficult areas of English for non-native speakers is the use
of articles. Two types of articles are used to modify **common nouns** (**proper
nouns** are rarely modified by articles).

- **Definite:** *the*
- **Indefinite:** *a/an* with singular nouns, and *some,* which functions as an
  indefinite article for plural **count nouns** and all **mass nouns.** (These and
  other technical terms are explained below.)

The choice among these articles—and the option of using no article at all—
is determined by three questions about the noun being modified by the article:

1. Is the noun a mass noun or count noun? If it is a count noun, is it singular or plural?

2. Does the noun give new information, or is the information already known?

3. Is the noun being used to make a generalization?

We will examine each of these three questions in turn.

Mass and Count Nouns.   Our first question about articles is

1. Is the noun a mass noun or count noun? If it is a count noun, is it
singular or plural?

The term **mass noun** (or **noncount noun**) refers to a category of nouns that have the following limitations:

- They cannot be used in the plural.
- They cannot be counted with number words.
- They cannot be used with the articles *a/an*.

Most nouns, of course, do not have these limitations. These unrestricted nouns are called **count nouns,** to distinguish them from mass nouns.

To illustrate the three limitations of mass nouns, we will use the pair of words *assignment* (count) and *homework* (mass). In each case the count noun is grammatical and the mass noun is ungrammatical:

(Plural)
Count: The *assignments* are due on Monday.
Mass: *The *homeworks* are due on Monday.

(Counted with Number Words)
Count: Three *assignments* are due on Monday.
Mass: * Three *homeworks* are due on Monday.

(a/an)
Count: An *assignment* is due on Monday.
Mass: * A *homework* is due on Monday.

(The prohibition of using *a/an* with mass nouns is actually a consequence of the prohibition against number words. Historically, the articles *a/an* are both derived from the number word *one*.)

The pair *assignment/homework* illustrates the enormous difficulty that non-native speakers have in determining which nouns are count nouns and which are mass nouns. The terms *assignment* and *homework* seem so much alike. However, as we will see below, there are some generalizations we can use to predict which nouns are mass nouns.

Mass nouns are typically used to refer to entire categories of things, while count nouns refer to specific instances. For example, the mass noun *homework* is a broader category than the count noun *assignment*. An *assignment* is one type of *homework*.

Here is another pair of words that illustrates the difference between count and mass nouns: *suitcase* (count) and *luggage* (mass).

(Plural)
Count: The *suitcases* are in the hall.
Mass: *The *luggages* are in the hall.

(Counted with Number Words)
Count: Three *suitcases* are in the hall.
Mass: *Three *luggages* are in the hall.

(a/an)
Count: A *suitcase* is in the hall.
Mass: *A *luggage* is in the hall.

Again, there is a predictable difference in meaning. The mass noun *luggage* is a kind of abstraction that refers to an entire category—objects used for carrying personal belongings, including backpacks, duffel bags, brief cases etc. The count noun *suitcase* refers to one particular kind of carrying device.

Some nouns can be used either way but with substantial shifts in meaning, for example, *beer*. As a mass noun, *beer* refers to the category of fermented malt beverages. As a count noun, a *beer* refers to a single can or bottle of beer.

(Plural)
Count: The *beers* in refrigerator are cold.
Mass: *Beer* can be pretty fattening.

(Counted with Number Words)
Count: There are three *beers* in the refrigerator.
Mass: There is *beer* in the refrigerator.

(a/an)
Count: Would you like a *beer*?
Mass: Do you drink *beer*?

> **The abstract category test.** If a noun is used to describe an entire abstract category of things, then it may be a mass noun.

Here is the abstract category test applied to the related nouns *experimentation* and *experiment* in the following sentence:

> *Experimentation* without an appropriate way to evaluate the result of the *experiment* is meaningless science.

In this sentence, *experimentation* is a mass noun that refers to the entire category of research. *Experiment* is a count noun that refers to an actual single activity. Native speakers of English can confirm this analysis by attempting to pluralize the two words. We can pluralize the count noun *experiment, but* not the mass noun *experimentation:*

> **Experimentations* without an appropriate way to evaluate the result of the *experiments* are meaningless science.

Non-native speakers, of course, do not have access to the language intuitions of the native speaker. They know that mass nouns cannot be pluralized, but they can only make educated guesses as to which nouns are mass and which are count.

Article Exercise #1: Identifying Mass Nouns by the Abstract Category Test _____

Each sentence contains one mass noun incorrectly used as a count noun. Underline the mass noun and make the necessary changes. Confirm your answers by briefly explaining the meaning of the mass noun. The first question is done as an example. (Answers to this exercise are on page 522.)

0. The dresses were made of silks.
   Answer: The dresses were made of silk.
   Confirmation: *Silk* is a mass noun that describes a category of fabric.

1. New roads mean increased traffics.

2. Russia has vast reserves of oils.

3. There was nothing but junks in the attic.

4. Carbon dioxides may contribute to global warming.

5. I learned the importance of relaxations in PE class.

6. Everyone knows that smokings are bad for your health.

7. Poor techniques affect the reliabilities of research findings.

8. The accidents caused a great deal of confusions.

9. After what happened, his distrusts were quite understandable.

10. He has been doing a lot of walkings to reduce his blood pressure.

Although it is difficult to predict which nouns are mass nouns, the majority of mass nouns do occur in relatively well-defined categories based on their meaning. Here are the major categories with some representative examples:

Mass Noun Categories
Abstractions: *faith, hope, charity, beauty, luck, knowledge . . .*
Natural phenomena: *gravity, electricity, space, matter . . .*
Weather terms: *weather, fog, rain, snow, pollution, thunder . . .*
Gerunds (-*ing* verb forms used as nouns): *smiling, wishing . . .*
Academic fields: *anthropology, chemistry, physics . . .*
Languages: *English, Chinese, Spanish, Russian . . .*
Food: *bread, butter, cheese, meat, jam, beef . . .*
Liquids and gases: *water, coffee, tea, air, oxygen . . .*
Materials: *gold, silver, wool, wood, cement, glass . . .*
Sports and games: *tennis, bridge, soccer, baseball . . .*

Article Exercise #2: Identifying Mass Nouns by Category

Underline the incorrectly used mass nouns and make the necessary changes. Confirm your answers by identifying the category of the mass noun from the above list. (Classify any mass noun that does not fit neatly into any of the specific categories as an Abstraction.) The first question is done as an example. (Answers to this exercise are on page 523.)

0. We received new informations.

   Answer: We received new information.

   Confirmation: *Information* is an abstraction.

1. You should eat several servings of fruits each day.

2. The kids love playing basketballs.

3. At the peak of the storm, the sky was filled with lightnings.

4. Would you like another helping of chickens?

5. When we went to Las Vegas, we really had good lucks.

6. The engines were producing excessive smokes.

7. Everything in the house was covered with dusts.

8. The audience reacted with great amusements.

9. The old battery couldn't produce enough energies.

10. I am studying literatures.

Sometimes we can use mass nouns in a plural form, but when we do so, they have a special meaning. Here is an example:

A stationery store may carry a dozen *inks*.

Normally, the mass noun *ink* cannot be made plural, as, for example, in the following sentence:

Darn it! *I got *inks* on my sleeve.

However, in the example about the stationery store, *inks* is plural in form but not in meaning. Instead, *inks* means something like "different kinds of ink." This "different kinds of" meaning is typical of mass nouns. Here are several more examples of mass nouns used in this manner:

We sorted out the *plastics*.

In France, we loved the different *breads*.

We are studying *religions* from around the world.

The distinction between mass and count nouns is critical for determining which type of indefinite article to use. Count nouns use *a/an* in the singular and *some* in the plural. Mass nouns use only *some*. However, the definite article *the* can be used with both count and mass nouns. The following table summarizes the use of articles:

Type of Noun	Definite Article	Indefinite Article
Count—singular	*the*	*a/an*
Count—plural	*the*	*some*
Mass	*the*	*some*

(Note: the indefinite article *some* is unstressed. Do not confuse this unstressed *some* with the emphatically stressed *some* that can be used to modify any kind of noun, including count nouns—for example, *Those were SOME cars!*)

Here are some examples that illustrate the table.

Count Noun—Singular
Definite article: *The* book is on *the* desk.
Indefinite article: *A* book is on *a* desk.

Count Noun—Plural
Definite article: *The* books are on *the* desks.
Indefinite article: *Some* books are on *some* desks.

Mass Noun
Definite article: *The* water in the pitcher is cold.
Indefinite article: I would like *some* water.

Article Exercise #3: Using Indefinite Articles with Count and Mass Nouns

In the underlined spaces, fill in the missing indefinite article and identify the noun being modified as Count-Sg, Count-Pl, or Mass. The first question is done as an example. (Answers to this exercise are on page 524.)

0. _____ teacher offered them _____ good advice.

    Answer: A   teacher offered them <u>some</u> good advice.
              Count-Sg   Mass

1. On _____ trip recently, we encountered _____ bad fog.

2. _____ dogs were chasing _____ squirrel.

3. I would like _____ bread and _____ butter.

4. With _____ luck, we should be there in time for _____ nice dinner.

5. I have _____ class this afternoon.

6. _____ situations are worse than others.

7. We got _____ gas at _____ filling station on the highway.

8. We took _____ friends to _____ soccer game.

9. There was still _____ hot water left in _____ container.

10. She has _____ information about the meeting.

New Information Versus Already Known Information.   Our second question about articles is

> 2. Does the noun give new information, or is the information already known?

What is the difference in meaning between the definite article *the* and the indefinite articles *a/an* and *some?* To get some idea of the difference, compare the following sentences:

    Definite article: I saw *the* truck parked nearby.
    Indefinite article: I saw *a* truck parked nearby.

Using the definite article *the* (*the truck,* in this example) means TWO things, BOTH of which must be true: (1) the writer has a particular truck in mind, and (2) the writer can reasonably assume that the reader knows WHICH truck the writer has in mind. In other words, using the definite article *the* with a noun means that the noun is known, established information.

    Using the indefinite article *a/an* or *some* (*a truck,* in this example) means that the writer knows that the information in the noun is new to the reader.

In this example, the writer assumes that the reader does NOT know ahead of time which truck the writer is talking about.

The choice of definite or indefinite article is thus dictated by assumptions the writer makes about the status of the information conveyed by the noun the article modifies. Simply put, writers follow this rule:

Established information:	Use the definite article (*the*)
New information:	Use the indefinite article (*a/an* or *some*)

What constitutes established information is not so simple. We will give three tests that will help you determine when a noun is established and thus requires the definite article *the*.

> **The previous-mention test.** Use *the* if the noun being modified has been previously mentioned.

The previous-mention test is the most common way of establishing a noun. Here is an example:

I saw *a* truck parked nearby. *The* truck had a flat tire.

Thus, the fundamental pattern of article use is the following:

- First mention of a noun: use *a/an* or *some*.
- All subsequent uses of the same noun: use *the*.

The second test is **the defined by modification test.**

> **The defined by modification test.** Use *the* if the noun is followed by a modifier that uniquely identifies the noun.

Here is an example of the first mention of a noun with the definite article:

I saw *the* truck that your Uncle Henry sold.

The post-noun modifier *that your Uncle Henry sold* uniquely defines which truck the writer is talking about (assuming, of course, that the writer can reasonably assume that the reader knew about Uncle Henry's selling his truck). Thus, the use of the definite article *the* is appropriate. If, in the same example, the writer had used the indefinite article *a*:

I saw *a* truck that your Uncle Henry sold.

the use of the indefinite article *a* would imply that Uncle Henry had sold a number of trucks, so the reader would have no way of knowing which of the trucks had been seen by the writer.

***

The normal expectations test. Use *the* if the noun being modified is identified by normal expectations.

***

The normal expectations test is the hardest of the tests to apply since it is difficult to define in any very precise way what normal expectations are. One kind of normal expectation is for things that are identified because they are unique. Here is an example:

The moon was just rising above *the* horizon.

We already know which moon and which horizon the sentence is about, because they are unique: there is only one moon and only one horizon. However, if you were writing a science fiction novel set on a planet with multiple moons, the following would be a plausible sentence:

A moon was just rising above the horizon.

More commonly, we identify things because we just expect them to be there. Here are some examples:

When I got home, I went into *the* kitchen, opened *the* refrigerator, and took out *a* can of coke.

Why did the writer use *the* with *kitchen* and *refrigerator?* The answer is that we have a normal expectation that houses will have kitchens and that kitchens will have refrigerators. There is no comparable expectation that the refrigerator will have cans of coke in it, so the writer used the indefinite article *a* with *can of coke.*

We use the definite article in some ways that are rather surprising when we think about them, for example:

We went shopping at *the* mall and then stopped at *the* post office to get some stamps.

We seem to have a normal expectation that cities will have malls and post offices. The same is true of many other public facilities:

We went to *the* bank
          the train station
          the airport
          the filling station
          the hospital
          the police station

(In my part of the country, many people have lake cabins. It is common for people talking about a third person, unknown to the listener, to say, "He went to *the* lake," as though it were a normal expectation that people have a lake to go to.)

Article Exercise #4: Using Definite Articles _____

For the underlined definite article, indicate which of the three tests best explains its use. In your answers, use Prev Men for previous mention, Mod for defined by modification, and Norm Exp for normal expectation. For normal expectation, briefly explain your answer. The first question is done as an example. (Answers to this exercise are on page 524.)

0. He went into the office and put a package on   the   desk.

  Answer: Norm Exp
                                               we expect offices to have desks

1. A truck pulled up beside us. Someone in the truck yelled at us.

2. Some of the books on *The New York Times* list of best-selling books have not yet been sold to the public.

3. I got into my car and turned on the radio.

4. We went to a Little League baseball game. The players were not great, but they were fun to watch.

5. I switched on a light and the bulb promptly burned out.

6. My cat nearly caught a bird. The bird barely escaped with its life.

7. I went into a phone booth and picked up the receiver.

8. I found the book that you had recommended.

9. We went to a football game in the new stadium.

10. Most fantasy novels involve a conflict between the forces of good and evil.

11. I have to hang up now; someone is at the door.

12. I had a strange dream last night. In the dream, I was diagramming sentences in Latin.

13. The index in our textbook is pretty helpful.

14. Most small meteors that hit our planet burn up in the atmosphere.

15. Did you see the headphones that I got yesterday?

Generalizations That Use No Articles.   Our third question about articles is

  3. Is the noun being used to make a generalization?

  The normal rule for English is that all common nouns need to be preceded by an article or other pre-noun modifier. There is one major exception.

We use mass nouns and plural count nouns WITHOUT articles or other pre-noun modifiers to signal that we are making a generalization. Here is an example of a mass noun and a plural count noun, each compared with the same noun when it is not being used to make a generalization:

Mass noun: *Cheese* is really salty.
                The *cheese* that I just bought is really salty.

The absence of any article with the mass noun *cheese* in the first example signals that the writer is making a generalization about ALL cheese. The article *the* in the second example tell us that the writer is talking only about some particular bit of cheese—the cheese that the writer just bought.

Plural count noun: *Textbooks* have really gotten to be expensive.
                        The *textbooks* in this course were really expensive.

The absence of any article with the plural count noun *textbooks* in the first example signals that the writer is making a generalization about ALL textbooks. The article *the* in the second example tells us that the writer is talking only about some particular group of textbooks.

How do non-native speakers know when it is appropriate not to use any article? In other words, what are some of the ways native speakers can tell that a sentence is a generalization? There are three tests that will help identify when a generalization is appropriate.

The adverb of frequency test. Nouns used to make generalizations often occur in sentences containing an adverb of frequency, such as *always, often, generally, frequently,* or *usually.*

Here are two examples of **the adverb of frequency test:**

Cats are **always** hanging around the barn.

The use of the adverb of frequency *always* helps us recognize that the plural count noun *cats* is being used to make a generalization. Therefore, omitting the article is appropriate.

We **usually** have *fish* on Fridays.

In the above example, the adverb of frequency *usually* helps us recognize that the mass noun *fish* is being used to make a generalization. Compare that sentence with the following, which does not make a generalization:

The *fish* we had Friday was really great.

> **The present tense test.** Nouns used to make generalizations typically occur in sentences in the present tense.

Here are two examples of **the present tense test:**

Water **seeks** its own level.

The fact that the verb *seeks* in this sentence is in the present tense is compatible with making a generalization, which in turn helps explain why the mass noun *water* is used without an article. Here is a comparable example with a plural count noun:

Goose feathers **make** the best pillows.

> **The no-post-noun modifier test.** Nouns used to make generalizations are rarely followed by post-noun modifiers.

Compare the following sentences using the **no post-noun modifiers test:**

Rain falls mainly on the plain in Spain.

The *rain* in Spain falls mainly on the plain.

In the first sentence, the absence of post-noun modifiers helps us recognize that the mass noun *rain* is being used to make a generalization and thus no article is required. In the second sentence the post-noun modifier *in Spain* means that the sentence is not making a generalization about all rain and that an article is required.

Article Exercise #5: Using Mass and Plural Count Nouns without Articles for Generalizations _____

Underline all nouns used to make generalizations and label them either Mass or Pl Ct. Confirm your answer by applying one or more tests that help identify the sentence as making a generalization. In your answer use Adv Freq for adverb of frequency, Pres for present tense, and No Mod for no post-noun modifier. The first question is done as an example. (Answers to this exercise are on page 525.)

0. It takes a two-thirds majority to override vetos.

   Answer: It takes a two-thirds majority to override <u>vetos</u>.
   Pl Ct

   Confirmation: Pres, No Mod

1. Conflicts are usually easier to start than to stop.

2. Transportation is always hard to arrange.

3. Hardly ever do we eat meat.

4. Ice cream always gives me a headache.

5. Discoveries are often accidental.

6. The discovery has led to controversy.

7. Generally, kitchens recover the cost of remodeling.

8. Coffee contains a lot of caffeine.

9. Tropical diseases are poorly understood. (Treat *tropical diseases* as a compound, i.e., a single word.)

10. Natural gas is formed by the process of decay. (Treat *natural gas* as a compound.)

Review of Articles   In order for non-native speakers to use articles correctly, they need to be aware of three variables that affect the use of articles with every common noun.

1. The nature of the noun. Is it a mass noun or a count noun? If it is a count noun, is it singular or plural?

The choice of indefinite article is particularly sensitive to the nature of the noun. Singular count nouns use *a/an* as their indefinite article. Mass nouns and plural count nouns use *some* as their indefinite article. One of the biggest problems non-native speakers have in using English articles is identifying mass nouns. Here is one test for identifying mass nouns.

The abstract category test. If a noun is used to describe an entire abstract category of things, then it may be a mass noun.

For example, *fruit* is a mass noun because it is the name of a category of food; the names of types of fruit, such as *apple, orange,* and *banana,* are typically used as count nouns.

Mass nouns tend to fall into the following categories:

Abstractions	Languages
Natural phenomena	Food
Weather terms	Liquids and gases
Gerunds	Materials
Academic fields	Sports and games

2. Does the noun give new information (indefinite article), **or is the information already known** (definite article)?

The rule for deciding between indefinite and definite is as follows:

Established information: Use the definite article (*the*)
New information: Use the indefinite article (*a/an* or *some*)

The trick, of course, is figuring out what constitutes "established" information. There are three tests that help determine when to use *the:*

The previous mention test. Once a noun has been introduced, subsequent uses of the same noun require *the*.

For example,

I saw *a* truck parked nearby. *The* truck had a flat tire.

The defined by modification test. Post-noun modifiers typically establish the meaning of a noun and thus require a definite article.

For example,

I saw *the* truck that your Uncle Henry sold.

The normal expectations test. Use the definite article if the noun being modified is identified by normal expectations.

This is by far the most difficult test to apply because the concept of "normal expectations" is inherently vague. One kind of normal expectation is for things that are identified because they are unique. Here is an example:

The moon was just rising above *the* horizon.

More commonly, we identify things because we just expect them to be there. Here are some examples:

When I got home, I went into *the* kitchen, opened *the* refrigerator, and took out *a* can of coke.

We expect houses to have kitchens and kitchens to have refrigerators.

3. Is the noun being used to make a generalization (no article)?
Mass nouns and plural count nouns are often used without articles when we are making generalizations. There are three tests that help identify sentences that make generalizations.

The adverb of frequency test. Adverbs of frequency, such as *often, always, usually,* and *generally,* are commonly found in sentences used for generalizations.

For example,

Usually adverbs of frequency occur in generalizations.

The present tense test. Almost always, sentences that make generalizations are in the present tense, as in the above example.

The no-post-noun modifiers test. Post-noun modifiers typically require a definite article to be used with the noun.

Here is a pair of examples that illustrate the difference between generalization and definite article usage:

Cheese is salty.

The *cheese* that I just bought is salty.

The absence of any post-noun modifiers with the noun *cheese* implies that the sentence is making a generalization. Conversely, the use of the post-noun modifier *that I just bought* dictates the use of *the* and also means that the sentence is not a generalization about all cheese.

Article Exercise #6: Review

Fill in the blanks with one of the following: a/an, some, the, or No Art (for no article). Briefly explain your choice. The first question is done as an example. (Answers to this exercise are on page 526.)

   0. _____ first question on the test was easy.

     Answer: The first question on the test was easy.
                 question is identified by post-noun modifiers

   1. I answered _____ ad in the newspaper.

   2. _____ opinions usually don't count for very much.

   3. I left _____ key to my room with the desk clerk.

   4. We saw _____ terrible accident on our way here.

   5. _____ winter that we had this year was unusually damp.

   6. Do you have _____ card?

   7. There must be _____ children next door.

   8. I think it was in _____ play that Shakespeare wrote.

   9. _____ accidents can usually be prevented.

  10. I just bought _____ new computer. _____ computer is a Mac.

11. There are ＿＿＿＿＿ candles in the top drawer.

12. ＿＿＿＿＿ pressure of a new job can be pretty intense.

13. ＿＿＿＿＿ phrase is a group of related words.

14. I found ＿＿＿＿＿ cat under my car. It looked like ＿＿＿＿＿ cat hadn't eaten in days.

15. We normally classify ＿＿＿＿＿ words by part of speech.

Comma Splices

See Run-on sentences.

Commas and Appositives

Appositives are nouns used to define or rename a preceding noun. For example, in the sentence

> My geology teacher, *Mr. Igneous,* took us on a field trip.

Mr. Igneous is an appositive that tells the reader who the writer's geology teacher is. If we turn the sentence around,

> Mr. Igneous, *my geology teacher,* took us on a field trip,

my geology teacher is an appositive phrase because it contains the appositive noun *teacher* and its modifiers.

Teaching Tip

The distinction between an appositive and an appositive phrase is a minor technicality, since they work exactly the same way. Point out the differences to your students and then use the term "appositive" to refer to both. (We will do the same in the following discussion.)

Beginning on page 171 of Chapter 5, there is a detailed discussion of appositives. Here is the test for identifying appositives from that discussion.

> **The appositive deletion test.** If either of two side-by-side nouns or noun phrases can be deleted, leaving a meaningful and grammatical sentence, then the second noun or noun phrase is an appositive to the first.

Here is the appositive deletion test applied to the two example sentences from above:

	My geology teacher, *Mr. Igneous,* took us on a field trip.
Test:	My geology teacher took us on a field trip.
	Mr. Igneous, *my geology teacher,* took us on a field trip.
Test:	Mr. Igneous took us on a field trip.

Obviously, the information contained in the appositive will be lost when we delete it, but what remains is both meaningful and grammatically complete. Therefore, the deleted portion was an appositive.

All normal appositives must be set off with commas. Thus, if the appositive deletion test identifies an appositive, it must be used with a comma.

Commas and Appositives Exercise #1: Identifying and Punctuating Appositives by the Appositive Deletion Test ____

Underline the appositives, and set them off with commas. Confirm your answers by applying the appositive deletion test. The first question is done as an example. (Answers to this exercise are on page 527.)

0. The book a present from my aunt was on the table.
   Answer: The book, a present from my aunt, was on the table.
   Confirmation: The book was on the table.

1. Miss Manners a newspaper columnist advised against it.

2. We took a train a new Amtrak sleeper across the county.

3. Mozart a child prodigy was already famous in his teens.

4. In the tropics there are many coral islands usually atolls.

5. The most famous atoll Bikini was used for testing atomic weapons.

6. Dorothy's enemy the Wicked Witch of the West suddenly appeared.

7. Her first publication an autobiographical short story was in 1983.

8. The theater a concrete warehouse had no air conditioning.

9. We had dinner with the Smiths old friends of my parents.

10. There was a rug a beautiful Persian in the attic.

11. A pickup a rusty old Chevy waited in the parking lot.

12. Katy their youngest daughter took us around the garden.

13. I got a new bike an Italian racer.

14. Emergency vehicles an ambulance and two police cars were at the scene of the accident.

15. The judge a middle-aged woman came into the courtroom.

16. Did you meet him Tom's college roommate?

17. SR 1008 a bill introduced by Senator Jones deals with traffic congestion.

18. Watch out for that truck the yellow one in the left lane.

19. Cleopatra my weird cousin's pet snake was missing again.

20. The coffee an expensive French roast tasted bitter to me.

The appositive deletion test is based on the fact that appositives are normally redundant; that is, they can be deleted without destroying the meaning of the remaining sentence. Sometimes, however, if the appositive is deleted, the meaning of the sentence is destroyed. This kind of appositive is called an **essential appositive.** Essential appositives cannot be deleted, and they are not set off with commas. Here is an example from Chapter 5:

Shakespeare's play *Hamlet* is one of his longest.

Hamlet is an appositive, but if we delete it, the sentence no longer makes sense because we do not know what play the sentence is talking about:

*Shakespeare's play is one of his longest.

Essential appositives are not that common. Nearly all appositives used by students are the normal redundant ones that need to be set off with commas. Discussion of essential appositives should be postponed until after students are completely comfortable recognizing and punctuating normal appositives. If an individual student is having trouble with essential appositives, have him or her do Phrase Exercise #9 in Chapter 5 to help see the difference between the two types of appositives.

Commas and Adjective Clauses

See Chapter 6, page 221.

Commas and Coordinate Adjectives

Beginning on page 26 of Chapter 2, there is a discussion of adjectives that modify nouns. These **modifying adjectives** are divided into two groups: **determiners** and **descriptive adjectives.** The determiners are things such as articles, numbers, and possessive nouns and pronouns. Determiners are mutually exclusive—typically there is no more than one per noun. Descriptive adjectives, however, are much more flexible. A noun can be modified by any number of descriptive adjectives.

Sometimes we use a comma to separate descriptive adjectives, and sometimes we do not. Here are some examples with multiple descriptive adjectives italicized:

The *six thin black* cats slipped through the door.

It was a *sunlit, windy* day in April.

Why do we not use any commas between the three descriptive adjectives in the first example, but we do use commas between the two descriptive adjectives in the second example?

The answer lies in the nature of the descriptive adjectives. There are at least five classes of descriptive adjectives. As long as no more than one adjective per class is modifying the same noun, we do not use commas to separate them. However, if TWO descriptive adjectives FROM THE SAME CLASS are modifying the same noun, they are called **coordinate adjectives,** and we must separate them with commas.

In the first example above, *six, thin,* and *black* all belong to different classes of descriptive adjectives, so they are not separated by commas. In the second example, *sunlit* and *windy* do belong to the same class, so they must be separated by a comma.

Here are the five classes of descriptive adjectives with examples:

(1)	*(2)*	*(3)*	*(4)*	*(5)*	
General	*Age*	*Color*	*Material*	*Origin*	*Noun*
wretched	old				textbooks
beautiful		red	cotton		prints
shiny	new			Swiss	coins
surviving			wooden		ships
long		blond			hair
little	old			Dutch	lady
wealthy	young				bachelor
special	aged	red		French	wines

The first class, General, is the open class. Most descriptive adjectives fall into this category. The other classes are sequenced in a fixed left-to-right order after the general class. Nearly all coordinate adjectives consist of two from the General category, as was the case in our example of *sunlit* and *windy*. Native speakers have a very strong sense of the classes, as is illustrated by the following exercise.

Commas and Coordinate Adjectives Exercise #1: Identifying Adjective Classes _____

Below are scrambled noun phrases. Put the adjectives and the noun back in their correct order. Underline each modifying adjective and put the name of its class under it. (There are no coordinate adjectives.) The first question is done as an example. (Answers to this exercise are on page 528.)

0. so-called problem Russian the

Answer: the <u>so-called</u> <u>Russian</u> problem
                General   Origin

1. ship a wooden old huge

2. primitive the societies first European

3. sensitive pink some tissue new

4. cape valuable feather red Sir Roderick's

5. evil that idol stone old

6. finish popular new its satin

7. continental innovative our design new

8. population entire urban the

9. broken several crates wooden

10. new problems these frightening technical

11. pizza our sausage hot

12. annual the dinner German third

13. old our desks two massive oak

14. explorers the European known first

15. cotton my clean shirt white

Teaching
Tip

The above exercise on classes of adjectives is a wonderful example of how much we all know intuitively about English. Give students the above exercise without showing them the classes. Ask them to sort the phrases into the correct word order. After they have done so, ask them how they were able to sort the phrases without consciously knowing any of the rules governing the sorting.

There are two tests for telling when descriptive adjectives are coordinate, i.e., belong to the same class.

> **The switched order test.** If you can switch the order of two
> descriptive adjectives, they are coordinate and require a comma.

The switched order test is based on the fact that adjectives that belong
to two different classes occur in a fixed left-to-right order and cannot be
switched. However, two adjectives from the same class have no intrinsic order
with respect to each other, and thus they can be switched. Here is an example:

His work has an *unworldly, haunted* quality.

If we can switch *unworldly* and *haunted*, they must belong to the same class.
If that is so, then the comma is correct:

His work has a *haunted, unworldly* quality.

Since the reversed order works fine, they are coordinate adjectives that require
a comma.
    The second test is **the *and* test.**

> **The *and* test.** If you can put *and* between two descriptive
> adjectives, they are coordinate and require a comma.

We can put *and* between coordinate adjectives, but not between adjectives that
belong to different classes. Here is an example of both situations:

           A *thin black* cat slipped through the door.
Test: *A *thin* **and** *black* cat slipped through the door.

Putting *and* between *thin* and *black* almost makes it sound like the sentence is describing two different cats. The failure of the *and* test tells us that *thin* and *black*
belong to two different classes and thus should not be separated by a comma.

           The lighthouse was on a flat, barren island.
Test: The lighthouse was on a *flat* **and** *barren* island.

The success of the *and* test tells us that *flat* and *barren* belong to the same class
and thus need to be separated by a comma.

Commas and Coordinate Adjectives Exercise #2: Identifying Coordinate Adjectives by the Switched Order Test and the *and* test

Underline the coordinate adjectives and put commas between them. Confirm your answers by both the switched order and *and* tests. The first question is done as an example. (Answers to this exercise are on page 529.)

0. The lad had a cheerful happy smile for everyone.

Answer: The lad had a cheerful, happy smile for everyone.

Confirmation:

Switched order: The lad had a happy, cheerful smile for everyone.

and test: The lad had a cheerful **and** happy smile for everyone.

1. He is a regular old crook.

2. Dracula had an ordinary normal childhood.

3. He answered Holmes' questions in halting accented English.

4. His suggestion provided an effective convenient solution.

5. He was a proper English butler of the old school.

6. He was a difficult obstinate child.

7. She decided that her basic black dress was appropriate.

8. Lady Mortock was smitten by the tall dark stranger.

9. It is a dirty dangerous job, but somebody has to do it.

10. She toyed with her beautiful new pearls.

11. We all noticed her delicate smooth complexion.

12. Holmes fixed the cabby with a steady cold eye.

13. Alexander had a terrible horrible day.

14. The original American musical was changed into a British novel.

15. We attended a disorganized unprofessional performance.

Commas and Coordinating Conjunctions

The coordinating conjunctions are best taught by the acronym FANBOYS:

For
And
Nor
Boys
Or
Yet
So

The punctuation problem with coordinating conjunctions results from confusion of two different functions: joining independent clauses (whole sentences) and joining parallel predicates or complements. Here is an example:

Joining two sentences:

John opened the refrigerator, **and** *he took out the milk.*
         sentence 1   sentence 2

Joining parallel predicates:

John *opened the refrigerator* **and** *took out the milk.*
          predicate 1   predicate 2

In the first example, *and* joins two SENTENCES together. This use of *and* is signaled by a comma before the *and*. In the second example, *and* joins two parallel PREDICATES—one beginning with the verb *opened* and the second beginning with the verb *took*.

   Some students may have difficulty distinguishing the two uses of *and* because they do not seem that different. Both example sentences mean exactly the same thing. In the second sentence, the reader still knows that it was John who took out the milk. In other words, there is an understood pronoun subject after the *and:*

John opened the refrigerator and (he) took out the milk.

This argument is logically correct, but it is irrelevant. We use a comma with coordinating conjunctions ONLY when the conjunction joins two complete independent clauses. Understood subjects do not count. This fact leads us to the following test.

The period test. Replace the coordinating conjunction with a period. If what follows is a complete sentence, then use a comma before the coordinating conjunction.

Here is the period test applied to our example sentences:

          John opened the refrigerator, and he took out the milk.
   Test: John opened the refrigerator. He took out the milk

Since what follows the period is a complete sentence, we know that we need a comma before the *and*.

          John opened the refrigerator and took out the milk.
   Test: John opened the refrigerator. *Took out the milk.

Since what follows the period cannot stand alone as a complete sentence, we know that we cannot put a comma before the *and*.

Commas and Coordinating Conjunctions Exercise #1: Punctuating Coordinating Conjunctions by the Period Test

Underline the coordinating conjunction and punctuate accordingly. Confirm your answers by applying the period test. The first question is done as an example. (Answers to this exercise are on page 530.)

0. Mary planned the wedding and made up the guest list.

　Answer: Mary planned the wedding <u>and</u> made up the guest list.

　Confirmation: Mary planned the wedding. *Made up the guest list.

1. It was a great restaurant and we had a wonderful meal.

2. Helen got into the car and she drove to the station.

3. I'm sure you are right but I can't help worrying about it.

4. The children were playing outside and making a lot of noise.

5. My father saved his bonus money and he bought a new boat.

6. Mary planned the wedding and she made up the guest list, too.

7. They should hurry for the game is about to start.

8. Henry jumped to his feet and ran to the door.

9. His family was poor but honest.

10. My parents got a new car and a new camper at the same time.

11. It was time to go but we weren't ready yet.

12. The police posted a sign and closed the road to through traffic.

13. She set the table and I lit the candles.

14. Jason answered the question and won a prize.

15. Answer the question and win a prize!

A particularly good way of teaching the use of commas with coordinating conjunctions is sentence combining. Sentence combining is a technique that gives students two (or more) simple sentences and asks them to combine the simple sentences together to form a single, more complex sentence. Here is an example:

The sergeant yelled at the recruits.

The sergeant told them to start over.

There are two solutions, one that retains the subject of the second sentence, the other that deletes the subject. The results mean the same thing, but they must be punctuated differently:

Second subject retained:

The sergeant yelled at the recruits, and *he/she* told them to start over.

Second subject not retained:

The sergeant yelled at the recruits and told them to start over.

The sentence-combining technique allows students to see how the difference in punctuation is a result of retaining or deleting the second subject.

Commas and Coordinating Conjunctions Exercise #2: Sentence Combining

Combine each pair of sentences two ways: (a) retain the subject of the second sentence; (b) delete the subject of the second sentence. Punctuate the coordinating conjunction appropriately. The first question is done as an example. (Answers to this exercise are on page 531.)

0. Rubin answered the phone.
   Rubin took the message

   Answer:

   (a) Rubin answered the phone, and he took the message.
   (b) Rubin answered the phone and took the message.

1. The governor vetoed the bill.
   The governor sent it back to the senate.

2. The performers dazzled the crowd.
   The performers amazed the critics.

3. The editor compiled a list of typographical errors.
   The editor sent the list to the grateful author.

4. The workers stacked the crates in the warehouse.
   The workers labeled them according to their contents.

5. The candidate invoked the names of the founding fathers.
   The candidate promised to follow in their footsteps.

6. The Boy Scouts synchronized their watches.
   The Boy Scouts oriented their maps.

7. The astrologer forecast the future of the stock market.
   The astrologer called his broker.

8. Dripping wet, Leon got out of the shower.
   Leon answered the phone for the third time.

9. A couple in a brand-new BMW wheeled into the filling station.
   The couple paid for their gas with nickels and dimes.

10. Holmes sent a wire to 221 Baker Street.
    Holmes told Watson to pack his service revolver.

Commas and Introductory Elements

Introductory elements are any words, phrases, or clauses that have been placed at the beginning of the sentence in front of the subject. Introductory elements are always modifiers—nearly always adverbs that modify the verb, but sometimes **participial phrases** that modify the subject. Here are some examples with the introductory element italicized and the subject in bold:

- Adverbs
  Single-word adverbs

    Reluctantly, the **company** went along with the proposal.

    Yesterday, **we** had a big snow storm in the area.

  Adverb prepositional phrases

    During the night, the **power** went out.

    In case of emergency, **you** can call this number.

  Adverb clauses

    When you get back, **we** will go out for dinner.

    Because I had a test, **I** decided to go to the library.

- Adjectives
  Participial phrases

    Grinning from ear to ear, the little **boy** pulled out a fish.

    Fingering his cutlass, **Captain Hook** welcomed them aboard.

In all of the examples, the introductory element has been set off with a comma. Most handbooks state that a comma is obligatory with adverb clauses and participial phrases, and recommended with single-word adverbs and prepositional phrases.

Most handbooks also advise that, as a practical matter, students should solve the problem of using commas with introductory elements by using a comma with ALL introductory elements. While this is a little bit of stylistic overkill with single-word adverbs, it is still very good advice.

The issue, then, is helping students recognize introductory elements. Here is a reliable technique.

> **The introductory-element deletion test.** Delete any suspected introductory material. If the sentence is still grammatically complete, then the material is introductory and should be set off with a comma.

The advantage of the introductory element deletion test is that it does not apply to **inverted sentences.** Inverted sentences are sentences in which a required part of the sentence has moved in front of the subject. The most common form of inverted sentence is the **existential *there*,** meaning "there exists." Here are some examples with the subject in italics:

There is a *fly* in my soup.

(= A fly is in my soup.)

There are many *fish* in the sea.

(= Many fish are in the sea.)

In these existential *there* sentences, the verb has been moved in front of the subject. If the material in front of the subject is deleted, the result is ungrammatical because there is then no verb:

*A fly in my soup.

*Many fish in the sea.

Another type of inverted sentence moves a required adverb to the front of the sentence for emphasis. Here is an example with the introductory element deletion test applied:

	Here you are!
Test:	*You are!

When we apply the introductory-element deletion test to actual introductory material, the results are obviously grammatical, though, of course, any information contained in the introductory element is lost:

	Reluctantly, the **company** went along with the proposal.
Test:	The company went along with the proposal.

	During the night, the **power** went out.
Test:	The power went out.

	When you get back, **we** will go out for dinner.
Test:	We will go out for dinner.

	Grinning from ear to ear, the little **boy** pulled out a fish.
Test:	The little boy pulled out a fish.

Commas and Introductory Elements
Exercise #1: Punctuating Introductory Elements
by the Introductory-Element Deletion Test _____

Underline the introductory elements and punctuate accordingly. Confirm your answers by applying the introductory-element deletion test. The first question is done as an example. (Answers to this exercise are on page 532.)

0. If you can make it give me a call.
Answer: If you can make it, give me a call.
Confirmation: Give me a call.

1. Rummaging in the trunk the wizard pulled out an old hat.

2. As soon as I got your message I put in the order.

3. Surely you must be joking.

4. In Japan they drive on the left side of the road.

5. Behind the brick was the coded message.

6. After all what difference did it make?

7. There were several comma errors in the paper.

8. On Tuesday we visited an old monastery.

9. Recalling Lady Dedlock's mysterious words Holmes called for the upstairs maid.

10. On Christmas day it began snowing in earnest.

11. All too soon we had to leave.

12. After eating a heavy meal I always get terribly sleepy.

13. What they did next was a big mistake.

14. Thanks to their efforts Disneyland was safe again.

15. From Key West to Miami is about 150 miles.

16. Since it was getting late we decided to head back.

17. In the poor light I could hardly read the sign.

18. There was really nothing I could say.

19. Somewhere over the rainbow skies are blue.

20. When it rains it pours.

Conjunctive Adverbs

See Chapter 6, page 237.

Dangling Modifiers

The most common form of dangling modifier is a **participle** form of the verb that is not properly attached to the word it modifies. (Participles and participial phrases are discussed in Chapter 5 beginning on page 183.) To recapitulate briefly, there are two types of participles: **present participles** and **past participles.** Here are some examples:

Verb	*Present Participle*	*Past Participle*
walk	walking	walked
sing	singing	sung
hope	hoping	hoped
have	having	had
be	being	been

As you can see, the present participle is completely regular. It is the base form of the verb plus -*ing*.

The past participle is much more difficult to recognize. With regular verbs, it is the base form of the verb plus -*ed*, making it look exactly like a past tense. With irregular verbs, the past participle form is unpredictable.

Participial phrases are merely participles together with their modifiers and/or complements. Participial phrases can be used as modifiers. The most common use is to modify nouns or pronouns as a special kind of adjective. Here is an example of an adjective participial phrase used properly, with the subject still in bold:

Having hiked all day, **I** couldn't wait to take off my backpack.

In this example, the participial phrase *having hiked all day* modifies the pronoun *I*.

Here is an example of a sentence containing a dangling modifier:

*Having hiked all day, my **backpack** was killing me.

The sentence is incorrect because the adjective participial phrase says something that the writer does not mean: the modifier makes it sound as though the backpack had hiked all day rather than the writer.

Here is another example of a dangling modifier that uses a past participle verb form:

Damaged beyond all repair, **I threw my watch away.

Again, the sentence is incorrect because the adjective participial phrase says something that the writer does not mean: that the writer was damaged beyond all repair. What the writer meant, of course, was that the watch was damaged beyond all repair.

Sometimes dangling modifiers result from a reduced form of an adverb clause, in which case the participial phrase is acting as an adverb modifying the verb. Here is an example of a grammatical adverb clause:

While I was jogging down Main Street, **I** saw the sun rise above the buildings.

We can reduce many adverb clauses by deleting the subject and the tensed verb:

While jogging down Main Street, **I** saw the sun rise above the buildings.

However, sometimes the reduction of an adverb clause can produce a dangling modifier. Here is an example of a grammatical adverb clause:

While I was jogging down Main Street, the **sun** rose above the buildings.

When we attempt to reduce this adverb clause, we create a dangling modifier:

*While jogging down Main Street, the **sun** rose above the buildings.

In this case, the dangling modifier makes it sound as though the sunrise were jogging down Main Street rather than the writer.

Fortunately, there is a simple test that we can use to see whether or not participial phrases, used either as adjectives or adverbs, are attached correctly:

The understood subject test. If the subject of the main sentence makes sense as the understood subject of the participle, then the participle is grammatical. If the subject of the main sentence does NOT make sense as the understood subject of the participle, then it is a dangling participle.

Here is the understood subject test applied to our example sentences:

Having hiked all day, **I** couldn't wait to take off my backpack.

Test: **I** had hiked all day. **I** couldn't wait to take off my backpack.

Result: The participial phrase is grammatical because *I* makes sense as the subject of *had hiked.*

Having hiked all day, my **backpack** was killing me.

Test: **My **backpack** had hiked all day. My **backpack** was killing me.

Result: The participial phrase is dangling because *my backpack* does NOT make sense as the subject of *had hiked.*

Damaged beyond all repair, **I** threw my watch away.

Test: **I* was damaged beyond all repair. **I** threw my watch away.

Result: *I* does not make sense as the understood subject of *was damaged.* Thus the sentence contains a dangling participial.

> *While jogging down Main Street,* **I** saw the sun rise above the buildings.

Test: While **I** was jogging down Main Street, **I** saw the sun rise above the buildings.

Result: The participial phrase is grammatical because *I* makes sense as the subject of *was jogging*.

> *While jogging down Main Street,* the **sun** rose above the buildings.

Test: *While the **sun** was jogging down Main Street, the **sun** rose above the buildings.

Result: The participial phrase is dangling because *the sun* does not make sense as the subject of *was jogging*.

Dangling Modifiers Exercise #1: Identifying Dangling Modifiers by the Understood Subject Test _____

Underline the dangling modifiers and replace the dangling modifier with a correct one (answers will vary). Confirm your analysis of modifiers by applying the understood subject test. The first question is done as an example. (Answers to this exercise are on page 533.)

0. Working all night, my term paper was almost finished.

Answer: <u>Working all night</u>, my term paper was almost finished.

Correction: Since I had worked all night, my term paper was almost finished.

Confirmation: *My term paper* does not make sense as the subject of *working all night.*

1. Waving good-bye to his mother, Philip's eyes grew misty.

2. Piled on the floor, I began sorting through my books.

3. Detouring through my old neighborhood, our house looked the same as ever.

4. Having matured, I now enjoy *The Flintstones.*

5. Being old Dodger fans, the outcome of the game pleased us.

6. Once considered only an average player, Don's game has improved enormously.

7. Hoping for a league championship, there was excitement in the air.

8. Disappointed by the unexpected defeat, we applauded the team's efforts nonetheless.

9. Working for old Mr. Green, he really taught us the value of a good day's work.

10. Finishing in 2 hours and 57 minutes, Ruth's first marathon was a terrific success.

11. Shining in the sun, the water looked very inviting.

12. Done with our project, we all went out for a pizza.

13. Running across the plowed field, my ankle twisted.

14. Made from a new plastic, you cannot easily tell these artificial flowers from the real ones.

15. Warped and twisted from the heat, I realized that my records were ruined.

Fragments

A fragment is a group of words that cannot stand alone and is therefore incorrectly punctuated as a complete sentence. Here are three typical fragments (in italics):

> Our cat has an annoying habit. *Leaving dead mice at our door.*

> I cleaned up the kitchen. *Because we were having visitors.*

> We lost the game. *By an unearned run in extra innings.*

Here are several observations about fragments that use the three examples above as illustrations.

- Fragment errors are not simply the result of students' ignorance of what constitutes a complete sentence. If fragment errors were merely the result of ignorance about the grammar of complete sentences, we would expect to find fragments sprinkled randomly throughout students' papers. In fact, fragment errors are rarely random. The vast majority of fragments occur in certain specific situations and for identifiable reasons. In other words, teaching the basic grammar of sentences—subjects and predicates—will not necessarily help many students to identify and correct their fragment errors.

- The most useful observation about fragments is that they are extensions of the sentence on their immediate left. Typically fragments are modifiers, either adjective structures that modify the last noun in the preceding sentence (as in the first example) or adverbs that modify the verb (as in the second and third examples).

- Fragments are created for emphasis. Most relatively inexperienced writers are attempting to imitate the pause that speakers would put in a sentence to emphasize a final key point—much like the pause before the punch line of a joke. Sometimes skilled writers do the same thing, but they are much more selective about it. Using fragments for emphasis is like using exclamation points—once in a while is fine, but don't do it very often.

- Most inexperienced writers are not consciously aware of fragments because they tend to hear what they write rather than see it on the page. Since fragments are extensions of the sentences on their left, they sound perfectly normal when they are read aloud together with the sentence on the left. For example, when the three fragment examples above are read aloud after the complete sentences on their left, the fragments sound normal.

- Correcting fragments once they have been spotted is easy. Nearly all fragment errors can be corrected merely by attaching them to the sentence on their left. (When you stop to think about it, what creates the fragment error is not the fragment itself, but the period that incorrectly terminates the sentence on the left.)

The problem is getting writers to SEE the fragments in the first place. The key to doing this is helping the writer to see the fragment in isolation from the sentence on the left. In other words, we overlook fragments because they are grammatically complete *when we combine them with the preceding sentence.* What we want students to do is see fragments isolated from the context of the previous sentence.

One way to help writers spot fragments is to encourage writers to proofread their sentences from right to left. Have the students use a 3 × 5 index card to cover up everything but the last sentence in a paragraph. If that sentence is grammatical, then move the card to reveal the sentence on its left. This is an effective, if tedious, technique for spotting fragments because it isolates the fragment from the sentence on its left.

Another effective technique for isolating fragments from the sentence on their left is the *I know that* test given on page 72 of Chapter 3. This technique exploits the fact that most complete sentences can be used as noun clauses following *I know that.* Turning a fragment into a noun clause isolates it from the previous sentence. Here is the *I know that* test applied to the three fragment examples above:

	Our cat has an annoying habit. *Leaving dead mice at our door.*
Test:	*I know that *leaving dead mice at our door.*
	I cleaned up the kitchen. *Because we were having visitors.*
Test:	*I know that *because we were having visitors.*
	We lost the game. *By an unearned run in extra innings.*
Test:	*I know that *by an unearned run in extra innings.*

Fragments Exercise #1: Identifying Fragments by the I know that Test _____

Underline fragments and then correct them by attaching them to the preceding sentence. Confirm your analysis by applying the *I know that* test to the fragment. The first question is done as an example. (Answers to this exercise are on page 534.)

0. My husband drives me crazy with the remote. Changing channels every two seconds.

Answer: My husband drives me crazy with the remote, <u>changing channels every two seconds</u>.

Confirmation: *I know that <u>changing channels every two seconds</u>.

1. I couldn't get started on my paper. Because I had nothing to say.

2. While everyone waited, I looked for my library card. Which I had left at home in my rush to get to the library.

3. We were awakened in the middle of the night. By the tornado-warning sirens.

4. Bambi fled. Hearing the approach of the hunter.

5. June 6, 1944. The day the allies landed in Normandy.

6. We took the kids to Grumpyland. Part of the Seven Dwarfs amusement complex.

7. I missed class because of a bad cold. Which was made worse by a sinus infection.

8. The conflict ended in 1987. When the rebels signed a treaty with the government.

9. We heard about the engagement. When her brother called last night.

10. He said he has stopped smoking. If you can believe what he says.

11. We went to Baltimore. Which has a restored inner harbor.

12. I finally found the office. Buried in the depths of a sub-basement.

13. He was fined $5,000. A huge sum at the time.

14. They didn't answer the phone. Even though they were home at the time.

15. We finally found the kids. Playing with the children next door.

Fused Sentences

See Run-on sentences.

Participles Used as Adjectives (ESL)

Participles are verb forms used as adjectives. There are two types of participles: **present participles** and **past participles.** For example, *boring* is a present participle and *bored* is a past participle. When they are used as adjectives, the two participles mean quite different things: there is a world of difference between a *boring teacher* and a *bored teacher*. A *boring teacher* bores his or her students; a *bored teacher* is a teacher whose students bore him or her.

While this distinction between present and past participles used as adjectives is rarely a problem for native speakers of English, it is a major problem for most non-native speakers of English. Non-native speakers are likely to write *boring teacher* when they really mean *bored teacher,* and vice versa.

Let us begin with a brief review of the difference between present and past participles:

Verb	Present Participle	Past Participle
walk	walking	walked
sing	singing	sung
hope	hoping	hoped
have	having	had
be	being	been

As you can see, the present participle is completely regular. It is the base form of the verb plus *-ing.*

The past participle is much more difficult to recognize. With regular verbs, it is the base form of the verb plus *-ed.* With irregular verbs, the past participle form is unpredictable.

The difference in meaning between the two participles used as adjectives comes from the relation of the noun being modified to the verb that underlies the participle. For example, the phrase

a *boring* teacher

comes from an underlying sentence in which the noun being modified (*teacher,* in this case) is the SUBJECT of the verb—the one doing the action:

The teacher is *boring* the students.

Conversely, the phrase

a *bored* teacher

comes from an underlying sentence in which the noun being modified (*teacher*) is the OBJECT of the verb—the one receiving the action—put into a **passive** sentence:

The teacher is *bored* by the students.   (passive)

The students *bore* the teacher.   (underlying active)

Here is a test that non-native speakers can use to decide whether to use the present or part participle form of a verb used as an adjective.

> **The *doing* test.** If the noun being modified is *doing* the action
> of the modifier, then use the *-ing* form of the modifier (the present
> participle). If the noun being modified is NOT *doing* the action,
> then use the past participle form.

Here are some examples of the *doing* test.

> The movie was about a *frightened* old house.
>
> Test: The house is doing the frightening. Nobody is frightening the house. Therefore, use the *-ing* present participle form.
>
> Correction: The movie was about a *frightening* old house.

> Their mothers reassured the *frightening* children.
>
> Test: The children are NOT doing the frightening. Therefore, do not use the *-ing* form.
>
> Correction: Their mothers reassured the *frightened* children.

> We gave a ten-minute break to the *exhausting* hikers.
>
> Test: The hikers were NOT doing the exhausting. Therefore, do not use the *-ing* form.
>
> Correction: We gave a ten-minute break to the *exhausted* hikers.

> The *exhausted* examinations were too much for the students.
>
> Test: The examinations are doing the exhausting. Therefore, use the *-ing* form.
>
> Correction: The *exhausting* examinations were too much for the students.

Participles Used as Adjectives Exercise #1: Identifying Participles by the Doing *Test* _____

Underline the participles and then correct them by writing the correct form below. Confirm your analysis by applying the *doing* test. The first question is done as an example. (Answers to this exercise are on page 535.)

0. You must replace any damaging furniture.

   Answer: You must replace any <u>damaging</u> furniture.
   damaged

   Confirmation: The furniture is NOT doing the damaging.

1. I thought it was a really amused movie.

2. It was certainly a terribly embarrassed accident.

3. The amusement park advertised its thrilled rides.

4. The sprawled suburbs went on for miles and miles.

5. The soaked rain brought the dry grass back to life.

6. I was really bothered by my injuring knee.

7. The diplomats issued the newly redrawing maps.

8. We bought some water-repelled rain garments.

9. It was a very amused incident.

10. After the hike, I soaked my blistering feet.

11. A delaying flight caused us to miss all of our connections.

12. The crew asked the remained passengers to leave the plane.

13. The policeman duly reported the alleging incident.

14. There was a revolved restaurant at the airport.

15. A watching pot never boils. (idiom)

Progressive Usage (ESL)

The progressive verb construction is discussed in Chapter 4 beginning on page 140. To recap briefly, the progressive construction is in two parts: the **helping verb** *be* (in the present, past, or future form) + the main verb in the present participle form. Here are some examples:

> I *am eating* now.
>
> The flags *are flapping* in the breeze.
>
> My shoes *were pinching* me all afternoon.
>
> I *will be seeing* them later.

The progressive is used to describe action in progress at some present, past, or future moment of time. Non-native speakers do not have any special problem with this use of the progressive construction.

However, non-native speakers do have a considerable problem with a group of exceptional verbs that cannot be used in the progressive constructions as one would expect them to be used. Here are some examples:

> *I *am knowing* the answer.
>
> *They *are having* a new car.
>
> *He *was owning* a house in the country.

The problem that the writers of the above sentences have encountered is that English has a group of exceptional verbs called **stative verbs.** Stative verbs differ from ordinary verbs in that they cannot be used in the progressive. Here is a pair of examples using the stative verb *own* and the ordinary verb *buy*.

> ***Progressive:***
> Stative: *We *are owning* a car.
> Ordinary: We *are buying* a car.

As you can see, the stative verb *own* and the ordinary verb *buy* are opposites. We cannot use a stative verb like *own* in the progressive, but we can use ordinary verbs like *buy* in the progressive quite naturally.

The difference between the two classes is a function of the peculiar meaning of stative verbs. Stative verbs, as the term "stative" implies, describe an ongoing, more or less permanent condition or STATE. Ordinary verbs, on the other hand, are time-bounded. That is, the actions that they refer to are temporary, time-bounded events that we expect to start and stop.

Going back to the two example verbs, the stative verb *own* describes the ongoing condition of ownership. When someone owns a car, that person owns the car for an indefinite period of time. We do not start and stop ownership on a momentary basis. However, the act of buying a car is a temporary process. The process may take minutes or weeks, but no matter how long the act of buying takes, it has a definite beginning and end.

The bottom line is that stative verbs refer to "timeless" states. This meaning is incompatible with the here-and-now meaning of the progressive. Consequently, we cannot use stative verbs in the progressive.

Stative verbs fall into certain broad categories of meaning. Here are some examples of the three most common categories of stative verbs:

- **Mental activity:** *believe, doubt, forget, imagine, know, mean*
- **Emotional condition:** *appreciate, care, dislike, envy, fear, hate, like, love, need, prefer, want*
- **Possession:** *belong to, contain, consist of, own, possess*

The ongoing state test. If a verb describes an ongoing state rather than a temporary activity, it may be a stative verb that cannot be used in the progressive.

Here is the ongoing state test applied to the example error sentences above.

	I am knowing the answer.
Test:	Knowing something is an on-going condition, not a temporary one.
Correction:	I *know* the answer.

	They are having a new car.
Test:	Having a car is an ongoing condition, not a temporary one.
Correction:	They *have* a new car.

	He was owning a house in the country.
Test:	Owning a house is an ongoing condition, not a momentary one.
Correction:	He *owned* a house in the country.

Progressive Usage Exercise #1: Identifying Stative Verbs by the Ongoing State Test

Underline all the progressives. If the progressive is incorrect, then write the corrected form below. Whether it is incorrect or not, confirm your analysis by applying the on-going state test. The first question is done as an example. (Answers to this exercise are on page 536.)

0. I am liking liver.

    Answer: I <u>am liking</u> liver.
               like

    Confirmation: Liking liver is an ongoing, not temporary condition.

1. I am believing that the answer is wrong.

2. It is seeming to be our best bet.

3. We are staying with some friends this weekend.

4. The boss is distrusting all expense vouchers.

5. The train is arriving on Track 7 now.

6. The solution is sounding pretty weak to me.

7. They are wanting us to approve their proposal.

8. It's raining.

9. She is loving coffee ice cream.

10. I am returning your call.

11. My heart is belonging to Daddy.

12. He is certainly acting the part.

13. No one is believing in the gold standard anymore.

14. I am hating what I do.

15. Thank you. I am appreciating your effort.

Pronoun Errors: *I/me we/us; he/him; she/her; they/them*

Most of the **personal pronouns** have two different forms: one when the pro-noun is used as a subject and one when it is used as an object. Occasionally, writers use a subject form when they should use an object form, and vice versa, for example,

    *Between you and I, liver turns my stomach.

In this example, the subject form *I* has been used incorrectly. Instead, the writer should have used the object form *me:*

    Between you and *me,* liver turns my stomach.

Here are the subject and object forms of all the personal pronouns. As you can see, with the exception of the 2nd-person pronoun *you,* they have one form when they are used as subjects and another form when they are used as objects.

	1st person		*2nd person*	*3rd person*		
Subject form:	I	we	you	he	she	they
Object form:	me	us	you	him	her	them

For example, we say

I saw *her.*

but not

*Me saw *she.*

The above mistake in pronoun form may seem far-fetched, because only a small child acquiring English as a first language or a beginning non-native speaker would make such a mistake. However, even the most sophisticated native speakers make subject–object pronoun errors in one particular construction. Here are several examples of the error. See if you can discover what grammatical features all these errors have in common before you look at the following discussion.

*You and *me* could go there next weekend.

*Fred and *him* are going to the store.

*Please save some for Kathy and *they.*

*I did it for you and *I.*

These sentences all share three grammatical features.

1. The errors occur in **compounds.** In grammar terminology, a compound is two elements of the same type joined by a coordinating conjunction. In the above examples, the errors occur in noun compounds, compounds in which nouns or pronouns are joined by the coordinating conjunction *and.*

2. The pronoun error is typically in the second element of the compound.

3. The first element in the compound is a word that does not show any difference in form whether it is used as a subject or an object. That is, the first element is either (a) a noun or (b) the pronoun *you,* which is the only personal pronoun that has the same form as a subject or an object.

What seems to cause this error is a breakdown in our ability to monitor our own sentences for grammatical correctness when the sentence contains a noun compound in which the first element does not change subject–verb form but the second element does.

The simplest way to help students monitor for this error is to have them get rid of the cause of the problem: the compound. There are two techniques for doing this. The first is the **first-element deletion test.**

The first-element deletion test. Delete the first element in a noun compound and use whatever pronoun sounds right for the second element.

Here is the first-element deletion test applied to the four examples above.

	*You and *me* could go there next weekend.
Test:	*I* could go there next weekend.
Correction:	You and *I* could go there next weekend.

	*Fred and *him* are going to the store.
Test:	*He* is going to the store.
Correction:	Fred and *he* are going to the store.

	*Please save some for Kathy and *they*.
Test:	Please same some for *them*.
Correction:	Please save some for Kathy and *them*.

	*I did it for you and *I*.
Test:	I did it for *me*.
Correction:	I did it for you and *me*.

The second way of eliminating the compound is to replace the compound with a plural pronoun.

The plural pronoun replacement test. Replace the compound with the appropriate plural pronoun. If the plural pronoun is a subject form, use the subject form in the compound. If the plural pronoun is an object form, use the object form in the compound.

Here is **the plural pronoun replacement test** applied to the four examples.

	*You and *me* could go there next weekend.	
Test:	*We* could go there next weekend.	(subject form)
Correction:	You and *I* could go there next weekend.	

	*Fred and *him* are going to the store.
Test:	*We* are going to the store. (subject form)
Correction:	Fred and *he* are going to the store.

	*Please save some for Kathy and *they.*
Test:	Please same some for *them.* (object form)
Correction:	Please save some for Kathy and *them.*

	*I did it for you and *I.*
Test:	I did it for *us.* (object form)
Correction:	I did it for you and *me.*

Usually the first-element deletion test is easier to use than the plural pronoun replacement test, because it requires less manipulation. The trouble with the plural pronoun replacement test is that the student has to convert the plural pronoun form (subject or object) back to the corresponding singular pronoun form. Sometimes, however, the plural pronoun replacement test is the only one that will fit the sentence. For example, when we attempt to apply the first-element deletion test to the following sentence, the result does not make any sense:

Between you and *I,* liver turns my stomach.

First element deletion test:

?Between *me,* liver turns my stomach.

However, the plural pronoun replacement test works fine:

	Between *us,* liver turns my stomach.
Correction:	Between you and *me,* liver turns my stomach.

The moral of the story is that students really need both tests. Then they can use the test that works best for any particular sentence.

Personal Pronoun Exercise #1: Identifying Correct Pronoun Form by the First-Element Deletion Test and the Plural Pronoun Replacement Test

Underline the incorrect personal pronouns and then correct them by writing the correct forms below. Confirm your analysis by applying BOTH the first-element deletion test and the plural pronoun replacement test. The first question is done as an example. (Answers to this exercise are on page 537.)

0. Ask the patient and he to step in, please.

Answer: Ask the patient and he to step in, please.

                                 him

Confirmation:

    1st element: Ask him to step in, please.

    Pl pronoun: Ask them to step in, please.

1. They gave it to you and she.

2. I hope that Fred and him can get along with each other.

3. The reason that we are late is that Harvey and me got lost.

4. The gift was originally intended for Sally and he.

5. Why did Mr. Smith ask you and I to leave?

6. My brother and me used to be good friends.

7. John and me want to be partners.

8. After Alice and he called, we had to change our plans.

9. Our visitors went with Alfred and I to the movies.

10. The outcome of the case surprised both Holmes and he.

11. Theo answered the phone because Louise and I had left already.

12. Ludwig proudly announced that Gretchen and him had won.

13. Only Philip and me would have been home at the time.

14. Above Dorrie and I was an ornate ceiling.

15. Near Holmes and I was the dark tower that we had seen earlier.

Pronoun Errors: *who* and *whom*

Who, whom, which, and *that* are **relative pronouns.** Relative pronouns begin **adjective** (or relative) **clauses.** Adjective clauses, as their name suggests, exist only to modify nouns. (See the treatment of adjective clauses in Chapter 6 beginning on page 216.) Here is an example of each relative pronoun with the adjective clause italicized and the relative pronouns in bold:

The weatherman ***who*** *is on Channel 7* is always wrong.

She married a man ***whom*** *she met at school.*

The alarm clock, ***which*** *I had forgotten to reset,* woke me.

I found it in the book ***that*** *you had lent me.*

    The four relative pronouns fall into two basic groups: *who* and *whom* are used for people; *which* and *that* are used for everything else—animals, objects, and abstractions. The most common relative pronoun error of less experienced writers is using *that* (less commonly, *which*) to refer to people, for example:

*The weatherman *that* is on Channel 7 is always wrong.

*She married a man *that* she met at school.

The reason for this error is easy to guess: with *that*, we do not have to chose between *who* and *whom*. *That* is so much easier to use than *who* and *whom* that *that* has become normal in informal spoken language. The problem, of course, is that beginning writers write what sounds normal to them. Thus, they carry over *that* into the more formal and conservative written language in a way that may not be appropriate. Accordingly, the best way to help students avoid the overuse of *that* is to show them how to use *who* and *whom*.

The choice between *that* and *which* depends on whether the adjective clause is **restrictive** or **nonrestrictive**. See the discussion on restrictive and nonrestrictive adjective clauses beginning on page 221 of Chapter 6. See also the discussion on *that* and *which* on page 225. Briefly summarized, most writers prefer to use *which* in nonrestrictive clauses. However, there is disagreement about restrictive clauses. Some writers strongly prefer to use *that*, while other writers use *that* and *which* interchangeably.

The grammatical rule governing *who* and *whom* is actually simple: if the relative pronoun is the subject of its clause, use *who*; if it is NOT the subject, use *whom*.

I know a man *who shaves while driving.*

I know a man *whom you may have met.*

I know a man *whom you went to school with.*

The issue then becomes, how can we help students recognize when the relative pronoun is a subject? **The verb–next test** is reasonably simple.

The verb–next test. If the next word following the relative pronoun is a verb, then use *who* because the relative pronoun is a subject.

Here is the verb–next test applied to the three example sentences.

I know a man *who shaves while driving.*

Test: The relative pronoun is followed by the verb *shaves,* so *who* is correct.

I know a man *whom you may have met.*

Test: The relative pronoun is followed by *you,* which is not a verb. Thus, *whom* is correct.

I know a man ***whom*** *you went to school with.*

Test: The relative pronoun is followed by *you,* which is not a verb. Thus, *whom* is correct.

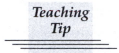

Teaching Tip

It helps students remember that *whom* is an object if you point out that historically the *m* in *whom* is the same object marker as in the object forms *him* and *them.*

There is one minor catch to using the verb–next test. Sometimes we can use an adverb BEFORE the verb, so that literally the next word is not the verb—it is an adverb modifying the verb. Here is an example:

I know a man *who **always** shaves while driving.*

In this sentence, the adverb *always* is modifying the verb *shaves.* As long as students understand that this rather trivial use of adverbs does not count when applying the verb–next test, then they will have no trouble with the test. (A more accurate way of phrasing the verb–next test would be that the relative pronoun is the subject if there is no other noun or pronoun between the relative pronoun and the verb, but this seems unnecessarily complex.)

Relative Pronoun Exercise #1: Choosing Between **who** and **whom** by the Verb–Next Test

Underline the instances of the incorrectly used relative pronoun *that* and put *who* or *whom* underneath (as appropriate). Confirm your answer by applying the verb–next test. The first question is done as an example. (Answers to this exercise are on page 539.)

0. I have a teacher that my father had.

    Answer: I have a teacher <u>that</u> my father had.
                         whom

    Confirmation: The relative pronoun is followed by the noun phrase *my father,* so the relative cannot be the subject.

1. I have teachers that love to diagram sentences.

2. We studied the Germans that invaded England in the 4th century.

3. The king met with the bishops that had opposed his policy.

4. Donald became a wealthy banker that everyone envied for his amusing anecdotes about the International Monetary Fund.

5. They employed an executive secretary that really ran the business.

6. The voters rejected the candidates that the party had nominated at the convention.

7. The story had been filed by a correspondent that the bureau had hired locally.

8. The plot involved rural sheriffs that kept wrecking their police cars.

9. Lady Lockheart graciously acknowledged the peasants that were permitted to watch their betters at play.

10. The manager called in the pitcher that they had recently acquired in a trade.

11. The long-suffering patients finally turned on the dentist that had ridiculed their brushing habits for so long.

12. The young woman that answered the phone took my order.

13. I called the couple that had answered the ad.

14. The clerk that I talked to found us a room.

15. The actors that were stage-front were blocking the other actors.

16. The insurance company needs the name of the mechanic that fixed your car.

17. Someone that I had met at the party called me up.

18. Writers that try to write completely outside their own experience always get into trouble.

19. He played the part of an aristocrat that everyone considered to be a complete idiot.

20. I know a person that would be perfect for the part.

Run-on Sentences (also Comma Splices and Fused Sentences)

Run-on sentence is a generic term referring to two **independent clauses** joined together as a single sentence without adequate punctuation. (Actually, a run-on sentence can have three or more independent clauses, but since additional independent clauses do not change the argument, we will ignore them from this point on.) There are two types of run-on sentences: **comma splices,** two independent clauses joined with only a comma; and **fused sentences,** two independent clauses joined with no punctuation at all. The distinction between comma splices and fused sentences is a distinction without a difference. They have the same cause, and they have the same treatment. Nevertheless, here are some examples of each type of run-on sentence, numbered for easy reference:

Comma Splice

1. *I got a new computer, it is an iMAC.

2. *I don't like to eat green peppers, they give me indigestion.

3. *Bluto drives me crazy, he never cleans up the kitchen.

Fused Sentence:

4. *She is finishing her degree soon she will graduate in June.

5. *My grades are OK I'm getting a 3.5.

6. *It was getting late I was beginning to get worried.

Run-on sentences happen for a reason: the two independent clauses are so closely related that writers do not want to break them up into two separate sentences. Typically, the first independent clause is a statement or a generalization that the second independent clause explains or elaborates on in some way. Let us now look again at the six example sentences and see how the second independent clause relates to the first.

1. *I got a new computer, it is an iMAC.

The first independent clause states that the writer got a computer, and the second clause tells the reader what kind of computer it is.

2. *I don't like to eat green peppers, they give me indigestion.

The second independent clause tells why the writer doesn't like to eat the green peppers mentioned in the first independent clause.

3. *Bluto drives me crazy, he never cleans up the kitchen.

The second independent clause tells why Bluto is driving the writer crazy.

4. *She is finishing her degree soon she will graduate in June.

The writer makes the generalization that a person is finishing soon. The second independent clause backs up that generalization by giving the actual date.

5. *My grades are OK I'm getting a 3.5.

The second independent clause supports the statement that the writer's grades are OK by giving the actual GPA.

6. *It was getting late I was beginning to get worried.

The two clauses imply cause and effect: it was late (cause), therefore, the writer was worried (result).

These six examples are quite typical run-ons. They show that their writers were attempting to connect closely related ideas. Rhetorically, it does make sense to put the two independent clauses together inside the boundaries of a single sentence. The problem is that the writers did not know the conventional technique for doing what they wanted: a semicolon.

Teaching
Tip

It might seem logical to also teach the technique of joining two independent clauses together by a comma and a coordinating conjunction in addition to the semicolon. However, relatively few run-ons make sense when joined with a co-ordinating conjunction. One of the causes of run-ons is the writers' awareness that coordinating conjunctions are not very effective ways of joining these independent clauses. In this sense, run-ons are a sign of the relative sophistication of the writers—they are no longer content with connecting ideas by *and*.

The error shows that the writers are no longer satisfied with writing sentences that express only one concept at a time. The writers are now beginning to explore more complex structures. What they need now is the punctuation tool that will enable them to do so—the semicolon.

Once writers who are producing run-on sentences have understood that the function of the semicolon is to join closely related independent clauses together in the same sentence, what they then need is a reliable way to identify sentences that contain two independent clauses.

> **The two periods test.** If two parts of a sentence can be broken apart and each punctuated with a period, then join the two parts with a semicolon.

Here is the two periods test applied to the six example sentences.

1.	*I got a new computer, it is an iMAC.
Test:	I got a new computer. It is an iMAC.
Correction:	I got a new computer; it is an iMAC.

2.	*I don't like to eat green peppers, they give me indigestion.
Test:	I don't like to eat green peppers. They give me indigestion.
Correction:	I don't like to eat green peppers; they give me indigestion.

3.	*Bluto drives me crazy, he never cleans up the kitchen.
Test:	Bluto drives me crazy. He never cleans up the kitchen.
Correction:	Bluto drives me crazy; he never cleans up the kitchen.

4.	*She is finishing her degree soon she will graduate in June.
Test:	She is finishing her degree soon. She will graduate in June.
Correction:	She is finishing her degree soon; she will graduate in June.

5.	*My grades are OK I'm getting a 3.5.
Test:	My grades are OK. I'm getting a 3.5.
Correction:	My grades are OK; I'm getting a 3.5.

6.	*It was getting late I was beginning to get worried.
Test:	It was getting late. I was beginning to get worried.
Correction:	It was getting late; I was beginning to get worried.

Run-On Sentences Exercise #1: Identifying Run-On Sentences by the Two Periods Test

Join the independent clauses with semicolons. Confirm your answers by applying the two periods test. The first question is done as an example. (Answers to this exercise are on page 540.)

 0. My computer is a life-saver I couldn't get along without it.

    Answer: My computer is a life-saver; I couldn't get along without it.

    Confirmation: My computer is a life-saver. I couldn't get along without it.

 1. English is a hybrid language it is related to both German and French.

 2. I'm going to have to get a new car, my old one is in the shop again.

 3. Don't eat your ice cream so quickly you'll get a headache.

 4. Children shouldn't see scary movies they have nightmares for weeks.

 5. The sale was a flop we hardly sold a thing.

 6. I don't like sitcoms on TV, they're all alike.

 7. He must have a cold his nose is running all the time.

 8. It was really cold this winter, the lake even froze over.

 9. I don't like that salsa it is too hot for me.

10. The forecast is for thunderstorms we should close the downstairs windows tonight.

11. I rarely watch the late show I don't want to stay up that late.

12. I have a copy of the book if you want to borrow it.

13. My sister is going to UCLA, my brother is going to USC.

14. I can't take that class I have a conflict with a required course.

15. Taking calculus is easy understanding it is hard.

16. They had a parfait, a dessert made with ice cream and syrup.

17. She's going to miss a couple of games she twisted her ankle in practice.

18. It is located near the interstate, about an hour's drive from here.

19. Las Vegas can't grow forever if nothing else, it can't get enough water to keep expanding.

20. Will Rogers said that you could always get a bank loan as long as you could show that you didn't need it.

For other ways of joining independent clauses, see also **Commas and Coordinating Conjunctions,** and **Semicolons and Conjunctive Adverbs.**

Subject–Verb Agreement

Subject–verb agreement requires that verbs in the present tense need to have a "3rd-person singular *s*" when the subject is singular. For example, compare the verbs in the following sentences:

> The book *seems* pretty difficult.

> The books *seem* pretty difficult.

In the first example, the verb *seem* has an added *s* because it is "in agreement with" its singular subject *book.* In the second example, the verb *seem* does not have an added *s* because it is in agreement with its plural subject *books.*

Part of the problem that many students have with subject–verb agreement is that the terminology is not as obvious as we might think. The subject of *seems* in the first example is not actually a 3rd-person pronoun at all; it is the noun *book.* It turns out that the term "3rd-person pronoun" can refer to either the actual 3rd-person pronouns *he,* she, or *it,* OR to a noun phrase that can be REPLACED by a 3rd-person pronoun:

> *The boy on the bus* looks like Elmer Fudd.
>   He

> *The woman* is looking our way.
>   She

> *The book* seems pretty difficult.
>   It

The rule governing the use of the 3rd-person singular *s* seems so fundamental to English that it is hard to imagine violating it. Yet anyone who has graded a set of student papers from grade school to college knows that subject–verb agreement is a major problem for some students.

One reason for making the error is psycholinguistic: the information contained in the 3rd-person singular s is simply not that important. Let us compare information conveyed by the *s* that marks the plural of nouns with information contained in the 3rd-person singular s:

Plural *s:*	The *books* seemed very hard.
3rd Pers Sg *s:*	The book *seems* very hard.

The *s* on *book* gives definable, new information: the *s* makes the word plural. What comparable information does the 3rd-person singular *s* give? The *s* on *seem* gives us the information that the subject must be either a 3rd-person singular pronoun or a noun phrase replaceable by a 3rd-person singular pronoun. This is hardly vital information, since we already know that *book* is the subject. We can delete the 3rd-person singular s without changing the meaning of the sentence:

*The book *seem* very hard.

The sentence is now nonstandard, but the actual meaning is exactly the same as the original sentence.

However, if we delete the *s* from the noun *book,* we significantly alter the information contained in the sentence by changing the number of the books involved:

The *book* seemed very hard.

The point of all this is that not all grammatical markers are equally important in terms of the information they convey. Our built-in language monitor prioritizes mistakes. It is particularly vigilant about mistakes of grammatical form that affect meaning (such as the plural s in *books*). These mistakes it notices and corrects immediately. Mistakes of form that do not affect meaning (such as the 3rd-person singular *s* in *seems*) are lower in the hierarchy of monitoring. If the monitor is being overwhelmed (as native speakers are under moments of stress and non-native speakers are most of the time), the monitor picks up the more important mistakes and lets the less important ones go by. Consequently, everything else being equal, we are far more likely to overlook our subject–verb agreement errors than we are to overlook errors that affect the meaning of what we are saying or writing.

One confirmation about the relative unimportance of the 3rd-person singular s is that, with the exception of the verb *be,* past-tense verbs do not agree with their subjects. For example, in the following sentences, the verb *seemed* is used with the singular subject *book* as well as the plural subject *books:*

The book *seemed* too difficult.

The books *seemed* too difficult.

We get along just fine in the past tense without marking subject–verb agreement, so why is it so important to mark subject–verb agreement in the present tense?

By far the most common specific cause of subject–verb agreement error is making the verb agree with a noun that is not actually the subject. However, before discussing misidentified subjects, let us deal with another cause of subject–verb error: identifying the subject correctly, but misidentifying the NUMBER of the subject.

Probably the most frequent error of this type occurs when students (usually but not always non-native speakers) mistakenly interpret a **mass** or **non-count** noun as a plural. (See "Articles" on page 318 for a discussion of these terms.) Here are some examples:

*The *luggage* are still at the station.

Pollution are making the cities unlivable.

*The *equipment* are in the gym.

In a way, these examples do not have subject–verb agreement errors at all. The writers knew perfectly well what the subjects were and made the verbs agree accordingly. The problem was that the writers assigned the wrong number to the subjects. The solution to this type of error has nothing to do with teaching students about subject–verb agreement; these students need more work on mass nouns.

Sometimes ESL students are tripped up by the differences between British and American English in the treatment of collective nouns. Collective nouns refer to groups (usually of people) that can be thought of in the plural as multiple individuals (British) or in the singular as an indivisible unit (American). Here are some examples:

British:	The team *are* on the field.
American:	The team *is* on the field.
British:	The orchestra *are* playing.
American:	The orchestra *is* playing.
British:	The government *are* pleased with the treaty.
American:	The government *is* pleased with the treaty.

Finally, sometimes non-native speakers are tripped up by the general wackiness of number in English. Consider, for example, how strange it is that the subjects in the following examples are singular:

A million *dollars* is a lot of money.

Everybody in the world knows about that.

Misidentified Subjects.   The most common cause of subject–verb agreement error, for native and non-native speakers alike, is making the verb agree with a noun or pronoun that is not actually the subject. To a great extent, the cause of this error is complexity. The longer and more complex the subject noun phrase is, the more likely we are to misidentify the subject. Part of the reason for this is also psycholinguistic. Most of us can hold five to seven words in verbatim, short-term memory. If the subject noun phrase is longer than five to seven words (or is especially grammatically complex), our brains recode the noun phrase in a simplified, condensed form. Here is a typical example:

> A group of yachts with brightly colored sails flying in the wind were entering the harbor.

This sentence contains a subject–verb agreement error. The verb *were* agrees with *yachts* rather than the actual subject *group*. In the research literature on grammatical error, this type of mistake is so common that it has its own name: "the nearest-noun agreement error." When we recode a long and/or complex subject noun phrase, we tend to remember only the semantically strongest noun that is nearest the verb. In the case of the above example, the nearest, strongest noun in the subject noun phrase is *yachts*.

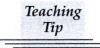

Teaching Tip

Put the sentence about the group of yachts on the board before students come into the classroom. After the class starts, erase the sentence. A few minutes later, ask the class if they remember what the sentence on the board was about. Nearly everyone will remember that it was about yachts. No one, unless they recall the sentence verbatim, will say that it was about a GROUP of yachts.

For most of our students, most of the time, subject–verb agreement errors are a function of the complexity of subject noun phrases. Students who write very simple sentences with subjects next to verbs rarely make subject–verb agreement errors (if they are able to add the 3rd-personal singular *s* at all, as all but some beginning ESL students can).

One reason that simple workbook exercises for subject–verb agreement error do not transfer very well to students' own writing is that workbook exercises tend to focus on relatively simple sentences. Even weaker students can usually monitor these sentences for subject–verb agreement. However, the errors reside in the very complexity of the students' own sentences, and no amount of work on simple sentences will do much good. What our students need is the ability to monitor the longer and more complex noun phrases.

One way to help students is by understanding the actual mechanisms for making noun phrases longer and more complex. Noun phrases are expanded in two ways: (1) additional adjectives in front of the head noun and

(2) post-noun modifiers. Of these two ways, only the latter is a source of significant growth. Basically, we make noun phrases longer and more complex by adding one or more of these four post-noun modifiers: prepositional phrases, adjective clauses, participial phrases, and appositive phrases. Here is how the head noun *group* was expanded in our example sentence:

> A **group** *of yachts*
> prepositional phrase
>
> > *with brightly colored sails*
> > prepositional phrase
> >
> > > *flying in the wind*
> > > participial phrase

As you can see, the effect of these three modifiers is to push the head noun (the simple subject *group*) farther and farther away from the verb.

What writers need to be able to do is check for subject–verb agreement by skipping over the post-noun modifiers that separate the actual subject (the **simple subject** in traditional terms) from the verb. If the hypothetical author of our example sentence had been able to skip over the post-noun modifiers, the author would have found this:

> *A *group* were entering the harbor.

This simplified version of the original sentence is obviously much easier to monitor for subject–verb agreement than the original.

Here is a technique for simplifying the subject noun phrase so that the actual simple subject is next to the verb: skip from the verb back to the first noun.

The first noun test. Skip back from the verb to the first noun in the sentence. Test that noun with the verb to see if it makes sense. If it does, then make sure the verb agrees with the number of that noun. If it does not make sense, go to the next noun.

The first noun test works because subject noun phrases are expanded by post-noun modifiers. The only time the first noun will not be the subject of the main clause is when an adverb prepositional phrase has been moved to the front of the sentence, for example:

> In the afternoons, the painters *go* to another job.
>
> Test: *Afternoons* **go** to another job.
> Test: *Painters* **go** to another job.

The first noun is *afternoon,* but that noun makes no sense as the subject of *go,* so we go to the next noun, *painters,* which obviously is the subject of *go.*

Here is a much more complex example in which the subject–verb error is in a subordinate clause:

> *Harold told them that his cottage, one of the many new houses in the ocean-side developments, *were* not damaged in the storm.

Test: *Harold **were** not damaged in the storm.

Test: The *cottage* **was** not damaged in the storm.

The first noun is *Harold,* but *Harold* is not a plausible subject. The next noun is cottage, which is a plausible subject of *were not damaged.*

Subject–Verb Agreement Exercise #1: Identifying Subjects by the First Noun Test _____

Find and underline the subjects of the italicized verbs, then correct the agreement error. Confirm your answers by applying the first noun test. The first question is done as an example. (Answers to this exercise are on page 541.)

   0. The advantages of this computer system *is* that you will not need upgrades for several years.

   Answer: The <u>advantages</u> of this computer system <u>are</u> that you will not need upgrades for several years.

   Confirmation: The <u>advantages are</u> that you will not need upgrades for several years.

   1. In our last three games, the average margin of our losses *have* been two points.

   2. The answers for the problems in the first section *is* on page 312.

   3. Only one finalist out of several hundred contenders *are* selected.

   4. In the last chapter, our hero, attacked by swarms of crazed bees, *were* swimming through the rat-infested sewers of New York.

   5. The time for cooking turkeys *depend* on the size of the birds.

   6. Speculation about the actions of the committee *have* dominated the news lately.

   7. In any event, the simplest solutions to a complex problem *is* the hardest to carry out.

   8. Three mistakes in a row *means* that you are out.

   9. Parking in the marked spaces *are* forbidden by city ordinance.

  10. As is usually the case, the people seated in the back row *needs* to move forward.

  11. The number of accidents caused by drunk drivers *increase* at night.

12. According to the catalog, one of these three classes *are* required for your major.

13. The heavy fall rain in the mountains *have* washed a lot of soil away.

14. The boxes in the back of the trailer *goes* in the storage room.

15. The belongings of the transit passenger *is* now available.

16. The radio shown in their new catalogs *were* just what we wanted.

17. The experts that we polled at the university *has* confirmed our opinion.

18. Parking in the downtown lots overnight *are* prohibited.

19. Pain in the joints of the fingers and toes *signal* arthritis.

20. A group of small children playing outside *delight* in keeping me from working.

Subject–Verb Agreement Errors in Existential Sentences.   One particular construction causes a disproportionate number of subject–verb agreement errors: existential sentences. Most languages have a grammatical construction called an existential sentence that is used for pointing out the existence of something. In English, the existential sentence uses the adverb there + a linking verb. Here are some examples:

> *There is* a fly in my soup.

> *There was* an old woman who lived in a shoe.

> *There seems* to be a problem with my bill.

> *There appears* to be no solution.

The grammar of existential sentences is unusual in that the actual subject FOLLOWS the verb. Here are the example sentences again, this time with the subject in bold:

> There *is* a **fly** in my soup.

> There *was* an old **woman** who lived in a shoe.

> There *seems* to be a **problem** with my bill.

> There *appears* to be no **solution.**

It is easy to show that the first noun following the verb is the subject. If we reverse the numbers in the examples above, i.e., change singular nouns to plural and vice versa, the verbs also change accordingly:

> There *is* a **fly** in my soup.

> There *are* **flies** in my soup.

There *was* an old **woman** who lived in a shoe.

There *were* some old **women** who lived in a shoe.

There *seems* to be a **problem** with my bill.

There *seem* to be some **problems** with my bill.

There *appears* to be no **solution.**

There *appear* to be no **solutions.**

One obvious cause for subject–verb agreement error in existential sentences is the unorthodox word order in which the subject follows the verb.

In addition, however, there is another, much more important reason why so many subject–verb agreement errors occur in this construction. In informal, spoken English, *there* functions as the apparent subject. As a result, the verbs in all existential sentences are singular in agreement with *there,* no matter what noun follows the verb. In other words, we find numerous instances of subject–verb errors like these in which the verb is singular but the actual subject noun is plural:

*There *is* **flies** in my soup.

*There *was* some old **women** who lived in a shoe.

*There *seems* to be some **problems** with my bill.

*There *appears* to be no **solutions.**

However, the reverse error in which a plural verb is used with a singular noun is quite rare:

*There *are* a **fly** in my soup.

*There *were* an old **woman** who lived in a shoe.

*There *seem* to be a **problem** with my bill.

*There *appear* to be no **solution.**

Knowing where to look for the error in existential sentences leads us to the following test.

> **The existential *there* test.** If a sentence contains an existential *there,* check to see if the noun following the verb is plural. If it is, make sure that the verb agrees with it.

Here is the existential there test applied to the most common types of errors:

	*There *is* **flies** in my soup.
Test:	*Flies is
Correction:	There are flies in my soup.
	*There *was* some old **women** who lived in a shoe.
Test:	*Women was
Correction:	There were some old women who lived in a shoe.
	*There *seems* to be some **problems** with my bill.
Test:	*Problems seems
Correction:	There seem to be some problems with my bill.
	*There *appears* to be no **solutions.**
Test:	*Solutions appears
Correction:	There appear to be no solutions.

Subject–Verb Agreement Exercise #2: Identifying Subjects in Existential There Sentences

Find and underline the subjects of the verbs in existential *there* sentences, then correct the agreement errors. Confirm your answers by applying the existential *there* test. The first question is done as an example. (Answers to this exercise are on page 543.)

0. There is millions of stars in our galaxy.

   Answer: There is millions of stars in our galaxy.

                                        are

   Confirmation: Millions of stars are.

1. There is dozens of books piled on the carpet.

2. There was many jobs still to do.

3. We discovered that there is some tools that we could use.

4. There is an old flashlight and some batteries in the trunk.

5. There was some dishes that looked OK.

6. There appears to be several possible solutions to the problem.

7. There is several movies that I would like to see.

8. Suddenly, there was several bright lights shining in the trees.

9. There is lakes all across this basin.

10. There seems to be noises coming from the back yard.

Part

III

Glossary
of Grammar Terms

This glossary gives the meaning and an example of every grammatical term used in this book. The terms in bold are other grammatical terms that you may need to look up in order to fully understand the definition.

Absolute adjective   An absolute adjective is an adjective that cannot be used with *very* and has no **comparative** or **superlative** forms. For example, the adjective *main* is an absolute adjective because we cannot say **the very main idea, *the mainer idea,* or **the mainest idea.* Either something is main or it is not. There are no degrees of being main.

Action verb   All verbs except **linking verbs** are action verbs. While many action verbs do indeed express an action carried out by the subject, many do not. The only characteristic that action verbs share is that they are not linking verbs. For example, in the sentence *The garden swarmed with bees,* the verb *swarmed* is considered an action verb even though the subject *garden* is not doing the swarming. *Swarm* is an action verb by default since *swarm* is not a linking verb.

Active   See **active voice.**

Active voice   The term "active voice" refers to the majority of sentences, in which the subject is the topic or "do-er" of the action, as opposed to **passive voice** sentences, in which the subject is the person or thing receiving the action. For example, in the active voice sentence *John saw Mary,* the subject *John* is doing the action of seeing. In the corresponding passive voice sentence *Mary was seen by John,* the subject *Mary* is not doing the seeing; she is still the person being seen.

Adjective   Adjectives play two roles: (1) **modifying adjectives** that modify the nouns that they precede, for example, *a young man,* and (2) **predicate adjectives** that follow **linking verbs,** for example *the actor looked young.* Most predicate adjectives have **comparative** and **superlative degrees,** for example, *younger, youngest* and *more beautiful, most beautiful.*

Adjective clause   Adjective clauses (also called "relative clauses") modify nouns. For example, in the sentence *The book that you bought was expensive,* the adjective clause *that you bought* modifies the noun *book.*

376

Adverb   Adverbs modify a verb (*spoke rapidly*), an adjective (*quite strong*), or another adverb (*pretty badly*). Adverbs that modify verbs are normally movable: *It will rain soon. Soon, it will rain.* Adverbs that modify verbs also answer **adverb questions.**

Adverb clause   Adverb clauses modify verbs, giving *when, where, why,* or *how* information. For example, in the sentence *I will meet you at the restaurant after my class is over,* the underlined adverb clause gives "when" information. Adverb clauses have the unusual property of being easily moved to the beginning of the **independent clause;** for example, *After my class is over, I will meet you at the restaurant.*

Adverb phrase   The term "adverb phrase" refers only to prepositional phrases used as adverbs. For example, in the sentence *I went home after work,* the prepositional phrase *after work* is called an "adverb phrase" since it functions as an adverb telling when the action happened. Do not use "adverb phrase" as a collective term for all types of adverbs.

Adverb question   Any word, phrase, or clause that answers an adverb question is acting as an adverb. The adverb questions are *when, where, why,* and *how.* For example, in the sentence *We walked home, home* is an adverb because it answers a *where* question: *Where did we walk?* Answer: *Home.*

Adverbial of place   In modern grammar, an adverbial of place is an adverb or adverb prepositional phrase that answers a *where* **adverb question.** Some verbs require an adverbial of place as their **complement.** The verb *put,* for example, requires a **noun phrase** + an adverbial of place complement: *I put the book on the table.* In other words, when you put something, you have to put it SOMEWHERE.

Agreement   Agreement refers to grammatically connected words. There are two main forms of agreement. (1) **Personal pronouns** and **reflexive pronouns** must agree with their **antecedents.** For example, in the sentence *John cut himself shaving,* the reflexive pronoun *himself* must agree with its antecedent *John* in number and gender (**John cut herself; *John cut themselves*). (2) Verbs must also agree with their subjects in number (**subject–verb agreement**). For example, in the sentence *She was expecting company,* the verb *was* must agree in number with its subject *she.*

Antecedent   see **pronoun antecedent.**

Appositive   An appositive is a noun that renames or further identifies a preceding noun. For example, in the sentence *My English teacher, Ms. Wright, went to school with my mother,* the appositive *Ms. Wright* further identifies who my English teacher is.

Appositive phrase   An appositive phrase is an **appositive** together with its modifiers. For example, in the following sentence, the appositive is in bold and the entire appositive phrase is underlined: *Ms. Wright, my English **teacher**, went to school with my mother.*

Article   Articles are a special class of adjectives. There are two types of articles: the **definite article** (*the*) and the **indefinite article** (*a/an*). Also see **determiner.**

Base form of adjective   Most adjectives have three forms: a base form that can be used with *very,* a **comparative** form, and a **superlative** form. For example, *very tall, taller, tallest;* and *very beautiful, more beautiful, most beautiful.* The base form is the dictionary-entry form of an adjective. Put negatively, the base form is the form that is not comparative or superlative.

Base form of verb   The base form of a verb is its dictionary-entry form. For example, the base form of *sang* is *sing.* The base form is the basis for all **infinitives** (*to sing*) and the basis of the **present tense** forms (*I sing, you sing, he sings, we sing, they sing*). The only exception is the verb *be,* whose present system is different than its base form *be:* (*I am, you are, he is, we are, they are*).

Cardinal number   Cardinal numbers are the names of the numbers: *one, two, three. . . .* The other kind of number (*first, second, third*) is called **ordinal number.**

Case   The term "case" refers to the grammatical function of nouns and pronouns in sentences. The cases are **subject, object,** and **possessive.** For example, in the sentence *She met him, she* is in the subject case and *him* is in the object case.

Clause   A clause contains at least one **subject** and one **finite verb** (a verb in agreement with its subject). If a clause can stand alone, it is called an **independent clause;** if a clause cannot stand alone, it is called a **dependent clause.** Clauses differ from **phrases** in that phrases do not have **finite verbs.**

Closed class   The term "closed class" refers to parts of speech (**pronoun, preposition, conjunction**) that can be defined by listing the membership of the class. The opposite of closed class is **open class.**

Command   See **exclamatory sentence.**

Common noun   The term "common noun" describes nouns used for categories of people, places, or things, as opposed to **proper nouns,** the names of specific individual persons, places, or things. For example, *woman* is a common noun, but *Martha Stewart* is a proper noun; *city* is a common noun, but *Chicago* is a proper noun; *company* is a common noun, but *General Electric* is a proper noun. Common nouns are not capitalized.

Comparative adjective   A comparative adjective is the form (**degree**) of adjective ending in *-er* or preceded by *more*. For example, in the following sentences, the underlined adjectives are in the comparative form: *Jason felt colder than ever; Jason felt more confident than ever.* Also see **base form** and **superlative form** of adjectives.

Complement   In traditional grammar, a complement is a noun, pronoun, or adjective required by a verb to make a complete sentence. For example, the verb *love* requires a noun or pronoun object as its complement: *John loves ice cream; John loves it.* (If the complement is deleted, the sentence is ungrammatical: **John loves.*) In modern grammar, the term "complement" is broadened to include any grammatical element (including prepositional phrases and adverbs) required by a verb. For example, the verb *put* requires both an object and an **adverbial of place** as its complement: *John put the book on the desk.* (Without the adverbial of place, the sentence is ungrammatical: **John put the book.*)

Complete subject   The complete subject is the entire subject phrase (the **simple subject** together with all its modifiers). For example, in the following sentence the complete subject is underlined and the simple subject is in bold: *A **boy** waiting at a bus stop saw the accident.* In modern grammar, the complete subject is called a subject **noun phrase.**

Complex sentence   A complex sentence consists of an **independent clause** and at least one **dependent clause.** For example, in the following sentence, the independent clause is in bold and the dependent clause is underlined: ***There was an old woman** who lived in a shoe.*

Compound   The term "compound" refers to two (or more) grammatical elements of the same type joined by a coordinating conjunction. The grammatical elements can be as small as individual words (*John and Mary went to town*), phrases (*We went over the river and through the woods*), or entire clauses (*John loves Mary, but Mary loves Sam*).

Compound sentence   A compound sentence contains two (or more) **independent clauses** but no subordinate clause, for example, *This little piggy had roast beef, but this little piggy had none.*

Compound-complex sentence   A compound-complex sentence contains a **compound sentence** and at least one **dependent clause.** In the following example, the compound sentence is underlined and the dependent clause is in bold: *John loves Mary, but Mary loves Sam **until somebody better comes along.***

Conjunction   A conjunction is a word that joins together grammatical units. There are two types of conjunctions: (1) **coordinating conjunctions,** words such as *and, but, or;*

and (2) **subordinating conjunctions,** words such as *when, since,* and *if* that begin **adverb clauses.**

Conjunctive adverb   A conjunctive adverb shows how the meaning of the second of two sentences is related to the meaning of the first sentence. For example, in the pair of sentences *We had planned to meet for lunch. However, I had to cancel,* the conjunctive adverb *however* signals that the second sentence contradicts in some way the meaning of the first sentence.

Coordinate adjectives   Coordinate adjectives are two adjectives from the same adjective class that must be separated by a comma, for example, *The weary, disillusioned daytrader slumped before his computer.*

Coordinating conjunction   A coordinating conjunction joins grammatical units of the same type, creating a **compound.** There are seven coordinating conjunctions; they can be remembered by the acronym FANBOYS: *for, and, nor, but, or, yet, so.*

Correlative conjunction   A correlative conjunction is a two-part **coordinating conjunction,** for example, *either . . . or; both . . . and; neither . . . nor.*

Count noun   A count noun is a common noun that has a plural form and can be used with number words, i.e., it can be counted. For example, *cat, goose, sheep* are all count nouns: *one cat/two cats; one goose/two geese; one sheep/two sheep.* Nouns that cannot be counted are called **mass nouns** or "noncount" nouns.

Declarative sentence   A declarative sentence is a statement (as opposed to an **interrogative, imperative,** or **exclamatory sentence**) punctuated with a period, as, for example, this sentence.

Degree   The term "degree" refers to the fact that most adjectives occur in three forms: a **base** form, a **comparative** form, and a **superlative** form. For example, the adjectives *tall* and *beautiful* have the following degrees: base forms: *tall, beautiful;* comparative forms: *taller, more beautiful;* superlative forms: *tallest, most beautiful.*

Demonstrative pronoun   The demonstrative pronouns are *this, that, these,* and *those* used as pronouns, not adjectives. For example, in the sentence *That is mine, that* is a demonstrative pronoun because it acts as the subject of the sentence. In the sentence *That porcupine is mine, that* is an adjective modifying the noun *porcupine.* (Some earlier grammars call demonstrative pronouns used as adjectives "demonstrative adjectives.")

Dependent clause   A dependent clause is a **clause** that cannot stand alone as a complete sentence (as opposed to an **independent clause,** which can stand alone). In the preceding sentence, *that cannot stand alone as a complete sentence* is a dependent clause. Dependent clauses are also called "subordinate clauses." There are three types of dependent clauses: **adjective clauses, adverb clauses,** and **noun clauses.**

Descriptive adjective   The term "descriptive adjective" includes all adjectives that follow **determiners,** the other class of adjectives. Descriptive adjectives (unlike determiners) can be used as **predicate adjectives.** For example, in the sentence *Susan appeared calm, calm* is a descriptive adjective. Most descriptive adjectives (also unlike determiners) have **comparative** and **superlative** forms, for example, *calmer, calmest.*

Determiner   The term "determiner" includes adjectives such as **articles, numbers,** and **possessives** that precede **descriptive adjectives.** For example, in the phrase *a calm pilot,* the article *a* is a determiner. Determiners (unlike descriptive adjectives) cannot be used as **predicate adjectives** and have no **comparative** or **superlative** forms.

Direct object   A direct object is a noun or pronoun used as the **object** of a verb. For example, in the sentence *John saw the accident,* the noun *accident* is the direct object of the verb *saw.* Also see **indirect object.**

Essential appositive   Most **appositives** are redundant; that is, they can be deleted without affecting the meaning of the sentence. However, if an essential appositive is deleted, the meaning of the resulting sentence is destroyed. For example, in the sentence *Shakespeare's play <u>Hamlet</u> is one of his greatest*, the essential appositive *Hamlet* cannot be deleted without making the sentence meaningless: **Shakespeare's play is one of his greatest*. Essential appositives are not set off with commas as normal appositives are.

Exclamatory sentence   An exclamatory sentence is a statement punctuated with an exclamation point instead of a period, for example: *I'm going to be late!*

Finite verb   See **tensed verb**.

Form   See **case**.

Fragment   See **sentence fragment**.

Future perfect tense   The future perfect tense consists of *will* + *have* + **past participle:** *She <u>will have been</u> here for a year by then.*

Future progressive   The future progressive consists of *will* + *be* + **present participle:** *She <u>will be staying</u> for another term.*

Future tense   In traditional grammar, the future tense consists of the helping verb *will* + **base form:** *I <u>will be</u> ready soon.* In modern grammar, the term "future tense" is not used; instead, *will* is treated as one of the five **modal verbs.**

Gender   The term "gender" refers to the uses of the pronouns *he/him* (masculine); *she/her* (feminine); and *it* (neuter).

Gerund   A gerund is the *-ing* form of a verb (the **present participle**) used as a noun. For example, in the sentence *Swimming is my favorite sport*, the present participle *Swimming* is used as a gerund. Also see **gerund phrase**.

Gerund phrase   A gerund phrase consists of a **gerund** together with its subject, complement, and/or modifiers. For example, in the following sentence, the gerund is in bold and the entire gerund phrase is underlined: <u>*John's* **swimming** *at the pool*</u> *keeps him in shape.*

Gradable adjective   The term "gradable" is used to describe adjectives that have **comparative** and **superlative** forms: *tall, taller, tallest; beautiful, more beautiful, most beautiful.* **Determiners** and **absolute adjectives** are not gradable.

Head   In modern grammar, the head of a **phrase** determines the nature of the phrase. For example, the head of a **noun phrase** is a noun. In other words, a phrase consists of its head together with the head's "subject," complement, and/or modifiers. For example, in the noun phrase *a young woman at the bus stop*, the head of the phrase is the noun *woman.*

Helping verb   The term "helping verb" is applied to all verbs used before another verb in multiple-verb constructions. Three helping verbs are used to form multiple-verb constructions: *will, have,* and *be. Will* is used to form the future "tenses" (*I <u>will</u> be there*). *Have* is used to form the perfect tenses (*I <u>have</u> been there*). *Be* is used to form the progressive (*I <u>am</u> going there*) and the passive (*John <u>was</u> seen by Mary*). In modern grammar, the list of helping verbs is expanded to include the remaining **modal verbs** (*can, may, must, shall*).

Imperative sentence   An imperative sentence must have an understood *you* as the subject. Imperative sentences may be punctuated with either a period (*Please close the door.*) or an exclamation point (*Close the door!*).

Indefinite pronoun   Indefinite pronouns refer to unspecified persons, things, or groups used as pronouns, not adjectives that modify nouns. For example, in the sentence *Many are called, many* is an indefinite pronoun because it is the subject; but in the sentence *Many hands make light work, many* is an adjective modifying the noun *hands.* Some typical indefinite pronouns are *all, any, each, every, few, many, much, one, some.* (Some earlier grammars call indefinite pronouns used as adjectives "indefinite adjectives.")

Independent clause   An independent **clause** can stand alone as a complete sentence, as, for example, this sentence. Independent clauses are also called "main clauses." Also see **dependent clause.**

Indirect object   A number of verbs take a second object, called the indirect object, in addition to the normal **direct object.** When a verb takes two objects, the indirect object always comes first and can be paraphrased with *to* or *for.* For example, in the sentence *John gave Mary a present, Mary* is the indirect object. The sentence can be paraphrased as *John gave a present* **to** *Mary.*

Infinitive   In traditional grammar, an infinitive is *to* + the **base form** of the verb, for example, *to see, to have, to be.* In modern grammar the term "infinitive" can also be used to refer to the base form by itself. Sometimes the base form with *to* is called a "marked infinitive" (*to see*) and the base form by itself is called an "unmarked infinitive" (*see*). Infinitives can also be used as nouns, adjectives, or adverbs.

Infinitive phrase   An infinitive phrase is an **infinitive** used as a noun together with the infinitive's subject, complement, and/or modifiers. For example, in the following sentence, the infinitive is in bold and the entire infinitive phrase is underlined: *For our team* **to win** *the game was our only goal.*

Infinitive verb phrase   In modern grammar, the term "infinitive verb phrase" is used to describe a type of **infinitive** that is one of the **complements** of a particular verb. For example, in the sentence *We finally got him to ask for a raise,* the infinitive phrase *to ask for a raise* is required by the verb *get.* In other words, one use of the verb *get* is to get somebody TO DO SOMETHING. The infinitive phrase is not being used as a noun because we cannot replace the infinitive phrase with the pronoun *it:* **We finally got him it.* (where *it = to ask for a raise*)

Inseparable phrasal verb   A **phrasal verb** is a kind of verb compound. An inseparable phrasal verb forms a compound with a particular preposition. For example, in the sentence *John looked after the kids,* the verb compound *looked after* has the unpredictable meaning of "supervised." This type of compound is called "inseparable" because the preposition cannot be moved after the object: **John looked the kids after.* Compare this type of verb compound with **separable phrasal verbs,** in which the second element of the compound can move after the object.

Interjection   An interjection is an exclamation inserted into a sentence for emphasis. For example, in the sentence *Wow, it's hot, wow* is an interjection. Interjections, unlike adverbs, play no grammatical role inside the sentence.

Interrogative pronoun   Interrogative pronouns begin questions that ask for information (as opposed to questions that can be answered by "yes" or "no"). The most common interrogative pronouns are *who, whom, when, where, which, why,* and *how,* for example: *Who are you? When, where, why,* and *how* are sometimes called "interrogative adverbs."

Interrogative sentence   An interrogative sentence asks a question and is always punctuated with a question mark, for example: *Is this an interrogative sentence?*

Intransitive verb   An intransitive verb is an **action verb** that does not require an **object.** For example, the verbs *die* and *sneeze* are intransitive verbs in the following sentences: *The old cow died last night. John sneezed loudly.*

Irregular verb   An irregular verb is a verb with one or more unpredictable forms. In particular, irregular verbs do not form their past tense with *-ed,* for example: *go–went; be–was/were; sing–sang; hit–hit.*

Linking verb   A linking verb is a verb that can take a **predicate adjective** as a complement, for example, *Fred was* <u>frantic</u>; *Susie seemed* <u>sad</u>; *Louise looked* <u>lonely</u>. The verb *be* is the most common linking verb. The other common linking verbs are verbs of sense perception (*appear, look, smell, taste*) or verbs that describe the condition of the subject (*The cook got angry; They became teachers*). All verbs that are not linking verbs are **action verbs.**

Main clause   See **independent clause.**

Main sentence line   In sentence diagramming, the main sentence line is the base line on which the required sentence components are drawn: the **simple subject,** the **verb,** and **complements.** All modifiers are drawn below the main sentence line.

Main verb   Every sentence must contain a main verb. The main verb may appear alone, or it may be preceded by one or more **helping verbs.** The main verb is always the rightmost verb in a sequence of verbs. For example, in the following sentence, the main verb is in bold and the helping verbs are underlined: *We will have been **working** on this project all night.* The main verb alone governs whatever **complements** are required to make a grammatical sentence.

Mass noun   The term "mass noun" is used for a large category of nouns that cannot be used in the plural, with number words, or with the indefinite article *a/an*, for example, **one homework, two homeworks, a homework; *one dirt, two dirt, a dirt.* Nouns that can be pluralized, counted, and used with *a/an* are called **count nouns.** Mass nouns are also called "noncount nouns."

Modal verb   The term "modal verb" is used in modern grammar to describe a group of five **helping verbs:** *can, may, must, shall,* and *will.* Modal verbs (used in either their present- or past-tense forms) are always followed by a verb in the **base form,** for example: *I can go. They might be late.* For historical reasons, traditional grammar recognized only *will*, which was considered to be the English equivalent of the future tense in Latin.

Modifying adjective   Modifying adjectives are adjectives used to modify nouns, for example, *an old man.* The other type of adjectives is **predicate adjectives.** There are two types of modifying adjectives: **descriptive adjectives** and **determiners.**

Noncount noun   See **mass noun.**

Nonfinite   See **nontensed verb form.**

Nonrestrictive adjective clause   A nonrestrictive adjective clause is an **adjective clause** that does not affect the meaning of the noun it modifies. For example, in the sentence *Sally's hair, which was dyed a fluorescent orange, naturally attracted attention*, the adjective clause *which was dyed a fluorescent orange* is nonrestrictive because the fact that Sally's hair was dyed florescent orange does not define WHOSE hair the sentence is about. Sally's hair would still be Sally's hair even if it were not fluorescent orange. Nonrestrictive adjective clauses are always set off with commas from the nouns they modify. Adjective clauses that do affect the meaning of the nouns they modify are called **restrictive clauses.**

Nonrestrictive modifier   The term "nonrestrictive modifier" is slightly broader than **nonrestrictive adjective clause** because the term also includes other nonrestrictive adjective structures such as nonrestrictive **participial phrases.** For example, in the sentence *Mr. Brown, betting his last dollar, won the pot*, the participial phrase *betting his last dollar* is a nonrestrictive modifier because it does not define who won the pot— Mr. Brown did, whether he bet his last dollar or not. Nonrestrictive modifiers are always set off with commas. Modifiers that do restrict are called **restrictive modifiers.**

Nontensed verb form   The term "nontensed verb" refers to all verb forms EXCEPT the ones in present- and past-tense forms. Using the verb *be* as an example, the four nontensed forms are the **base form** (*be*), the **infinitive** (*to be*), the **present participle** (*being*), and the **past participle** (*been*).

Nontensed verb phrase In modern grammar, a nontensed verb phrase is a verb **complement** that contains one of the four **nontensed verbs:** a **base form,** an **infinitive,** a **present participle,** or a **past participle.** For example, in the sentence *I saw him working in the den,* the nontensed verb phrase *working in the den* is a complement of *saw.* In this particular example, the nontensed verb phrase contains a present participle.

Noun In traditional grammar, a noun is defined as the name of a person, place, or thing. Nouns also have certain properties by which they can be identified: most nouns can be used with *the,* have plural forms, and can always be replaced by pronouns. For example, the noun *cat* can be used with *the* (*the cat*), used in the plural (*cats*), and be replaced by the pronoun *it.*

Noun clause A noun clause is a **clause** that plays a noun role in a sentence; that is, the noun clause plays the role of subject, object of a verb, or object of a preposition. For example, in the sentence *What he meant was a complete mystery,* the noun clause *What he meant* plays the role of subject. There are two types of noun clause: ***that-type*** and ***wh-type.***

Noun phrase The term "noun phrase" is widely used in modern grammar as a collective term for any grammatical structure that plays a noun role. Most noun phrases are headed (see **head**) by a noun (with or without accompanying modifiers). For example, the noun phrase *the boy in the picture* is headed by the noun *boy.* Pronouns are also considered noun phrases since they play noun roles.

Object An object is a noun (or pronoun) required by a verb or preposition. In the sentence *John saw Mary, Mary* is the object of the verb *saw.* However, not all nouns following verbs are objects: **linking verbs** do not take objects; they are used with **predicate nominatives.** Prepositions must always be followed by a noun (or pronoun) that acts as the preposition's object, for example, *under the <u>desk;</u> after the <u>party,</u> near <u>them.</u>*

Object complement An object complement is a noun (or pronoun) that follows a **direct object** and renames or describes it. For example, in the sentence *She called Fred a fool,* the noun *fool* is an object complement that describes the object *Fred.*

Open class The term "open class" refers to the four parts of speech (**nouns, verbs, adjectives, adverbs**) that cannot be defined by listing the membership of the class. Each of these parts of speech must be defined by defining characteristics shared by all the members. For example, all verbs share the unique characteristic of having a past tense. The opposite of open class is **closed class.**

Ordinal number The ordinal numbers are *first, second, third.* . . . One way to remember the term "ordinal" is that ordinal numbers refer to the "order" of things. The other form of number is **cardinal** (*one, two, three* . . .).

Participle The term "participle" is a generic term covering the two participle verb forms: the **present participle** and the **past participle.**

Participial phrase A participial phrase is a **phrase** containing either a **present participle** or a **past participle** together with the participle's complements and/or modifiers. Participial phrases are used as adjectives following the nouns they modify. For example, in the following sentence, the participle is in bold and the entire participle phrase is underlined: *The woman **taking** <u>notes in court</u> was a reporter.* The participial phrase modifies the noun *woman.*

Parts of speech The conventional seven parts of speech are **noun, adjective, pronoun, verb, adverb, preposition,** and **conjunction.** Sometimes the **interjection** is included as the eighth part of speech.

Passive See **passive voice.**

Passive voice   In a passive voice sentence, the subject is not the person or thing doing the action; the subject is the recipient of the action. For example, in the passive voice sentence *Mary was seen by John,* the subject *Mary* is not doing the seeing, she is the person being seen. The most common version of the passive voice is formed by the helping verb *be* + **past participle.** In the example above, *Mary was seen by John, was* is the past tense of *be* and *seen* is the past participle form of *see.* Sentences that are not in the passive voice are in the **active voice.**

Past participle   In **regular verbs,** the past participle ends in -*ed.* In **irregular verbs,** the form of the past participle is quite unpredictable: *sing–sung; tell–told; see–seen; wake–woken; be–been.* The best way to identify the past participle of a verb is to put the verb after the helping verb *have: have walked; have told; have seen, have spoken; have been.*

Past perfect tense   The past perfect tense consists of *had* + **past participle,** for example, *John had seen the movie before.*

Past progressive   The past progressive consists of *was/were* + **present participle,** for example, *John was watching TV.*

Past tense   The past tense is used for completed action. In **regular verbs** the past tense is formed by adding -*ed* to the **base form,** for example, *walk–walked; pin–pinned; part–parted.*

Perfect tense   The three perfect tenses are formed by the helping verb *have* (in some form) + **past participle.** The form of *have* (present, past, or future) determines the perfect tense. The three perfect tenses are the **present** perfect (*John has seen the movie*), the **past perfect** (*John had seen the movie*), and the **future perfect** (*John will have seen the movie*).

Personal pronoun   The personal pronouns (in their subject forms) are *I, you, he, she, it, they, you* (plural), and *we.*

Phrasal verb   In modern grammar, the term "phrasal verb" refers to the large number of verbs that form idiomatic compounds with particular adverbs or prepositions. For example, the phrasal verb *give up* can mean "quit" (*The police gave up*); the phrasal verb *call on* can mean "visit" (*Miss Manners called on her friends*). Also see **separable phrasal verb** and **inseparable phrasal verb.**

Phrase   In traditional grammar, a phrase is a group of words that acts as a single part of speech; for example, prepositional phrases act as either adjectives or adverbs. A phrase differs from a clause in that a phrase does not contain a subject–verb relationship. In modern grammar, the term "phrase" is defined somewhat differently. A phrase can be just the single **head** word or the head word together with complements and/or modifiers.

Possessive noun   A possessive noun adds *'s* or *s'* to the subject form of the noun, for example: *Mary–Mary's; child–children's; boy–boys'.* Possessive nouns are usually noun modifiers: for example, *I found Mary's book;* though sometimes they can be used as pronouns: for example, *I found Mary's.*

Possessive pronoun   Possessive pronouns have two forms: one used as an adjective to modify a following noun, the other used as a true pronoun that stands in place of a noun. For example, in the sentence *I found my porcupine,* the possessive pronoun *my* is used as an adjective modifying the noun *porcupine.* In the sentence *I found mine,* the possessive pronoun *mine* functions as a true pronoun, the object of the verb *found.* Here are the two forms of the possessive personal pronouns:

Adjective: *my, your, his, her, its, our, your, their*

Pronoun: *mine, your, his, hers, its, ours, yours, theirs*

(Some earlier grammars call possessive pronouns used as adjectives "possessive adjectives.")

Predicate   The term "predicate" (also called the "complete predicate") refers to the portion of the sentence that follows the **complete subject.** The predicate consists of the **main verb** together with any helping verbs, complement, and/or modifiers. For example, in the following sentence the predicate is underlined and the main verb is in bold: *The rowdy children were **playing** in the yard again.* Occasionally the term "simple predicate" is used to identify just the main verb and helping verbs (if any).

Predicate adjective   A predicate adjective is an adjective used as the **subject complement** of a **linking verb,** for example, *Sam was sad, and William was weary.*

Predicate nominative   A predicate nominative is a noun (or pronoun) used as the **subject complement** of a **linking verb,** for example, *Sam was a sailor, and William was a waiter.* Do not refer to predicate nominatives as "objects." The term "object" can only be applied to the complements of **transitive verbs.**

Preposition   Prepositions are the "little words" that are used to form **prepositional phrases,** for example, *in the afternoon, near the river.* Some prepositions have spatial meanings, for example, *across, above, below, in, on, over, under.* Most prepositions, however, cannot be easily categorized by meaning, for example, *against, as, but, concerning, except, out, with.* In addition to single-word prepositions, there are also many compound prepositions, for example, *as of, aside from, next to, in spite of, on account of.*

Prepositional phrase   A prepositional phrase consists of a **preposition** plus its noun (or pronoun) object. Prepositional phrases act as either (1) adjectives (also called "adjective phrases"), for example, in the sentence *A man in a yellow car turned left,* the prepositional phrase *in a yellow car* modifies the noun *man,* or (2) adverbs (also called "adverb phrases"), for example, in the sentence *A car had broken down in the left lane,* the prepositional phrase *in the left lane* is an adverb phrase that tells where the car had broken down.

Present participle   The present participle is formed by adding *-ing* to the **base form** of a verb: *seeing, knowing, being, having.* The present participle is the only verb form that is completely regular—zero exceptions.

Present participle verb phrase   In modern grammar, the term "present participle verb phrase" is used to describe a type of **present participle** that is one of the **complements** of a particular verb. For example, in the sentence *We heard him fixing breakfast,* the present participle *fixing breakfast* is required by the verb *hear.* In other words, one use of the verb *hear* is to hear somebody DOING SOMETHING. The present participle phrase is not being used as a noun because we cannot replace the present participle phrase with the pronoun *it:* *We heard him it.

Present perfect tense   The present perfect tense consists of the present tense of *have* (*have, has*) + **past participle,** for example, *John has gone to town.*

Present progressive   The present progressive consists of some present tense form of the verb *be* (*am, are, is*) + **present participle,** for example, John *is going* to town.

Present tense   The present tense has a distinctive *-s* ending when the subject is a **third-person singular** pronoun (or a complete subject that can be replaced by a third-person singular pronoun, for example, *The young man loves asparagus. He loves asparagus.* With all other subjects, the present tense is identical to the **base form.** (The verb *be* is unique; its present tense forms are *I am, you are, he/she/it is; we/you/they are.*) The present tense rarely means "present time." We usually use the present tense for statements of fact or generalizations. For example, the present tense in the sentence *Two plus two is four* does not mean "right now."

Progressive   The term "progressive" is a collective name for a number of verb constructions that use some form of the verb *be* as a helping verb followed by a present participle, for example, *I am going* (**present progressive**), *I was going* (**past progressive**); and *I will be going* (**future progressive**). For historical reasons, the progressive is not called a "tense" in traditional grammar.

Pronominal adverb   Pronominal adverbs are adverbs that act as **relative pronouns** in adjective clauses. For example, in the following sentence the pronominal adverb is in bold and the adjective clause is underlined: *I know a place **where** we can get a good cup of coffee.* The pronominal adverb *where* modifies the noun *place.* Here are two more examples of pronominal adverbs (underlined): *the day when I left; the reason why they did it.* (Sometimes pronominal adverbs are called "relative adverbs.")

Pronoun   The term "pronoun" refers to a group of words that can play the grammatical role of nouns; that is, pronouns can act as subjects or objects. The most important class of pronouns is the **personal pronoun** (*I, you, he, she, it, we, you* [plural], *they*). For example, in the sentence *I see you*, the subject is the pronoun *I* and the object is the pronoun *you.* The remaining pronoun classes are **demonstrative, indefinite, interrogative, reflexive,** and **relative.**

Pronoun agreement   See **agreement.**

Pronoun antecedent   **Personal** and **reflexive pronouns** derive their meaning from their antecedents—some person or thing mentioned earlier in the sentence or even in a previous sentence, from which the pronoun takes its meaning. For example, in the sentences *My cousins live next door. They just moved here*, the antecedent of the personal pronoun *they* is *cousins.* In the sentence *John cut himself*, the antecedent of the reflexive pronoun *himself* is *John.*

Proper noun   The name of particular persons, places, or things. Proper nouns are always capitalized, for example, *Bob Smith, Detroit, the Ford Motor Company.* **Common nouns** refer to general categories and are not capitalized.

Quantifier   Quantifiers are a subclass of **determiners.** Common quantifiers are *few, some, many, much, several*, for example, *a few questions, some answers, many questions.*

Reflexive pronoun   Reflexive pronouns always end in *-self* or *-selves.* The reflexive pronouns are *myself, yourself, himself, herself, itself, ourselves, yourselves,* and *themselves.* Reflexive pronouns must have an antecedent in the same sentence. For example, in the sentence *I found out the answer for myself*, the antecedent of the reflexive pronoun *myself* is *I.* Reflexive pronouns can also be used for emphasis, for example, the use of *myself* in the following sentence is emphatic: *I wouldn't kiss Miss Piggy myself.* Unlike the normal use of reflexives, these emphatic reflexives can be moved or deleted.

Regular verb   Regular verbs form their past tense and **past participle** forms by adding *-ed* to the **base form**, for example, talk–*talked* (past)–have *talked* (past participle).

Relative clause   See **adjective clause.**

Relative pronoun   **Adjective clauses** begin with relative pronouns; for example, in the following sentence, the relative pronoun is in bold and the entire adjective clause is underlined. *It was an idea **whose** time had come.* The relative pronouns are *who, whom, whose, which,* and *that* (plus the **pronominal adverbs** that also begin adjective clauses).

Restrictive adjective clause   A restrictive adjective clause is an **adjective clause** that affects the meaning of the noun it modifies. For example, in the sentence *A book that he had ordered came today*, the adjective clause *that he had ordered* identifies WHICH book the speaker is talking about. Restrictive adjective clauses are never set off with commas from the nouns they modify. Adjective clauses that do not affect the meaning of the nouns they modify are called **nonrestrictive adjective clauses.**

Restrictive modifier   The term "restrictive modifier" is slightly broader than **restrictive adjective clause** because the term also includes other restrictive adjective structures such as restrictive **participial phrases.** For example, in the sentence *The people waiting in line are getting tickets,* the restrictive participial phrase *waiting in line* identifies WHICH people that speaker is talking about. Restrictive modifiers are never set off with commas. Modifiers that do not restrict are called **nonrestrictive modifiers.**

Sentence   In traditional grammar, a sentence is defined as expressing a complete thought. Another definition is that a sentence is a grammatical unit that can stand alone. A sentence contains a **subject** and a **finite verb** and is not included in some larger structure (as a **dependent clause** would be). Sentences are also called "complete sentences."

Sentence fragment   A sentence fragment is a piece of a sentence, punctuated as though it were a complete sentence. For example, the construction *I shut off my computer. Without saving my work first* contains the fragment *without saving my work first.*

Separable phrasal verb   A phrasal verb is a kind of verb compound. A separable phrasal verb is a **transitive verb** that forms a compound with a particular adverb. For example, in the sentence *John looked up the word,* the phrasal verb *look up* means "find in a dictionary or other research work." The unique feature about separable phrasal verbs is that the adverb can be moved after the object: *John looked the word up.* Compare this type of verb compound with **inseparable phrasal verbs,** in which the second element of the compound cannot be moved after the object.

Simple sentence   A simple sentence is a sentence that consists of only a single **independent clause** and has no **dependent clauses,** for example, *This is a simple sentence.*

Simple subject   The simple subject is the actual noun or pronoun within the **complete subject** that the verb agrees with. For example, in the following sentence the complete subject is underlined and the simple subject is in bold: *A **boy** waiting at a bus stop saw the accident.* In modern grammar, the simple subject is called the **head** of the subject **noun phrase.**

Subject   The subject of a sentence is what the sentence is about. The term "subject" is ambiguous: it can refer to the entire subject phrase, called the **complete subject,** or just to the individual noun or pronoun within the complete subject that the verb agrees with, called the **simple subject.** For example, in the following sentence the simple subject is in bold and the complete subject is underlined: *The **porcupine** that you bought seems to have disappeared.* Also see **subject of gerund** and **subject of infinitive.**

Subject complement   A subject complement is the **complement** that follows a **linking verb.** There are two types of subject complements: **predicate nominatives** (*John is a teacher*) and **predicate adjectives** (*John is busy*).

Subject of gerund   A **gerund** is a present participle used as a noun. Gerunds are derived from verbs whose underlying subject may be retained as a possessive. For example, in the sentence ***Sally's** answering the phone was a surprise, Sally's* is the "subject" of the gerund *answering.*

Subject of infinitive   When an **infinitive** is used as a noun, adjective, or adverb, the subject of the underlying verb may be retained as the object of the preposition *for.* For example, in the sentence *For **Sally** to answer the phone was a surprise,* Sally is the "subject" of the infinitive *to answer.*

Subject–verb agreement   The **finite verb** in every **clause** must agree with the subject. If the subject is a **third-person pronoun** (or a noun that can be replaced by a third-person pronoun), then all present tense verbs must have an -*s* ending, for example, *She sells sea shells.* Conversely, if the subject of a present tense verb is NOT a third-person pronoun (or a noun that can be replaced by a third-person pronoun), then the verb cannot have an -*s* ending, for example, *They sell sea shells.* The verb *be* also has subject–verb agreement in the past tense, for example, *She was selling sea shells; They were selling sea shells.*

Subordinate clause   See **dependent clause.**

Subordinating conjunction   Subordinating conjunctions begin **adverb clauses.** For example, in the following sentence the subordinating conjunction is in bold and the entire adverb clause is underlined: *I hung up the phone **after** I had been on hold for ten minutes.*

Superlative adjective   A superlative adjective is the form (**degree**) of adjective ending in *-est* or preceded by *most.* For example, in the following sentences, the underlined adjectives are in the superlative form: *It was the coldest night of the year; She says the most outrageous things.* Also see **base form** and **comparative form** of adjectives.

Tense   The term "tense" has several meanings. (1) It can refer to the TIME in which the action of the sentence takes place: present tense (= present time); past tense (= past time); future tense (= future time). (2) "Tense" can also refer to the **verb form** of the six tenses of traditional grammar: **present tense, past tense, future tense, present perfect tense, past perfect tense,** and **future perfect tense.** (3) In modern grammar, the term "tense" refers only to **tensed verb** forms—the present tense and the past tense.

Tense marker   There are two tense markers: (1) the third-person singular *-s* that signals present-tense verbs *(He loves asparagus)*; and (2) the past-tense marker *(-ed* for regular verbs) that signals past-tense verbs *(He loved asparagus).*

Tensed verb form   In modern grammar, the term "tensed verb" refers to verb forms that can be used without helping verbs. There are only two tensed verb forms: the present and past tense. The tensed verb forms are also the only verb forms that can show subject–verb agreement. All other verb forms are called **nontensed.**

That*-type noun clause**   The term "that-type noun clause" refers to a category of **noun clauses** beginning with *that, if,* or *whether.* In the following sentence, the "that-type" word is in bold and the entire noun clause is underlined: *We debated about **whether we should go. The other category of noun clauses is called a ***wh*-type noun clause.**

Third-person singular   The term "third-person singular" refers both to the three third-person singular pronouns *he, she, it* and to subjects that can be replaced by *he, she, it.* For example, in the sentence *The mysterious fire in the hotel is being investigated,* the subject *the mysterious fire in the hotel* is considered to be a third-person singular subject because it can be replaced by *it: It is being investigated.*

Transitive verb   A transitive verb is an **action verb** that requires an **object,** for example, *Harry met Sally.* The transitive verb *meet* requires an object. If we delete the object *Sally,* the resulting sentence becomes ungrammatical: **Harry met.*

Verb   In traditional grammar, a verb is defined as a word that expresses action (*Jack jumped over the candle stick*) or describes the subject (*Jack is nimble*). In modern grammar, a verb is defined by its unique ability to be used in a present-tense or past-tense form.

Verb complement   A verb complement is whatever grammatical structure is required by a particular verb to make a complete sentence. For example, a **transitive verb** must have an object. In traditional grammar, the verb complements are limited to nouns (and pronouns) and predicate adjectives. In modern grammar, the term "verb complement" is used more broadly to include other structures such as **adverbial phrases, prepositional phrases,** and **nontensed verb phrases.** For example, the verb *depend* requires as its complement a prepositional phrase beginning with *on: Jason depended on his spell checker.*

Verb form   There are six verb forms. Using the verb *be* as an example, the six verb forms are **present** (*am, is, are*), **past** (*was, were*), **base** (*be*), **infinitive** (*to be*), **present participle** (*being*), and **past participle** (*been*). The term "verb form" refers only to the actual form of a verb, not to what that form might mean. For example, in the sentence *It might rain* *tomorrow,* the verb *might* is the past tense form of the verb *may.* However, in this sentence, the use of the past-tense form has nothing to do with the meaning of past time.

Verb phrase In modern grammar, the term "verb phrase" means the main verb together with all of its complements (if any). For example, in the sentence *John put the milk on the table at breakfast,* the verb phrase consists of the verb *put* together with its complements the noun phrase *the milk* and the obligatory adverbial of place *on the table.* The term "verb phrase" is also used in traditional grammar, but with a quite different meaning. In traditional grammar, the term refers to the main verb together with all of its helping or auxiliary verbs.

Verb tense See **tense.**

Verbal The term "verbal" is a collective term for three **nontensed verb forms** used as other parts of speech: (1) **gerunds** (**present participles** used as nouns, for example, *Swimming is my favorite sport;* (2) **participles** (present or past participles used as adjectives, for example, *The man laughing is my uncle*); and (3) **infinitives** used as nouns, adjectives, or adverbs. For example, in the sentence *To fly has always been mankind's dream,* the infinitive *to fly* is a noun.

Verbal phrase A verbal phrase is a phrase containing a **verbal** together with the verbal's subject, complements, and/or modifiers. There are three types of verbal phrases. In the following examples, the verbal is in bold and the entire verbal phrase is underlined: (1) **gerund** (*Swimming at the pool is my favorite sport;* (2) **participial** (*The man sneezing uncontrollably is my uncle;* and (3) **infinitive** (*To fly to the moon has always been mankind's dream.*)

Voice The term "voice" is used to distinguish the **passive voice** (*John was rejected by Mary*) from the **active voice** (*Mary rejected John*).

Wh-type noun clause The term "*wh*-type noun clause" refers to a category of **noun clauses** beginning with words such as *who, whom, whose, when, where, why, wherever,* most of which begin with the letters *wh.* In the following sentence, the *wh*- word is in bold and the entire noun clause is underlined: *We debated about **what** we should say.* The other category of noun clauses is called ***that*-type noun clauses.**

Answers to Exercises

Chapter 2

Noun Exercise #1: Identifying Nouns by the the Test

1. the authority
2. the length
3. the concession
4. the discovery
5. the performance

Noun Exercise #2: Identifying Nouns by the the Test

1. The <u>instrument</u> measures the <u>velocity</u> (of the wind).
2. They registered the <u>protest</u> against the <u>ruling</u>.
3. I was attracted to the <u>fabric</u> by the <u>texture</u>.
4. The <u>machines</u> recorded the <u>discontinuity</u>.
5. The <u>problems</u> were uncovered after the <u>inspection</u>.
6. The <u>departure</u> of the <u>friends</u> (we have) is always sad.
7. The <u>waiter</u> brought us the <u>phone</u>.
8. The <u>moon</u> was just rising over the <u>hills</u>.
9. We all admired the <u>drawing</u> she got on the <u>trip</u>.
10. The bought the <u>safe</u> to protect the <u>valuables</u> (that they have).

Noun Exercise #3: Identifying Nouns by the Plural Test

1. The <u>experiment</u> with the <u>mouse</u> was going well.
   Confirmation: The <u>experiments</u> with the <u>mice</u> were going well.
2. The <u>policeman</u> told us that the <u>bridge</u> was out.
   Confirmation: The <u>policemen</u> told us that the <u>bridges</u> were out.
3. The <u>lawyer</u> argued for the <u>claim</u>.
   Confirmation: The <u>lawyers</u> argued for the <u>claims</u>.

4. The <u>poem</u> appeared in the new <u>anthology</u>.

   Confirmation: The <u>poems</u> appeared in the new <u>anthologies</u>.

5. Snow White took out a <u>finger bowl</u> for the <u>dwarf</u>.

   Confirmation: Snow White took out some <u>finger bowls</u> for the <u>dwarves</u>.

6. The <u>governor</u> held a <u>press conference</u>.

   Confirmation: The <u>governors</u> held some <u>press conferences</u>.

7. A <u>flower</u> was poking up through the <u>snowbank</u>.

   Confirmation: Some <u>flowers</u> were poking up through the <u>snowbanks</u>.

8. My <u>dream</u> was very unsettling.

   Confirmation: My <u>dreams</u> were very unsettling.

9. The <u>fly</u> was buzzing around in the <u>window</u>.

   Confirmation: The <u>flies</u> were buzzing around in the <u>windows</u>.

10. The <u>speech</u> put the <u>audience</u> to sleep.

    Confirmation: The <u>speeches</u> put the <u>audiences</u> to sleep.

Noun Exercise #4: Identifying Nouns

1. A good <u>plumber</u> can fix any <u>sink</u> ever made.
      common   common

   Confirmation: Good <u>plumbers</u> can fix any <u>sinks</u> ever made.

2. A <u>pound</u> of <u>hamburger</u> will not feed us.
      common   common

   Confirmation: Two <u>pounds</u> of the <u>hamburger</u> (you bought) will not feed us.

3. <u>College professors</u> are always looking for <u>grants.</u>
      common   common

   Confirmation: Both nouns are already plural.

4. The good <u>fairy</u> granted her <u>wish</u> to play <u>quarterback.</u>
      common   common   common

   Confirmation: The good <u>fairies</u> granted her <u>wishes</u> to play the <u>quarterback</u>.

5. <u>Economists</u> were issuing dire <u>predictions</u> at regular <u>intervals.</u>
      common   common   common

   Confirmation: All three nouns are already plural.

6. Napoleon's <u>army</u> advanced rapidly on <u>Moscow.</u>
      common   proper

   Confirmation: Napoleon's <u>armies</u> advanced rapidly on Moscow.

   (Note: <u>Napoleon's</u> is not used here as a noun; it is used as an adjective modifying <u>army</u>.)

7. He forgot to telephone his <u>office</u> about the <u>meeting.</u>
      common   common

   Confirmation: He forgot to telephone his <u>offices</u> about the <u>meetings.</u>

8. His <u>interpretation</u> of the <u>law</u> was challenged in <u>court.</u>
       common   common   common

   Confirmation: His <u>interpretations</u> of the <u>laws</u> were challenged in the <u>courts.</u>

9. The <u>class</u> grimly wrote yet another <u>essay.</u>
      common   common

   Confirmation: The <u>classes</u> grimly wrote yet more <u>essays.</u>

10. A <u>student</u> showed a <u>drawing</u> he had purchased in <u>Venice</u>.
       common   common   proper

   Confirmation: The <u>students</u> showed the <u>drawings</u> they had purchased
   in Venice.

Adjective Exercise #1: Identifying Modifying Adjectives by the Pair Test

1. <u>My</u> <u>first</u> class is in <u>an</u> <u>old</u> theater.
   Confirmation: my class, first class; a(n) theater, old theater

2. <u>Tall</u> <u>prickly</u> weeds were choking out <u>the</u> <u>vegetable</u> garden.
   Confirmation: tall weeds, prickly weeds; the garden, vegetable garden
   (Note: <u>vegetable garden</u> can also be treated as a compound noun.)

3. <u>A</u> <u>horrid</u> <u>new</u> crime wave was sweeping <u>the</u> <u>entire</u> kingdom.
   Confirmation: a crime wave, horrid crime wave, new crime wave; the
                  kingdom, entire kingdom

4. <u>Several</u> <u>discount</u> <u>department</u> stores had specials on <u>the</u> <u>upright</u> freezer.
   Confirmation: several stores, discount stores, department stores (<u>department
                  stores</u> could also be a compound noun); the freezer, upright
                  freezer (<u>upright freezer</u> could also be a compound noun)

5. <u>An</u> <u>old</u> <u>sun-burned</u> man was leaning against <u>the</u> <u>weathered</u> fence.
   Confirmation: a(n) man, old man, sun-burned man; the fence,
                  weathered fence

6. <u>The</u> <u>wine</u> store specialized in very <u>expensive</u> <u>French</u> wines.
   Confirmation: the store, wine store (<u>wine store</u> could also be a compound
                  noun); expensive wines; French wines (<u>French wines</u> could
                  also be a compound noun)

7. We had <u>a</u> <u>nice</u> evening with <u>some</u> <u>old</u> friends.
   Confirmation: a(n) evening, nice evening; some friends, old friends

8. <u>The</u> <u>desperate</u> company finally called in <u>an</u> <u>outside</u> consultant.
   Confirmation: the company, desperate company; a(n) consultant,
                  outside consultant

9. An ominous dark shadow passed by the open window.

   Confirmation: a(n) shadow, ominous shadow, dark shadow; the window, open window

10. Aware of his weak backhand, John relied on his excellent first serve.

    Confirmation: his backhand, weak backhand; his serve, excellent serve, first serve (first serve could also be a compound noun)

Adjective Exercise #2: Classifying Determiners

1. There were several messages on our answering machine.
   Quant   Poss

2. This test will cover the last chapter.
   Dem   Art   #

3. We delivered two packages to that address.
            #   Dem

4. I left my wallet at home.
        Poss

5. There were ninety-nine bottles of beer on the wall.
           #   Art

6. John's car was an old Ford with two cracked windows.
   Poss   Art   #

7. Most computers are now hooked up to a server.
   Quant   Art

8. I ordered some coffee and the last piece of pie.
       Quant   Art   #

9. All roads lead to Rome.
   Quant

10. I didn't have much money with me.
         Quant

Adjective Exercise #3: Identifying Gradable Adjectives

1. A very cold wave suddenly crashed over the very wet deck.
      colder, coldest   wetter, wettest

2. The very weary firefighters slowly collected their very grimy equipment.
      wearier, weariest   grimier, grimiest

3. His very nervous laugh seemed to fill the room.
      more nervous, most nervous

4. The very unpleasant ceremony finally came to an end.
      more unpleasant, most unpleasant

5. All work and no play makes Jack a very dull boy.
                              duller, dullest

6. A very large very ornate chandelier hung in the center of the very large room.
   larger,   more ornate,   larger, largest
   largest   most ornate

7. Holmes investigated the very mysterious disappearance of Lady Greer's very rare manuscript.
                                       more mysterious,
              rarer, rarest   most mysterious

8. We paddled the very heavy boat across the very still waters of the pond.
                   heavier, heaviest   stiller, stillest

9. The very tired children were waiting in a very long line.
       more tired, most tired   longer, longest

10. The very heavy rain caused very severe damage.
        heavier, heaviest   more severe, most severe

Adjective Exercise #4: Identifying Absolute Adjectives

1. They must think that I am a complete idiot.
   *very complete idiot, *more complete, *most complete

2. We listed the chief reasons for going ahead with the project.
   *very chief reasons, *chiefer, *chiefest

3. He finally got a full-time job at the plant.
   *very full-time job, *more full-time, *most full-time

4. The students finally found the correct answer to the problem.
   *very correct answer, *more correct, *most correct

5. My uncle raises giant pumpkins on his farm.
   *very giant pumpkins, *gianter, *giantest

Adjective Exercise #5: Identifying Nouns and Modifying Adjectives

1. His first book was about rural development in upstate New York.
2. The topic interested only a few specialists.
3. Eighteenth-century Latin grammar is the source of modern grammar.
4. The unexpected rainstorm completely ruined my new shoes.
5. A successful swindler often has polite manners.
6. The purchasing committee debated endlessly about the kind of computer.
7. His insulting behavior almost created a major diplomatic incident.
8. The possible junior partnership interested my sister.
9. Watson gave Holmes a far-fetched explanation of Lady Danforth's mysterious disappearance.
10. My cousin actually won a valuable prize in a publisher's sweepstake.

11. I made only one mistake, but it was a bad one.

12. Our new car gets poor mileage.

13. I'll have the roast chicken and a tossed salad.

14. The vacant lot was covered with countless unsightly, rank weeds.

15. A good salesperson can get by with a winning smile and pressed clothes.

16. The witness's confusing statement hindered the entire investigation.

17. That was my first consideration.

18. The committee was impressed by the candidate's broad knowledge.

19. A dozen people were packed into that old stationwagon.

20. We finally found the right key in a beat-up old dresser.

Pronoun Exercise #1: Use of Possessive Pronouns

1. We left our car at home and took a taxi to their apartment.
      Adj   Adj

2. His company is bigger than ours.
   Adj   Pro

3. Our cat got its tail caught in the screen door.
   Adj   Adj

4. Theirs is a highly unusual story.
   Pro

5. Her house is about the same size as mine.
   Adj   Pro

Pronoun Exercise #2: Identifying Personal Pronouns

1. The high quality of the workshop surprised us.
                                             1-Pl-Obj

2. Give me your address, will you? (Note: *your* is an adjective.)
      1-Sg-Obj   2-Sg-Sub

3. We took the plants inside to keep them from freezing.
   1-Pl-Sub   3-Pl-Obj

4. They gave it to   him for his birthday.
   3-Pl-Sub 3-Sg-Obj 3-Sg-Obj

5. I am a friend of hers.
   1-Sg-Sub   3-Sg-Poss

6. We hope that you and your friends can join us this summer.
   1-Pl-Sub   2-Sg-Sub   1-Pl-Obj

7. She took her roommate to see it last night.
   3-Sg-Sub   3-Sg-Obj

8. Do you know where yours is?
     2-Sg-Sub   2-Sg-Poss

9. It is up to you.
   3-Sg-Sub   2-Sg-Obj

10. We only want what is ours.
    1-Pl-Sub   1-Pl-Poss

Pronoun Exercise #3: Personal Pronoun Terminology

1. Excuse me, that coat is mine.
       1-Sg-Obj   1-Sg-Pos

2. He/she gave them the book back.
   3-Sg-Sub   3-Pl-Obj

3. We saw you at the movie last night.
  1-Pl-Sub 2-Sg-Obj

4. The cat left them on the porch.
            3-Pl-Obj

5. Give them to me.
      3-Pl-Obj 1-Sg-Obj

6. What's mine is mine. What's yours is yours.
      1-Sg-Pos 1-Sg-Pos   2-Sg-Pos 2-Sg-Pos

7. He/she really gave him/her the brush-off.
   3-Sg-Sub   3-Sg-Obj

8. You never know, do you?
  2-Sg-Sub   2-Sg-Sub

9. We sold it to them.
  1-Pl-Sub 3-Sg-Obj   3-Pl-Obj

10. Where did they get them?
         3-Pl-Sub 3-Pl-Obj

Pronoun Exercise #4: Identifying Nouns by the Pronoun Replacement Test

1. The commander postponed the planned attack.
   He/she   it

2. The obnoxious waiter finally brought our tepid dinners.
        He   them

3. The French language is even more difficult to spell than English is.
      It   it

4. The old bridges were badly in need of extensive repair.
   They   it

5. The busy tugboats pushed the liner into its appointed berth.
     They   it   it

6. The chill November <u>rain</u> never seemed to let up.
   It

7. The overworked <u>teacher</u> couldn't correct <u>any more student essays</u>.
   He/she   them

8. The <u>day</u> was turning out to be fine after all.
   It

9. The <u>driver</u> took <u>the passengers</u> back to <u>their hotel</u>.
   He/she   them   it

10. <u>My hands and feet</u> were absolutely frozen.
    They

11. We had <u>tuna sandwiches</u> for <u>our lunch</u>.
    them   it

12. The <u>museum guards</u> were in <u>dark gray uniforms</u>.
    They   them

13. A <u>200% mark-up</u> seemed excessive.
    It

14. With <u>any luck</u> <u>the meeting</u> will be over soon.
    it   it

15. The <u>children</u> had <u>very bad sore throats</u>.
    They   them

16. The <u>garage</u> replaced <u>the left front wheel</u>.
    It   it

17. The <u>upper trail</u> leads to <u>some very nice lakes</u>.
    It   them

18. The <u>hiring committee</u> will be conducting <u>several interviews</u>.
    It/They   them

19. Over <u>the weekend</u>, <u>my parents</u> stayed with <u>my aunt and uncle</u>.
    it   they   them

20. According to <u>my grandfather</u>, <u>nobody's property</u> was safe while
    him   it

    <u>the legislature</u> was in <u>session</u>.
    it   it

Pronoun Exercise #5: Using Reflexive Pronouns

1. Be careful, you will hurt <u>yourself</u>.
2. We entered <u>ourselves</u> in a drawing.
3. The propeller tangled <u>itself</u> in some weeds along the bank.
4. My aunt and uncle had <u>themselves</u> painted by a well-known local artist.
5. I talked <u>myself</u> into taking a course in astrophysics.

Pronoun Exercise #6: Identifying Reflexive Pronouns and Their Antecedents

1. The <u>driveway</u> curved back on <u>itself</u>.
2. Because of a potential conflict of interest, the <u>judge</u> excused <u>herself</u>.
3. Several <u>skiers</u> injured <u>themselves</u> badly on the icy slope.
4. Thelma told <u>Louise</u> to assert <u>herself</u>.
5. <u>We</u> didn't want to compete against <u>ourselves</u>.
6. Sam told <u>Effie</u> to address the letter to <u>herself</u>.
7. <u>Stan and Ollie</u> got <u>themselves</u> into another fine mess.
8. The constant racket forced <u>us</u> to keep repeating <u>ourselves</u>.
9. Miss Manners helped <u>her</u> improve <u>herself</u>.
10. The clerk told <u>John</u> to help <u>himself</u>.
11. TRICK QUESTION: All these sentences have an understood *you* as the subject, which also serves as the antecedent for the reflexives.

Pronoun Exercise #7: Identifying Emphatic (Intensive) Reflexive Pronouns

1. The defeated rebels eventually turned on <u>themselves</u>.
   Obj

   Confirmation: *The defeated rebels eventually turned on ~~themselves~~.

2. The defeated rebels eventually acknowledged defeat ~~themselves~~.
   EMPH

   Confirmation: The defeated rebels <u>themselves</u> eventually acknowledged defeat.

3. I saw <u>myself</u> in the play.
   OBJ

   Confirmation: *I ~~myself~~ saw in the play.

4. I <u>myself</u> know that I can make mistakes.
   EMPH

   Confirmation: I know that I can make mistakes.

5. Finally, we can only depend on <u>ourselves</u>.
   OBJ

   Confirmation: *Finally, we can only depend on ~~ourselves~~.

6. We finally talked <u>ourselves</u> into doing it.
   Obj

   Confirmation: *We finally talked ~~ourselves~~ into doing it.

7. You gave it to me <u>yourself</u>!
   EMPH

   Confirmation: You ~~yourself~~ gave it to me!

8. Dorothy <u>herself</u> did not believe in witches.
        EMPH

    Confirmation: Dorothy did not believe in witches ~~herself~~.

9. The vice president cast the deciding vote <u>himself</u>.
                                              EMPH

    Confirmation: The vice president ~~himself~~ cast the deciding vote.

10. I locked <u>myself</u> out of my room.
            OBJ

    Confirmation: *I ~~myself~~ locked out of my room.

Pronoun Exercise #8: Distinguishing Indefinite Pronouns from Adjectives

1. <u>All</u> packages must be checked at the desk.
   ADJ

2. <u>Many</u> are called, but <u>few</u> are chosen.
    PRO   PRO

3. <u>Some</u> people do not know how lucky they are.
    ADJ

4. I wanted to get <u>another</u> box, but they didn't have <u>one</u>.
                    ADJ   PRO

5. <u>Neither</u> <u>one</u> was what I wanted.
    ADJ   PRO

6. Please get me <u>another</u>.
                 PRO

7. I don't get <u>any</u> respect.
               ADJ

8. <u>Few</u> passenger trains stop here anymore.
    ADJ

9. <u>Most</u> are just freight trains.
    PRO

10. <u>All</u> calls are routed to the secretary.
    ADJ

Pronoun Exercise #9: Distinguishing Demonstrative Pronouns from Adjectives

1. I didn't agree to do <u>that</u>.
                        PRO

2. <u>Those</u> cookies are getting stale.
    ADJ

3. I would like to buy <u>this</u> one.
                       ADJ

4. Is <u>this</u> the face that launched a thousand ships?
   PRO

5. <u>These</u> are the times that try men's souls.
   PRO

6. Do you want <u>this</u> one or <u>that</u> one?
                 ADJ   ADJ

7. <u>These</u> pencils all need sharpening.
   ADJ

8. <u>That</u> is what you think!
   PRO

9. <u>Those</u> questions were certainly hard.
   ADJ

10. Did you get answers to <u>these</u>?
                             PRO

Pronoun Exercise #10: Identifying Pronouns

1. <u>He</u> asked about <u>that</u>.
   PERS   DEMON

2. <u>One</u> for <u>all</u> and <u>all</u> for <u>one</u>.
   INDEF INDEF INDEF INDEF

3. Are <u>you</u> sure about your answers?
        PERS

4. Her choice of words surprised <u>us</u>.
                                  PERS

5. <u>I</u> wouldn't go to that movie if <u>it</u> were the last <u>one</u> on earth.
   PERS   PERS   INDEF

6. <u>Nobody</u> knows the trouble <u>I</u> have seen.
    INDEF   PERS

7. That contraption of <u>yours</u> will never get off the ground, Wilbur.
                        PERS

8. Can <u>we</u> get <u>you</u> <u>anything</u> at the store?
       PERS   PERS   INDEF

9. Another victory like <u>that</u> and <u>we</u> are done for.
                         DEMON   PERS

10. Would <u>you</u> like another <u>one</u>?
          PERS   INDEF

11. <u>He</u> is a friend of her sister.
    PERS

12. <u>They</u> are friends of <u>ours</u>.
    PERS   PERS

13. <u>Someone</u> took <u>all</u> of the clean cups.
INDEF   INDEF

14. All the clean cups are over there.

15. Your logic is impeccable, but <u>it</u> is despicable.
PERS

16. <u>No one</u> knows that <u>they</u> did <u>it</u>.
INDEF   PERS   PERS

17. His friends are not very realistic about those things.

18. <u>We</u> don't have much food left in that container.
PERS

19. <u>I</u> would like <u>these</u> to go, please.
PERS   DEMON

20. <u>Much</u> of that egg is perfectly good.
INDEF

Verb Exercise #1: Identifying Verbs by Shifting Tense

1. They <u>score</u> more points in the second half.
Confirmation: Past: <u>scored</u>   Future: <u>will score</u>

2. Critics <u>characterize</u> his plots as simplistic.
Confirmation: Past: <u>characterized</u>   Future: <u>will characterize</u>

3. The cookies <u>have</u> too much sugar in them.
Confirmation: Past: <u>had</u>   Future: <u>will have</u>

4. The rules <u>generate</u> a number of sentences.
Confirmation: Past: <u>generated</u>   Future: <u>will generate</u>

5. South-bound trains usually <u>depart</u> from Platform 2.
Confirmation: Past: <u>departed</u>   Future: <u>will depart</u>

6. Red wines generally <u>improve</u> with age.
Confirmation: Past: <u>improved</u>   Future: <u>will improve</u>

7. Time and tide <u>wait</u> for no man.
Confirmation: Past: <u>waited</u>   Future: <u>will wait</u>

8. They usually <u>attain</u> their goals on time.
Confirmation: Past: <u>attained</u>   Future: <u>will attain</u>

9. The aches and pains <u>persist</u> for several days.
Confirmation: Past: <u>persisted</u>   Future: <u>will persist</u>

10. Crop rotation and good tilling habits <u>reduce</u> erosion.
Confirmation: Past: <u>reduced</u>   Future: <u>will reduce</u>

11. The rabbits <u>need</u> a lot of water and fresh food.
    Confirmation: Past: <u>needed</u>   Future: <u>will need</u>

12. The sales people typically <u>exaggerate</u> about their successes.
    Confirmation: Past: <u>exaggerated</u>   Future: <u>will exaggerate</u>

13. The wines <u>go</u> well with the food.
    Confirmation: Past: <u>went</u>   Future: <u>will go</u>

14. Grammarians <u>classify</u> words by part of speech categories.
    Confirmation: Past: <u>classified</u>   Future: <u>will classify</u>

15. Rolling stones <u>gather</u> no moss.
    Confirmation: Past: <u>gathered</u>   Future: <u>will gather</u>

Adverb Exercise #1: Identifying Adverbs That Modify Verbs by the Adverb Question Test

1. The vet had examined the horse <u>recently</u>.
   Adverb question: When had the vet examined the horse?
   Adverb answer: Recently.

2. The ants were crawling <u>everywhere</u>.
   Adverb question: Where were the ants crawling?
   Adverb answer: Everywhere.

3. He <u>quickly</u> unzipped the tent flap.
   Adverb question: How did he unzip the tent flap?
   Adverb answer: Quickly.

5. She answers all the questions <u>correctly</u>.
   Adverb question: How does she answer all the question?
   Adverb answer: Correctly.

6. The operator will return your call <u>soon</u>.
   Adverb question: When will the operator return your call?
   Adverb answer: Soon.

7. They <u>gradually</u> became accustomed to the high altitude.
   Adverb question: How did they become accustomed to the high altitude?
   Adverb answer: Gradually.

8. We <u>rarely</u> watch TV.
   Adverb question: How often do we watch TV?
   Adverb answer: Rarely.

9. Leon <u>invariably</u> sleeps through his 8 o'clock class.
   Adverb question: How often does Leon sleep through his 8 o'clock class?
   Adverb answer: Invariably.

10. There will be a full moon <u>tonight</u>.

    Adverb question: When will there be a full moon?

    Adverb answer: Tonight.

Adverb Exercise #2: Identifying Adverbs That Modify Verbs by the Adverb Movement Test

1. Toto is <u>usually</u> a good little dog.

   Confirmation: <u>Usually</u>, Toto is a good little dog.

2. The teller <u>carefully</u> examined the signatures on the check.

   Confirmation: The teller examined the signatures on the check <u>carefully</u>.

3. He <u>reluctantly</u> counted out the cash and gave it to me.

   Confirmation: <u>Reluctantly</u>, he counted out the case and gave it to me.

4. They will twist in the wind <u>slowly</u>.

   Confirmation: They will <u>slowly</u> twist in the wind.

5. The lawyer looked at the defendant <u>knowingly</u>.

   Confirmation: The lawyer looked <u>knowingly</u> at the defendant.

6. The bird <u>repeatedly</u> fluttered at his reflection in the window.

   Confirmation: <u>Repeatedly</u>, the bird fluttered at his reflection in the window.

7. We <u>routinely</u> check the files for errors.

   Confirmation: We check the files for errors <u>routinely</u>.

8. <u>Magically</u>, the key opened the door.

   Confirmation: The key opened the door <u>magically</u>.

9. We will find out the truth <u>ultimately</u>.

   Confirmation: <u>Ultimately</u>, we will find out the truth.

Adverb Exercise #3: Identifying Adverbs That Modify Adjectives by the Pair Test

1. <u>Their</u> proposal brought <u>a</u> very <u>swift</u> response.
                                ADV

   Confirmation: *very response

2. <u>A</u> day in <u>the</u> country was <u>an</u> extremely <u>good</u> plan.
                                          ADV

   Confirmation: *extremely plan

3. They bought <u>a</u> quite <u>beautiful</u> <u>old</u> print.
                      ADV

   Confirmation: *quite print

4. <u>Their</u> <u>first</u> <u>rafting</u> trip had been <u>a</u> really <u>terrifying</u> experience.
                                                        ADV

   Confirmation: *really experience

5. <u>The</u> administration proposed <u>a</u> surprisingly <u>bold</u> <u>diplomatic</u> initiative.
                                     ADV

    Confirmation: *surprisingly initiative

6. I thought it was <u>a</u> very <u>funny</u> movie.
                        ADV

    Confirmation: *very movie

7. Donald memorized tediously <u>long</u> lists.
                         ADV

    Confirmation: *tediously lists

8. <u>The</u> perpetually <u>damp</u> <u>British</u> weather became depressing.
                ADV

    Confirmation: *perpetually weather

9. In <u>an</u> <u>early</u> story, <u>an</u> apparently <u>naive</u> <u>young</u> woman outwitted Holmes.
                                   ADV

    Confirmation: *apparently woman

10. <u>A</u> <u>good</u> <u>mystery</u> writer makes us miss <u>the</u> obviously <u>important</u> facts.
                                           ADV

    Confirmation: *obviously facts

Adverb Exercise #4: Identifying Adverbs That Modify Other Adverbs

1. We will be done <u>pretty</u> <u>soon</u>.
                  ADV

2. We played <u>surprisingly</u> <u>well</u>.
              ADV

3. She talks <u>so</u> <u>softly</u>.
         ADV

4. The changes have occurred <u>somewhat</u> <u>irregularly</u>.
                         ADV

5. Harvard fought <u>rather</u> <u>fiercely</u>.
           ADV

Adverb Exercise #5: Identifying Adverbs

1. The <u>savagely</u> stinging bugs <u>nearly</u> ruined our camping trip.

2. <u>Unusually</u> glib strangers <u>naturally</u> arouse our suspicions.

3. They <u>nearly</u> <u>always</u> come to see us <u>afterwards</u>.

4. <u>Recently</u>, we sent you our <u>newly</u> published report.

5. <u>Nearly</u> every reporter had filed a <u>totally</u> misleading story.

6. <u>Too</u> many cooks spoil the broth.

7. She smiled <u>very</u> <u>sweetly</u>.

8. <u>Invariably</u> Uncle Andrew makes a <u>truly</u> embarrassing speech.

9. The <u>disgustingly</u> dirty water <u>eventually</u> evaporated.

10. The <u>unusually</u> dry summer threatened many crops <u>here</u>.

11. The <u>badly</u> beaten army <u>hastily</u> withdrew from the field.

12. <u>Unfortunately</u>, I have to return <u>there</u> <u>tonight</u>.

13. The <u>incredibly</u> loud noise <u>completely</u> overwhelmed us.

14. <u>Personally</u>, I think she <u>finally</u> made a <u>very</u> good choice.

15. The unscheduled conference made us look foolish.

Conjunction Exercise #1: Identifying Coordinating Conjunctions

1. We were tired, <u>so</u> we went home early.

2. This is <u>either</u> very good cheese <u>or</u> very bad meat.

3. I'm sure that he is OK, <u>but</u> I can't help worrying.

4. We got into the car <u>and</u> drove to the station.

5. Did you want <u>coffee</u>, <u>tea</u>, <u>or</u> milk?

6. <u>Not only</u> did Holmes fool Watson, <u>but also</u> he fooled Inspector Lestrade.

7. Thanks to careful planning <u>and</u> more than our share of good luck, we were successful.

8. John <u>neither</u> drinks <u>nor</u> watches daytime TV.

9. <u>Either</u> you give me my money back, <u>or</u> I will take you to court.

10. Unfortunately, I am <u>neither</u> rich <u>nor</u> famous.

11. They had better hurry, <u>for</u> the game is about to start.

12. He is <u>either</u> a fool <u>or</u> a knave.

13. Time <u>and</u> tide wait for no man.

14. It was getting late, <u>so</u> I decided to quit.

15. <u>Either</u> a Pepsi <u>or</u> a Coke is OK.

Review Exercise #1: Identifying Parts of Speech

1. Almost all professional writers keep a daily journal.
   Adv   Adj   Adj   N   V Adj Adj   N

2. The FDA carefully evaluated the new drug.
   Adj N   Adv   V   Adj Adj   N

3. They rebuilt the old gym and completely restored the chemistry lab.
   P   V   Adj Adj N C   Adv   V   Adj   Adj   N

4. Holmes finally located the missing gun and incriminating letters.
   N   Adv   V   Adj   Adj   N   C   Adj   N

5. The plane circled the field and then landed smoothly.
   Adj   N   V   Adj   N   C   Adv   V   Adv

6. The Constitution protects free speech.
   Adj   N   V   Adj   N

7. <u>Count Dracula</u> appreciated her friendly attitude and unlocked windows.
        N   V   Adj   Adj   N   C   Adj   N

8. A new conductor led the orchestra today.
   Adj Adj   N   V   Adj   N   Adv

9. Unfortunately, the tuba player had a bad cold and missed some notes.
       Adv   Adj Adj   N   V Adj Adj   N   C   V   Adj   N

10. I always have a good time there.
    P   Adv   V Adj Adj   N   Adv

11. The waitress pocketed the tip and smiled politely.
    Adj   N   V   Adj N   C   V   Adv

12. John came home late last Thursday.
      N   V   Adv   Adv Adv   Adv

13. The cleaner nearly ruined my blue sweater.
    Adj   N   Adv   V   Adj   Adj   N

14. The class passed the examination easily.
    Adj   N   V   Adj   N   Adv

15. Fortunately, every dark cloud has a silver lining.
        Adv   Adj   Adj   N   V Adj Adj   N

16. Our cat loves fresh fish or old catfood.
    Adj   N   V   Adj   N   C   Adj   N

17. My mother loudly announced our engagement.
    Adj   N   Adv   V   Adj   N

18. Every graduate faces a frightening and thrilling new beginning.
    Adj   N   V Adj   Adj   C   Adj   Adj   N

19. Theirs was a very odd but happy marriage.
       P   V Adj Adv   Adj   C   Adj   N

20. The black jacket is mine.
    Adj   Adj   N   V   P

Review Exercise #2: Identifying Parts of Speech

1. The reporters interviewed the rookie cop and the witnesses.
   Adj   N   V   Adj   Adj   N   C   Adj   N

2. Jason missed the bus again today.
     N   V   Adj N   Adv   Adv

3. The commission certainly expected a more favorable outcome.
   Adj   N   Adv   V   Adj Adv   Adj   N

4. Holmes always quizzed Watson and Inspector Lestrade unmercifully.
   N   Adv   V   N   C   N   Adv

5. Godzilla ordered the poached fish and artichokes.
   N   V   Adj   Adj   N   C   N

6. Sally sold Sarah and Susan some sardine sandwiches.
   N   V   N   C   N   Adj   Adj   N

7. Both John and I completed the final project.
   C   N   C   P   V   Adj Adj   N

8. You left your coat.
   P   V   Adj   N

9. Very few detectives resemble Sam Spade.
   Adv Adj   N   V   N

10. Only the brave deserve the fair.
    Adj Adj   N   V   Adj   N

11. The company hired too many consultants and outside experts.
    Adj   N   V   Adv   Adj   N   C   Adj   N

12. I finally found my book, but Ralph lost his.
    P Adv   V   Adj   N   C   N   V   P

13. I caught the first ball, but missed the second.
    P   V   Adj Adj   N   C   V   Adj   N

14. He gave himself a truly awful haircut.
    P   V   P   Adj Adv   Adj   N

15. His carelessness nearly caused a serious accident.
    Adj   N   Adv   V   Adj   Adj   N

16. Superman leapt pretty tall buildings.
    N   V   Adv   Adj   N

17. The police finally arrested Bugsy.
    Adj   N   Adv   V   N

18. They replaced the cracked and broken windows.
    P   V   Adj   Adj   C   Adj   N

19. The basketball coach picked only the tallest players.
    Adj   Adj   N   V   Adv Adj   Adj   N

20. The outcome was amazing.
    Adj   N   V   Adj

Chapter 3 _____

*Sentence Exercise #1: Using the **I know that** Test to Distinguish Fragments and Complete Sentences*

1. Whatever you say

    Fragment: *I know that <u>whatever you say</u>.

2. We were completely confused

    Complete sentence: I know that <u>we were completely confused</u>.

3. On top of old smoky

    Fragment: *I know that <u>on top of old smoky</u>.

4. More or less

    Fragment: *I know that <u>more or less</u>.

5. Not a chance

    Fragment: *I know that <u>not a chance</u>.

6. I will go if you can

    Complete sentence: I know that <u>I will go if you can</u>.

7. I couldn't believe it

    Complete sentence: I know that <u>I couldn't believe it</u>.

8. Last evening when you called

    Fragment: *I know that <u>last evening when you called</u>.

9. He doesn't have a clue

    Complete sentence: I know that <u>he doesn't have a clue</u>.

10. At the office

    Fragment: *I know that <u>at the office</u>.

Sentence Exercise #2: Third-Person Pronoun Test for Identifying Complete and Simple Subjects

1. <u>A first-class <u>education</u></u> is worth its weight in rubies.

       It

2. <u>The modern art <u>world</u></u> was shocked by Fred's use of bananas.

       It

3. <u>The <u>program</u></u> has been canceled.

   It

4. <u>The <u>unions</u> in that industry</u> have always opposed open shops.

     They

5. <u>A <u>stitch</u> in time</u> saves a lot of extra stitches.

   It

6. The <u>announcement</u> will be made this week.
         It

(Note: *this week* is an adverb expression, as we can tell when we try to replace it with a pronoun: *The announcement will be made *it*.)

7. The <u>proposed new industry standards</u> are likely to be controversial.
         They

8. The <u>economic conditions of the country</u> depend on the balance of trade.
         They

9. The <u>opportunity for the launches</u> is limited.
         It

10. The <u>buildings near the river</u> have become quite valuable.
          They

11. The <u>treasurer</u> made a sudden trip to Brazil.
      He/she

12. The <u>tax for purchases made after January 1</u> has been lowered.
          It

13. As always, <u>the list of suspects in her novel</u> is overwhelming.
          it

14. The <u>new lamp in the den</u> doesn't give enough light.
          It

15. Increasingly, <u>the internationalization of trade</u> makes us
          It

an economic global village.

Sentence Exercise #3: Putting Sentences Back into Normal Order

1. At first <u>the focus</u> is hard to adjust.
       it

   Normal order: The focus is hard to adjust at first.

2. By using a coat hook, <u>the young woman</u> managed to open the car.
         she

   Normal order: The young woman managed to open the car by using a coat hook.

3. Later in the day, <u>the cashier</u> noticed the missing bills.
        he/she

   Normal order: The cashier noticed the missing bills later in the day.

4. This afternoon <u>the director</u> has several appointments.
        he/she

   Normal order: The director has several appointments this afternoon.

5. Today <u>Adam</u> bought some apples.
       he

   Normal order: Adam bought some apples today.

6. With surprising speed <u>the little girl</u> climbed into the canoe.
                              she

   Normal order: The little girl climbed into the canoe with surprising speed.

7. Recently <u>a member of our sales staff</u> contacted you.
                   he/she

   Normal order: A member of our sales staff contacted you recently.

8. With a flourish <u>the detective</u> pulled out his service revolver.
                        he

   Normal order: The detective pulled out his service revolved with a flourish.

9. Somewhere <u>the sun</u> is shining.
                   it

   Normal order: The sun is shining somewhere.

10. Most of the time <u>your answer</u> would be right.
                          it

   Normal order: Your answer would be right most of the time.

Sentence Exercise #4: Identifying Verbs and Predicates

1. The students <u>found the answer on the Internet</u>.
   Confirmation: They will find the answer on the Internet.

2. The cry of the hound of the Baskervilles <u>echoed across the moor</u>.
   Confirmation: It will echo across the moor.

3. The garage <u>normally has the car ready by noon</u>.
   Confirmation: It normally will have the car ready by noon.

4. The police <u>usually rely only on verifiable information</u>.
   Confirmation: They usually will rely only on verifiable information.

5. The TV <u>was on at full volume</u>.
   Confirmation: It will be on at full volume.

6. The line at the restaurant <u>stretched out the door</u>.
   Confirmation: It will stretch out the door.

7. The new car <u>cost an arm and a leg</u>.
   Confirmation: It will cost an arm and a leg.

8. Baseball games <u>usually last about two and a half hours</u>.
   Confirmation: They usually will last about two and a half hours.

9. The state flower of Tennessee <u>is the iris</u>.

   Confirmation: It will be the iris.

10. The operating system of my new computer <u>really is a total mystery to me</u>.

    Confirmation: It really will be a total mystery to me.

Sentence Exercise #5: Recognizing Forms of the Linking Verb **be**

1. They <u>were</u> in very bad shape.

3rd-Pl-Past

2. I <u>am</u> not your sweet baboo!

1st-Sg-Pres

3. You <u>will be</u> a menace to the general public.

2nd-Sg-Future

4. They <u>were</u> such good friends.

3rd-Pl-Past

5. I <u>am</u> an only child.

1st-Sg-Pres

6. They <u>are</u> mistaken about that.

3rd-Pl-Pres

7. You <u>were</u> such a big pain in the neck.

2nd-Pl-Past

8. He <u>was</u> able to leap tall buildings at a single bound.

3rd-Sg-Past

9. You <u>will be</u> sixteen next month.

2nd-Sg-Future

10. You <u>are</u> ready to go now.

2nd-Pl-Pres

Sentence Exercise #6: Using **very**, the Comparative, and the Superlative to Identify Predicate Adjectives

1. Her entry was <u>graceful</u>.

   Confirmation: very graceful, more graceful, most graceful

2. His sense of humor is <u>strange</u>.

   Confirmation: very strange, stranger, strangest

3. The investigation seemed <u>thorough</u>.

   Confirmation: very thorough, more thorough, most thorough

4. Their gestures were often <u>dramatic</u>.

   Confirmation: very dramatic, more dramatic, most dramatic

5. The approach to the problem seems <u>practical</u>.
   Confirmation: very practical, more practical, most practical

6. The children got <u>angry</u>
   Confirmation: very angry, angrier, angriest

7. The society has been <u>active</u> for many years.
   Confirmation: very active, more active, most active

8. At that altitude, the air becomes <u>thin</u>.
   Confirmation: very thin, thinner, thinnest

9. The proposal seems <u>interesting</u>.
   Confirmation: very interesting, more interesting, most interesting

10. The person on the phone sounded <u>upset</u> to me.
    Confirmation: very upset, more upset, most upset

Sentence Exercise #7: Using the **very** Test to Distinguish Predicate Adjectives from Verbs

1. The children were very <u>amusing.</u>   (predicate adjective)

2. *The children were very <u>sleeping.</u>   (verb)

3. *The axle was very <u>turning.</u>   (verb)

4. The play was very <u>challenging.</u>   (predicate adjective)

5. *Our car was very <u>stolen.</u>   (verb)

6. *The incident was very <u>reported</u> to the police.   (verb)

7. The police were very <u>involved</u> in the case.   (predicate adjective)

8. *The lawyer's motion was very <u>rejected.</u>   (verb)

9. The lawyer's motion was not very <u>well presented.</u>   (predicate adjective)

10. *Unfortunately, the case was very <u>thrown</u> out of court.   (verb)

Sentence Exercise #8: Identifying Linking Verbs and Subject Complements

1. Throughout the ordeal, Holmes <u>remained</u> <u>calm</u>.
   Pred Adj

2. The driver <u>was</u> <u>drunk</u>.
   Pred Adj

3. Hearing the news, the general <u>grew</u> <u>furious</u>.
   Pred Adj

4. Aunt Sally <u>got</u> <u>angry</u> at her car.
   Pred Adj

5. Her car <u>is</u> a <u>Ford</u>.
   Pred Nom

6. The cat goes crazy during thunderstorms.
       Pred Adj

7. I am mad at myself for saying that.
      Pred Adj

8. Rudolph remained a private for several more months.
                    Pred Nom

9. Later that year, Lady Windermere fell dangerously ill.
                                             Pred Adj

10. In the *Hitchhiker's Guide to the Galaxy*, the answer to the meaning of life is 42.
                                                                      Pred Nom

11. At first the idea sounded strange to me.
                              Pred Adj

12. After the blow-out, the tire resembled a pancake.
                                          Pred Nom

13. Aunt Sally was upset.
              Pred Adj

14. Louise looked angry.
             Pred Adj

15. The dinner was a complete mess.
                            Pred Nom

Sentence Exercise #9: Distinguishing Intransitive and Transitive Verbs

1. I shot an arrow into the air.
     Vt   it

2. Leon smiled at the dentist.
            Vi

   (Note: We can replace *the dentist* with a pronoun, but the substitution merely proves that *dentist* is a noun. The replacement does not show that *dentist* is functioning as the object of the verb. In fact, *dentist* is the object of the preposition *at*.)

3. The judge suppressed the evidence.
                Vt   it

4. The prosecution objected to the judge's action.
                     Vi

   (*Action* is the object of the preposition *to*.)

5. The infection damaged the crops in the area.
                   Vt   them

6. The planets revolve around the earth.
               Vi

   (*Earth* is the object of the preposition *around*.)

7. Adrian <u>added</u> <u>chlorine</u> to the pool.
        Vt   it

8. The report will <u>emphasize</u> <u>the need for better fiscal control</u>.
            Vt   it

9. The car slowly <u>backed</u> down the driveway.
           Vi

10. That <u>concludes</u> <u>the meeting</u>.
      Vt   it

Sentence Exercise #10: Identifying Indirect Objects by the to/for Paraphrase Test

1. Holmes finally told <u>Watson</u> the killer's <u>name</u>.

   Confirmation: Holmes finally told the killer's name to Watson.

2. Paul fixed <u>her</u> an elegant <u>dessert</u>.

   Confirmation: Paul fixed an elegant dessert for her.

3. He saved <u>us</u> <u>some</u>.

   Confirmation: He saved some for us.

4. Professor Fiditch taught the grateful <u>students</u> <u>grammar</u>.

   Confirmation: Professor Fiditch taught grammar to the grateful students.

5. Throw the <u>dog</u> a <u>bone</u>!

   Confirmation: Throw a bone to the dog!

6. I ordered <u>us</u> some <u>dinner</u>.

   Confirmation: I ordered some dinner for us.

7. The Fairy Godmother granted <u>Cinderella</u> three <u>wishes</u>.

   Confirmation: The Fairy Godmother granted three wishes to Cinderella.

8. Cinderella told the <u>Prince</u> her <u>secret</u>.

   Confirmation: Cinderella told her secret to the Prince.

9. Marsha told John to leave her alone.

   (No indirect object)

10. The restaurant reserved the <u>couple</u> a <u>table</u> by the window.

    Confirmation: The restaurant reserved a table by the window for the couple.

Sentence Exercise #11: Identifying Object Complements

1. Bill's idea made him <u>rich</u>.

2. Bill's idea made him a <u>billionaire</u>.

   Confirmation: *Bill's idea made a billionaire to/for him.

3. The Justice Department considered Bugsy a <u>crook</u>.

   Confirmation: *The Justice Department considered a crook to/for Bugsy.

4. Bugsy believed himself <u>innocent</u>.

5. Judy painted the living room <u>pink</u>.

6. The President appointed his brother <u>Attorney General</u>.

   Confirmation: *The President appointed Attorney General to/for his brother.

7. She really made her mother <u>angry</u>.

8. I told them the truth. (indirect object + direct object)

   Confirmation: I told the truth to them.

9. They named the baby <u>Theo</u>.

   Confirmation: *They named Theo to/for the baby.

10. We chose the baby a present. (indirect object + direct object)

    Confirmation: We chose a present for the baby.

Sentence Exercise #12: Identifying Action Verb Complements

1. The company <u>employs</u> ten <u>workers</u>.
   Vt · DO

2. I will <u>arrange</u> a <u>meeting</u> with them.
   Vt · DO

3. The green container will <u>leak</u>.
   Vi

4. They <u>refused</u> the <u>offer</u>.
   Vt · DO

5. My brother <u>sent</u> <u>me</u> a <u>package</u>.
   Vt · IO · DO

6. The little girl <u>stared</u> at the food on her plate.
   Vi

7. <u>Save</u> <u>me</u> <u>some</u>.
   Vt · IO · DO

8. The earthquake <u>shook</u> the <u>house</u>.
   Vt · DO

9. The movie <u>made</u> <u>me</u> <u>sleepy</u>.
   Vt · DO · OC

10. The bank <u>loaned</u> the <u>company</u> two million <u>dollars</u>.
    Vt · IO · DO

11. Time and tide <u>wait</u> for no man.
    Vi

12. Holmes <u>offered</u> <u>Watson</u> some <u>advice</u>.
    Vt · IO · DO

13. Joanne <u>found</u> the <u>answer</u> to her question on the internet.
             Vt   DO

14. You <u>gave</u> <u>me</u> a <u>scare</u>.
         Vt IO   DO

15. I <u>gave</u> a <u>contribution</u> at the office.
      Vt   DO

16. Sleeping Beauty <u>considered</u> the <u>dwarves</u> <u>idiots</u>.
                 Vt   DO   OC

17. I finally <u>got</u> the <u>answer</u>.
          Vt   DO

18. <u>Tell</u> <u>me</u> a <u>story</u>.
     Vt IO   DO

19. The ghost <u>accused</u> <u>Scrooge</u> of being a miser.
           Vt   DO

20. We <u>talked</u> about your suggestion.
       Vi

Sentence Exercise #13: Identifying Verbs and Their Complements

1. The ship <u>sank</u>.
       Vi

2. The torpedo <u>sank</u> the <u>ship</u>.
           Vt   DO

3. The teacher <u>read</u> the <u>class</u> a <u>story</u>.
          Vt   IO   DO

4. William <u>was</u> a <u>waiter</u>.
       LV   PN

5. William <u>was</u> <u>weary</u>.
       LV   PA

6. These sentences <u>are</u> <u>rich</u> in complements.
           LV PA

7. We <u>completed</u> the first <u>portion</u> of the test.
      Vt   DO

8. The post office <u>returned</u> the <u>package</u> to Marty.
          Vt   DO

9. Cinderella <u>grew</u> <u>fat</u> in her old age.
        LV PA

10. Alice <u>brought</u> <u>Fred</u> a new dish <u>towel</u> for Father's Day.
        Vt   IO   DO

11. The President <u>appointed</u> <u>her</u> <u>Ambassador to the United Nations</u>.
           Vt   DO   OC

12. The cheese <u>smells</u> <u>moldy</u>.
          LV   PA

13. The agent <u>sold</u> <u>them</u> a new <u>house</u>.
             Vt   IO   DO

14. Today, Leon <u>turned</u> <u>30</u>.
                  LV PN

15. Aunt Sally <u>fit</u> the last <u>piece</u> into the puzzle.
              Vt   DO

Sentence Exercise #14: Identifying Verbs and Their Complements

1. Everyone <u>likes</u> <u>chocolate</u>.
          Vt   DO

2. No one <u>noticed</u> the <u>incident</u> in Lady Crumhorn's drawing room.
          Vt   DO

3. With deep regret, Charles <u>declined</u> a second <u>helping</u>.
                Vt   DO

4. Leon eventually <u>became</u> a famous and beloved <u>grammarian</u>.
            LV   PN

5. The tenor <u>sounded</u> <u>flat</u> to me.
           LV   PA

6. We <u>walked</u> to the end of the pier.
      Vi

7. They <u>offered</u> <u>us</u> a <u>lift</u> back to town.
       Vt   IO   DO

8. The play <u>received</u> great <u>reviews</u>.
          Vt   DO

9. They <u>lied</u> to us.
       Vi

10. Marley <u>gets</u> <u>upset</u> easily.
         LV   PA

11. With a flourish, the magician <u>produced</u> a <u>tuba</u> out of thin air.
                      Vt   DO

12. They <u>picked</u> <u>me</u> <u>first</u>.
        Vt   DO OC

13. They <u>were</u> <u>uninterested</u> in my ideas.
        LV   PA

    (Note: We can tell *uninterested* is an adjective by the *very* test—*very uninterested*—and by the fact that we cannot use *uninterest* as a verb: *"They uninterested in my idea.")

14. The waiter <u>slipped</u> <u>us</u> the <u>bill</u>.
           Vt   IO   DO

15. You <u>look</u> <u>good</u>.
       LV   PA

Sentence Exercise #15: Classifying Sentences by Purpose

1. Well, what do you know about that?   Answer: Interrogative

2. It seems pretty simple to me!   Answer: Exclamatory

3. That's what you think.   Answer: Declarative

4. Holmes warned Watson to stay back.   Answer: Declarative

5. To get the mean, total the data and divide by the number of observations.
   Answer: Imperative

6. Is everything OK here?   Answer: Interrogative

7. Return to headquarters at once!   Answer: Imperative

8. You must be good while we're gone.   Answer: Declarative

9. Blend in the cream cheese until smooth.   Answer: Imperative

10. Publish or perish!   Answer: Imperative

Sentence Exercise #16: Diagramming the Basic Sentence

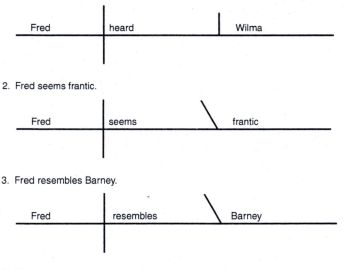

1. Fred heard Wilma.

| Fred | heard | Wilma |

2. Fred seems frantic.

| Fred | seems | frantic |

3. Fred resembles Barney.

| Fred | resembles | Barney |

4. Barney coughed.

| Barney | coughed |

5. Fred gave Barney measles.

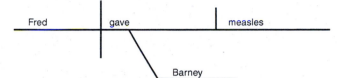

6. Wilma was angry.

7. Fred left.

8. Barney resented Fred.

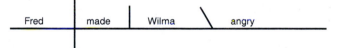

9. Fred made Wilma angry.

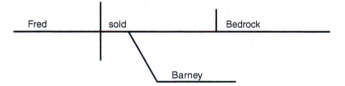

10. Fred sold Barney Bedrock.

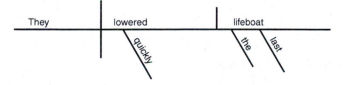

Sentence Exercise #17: Diagramming the Basic Sentence

1. They quickly lowered the last lifeboat.

2. Popeye nearly always split his infinitives.

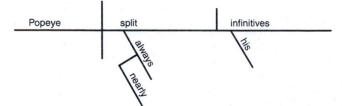

3. The room was a complete mess.

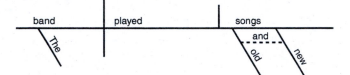

4. The band played new and old songs.

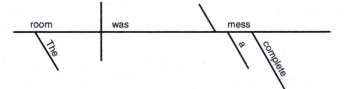

5. The event became an urban legend.

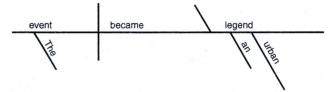

6. The teacher appointed Marvin the room monitor.

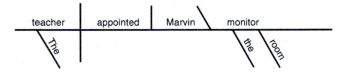

7. The phones rang loudly and endlessly.

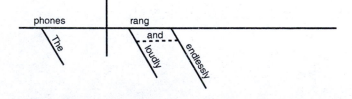

8. Dagwood made himself a huge sandwich.

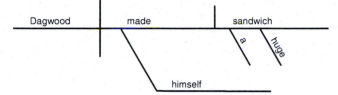

9. The hiker was quite badly hurt.

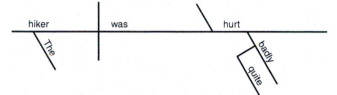

10. That class always gives me a very bad headache.

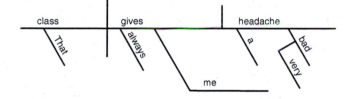

Sentence Exercise #18: Diagramming the Basic Sentence

1. Most politicians kiss babies and shake hands.

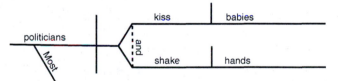

2. Ralph's comment was not appropriate.

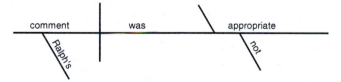

Note: *not* could also modify *was*.

3. We went home and changed clothes.

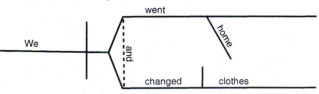

4. Answer the phone.

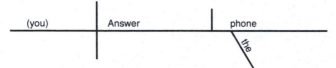

5. He tapped his glass and cleared his throat loudly.

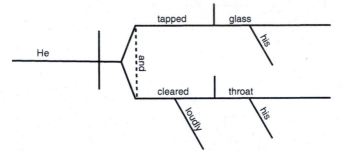

6. Joan and I sanded that old desk yesterday.

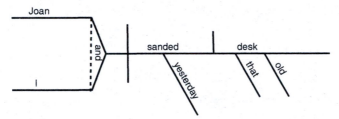

7. The residents were constantly complaining and whining.

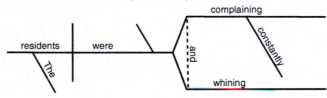

(Note: If you interpret *constantly* as modifying both *complaining* and *whining*, then *constantly* is attached to the main sentence line before the branch.)

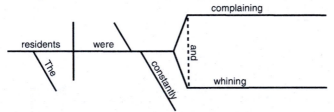

8. It drove Ford crazy.

9. Are you coming?

10. Did you get my message?

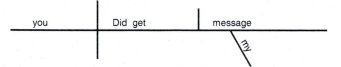

11. When are we leaving?

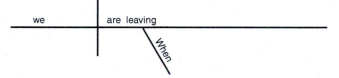

12. The Count politely took a very small bite.

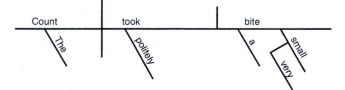

13. The plumber flooded the basement and the garage.

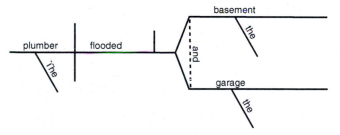

14. Lady Grenville greeted the humble peasants gracefully.

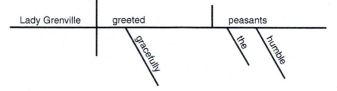

15. I must have been dreaming.

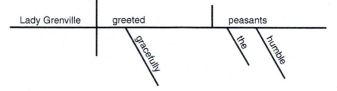

Sentence Exercise #19: Diagramming the Basic Sentence

1. Did she find Anne an apartment?

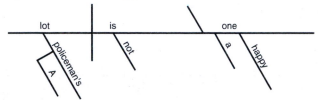

2. A policeman's lot is not a happy one.

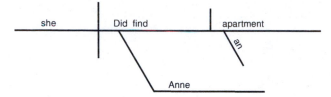

(Note: *A* could also modify *lot*.)

3. I had a really terrible cold recently.

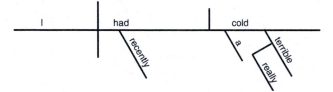

4. Wasn't the rainy landscape gloomy and depressing?

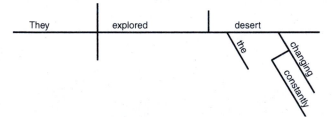

5. They explored the constantly changing desert.

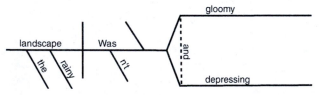

6. Tarzan and Jane loathe bananas.

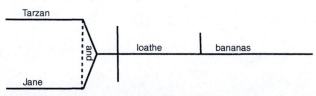

7. Did you take your pills?

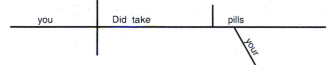

8. The mysterious red stain had appeared again.

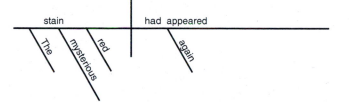

9. The dog gave Holmes an idea.

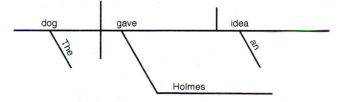

10. I am getting tired.

11. What are you saying?

12. The office resembled a bad movie set.

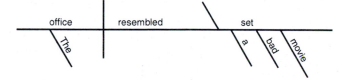

13. What did you do then?

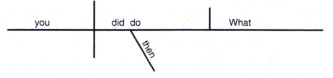

14. The press considered Senator Fogg a big windbag.

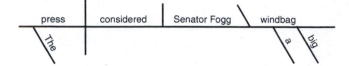

15. Naturally, he had wanted a full-time job and reasonable pay.

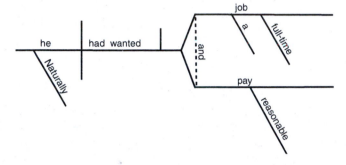

Chapter 4

Verb Exercise #1: Identifying Base Forms by the be Replacement Test

1. I can't <u>get</u> ready by then.
        BASE
Confirmation: I can't <u>be</u> ready by then.

2. They never <u>become</u> very good players.
                PRES
Confirmation: *They never <u>be</u> very good players.

3. You wouldn't <u>want</u> that.
                BASE
Confirmation: You wouldn't <u>be</u> that.

4. You shouldn't let it <u>upset</u> you.
                    BASE
Confirmation: You shouldn't let it <u>be</u> (a problem).

5. The butler will <u>see</u> you out.
                    BASE
Confirmation: The butler will <u>be</u> (ready soon).

6. Sarah helped us <u>get</u> prepared.
                    BASE
Confirmation: Sarah helped us <u>be</u> prepared.

7. It couldn't <u>come</u> at a worse time.
                BASE
Confirmation: It couldn't <u>be</u> at a worse time.

8. Have John <u>take</u> you home.
    BASE

    Confirmation: Have John <u>be</u> (on time).

9. Sometimes, the easiest things <u>appear</u> the most difficult.
    PRES

    Confirmation: *Sometimes, the easiest things <u>be</u> the most difficult.

10. Let me <u>help</u> you.
    BASE

    Confirmation: Let me <u>be</u> (the first to know).

Verb Exercise #2: Identifying Verb Forms

1. forget: forgets, forgot, to forget, forgetting, have forgotten

2. choose: chooses, chose, to choose, choosing, have chosen

3. come: comes, came, to come, coming, have come

4. protest: protests, protested, to protest, protesting, have protested

5. fade: fades, faded, to fade, fading, have faded

6. buy: buys, bought, to buy, buying, have bought

7. go: goes, went, to go, going, have gone

8. run: runs, ran, to run, running, have run

9. fulfill: fulfills, fulfilled, to fulfill, fulfilling, have fulfilled

10. substitute: substitutes, substituted, to substitute, substituting, have substituted

11. dig: digs, dug, to dig, digging, have dug

12. concede: concedes, conceded, to concede, conceding, have conceded

13. dream: dreams, dreamed (dreamt), to dream, dreaming, have dreamed (dreamt)

14. spend: spends, spent, to spend, spending, have spent

15. inquire: inquires, inquired, to inquire, inquiring, have inquired

16. do: does, did, to do, doing, have done

17. sell: sells, sold, to sell, selling, have sold

18. split: splits, split, to split, splitting, have split

19. have: has, had, to have, having, have had

20. be: is, was/were, to be, being, have been

Verb Exercise #3: Identifying Verb Forms

1. I <u>have</u> already <u>read</u> that book.
    Pres   Past Part

2. They <u>criticized</u> the plot unmercifully.
   Past

3. He <u>was</u> <u>scratching</u> his head.
   Past   Pres Part

4. You <u>are</u> merely <u>prolonging</u> the situation.
   Pres   Pres Part

5. The doctor <u>had</u> just <u>administered</u> the test.
   Past   Past Part

6. We <u>have</u> <u>had</u> a very good time.
   Pres Past Part

7. They <u>wanted</u> him <u>to come</u> back.
   Past   Inf

8. The bridge <u>was</u> slowly <u>collapsing</u> into the river.
   Past   Pres Part

9. The cars <u>merge</u> onto the freeway at a very high speed.
   Pres

10. We <u>had</u> <u>been</u> <u>studying</u> for hours.
    Past Past Part Pres Part

11. The instructor <u>made</u> us <u>try</u> it again.
    Past   Base

12. I <u>wasn't</u> <u>going</u> <u>to do</u> anything.
    Past   Pres Part Inf

13. The band <u>was</u> <u>featuring</u> the loudest amplifiers in the known universe.
    Past Pres Part

14. The chair <u>demanded</u> that he <u>be</u> quiet.
    Past   Base

15. We <u>wanted</u> you <u>to be</u> happy.
    Past   Inf

16. I <u>hate</u> them <u>interrupting</u> all the time.
    Pres   Pres Part

17. The professor <u>let</u> her <u>give</u> the answer.
    Past   Base

18. The children <u>have</u> <u>been</u> <u>watching</u> too much TV.
    Pres Past Part Pres Part

19. I <u>get</u> it.
    Pres

20. We <u>heard</u> him <u>ringing</u> the doorbell.
    Past   Pres Part

Verb Exercise #4: Identifying Uses of the Present Tense

1. Fortune cookies are unknown in China.
   Fact

2. There are 64 squares on a standard checker or chess board.
   Fact

3. The governor is soft on crime.
   Generalization

4. Las Vegas, Nevada, is one of the fastest-growing cities in the country.
   Fact

5. The new drug reduces the risk of stroke by 50%.
   Fact

6. Everyone needs to take that drug.
   Generalization

7. John Wayne's last movies are ridiculous because he is too old and fat
   for the roles.   Generalization   Fact

8. The reservoir holds 100 million gallons of water.
   Fact

9. A good supervisor knows when to ignore little problems.
   Generalization

10. While pickup trucks are a lot cheaper than cars, they are less safe.
    Fact   Fact

Verb Exercise #5: Using Present and Past Tenses

1. The play deal with extremely complex themes.
   deals

2. Many critics think that Hamlet be Shakespeare's most difficult play.
   think   is

3. One problem be that apparently Shakespeare revise it a number of times.
   is   revised

4. The modern text combine a number of different revisions.
   combines

5. Until recent times, people believe that illness be caused by imbalances of
   humors in the blood.   believed   is/was?

6. In the 1620s William Harvey, a British physician, discover the circulation
   of blood.   discovered

7. Harvey's discovery destroy the basis for bloodletting, the main treatment for
   most illnesses.   destroyed

8. Nevertheless, the practice of bloodletting continue for a long time.
                                               continued

9. In fact, George Washington <u>be</u> bled to death.
             was

10. It <u>be</u> amazing how conservative medical practices <u>be</u> even today.
       is   are

Verb Exercise #6: Modals and Base Forms

1. She <u>can sing</u> in the church choir.
2. I <u>could answer</u> the question.
3. The train <u>may be</u> on time for a change.
4. It <u>might be</u> raining.
5. Fred <u>must do</u> the dishes for a change.
6. General MacArthur is famous for saying, "I <u>shall return</u>."
7. We <u>should be</u> leaving soon.
8. I <u>will be</u> seeing you.
9. We thought that there <u>would be</u> time for that later.
10. You <u>should take</u> an umbrella.

Verb Exercise #7: Using the Present Perfect

1. Freddy Fireball <u>has been</u> a great pitcher.
2. Recently I <u>have invested</u> a lot of money in mutual funds.
3. The reviewers <u>have criticized</u> his recent movies.
4. You <u>have hurt</u> their feelings.
5. The phone <u>has been</u> out all afternoon.
6. We <u>have been</u> here so long that I think our waiter must have gone home.
7. It <u>has snowed</u> off and on all winter.
8. Your carelessness <u>has</u> just <u>caused</u> an accident!
9. Thelma <u>has read</u> every book that Louise ever wrote.
10. The mysterious hound <u>has appeared</u> on the moor several times.

Verb Exercise #8: Drawing Timelines for the Past Perfect

1. The curtain had gone up before the audience was seated.

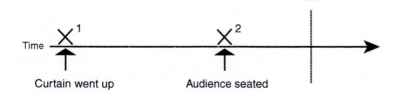

2. The driver had suffered a heart attack before the accident happened.

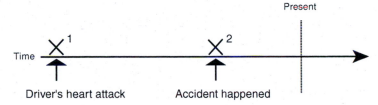

3. I had read the book before I saw the movie.

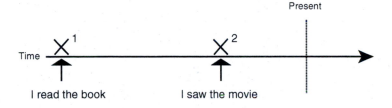

4. The cruise ship returned to port after the captain had discovered a fuel leak.

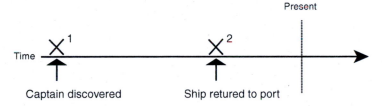

5. I had fixed dinner before I picked them up at the hotel.

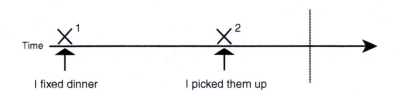

6. The concert was cancelled because the performers' plane had been grounded by bad weather.

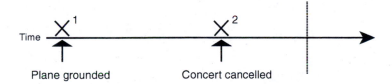

7. Apparently Shakespeare had writen his first play before he went to London.

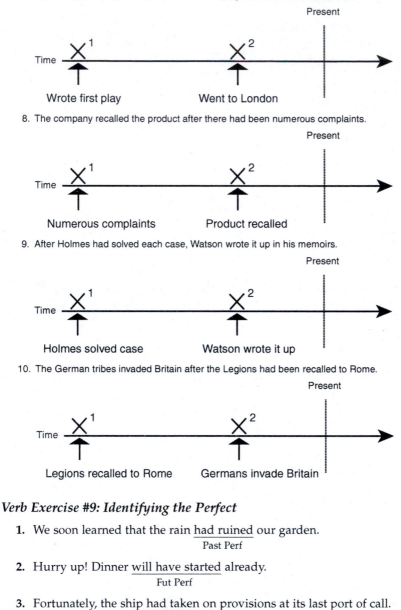

8. The company recalled the product after there had been numerous complaints.

9. After Holmes had solved each case, Watson wrote it up in his memoirs.

10. The German tribes invaded Britain after the Legions had been recalled to Rome.

Verb Exercise #9: Identifying the Perfect

1. We soon learned that the rain <u>had ruined</u> our garden.
   Past Perf

2. Hurry up! Dinner <u>will have started</u> already.
   Fut Perf

3. Fortunately, the ship <u>had taken</u> on provisions at its last port of call.
   Past Perf

4. The cells <u>have reproduced</u> themselves in the laboratory.
   Pres Perf

5. The newspapers <u>will have got</u> the story by now.
   Fut Perf

6. Prompt action <u>had minimized</u> the damage.
   Past Perf

7. The two companies <u>have merged</u> to form a new corporation.
   Pres Perf

8. The collision with the iceberg <u>had punched</u> a hole below the waterline.
   Past Perf

9. He <u>has</u> always <u>blamed</u> himself for the incident.
   Pres Perf

10. By the time we get back, the flood water <u>will</u> already <u>have reached</u> the house.
    Fut Perf

Verb Exercise #10: Identifying the Progressive

1. The strike <u>was crippling</u> the plant's output.
   Past Prog

2. The electrician <u>will be putting</u> in the wires this afternoon.
   Fut Prog

3. The wine stain <u>was soaking</u> into the tablecloth.
   Past Prog

4. Sorry, I can't make it. I<u>'m working</u> this evening.
   Pres Prog

5. The defense argued that the prosecutor <u>was suppressing</u> evidence.
   Past Prog

6. Tomorrow I <u>will be flying</u> out to Seattle.
   Fut Prog

7. She <u>is</u> currently <u>supervising</u> six employees.
   Pres Prog

8. Dorothy made it clear that she <u>was taking</u> her little dog with her.
   Past Prog

9. We <u>will be spraying</u> the park for beetles tomorrow.
   Fut Prog

10. I<u>'m getting</u> ready now.
    Pres Prog

Verb Exercise #11: Identifying Verb Constructions

1. Time and tide <u>wait</u> for no man.
   Pres

2. The president <u>had resigned</u> after the no-confidence vote.
   Past Perf

3. They <u>will drive</u> a very hard bargain.
   Fut

4. The machine <u>smoothes</u> the ice for the skaters.
                Pres

5. I <u>burned</u> myself.
   Past

6. The electrician <u>should finish</u> this afternoon.
              Modal

7. The game <u>will have ended</u> by now.
       Fut Perf

8. We <u>are</u> now <u>bidding</u> for lot #127.
     Pres Prog

9. I <u>will send</u> it by overnight delivery.
   Fut

10. The glare from the sun <u>was</u> really <u>bothering</u> me.
       Past Prog

11. The engineers <u>will be pumping</u> water out for a week.
     Fut Prog

12. I <u>had</u> badly <u>underestimated</u> the costs of the damages.
    Past Perf

13. I'<u>m melting</u>!
   Pres Prog

14. Steam <u>was coming</u> out of the pipes.
    Past Prog

15. We <u>will have played</u> every team in the league.
   Fut Perf

16. You <u>can be</u> sure of that.
   Modal

17. The phone <u>is ringing</u>.
    Pres Prog

18. I'<u>m</u> sorry about that.
  Pres

19. Finally I <u>had finished</u> my homework.
   Past Perf

20. Houston, we <u>have</u> a problem.
   Pres

Verb Exercise #12: Identifying Passives

1. Attila the Hun <u>was criticized</u> by the social committee.
Confirmation: The social committee criticized Attila the Hun.

2. The opening <u>was concealed</u> by a wooden screen.
Confirmation: A wooden screen concealed the opening.

3. Bugsy's sentence <u>was commuted</u> by the Governor.
Confirmation: The Governor commuted Bugsy's sentence.

4. Sleeping Beauty <u>was sued</u> by seven plaintiffs.

Confirmation: Seven plaintiffs sued Sleeping Beauty.

5. Large debts <u>were incurred</u> by my client.

Confirmation: My client incurred large debts.

6. The painting <u>was greatly</u> admired.

Confirmation: (Everybody) greatly admired the painting.

7. The country <u>was unified</u> by the new President.

Confirmation: The new President unified the country.

8. The robot <u>is programmed</u> to use a Hula-Hoop.

Confirmation: (Somebody) programs the robot to use a hula-hoop.

9. We <u>were embarrassed</u> by the regrettable incident.

Confirmation: The regrettable incident embarrassed us.

10. My resolve <u>was weakened</u> by the chocolate cheesecake.

Confirmation: The chocolate cheesecake weakened my resolve.

Verb Exercise #13: Converting Active-Voice Sentences into Passives

1. The children <u>were</u> really <u>scared</u> by the movie.

2. The trucks <u>were halted</u> by the guard.

3. A good game <u>was pitched</u> by the rookie.

4. He <u>was confined</u> to his quarters by them.

5. The art world <u>was rocked</u> by the exhibit.

6. The new tax loophole <u>was exploited</u> by everyone.

7. The original decision <u>was upheld</u> by the appeals court.

8. Our windshield <u>was shattered</u> by a rock.

9. His sense of humor <u>is admired</u> by them.

10. The Christmas tree <u>was decorated</u> in record time by us.

Verb Exercise #14: Identifying Complex Verb Constructions

1. The senator's aides <u>are denying</u> the statement.

   Present progressive

2. They <u>will have finished</u> by now.

   Future Perfect

3. I've <u>been working</u> on the railroad.

   Present Perfect Progressive

4. The doctor <u>prescribed</u> a non-aspirin pain reliever.

   Past

5. I <u>will be</u> very busy all afternoon.
Future/Modal

6. The commercials always <u>ruin</u> movies on TV.
Present

7. I <u>had been thinking</u> about it.
Past Perfect Progressive

8. They <u>will have invested</u> a fortune in it.
Future Perfect

9. He <u>had</u> nearly <u>wrecked</u> the stereo.
Past Perfect

10. The children <u>will have been sleeping</u> all afternoon.
Future Perfect Progressive

11. I <u>should have known</u> better.
Modal Perfect

12. There <u>will be</u> a small reception afterwards.
Future/Modal

13. <u>I've had</u> it.
Present Perfect

14. We <u>must be going</u> now.
Modal Progressive

15. Some rain <u>might have been getting</u> into the ceiling.
Modal Perfect Progressive

Verb Exercise #15: Identifying Complex Verb Constructions with the Passive

1. The dog <u>was being washed</u> by the whole family.
Past Progressive Passive

2. The writer <u>has been threatened</u> by his cruel editor.
Present Perfect Passive

3. Children <u>must be accompanied</u> by an adult.
Modal Passive

4. The gun <u>had been owned</u> by a retired policeman.
Past Perfect Passive

5. Corla's embarrassing slip <u>will be noticed</u> by everyone.
Future/Modal Passive

6. The judge <u>was being interviewed</u> by a reporter.
Past Progressive Passive

7. A serious accident <u>had been prevented</u>.
Past Perfect Passive

8. The presentation was being recorded.
   Past Progressive Passive

9. The plan should be approved.
   Modal Passive

10. The appointment will be announced tomorrow.
   Future/Modal Passive

Verb Exercise #16: Review Exercise

1. The students have been diagramming sentences.
   Present Perfect Progressive

2. The advertisement will attract a crowd.
   Future/Modal

3. The clutch engages the gears.
   Present

4. They have filed a motion.
   Present Perfect

5. The design must be approved.
   Modal Passive

6. He was a fool.
   Past

7. His claim is stretching the truth.
   Present Progressive

8. We should have warned them.
   Modal Perfect

9. The Smiths would have been watching TV.
   Modal Perfect Progressive

10. The children were frightened by Godzilla.
   Past Passive

11. Holmes is checking Lord Bumfrey's story.
   Present Progressive

12. Bugsy had acquired a large fortune by devious means.
   Past Perfect

13. The combination may have been changed.
   Modal Perfect Passive

14. Lady Smithers could have taken the pearls.
   Modal Perfect

15. Leon loves Lily.
   Present

16. Sir Desmond had had his answer.
   Past Perfect

17. The butler <u>should have polished</u> the silver.
    Modal Perfect

18. The Legionnaires <u>ordered</u> clam juice.
    Past

19. The meeting <u>was</u> rudely <u>interrupted</u>.
    Past Passive

20. I <u>am</u> tired now.
    Past (*Tired* is a predicate adjective: *very tired.*)

Chapter 5

Phrase Exercise #1: Identifying Prepositional Phrases by Noun Roles

1. <u>He</u> answered the reporters' <u>questions</u> (during the <u>flight</u>).
   Subj   Verb-Comp   Obj-Prep

2. The <u>computers</u> (in the <u>library</u>) were replaced (over <u>Christmas</u>).
       Subj   Obj-Prep   Obj-Prep

3. <u>We</u> got <u>curtains</u> (for the <u>windows</u>) (in the living <u>room</u>).
   Subj   Verb-Comp   Obj-Prep   Obj-Prep

4. (Except for the <u>ending</u>), I liked your <u>ideas</u> (about your <u>paper</u>).
       Obj-Prep Subj   Verb-Comp   Obj-Prep

5. <u>I</u> haven't had a <u>minute</u> (to <u>myself</u>) (since <u>lunch</u>).
   Subj   Verb-Comp   Obj-Prep   Obj-Prep

6. The <u>cars</u> (in the <u>lot</u>) have already been washed.
       Subj   Obj-Prep

7. A <u>friend</u> (of <u>mine</u>) received an <u>award</u> (for her <u>writing</u>).
     Subj   Obj-Prep   Verb-Comp   Obj-Prep

8. John's <u>attitude</u> (toward the <u>project</u>) is the main <u>problem</u>.
          Subj   Obj-Prep   Verb-Comp

9. <u>We</u> got a good <u>table</u> (near the <u>window</u>).
   Subj   Verb-Comp   Obj-Prep

10. (In the <u>afternoon</u>), <u>we</u> had a big <u>thunderstorm</u>.
        Obj-Prep   Subj   Verb-Comp

Phrase Exercise #2: Identifying Adjective Phrases by the Pronoun Replacement Test

1. Tickets <u>to Seattle</u> cost $338 round-trip.

   Confirmation: <u>Tickets to Seattle</u> cost $338 round-trip.
                      They

2. The apartment <u>in the basement</u> was all that I could afford.

   Confirmation: <u>The apartment in the basement</u> was all that I could afford.
                        It

3. A book by Toni Morrison was required.

   Confirmation: A book by Toni Morrison was required.
   It

4. The lamp next to my desk isn't working.

   Confirmation: The lamp next to my desk isn't working.
   It

5. Two hours between classes doesn't give me much time.

   Confirmation: Two hours between classes doesn't give me much time.
   It

6. We should eat the apples in the refrigerator first.

   Confirmation: We should eat the apples in the refrigerator first.
   them

7. Several pictures at that gallery caught our eye.

   Confirmation: Several pictures at that gallery caught our eye.
   They

8. Some instructors in white lab coats asked what we wanted.

   Confirmation: Some instructors in white lab coats asked what we wanted.
   They

9. I needed to find a book about Sicily.

   Confirmation: I needed to find a book about Sicily.
   it

10. The first of the month will be here soon.

    Confirmation: The first of the month will be here soon.
    It

Phrase Exercise #3: Identifying Adjective Prepositional Phrases by the Which Test

1. The meeting at the hotel lasted only a few minutes.
   Confirmation: Which meeting? The one at the hotel.

2. The computers in the library were updated recently.
   Confirmation: Which computers? The ones in the library.

3. All prepositional phrases in these sentences should be underlined.
   Confirmation: Which prepositional phrases? The ones in these sentences.

4. The award for her writing was a pleasant surprise.
   Confirmation: Which award? The one for her writing.

5. I framed the picture of my parents.
   Confirmation: Which picture? The one of my parents.

6. The meeting about class schedules has been postponed.
   Confirmation: Which meeting? The one about class schedules.

7. I found several books <u>by our teacher</u> in the library.

   Confirmation: Which books? The ones <u>by our teacher</u>. (Note: *in the library* is also a prepositional phrase, but it is not an adjective phrase. It is an adverb phrase that tells where the books were found.)

8. The new computers <u>at work</u> are much faster than the old ones.

   Confirmation: Which computers? The ones <u>at work</u>.

9. I never got used to the winters <u>in the Midwest</u>.

   Confirmation: Which winters? The ones <u>in the Midwest</u>.

10. The class <u>in advanced Spanish</u> was canceled.

   Confirmation: Which class? The one <u>in advanced Spanish</u>.

Phrase Exercise #4: Identifying Adverb Prepositional Phrases by the Adverb Question Test

1. I took algebra <u>in community college</u>.

   Confirmation: Where did I take algebra? <u>In community college</u>.

2. We painted the kitchen ceiling <u>with a roller</u>.

   Confirmation: How did we paint the kitchen ceiling? <u>With a roller</u>.

3. She finished her paper <u>after class</u>.

   Confirmation: When did she finish her paper? <u>After class</u>.

4. The freeway goes <u>by the airport</u>.

   Confirmation: Where does the freeway go? <u>By the airport</u>.

5. I stood there <u>like a fool</u>.

   Confirmation: How did I stand there? <u>Like a fool</u>.

6. It must have rained <u>during the night</u>.

   Confirmation: When must it have rained? <u>During the night</u>.

7. Our doors always stick <u>in wet weather</u>.

   Confirmation: When do our doors always stick? <u>In wet weather</u>.

8. I got a ticket <u>for parking there</u>.

   Confirmation: Why did I get a ticket? <u>For parking there</u>.

9. We ate breakfast <u>at McDonald's</u> this morning.

   Confirmation: Where did we eat breakfast this morning? <u>At McDonald's</u>.

10. I scheduled all my classes <u>in the afternoon</u>.

   Confirmation: When did I schedule all my classes? <u>In the afternoon</u>.

Phrase Exercise #5: Identifying Adverb Prepositional Phrases by the Adverb Phrase Movement Test

1. We are going to watch a program <u>at eight</u>.

   Confirmation: <u>At eight</u>, we are going to watch a program.

2. I need to get home <u>after class</u>.

   Confirmation: <u>After class</u>, I need to get home.

3. I nearly fell asleep <u>during the lecture</u>.

   Confirmation: <u>During the lecture</u>, I nearly fell asleep.

4. There was a small grocery store <u>behind the post office</u>.

   Confirmation: <u>Behind the post office</u>, there was a small grocery store.

5. We will begin the presentation <u>in just a minute</u>.

   Confirmation: <u>In just a minute</u>, we will begin the presentation.

6. We discussed the problem <u>before lunch</u>.

   Confirmation: <u>Before lunch</u>, we discussed the problem.

7. John found the missing letter <u>in a desk drawer</u>.

   Confirmation: <u>In a desk drawer</u>, John found the missing letter.

8. The wind began to rise <u>toward dawn</u>.

   Confirmation: <u>Toward dawn</u>, the wind began to rise.

9. The lawyer addressed the jury <u>with barely concealed outrage</u>.

   Confirmation: <u>With barely concealed outrage</u>, the lawyer addressed the jury.

10. The streets had become completely empty <u>but for a few delivery trucks</u>.

    Confirmation: <u>But for a few delivery trucks</u>, the streets had become completely empty.

Phrase Exercise #6: Identifying Adverb Phrases

1. They are very <u>efficient</u> at their jobs.

Adjective

   Confirmation: *How are they very efficient? *At their jobs?

*At their jobs, they are very efficient.

2. The soldiers <u>paraded</u> across the field.

Verb

   Confirmation: Where did the soldiers parade? Across the field.

Across the field the soldiers paraded.

3. She returned our call <u>late</u> in the evening.

Adverb

   Confirmation: *When did she return our call late? *In the evening.

*In the evening, she returned our call late.

4. I felt <u>guilty</u> at our behavior.

Adjective

   Confirmation: *How did I feel guilty? *At our behavior.

*At our behavior, I felt guilty.

5. Everybody was <u>upset</u> about the accident.
                    Adjective

   Confirmation: *Why was everybody upset? *About the accident.
                 *About the accident, everybody was upset.

6. The judge <u>supported</u> the defense <u>in the Brown case</u>.
                Verb

   Confirmation: When did the judge support the defense? In the Brown case.
                 In the Brown case, the judge supported the defense.

7. The ruling seemed <u>favorable</u> to the prosecution.
                       Adjective

   Confirmation: *When did the ruling seem favorable? *To the prosecution.
                 *To the prosecution, the ruling seemed favorable (Note: This
                 sentence is grammatical but with a different meaning—"As far as
                 the prosecution was concerned, the ruling seemed favorable.")

8. We left <u>early</u> in the morning.
             Adverb

   Confirmation: *When did we leave early? *In the morning.
                 *In the morning we left early.

9. We were <u>ready</u> for any problem.
             Adjective

   Confirmation: *How were we ready? *For any problem.
                 *For any problem, we were ready.

10. The offer seemed <u>comparable</u> with the previous offer.
                       Adjective

    Confirmation: *How did the offer seem comparable? *With the previous offer.
                  *With the previous offer, the offer seemed comparable.

Phrase Exercise #7: Identifying Adjective and Adverb Prepositional Phrases

1. I liked your paper <u>about the Civil War</u>.
                         Adj

   Confirmation: I liked <u>your paper about the Civil War</u>.
                                                    it   (pronoun replacement test)

2. They crossed the road <u>during the night</u>.
                            Adv   modifying verb *crossed*

   Confirmation: <u>During the night</u>, they crossed the road.
                   Adv   (adv movement test)

3. The proposal <u>for a new bridge</u> has become quite controversial.
                   Adj

   Confirmation: <u>The proposal for a new bridge</u> has become quite controversial.
                                      It   (pronoun replacement test)

4. I liked your paper <u>except for the ending</u>.

                            Adv   (modifying the verb *liked*)

   Confirmation: <u>Except for the ending</u>, I liked your paper.

                           Adv   (adverb movement test)

5. The governor issued a statement <u>concerning the trial</u>.

                                       Adj

   Confirmation: The governor issued <u>a statement concerning the trial</u>.

                                                        it   (pronoun replacement test)

6. We washed the plants <u>with great care</u>.

                           Adv   (modifying the verb *washed*)

   Confirmation: How did we wash the plants? <u>With great care</u>.

                                          Adv   (question)

7. The building <u>behind ours</u> has become vacant.

                       Adj

   Confirmation: <u>The building behind ours</u> has become vacant.

                                It   (pronoun replacement test)

8. I was very upset <u>at the time</u>.

                       Adv   (modifying the verb *was*)

   Confirmation: <u>At the time</u>, I was very upset.

                       Adv   (adverb movement test)

9. The rebellion <u>in 1845</u> caused many Germans to immigrate.

                       Adj

   Confirmation: <u>The rebellion in 1845</u> caused many Germans to immigrate.

                              It   (pronoun replacement test)

10. The meeting <u>on Tuesday</u> has been canceled.

                       Adj

   Confirmation: <u>The meeting on Tuesday</u> has been canceled.

                              It   (pronoun replacement test)

11. I couldn't understand his attitude <u>toward the play</u>.

                                 Adj

   Confirmation: I couldn't understand <u>his attitude toward the play</u>.

                                                   it   (pronoun replacement test)

12. We might have some rain <u>during the game</u>.

                           Adv   (modifying the verb *have*)

   Confirmation: <u>During the game</u>, we might have some rain.

                       Adv   (Adverb movement test)

13. The relentless inflation <u>after WWI</u> destroyed Germany's economy.

                       Adj

   Confirmation: <u>The relentless inflation after WWI</u> destroyed G's economy.

                              It   (pronoun replacement test)

14. Holmes examined the cloak <u>with great care</u>.

                           Adv   (adverb modifying the verb *examined*)

   Confirmation: <u>With great care</u>, Holmes examined the cloak.

                       Adv   (Adverb movement test)

15. Holmes examined the cloak <u>with the torn fringe</u>.

   Adj

   Confirmation: Holmes examined <u>the cloak with the torn fringe</u>.

   it   (pronoun replacement test)

16. The decision was favorable <u>to the opposition</u>.

   Adv   (modifying the adjective *favorable*)

   Confirmation: *How was the decision favorable? *To the opposition.

   (Adverb question test fails)

17. I returned the car early <u>in the morning</u>.

   Adv   (modifying the adverb *early*)

   Confirmation: *<u>In the morning</u>, I returned the car early.

   (Adverb movement test fails)

18. We grew angry <u>at the unnecessary delay</u>.

   Adv   (modifying the adjective *angry*)

   Confirmation: *At the unnecessary delay, we grew angry.

   (Adverb movement test fails)

19. I searched the Web <u>for an answer</u>.

   Adv   (modifying verb *searched*)

   Confirmation: Why did I search the Web? <u>For an answer</u>.

   Adv   (Adverb question test)

20. Washing dishes is hard <u>on your hands</u>.

   Adv   (modifying the adjective *hard*)

   Confirmation: *<u>On your hands</u>, washing dishes is hard.

   (Adverb movement test fails)

Phrase Exercise #8: Diagramming Prepositional Phrases

1. I knew all the people at the party.

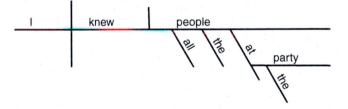

2. The house on the corner is vacant.

3. The carrier delivered a package to our new address.

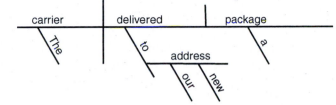

4. We went to the library.

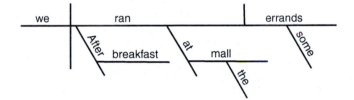

5. After breakfast, we ran some errands at the mall.

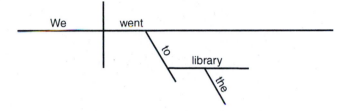

6. Naturally, Watson was misled by the clue.

(a) *was misled* is a passive

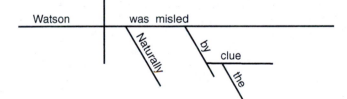

(b) *misled* is a predicate adjective

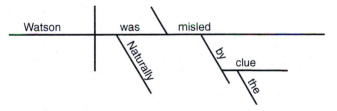

7. With great relish, he discussed the causes of the problem.

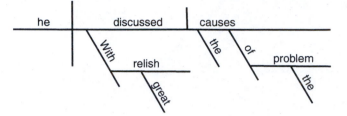

8. They issued a retraction of their previous press-release at the next meeting.

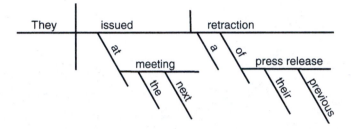

9. The European Union boycotted the importation of beef from the United States.

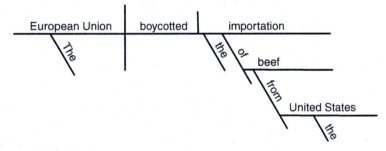

10. After dinner, we watched some TV at a friend's house.

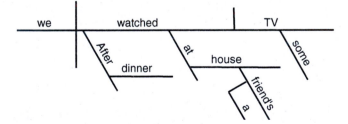

11. My cousin was active in politics after graduation.

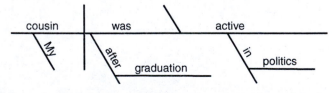

12. I suggested some revisions to the plans for the new office.

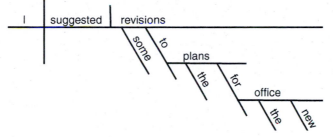

13. The count was polite to everyone in the vault.

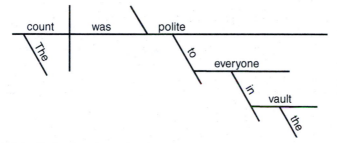

14. It had rained earlier in the day.

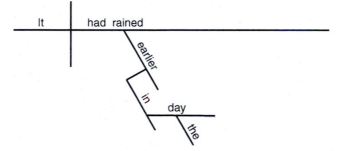

15. I saw the movie about the killer tomatoes.

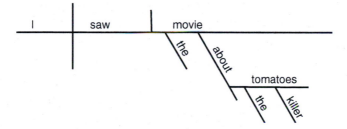

Phrase Exercise #9: Identifying Appositive Phrases by the Appositive Deletion Test

1. He gave his daughter a new toy, <u>a stuffed teddy bear</u>.

    Confirmation: He gave his daughter a new toy.

                    He gave his daughter <u>a stuffed teddy bear</u>.

2. PDQ Bach, <u>an imaginary son of JS Bach</u>, composed *The Stoned Guest*.

   Confirmation: PDQ Bach composed *The Stoned Guest*.
   <u>An imaginary son of JS Bach</u> composed *The Stoned Guest*.

3. Atolls, <u>small coral islands</u>, cover tropical waters.

   Confirmation: Atolls cover tropical waters.
   <u>Small coral islands</u> cover tropical waters.

4. Watson, <u>a slightly comic figure</u>, is the perfect foil for Holmes.

   Confirmation: Watson is the perfect foil for Holmes.
   <u>A slightly comic figure</u> is the perfect foil for Holmes.

5. Calvin Coolidge, <u>the 30th President</u>, was known as "Silent Cal."

   Confirmation: Calvin Coolidge was known as "Silent Cal."
   <u>The 30th</u> President was known as "Silent Cal."

6. The theater, <u>one of the old movie palaces</u>, was undergoing renovation.

   Confirmation: The theater was undergoing renovation.
   <u>One of the old movie palaces</u> was undergoing renovation.

7. Mr. Brown, <u>a friend of my grandfather's</u>, refused to use electric lights.

   Confirmation: Mr. Brown refused to use electric lights.
   <u>A friend of my grandfather's</u> refused to use electric lights.

8. The test, <u>a multiple-choice philosophy exam</u>, proved to be easy.

   Confirmation: The test proved to be easy.
   <u>A multiple-choice philosophy exam</u> proved to be easy.

9. The police found his last address, <u>an old hotel in Denver</u>.

   Confirmation: The police found his last address.
   The police found <u>an old hotel in Denver</u>.

10. The first talking motion picture, *The Jazz Singer*, appeared in 1927.

    Confirmation: The first talking motion picture appeared in 1927.
    The Jazz Singer appeared in 1927.

Phrase Exercise #10: Distinguishing Redundant and Essential Appositive Phrases

1. The Greek poet <u>Homer</u> was blind. (Essential)

   Confirmation: *The Greek poet was blind.

2. Children love tortillas, <u>a type of cornmeal pancake</u>.

   Confirmation: Children love tortillas.

3. Mr. Smith, <u>a teacher at our school</u>, greatly admires appositives.

   Confirmation: Mr. Smith greatly admired appositives.

4. My friend <u>Amy</u> wants to become a dentist. (Essential)

   Confirmation: My friend wants to become a dentist.

5. Noel Coward wrote *Private Lives*, his best-known play, in 1930.

   Confirmation: Noel Coward wrote *Private Lives* in 1930.

6. The novel *Pride and Prejudice* is required for the course. (Essential)

   Confirmation: The novel is required for the course.

7. They moved to Olympia, the capital of Washington State.

   Confirmation: They moved to Olympia.

8. The novelist William Faulkner became a successful film writer. (Essential)

   Confirmation: The novelist became a successful film writer.

9. She is going out with Richard, a guy in her geology class.

   Confirmation: She is going out with Richard.

10. A small start-up company Apexx made the headlines. (Essential)

    Confirmation: A small start-up company made the headlines.

Phrase Exercise #11: Diagramming Appositives and Appositive Phrases

1. Cereal, an American invention, is now a universal breakfast.

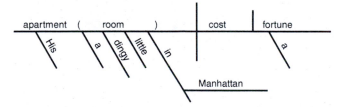

2. His apartment, a dingy little room in Manhattan, cost a fortune.

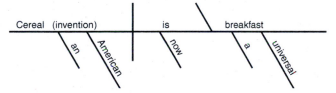

3. Mrs. McCormick, the first foreign-affairs reporter, wrote only about Europe.

4. We got new dishes, some beautiful pottery from Mexico.

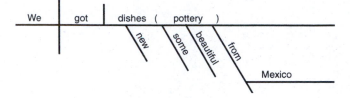

5. The driver, a new arrival, couldn't find the address.

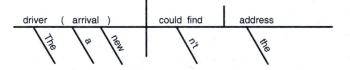

6. The plane, an old DC-3, was waiting at the airstrip.

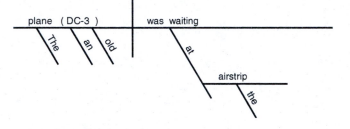

7. I contacted the salesman at his e-mail address, greed.com.

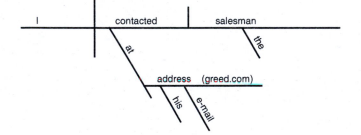

8. Please bring that briefcase, the one with a red tag.

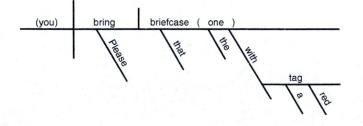

9. Have you met my friend Sarah?

10. She asked Mrs. Brown, our English teacher, a hard grammar question.

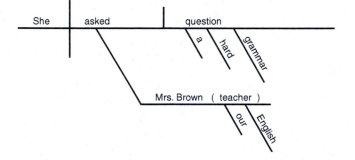

Phrase Exercise #12: Identifying Gerunds and Gerund Phrases by the it Test

1. Their main job is protecting the President.
   It   it

2. We talked about our going out for something to eat.
                         it

3. Seeing is believing.
   It   it

4. His always being late gets him into unnecessary trouble.
           It

5. I usually avoid working after dinner.
               it

6. They are always complaining about their having to do the dishes.
                        it

7. Getting stuck in traffic was a real pain.
        It

8. My goal is studying classical Greek in Athens.
             it

9. Alicia learned English by listening to the radio.
                   it

10. My adjusting the antenna did not help the reception.
        It

Phrase Exercise #13: Identifying Gerunds by the Possessive Subject Test

1. <u>Playing</u> tennis helps keep me in shape.

   Confirmation: My <u>playing</u> tennis helps keep me in shape.

2. I didn't like <u>missing</u> so many classes.

   Confirmation: I didn't like my <u>missing</u> so many classes.

3. They insisted on <u>telling</u> us the plot of the entire movie.

   Confirmation: They insisted on their <u>telling</u> us the plot of the entire movie.

4. <u>Leaving</u> for summer vacation requires a lot of preparation.

   Confirmation: Our <u>leaving</u> for summer vacation requires a lot of preparation.

5. She had a good reason for not <u>going</u> to class yesterday.

   Confirmation: She had a good reason for her not <u>going</u> to class yesterday.

6. <u>Producing</u> a good dinner is a major undertaking.

   Confirmation: Our <u>producing</u> a good dinner is a major undertaking.

7. The company was worried about <u>expanding</u> so quickly.

   Confirmation: The company was worried about their <u>expanding</u> so quickly.

8. We enjoyed <u>participating</u> in the festivities.

   Confirmation: We enjoyed our <u>participating</u> in the festivities.

9. <u>Appointing</u> the committee proved surprisingly difficult.

   Confirmation: Their <u>appointing</u> the committee proved surprisingly difficult.

10. I liked <u>getting</u> there early.

    Confirmation: I liked our <u>getting</u> there early.

Phrase Exercise #14: Diagramming Gerunds and Gerund Phrases

1. Answering the phone takes all morning.

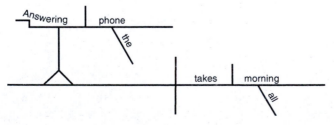

2. I worried about finishing my paper on time.

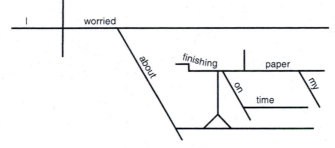

3. Making an outline is always the first step in writing a paper.

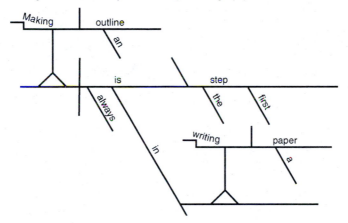

4. The prosecutor's accusing Bugsy of perjury caused a mistrial.

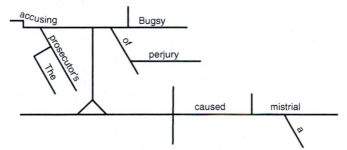

5. I appreciated his getting good information.

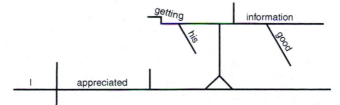

6. Getting their cooperation in this matter was not easy.

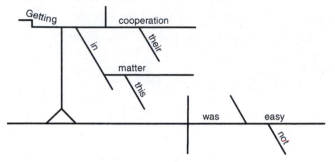

(Note: *Not* could also modify *was.*)

7. Leon often regretted his picking a fight with all those Marines.

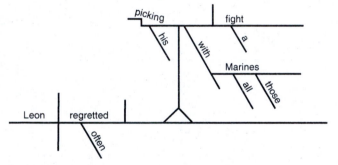

8. Don't bother about washing the dishes now.

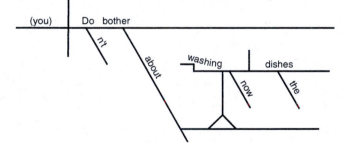

9. He muttered something about finding the Maltese Falcon.

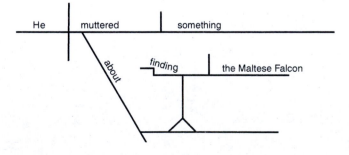

10. Lowering the interest rate usually spurs consumers' spending.

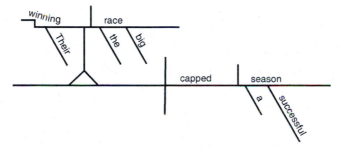

11. Their winning the big race capped a successful season.

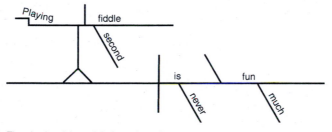

12. Playing second fiddle is never much fun.

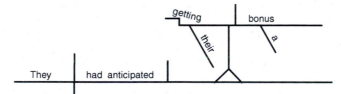

13. They had anticipated their getting a bonus.

14. I hate meeting tight deadlines.

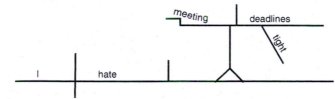

15. We laughed at Leon's retelling of the incident.

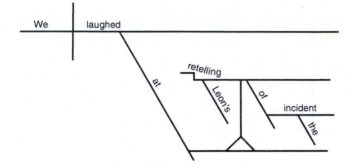

Phrase Exercise #15: Identifying Participial Phrases by the Pronoun Replacement Test

1. The place was a gloomy old brick factory <u>built in the nineteenth century</u>.
   Confirmation:
   The place was <u>a gloomy old brick factory built in the nineteenth century</u>.
   it

2. The document <u>summarizing the proposal</u> was finally finished.
   Confirmation: <u>The document summarizing the proposal</u> was finally finished.
   It

3. Several trees <u>weakened by the relentless storm</u> came down during the night.
   Confirmation:
   <u>Several trees weakened by the relentless storm</u> came down during the night.
   They

4. The room <u>adjoining ours</u> was much larger.
   Confirmation: <u>The room adjoining ours</u> was much larger.
   It

5. The workers <u>terminated after the strike</u> sued the employer.
   Confirmation: <u>The workers terminated after the strike</u> sued the employer.
   They

6. We disconnected the cables <u>leading to the power source</u>.
   Confirmation: We disconnected <u>the cables leading to the power source</u>.
   them

7. The council adopted the proposal <u>submitted by the subcommittee</u>.
   Confirmation:
   The council adopted <u>the proposal submitted by the subcommittee</u>.
   it

8. The peasants found the accents <u>cultivated by the local aristocracy</u> to be laughable.

   Confirmation:

   The peasants found <u>the accents cultivated by the local aristocracy</u> to be laughable.   them

9. The runners <u>competing in the first event</u> were called to the announcer's booth.

   Confirmation:

   <u>The runners competing in the first event</u> were called to the announcer's booth.
         They

10. We collected the paper cups <u>discarded by the runners</u>.

    Confirmation: We collected <u>the paper cups discarded by the runners.</u>
                 them

Phrase Exercise #16: Identifying Participial Phrases by the Understood–Subject Test

1. <u>Picking their spot carefully</u>, the <u>hikers</u> set up camp.

   Confirmation: Who was picking their spot carefully? The hikers were.

2. The <u>professor</u> made his point, <u>gesturing at the figures on the blackboard</u>.

   Confirmation: Who was gesturing at the figures on the blackboard? The professor was.

3. <u>Worried about his grades</u>, <u>Chadwick</u> decided he had better get to work.

   Confirmation: Who was worried about his grades? Chadwick was.

4. The <u>runner</u> slid into second base, <u>easily ducking under the tag</u>.

   Confirmation: Who easily ducked under the tag? The runner did.

5. <u>Giving me a dirty look</u>, <u>she</u> concluded her prepared remarks.

   Confirmation: Who gave me a dirty look? She did.

6. I remembered the strange <u>sound</u> <u>occurring in the night</u>.

   Confirmation: What occurred in the night? A sound did.

7. <u>Closing his book</u>, the <u>teacher</u> signaled the end of class.

   Confirmation: Who closed his book? The teacher did.

8. How could <u>he</u> have paid the fine, <u>being completely broke</u>?

   Confirmation: Who was completely broke? He was.

9. <u>Scrooge</u> took a deep breath, <u>realizing that he shouldn't get upset over small matters</u>.

   Confirmation: Who realized that he shouldn't get upset? Scrooge did.

10. The <u>events</u> <u>scheduled for the afternoon</u> were postponed.

    Confirmation: What was scheduled for the afternoon? The events were.

Phrase Exercise #17: Diagramming Participial Phrases

1. The student answering the first question did a good job.

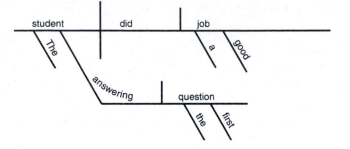

2. Upset by their carelessness, the director reprimanded the actors sharply.

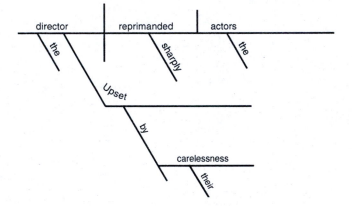

3. The actors took their places, gumbling under their breath.

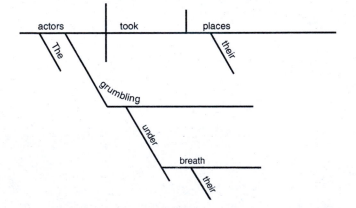

4. The children, experiencing really cold weather for the first time, huddled together.

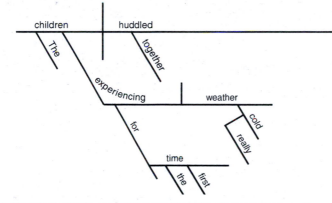

5. Inspector Lastrade, completely misled by Holmes's suggestions, made absurd accusations.

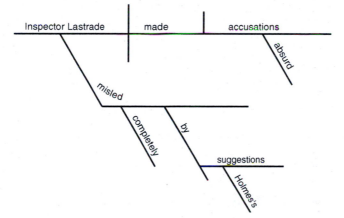

6. I opened the refrigerator, looking for a quick snack.

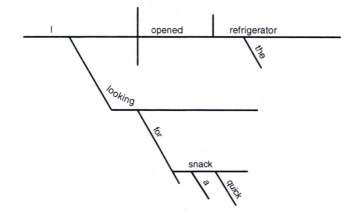

7. Confusing enthusiasm with talent, Leon quit his day job.

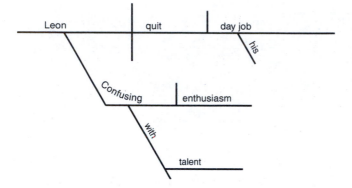

8. Disturbed by her weight, Sleeping Beauty began an exercise program.

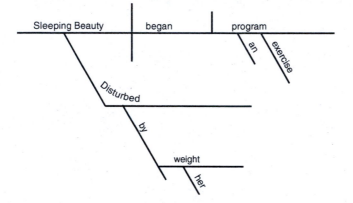

9. They were studying Italian, motivated by their planned trip to Italy.

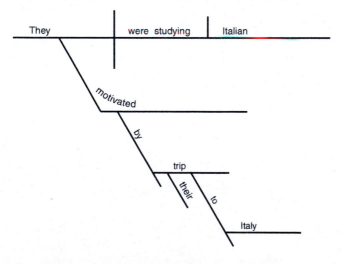

10. Underscoring his concern, Senator Fogg commissioned a survey.

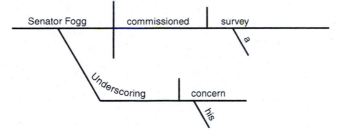

11. Scrooge, frightened by his strange dreams, slept very badly.

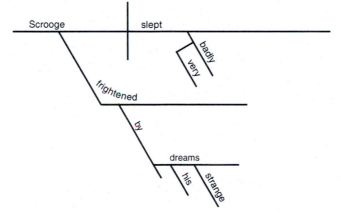

12. Tiny Tim skipped through the town, strumming his ukulele.

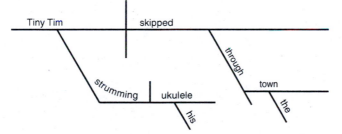

13. Batting her eyes flirtatiously, Miss Piggy answered the reporters' questions.

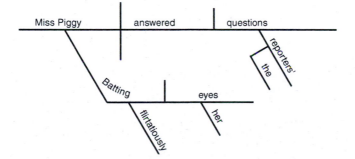

14. We talked to the children playing in the park.

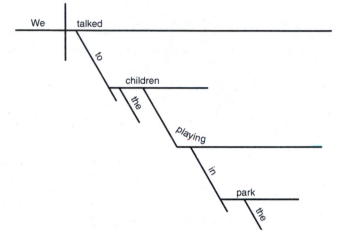

15. I asked the woman standing next to me a question.

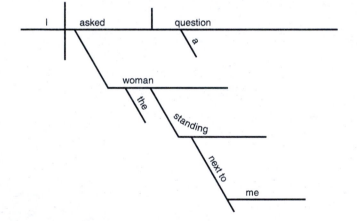

Phrase Exercise #18: Distinguishing Participles and Participial Phrases from Gerunds and Gerund Phrases by the Deletion Test

1. <u>Handing in my exam</u> was the easy part of the test.

   Gerund phrase

   Confirmation: *~~Handing in my exam~~ was the easy part of the test.

2. <u>Keeping an eye on the time</u>, I wrote as fast as I could.

   Participial phrase

   Confirmation: ~~Keeping an eye on the time~~, I wrote as fast as I could.

3. <u>Keeping an eye on the time</u> is a good idea.

   Gerund phrase

   Confirmation: *~~Keeping an eye on the time~~ is a good idea.

4. Thinking about the problem gave me a headache.
       Gerund phrase

   Confirmation: *~~Thinking about the problem~~ gave me a headache.

5. Thinking about the problem, I came up with a possible solution.
       Participial phrase

   Confirmation: ~~Thinking about the problem~~, I came up with a possible solution.

6. Asking the question is not the same as an answer.
       Gerund phrase

   Confirmation: *~~Asking the question~~ is not the same as an answer.

7. Asking the question, he looked around for someone to answer.
       Participial phrase

   Confirmation: ~~Asking the question~~, he looked around for someone to answer.

8. I learned a lot, writing the paper.
       Participial phrase

   Confirmation: I learned a lot, ~~writing the paper~~.

9. I learned about writing the paper.
       Gerund phrase

   Confirmation: *I learned about ~~writing the paper~~.

10. They left the room complaining about the test.
       Participial phrase

    Confirmation: They left the room ~~complaining about the test~~.

Phrase Exercise #19: Identifying Infinitives and Infinitive Phrases Used as Nouns by the It *Test*

1. Their main job is to protect the President.

   Confirmation: Their main job is <u>to protect the President</u>.
                                      it

2. For her to win so easily encouraged the whole team.

   Confirmation: <u>For her to win so easily</u> encouraged the whole team.
                  It

3. We expected to be done by now.

   Confirmation: We expected <u>to be done by now</u>.
                              it

4. The best opportunity was for them to lead hearts.

   Confirmation: The best opportunity was <u>for them to lead hearts</u>.
                                           it

5. To keep on smoking now seemed foolish.

   Confirmation: <u>To keep on smoking now</u> seemed foolish.
                  It

6. He claimed <u>to be a friend of hers</u>.

   Confirmation: He claimed <u>to be a friend of hers</u>.
   it

7. I like <u>to eat French fries with mustard</u>.

   Confirmation: I like <u>to eat French fries with mustard</u>.
   it

8. <u>For us to take such an early flight</u> meant we left before dawn.

   Confirmation: <u>For us to take such an early flight</u> meant we left before dawn.
   It

9. <u>To do the right thing</u> is important.

   Confirmation: <u>To do the right thing</u> is important.
   It

10. <u>To miss an inch</u> is <u>to miss a mile</u>.

    Confirmation: <u>To miss an inch</u> is <u>to miss a mile</u>.
    It   it

Phrase Exercise #20: Identifying Infinitives and Infinitive Phrases Used as Adjectives by the Pronoun Replacement Test

1. The schedule <u>for us to go on field trips</u> is posted on the door.

   Confirmation: <u>The schedule for us to go on field trips</u> is posted on the door.
   It

2. Here is a list of the drugs <u>to avoid during pregnancy</u>.

   Confirmation: Here is a list of <u>the drugs to avoid during pregnancy</u>.
   them

3. I got the books <u>to read for class</u>.

   Confirmation: I got <u>the books to read for class</u>.
   them

4. The plot <u>to overthrow the king</u> was discovered.

   Confirmation: <u>The plot to overthrow the king</u> was discovered.
   It

5. I bought a gift <u>for us to take to the housewarming</u>.

   Confirmation: I bought <u>a gift for us to take to the housewarming</u>.
   it

6. That is the edition <u>to get</u>.

   Confirmation: That is <u>the edition to get</u>.
   it

7. I set a goal <u>for myself to reach</u>.

   Confirmation: I set <u>a goal for myself to reach</u>.
   it

8. They had quite a story <u>to tell us</u>.

   Confirmation: They had <u>quite a story to tell us</u>.
   it

9. We had the good fortune <u>to be in just the right place</u>.

   Confirmation: We had <u>the good fortune to be in just the right place</u>.
   $$\text{it}$$

10. She was the first woman <u>to serve as governor</u>.

    Confirmation: She was <u>the first woman to serve as governor</u>.
    $$\text{it}$$

Phrase Exercise #21: Identifying Infinitives and Infinitive Phrases That Modify Verbs by the Why Test and the Adverb Movement Test

1. He brought up the issue <u>to provoke an argument</u>.

   Why test: Why did he bring up the issue? To provoke an argument.

   Adverb Movement test: To provoke an argument, he brought up the issue.

2. The new drug shrinks the blood vessels <u>to deprive the cancer cells of oxygen</u>.

   Why test: Why does the new drug shrink the blood vessels? To deprive the cancer cells of oxygen.

   Adverb movement test: To deprive the cancer cells of oxygen, the new drug shrinks the blood vessels.

3. There had to be a consensus <u>for them to reach an agreement</u>.

   Why test: Why did there have to be a consensus? For them to reach an agreement.

   Adverb movement test: For them to reach an agreement, there had to be a consensus.

4. We took the kids to the harbor <u>for them to see the sailboats</u>.

   Why test: Why did we take the kids to the harbor? For them to see the sailboats.

   Adverb movement test: For them to see the sailboats, we took the kids to the harbor.

5. I turned off the water <u>to fix a leak in a pipe</u>.

   Why test: Why did I turn off the water? To fix a leak in a pipe.

   Adverb movement test: To fix a leak in a pipe, I turned off the water.

6. We added some extra time <u>for them to comply with the new regulations</u>.

   Why test: Why did we add some extra time? For them to comply with the new regulations.

   Adverb movement test: For them to comply with the new regulations, we added some extra time.

7. Congress raised salaries in the military <u>to help retain more officers</u>.

   Why test: Why did Congress raise salaries in the military? To help retain more officers.

   Adverb movement test: To help retain more officers, Congress raised salaries in the military.

8. She is staying off her foot <u>to give it a chance to heal</u>.

   Why test: Why is she staying off her foot? To give it a chance to heal.

   Adverb movement test: To give it a chance to heal, she is staying off her foot.

9. We got a video camera <u>for them to see what they were doing</u>.

   Why test: Why did we get a video camera? For them to see what they were doing.

   Adverb movement test: For them to see what they were doing, we got a video camera.

10. The judge delayed the trial <u>for the defendant to get a new lawyer</u>.

    Why test: Why did the judge delay the trial? For the defendant to get a new lawyer.

    Adverb movement test: For the defendant to get a new lawyer, the judge delayed the trial.

Phrase Exercise #22: Identifying Infinitives and Infinitive Phrases That Modify Verbs by the In Order Test

1. France fought England <u>to protect her colonies in America</u>.

   Confirmation: France fought England in order <u>to protect her colonies in America</u>.

2. We sprayed the fruit trees <u>to prevent rust and scale</u>.

   Confirmation: We sprayed the fruit trees in order <u>to prevent rust and scale</u>.

3. The committee called a recess <u>for the negotiators to consult with their embassies</u>.

   Confirmation: The committee called a recess in order <u>for the negotiators to consult with their embassies</u>.

4. Senator Fogg attacked his opponent <u>to cloud the issues</u>.

   Confirmation: Senator Fogg attacked his opponent in order <u>to cloud the issues</u>.

5. They needed a pump <u>for them to drain the pool</u>.

   Confirmation: They needed a pump in order <u>for them to drain the pool</u>.

6. We closed the blinds <u>for the children to fall asleep</u>.

   Confirmation: We closed the blinds in order <u>for the children to fall asleep</u>.

7. Wash them in cool water <u>to prevent them from shrinking</u>.

   Confirmation: Wash them in cool water in order <u>to prevent them from shrinking</u>.

8. There was a fee <u>for us to enroll in the program</u>.

   Confirmation: There was a fee in order <u>for us to enroll in the program</u>.

9. The plans were revised <u>to make more space in the living room</u>.

   Confirmation: The plans were revised in order <u>to make more space in the living room</u>.

10. I sold the bonds <u>to invest in a new mutual fund</u>.

Confirmation: I sold the bonds in order <u>to invest in a new mutual fund</u>.

Phrase Exercise #23: Identifying Infinitives and Infinitive Phrases Used as Adverbs

1. They are ready <u>for us to leave</u>.
               Pred Adj

Adverb movement test: *For us to leave, they are ready.

In order test: *They are ready in order for us to leave.

2. They took a trip <u>to use up their frequent flyer miles</u>.
                  Verb

Adverb movement test: To use up their frequent flyer miles, they took a trip.

In order test: They took a trip in order to use up their frequent flyer miles.

3. I was not able <u>to finish my paper on time</u>.
                 Pred Adj

Adverb movement test: *To finish my paper on time, I was not able.

In order test: *I was not able in order to finish my paper on time.

4. The rules were put in place <u>to ensure fair competition</u>.
                     Verb

Adverb movement test: To ensure fair competition, the rules were put into place.

In order test: The rules were put into place in order to ensure fair competition.

5. Nonsense, I am happy <u>to do it</u>.
               Pred Adj

Adverb movement test: *To do it, I am happy.

In order test: *I am happy in order to do it.

6. We need a key <u>to unlock the garage door</u>.
             Verb

Adverb movement test: To unlock the garage door, we need a key.

In order test: We need a key in order to unlock the garage door.

7. It is rude <u>for the hostess to call her guests bad names</u>.
                  Pred Adj

Adverb movement test: *For the hostess to call her guests bad names, it is rude.

In order test: *It is rude in order for the hostess to call her guests bad names.

8. They retired early <u>to take advantage of the buy-out</u>.
                 Verb

Adverb movement test: To take advantage of the buy-out, they retired early.

In order test: They retired early in order to take advantage of the buy-out.

9. I am pleased <u>to make the following announcement</u>.
                        Pred Adj

Adverb movement test: *To make the following announcement, I am pleased.

In order test: *I am pleased in order to make the following announcement.

10. It was nice <u>to see them again</u>.
                    Pred Adj

Adverb movement test: *To see them again, it was nice.

In order test: *It was nice in order to see them again.

Phrase Exercise #24: Identifying Infinitives and Infinitive Phrases

1. The plan is <u>for you to leave your car at the station</u>.
                            Noun

Confirmation: The plan is <u>for you to leave your car at the station</u>.
                                                            it

2. They bought some tape <u>to mail the box</u>.
                            Adv   modifying verb

Confirmation: They bought some tape in order to mail the box.

3. Leon planned <u>for them to have a romantic dinner</u>.
                        Noun

Confirmation: Leon planned <u>for them to have a romantic dinner</u>.
                                                        it

4. Napoleon hung a few generals occasionally <u>to encourage the others</u>.
                                                    Adv   modifying verb

Confirmation: To encourage the others, Napoleon hung a few generals
                occasionally.

5. Aunt Sally is in the mood <u>to play Monopoly</u>.
                                    Adj

Confirmation: Aunt Sally is in <u>the mood to play Monopoly</u>.
                                                    it

6. Toto ran behind the curtain <u>to expose the wizard</u>.
                                    Adv   modifying verb

Confirmation: Toto ran behind the curtain in order to expose the wizard.

7. John was eager <u>to take the test</u>.
                        Adv   modifying predicate adjective *eager*

Confirmation: *To take the test, John was eager.

8. They waited there politely <u>for us to introduce the stranger</u>.
                                    Adv   modifying verb

Confirmation: They waited there politely in order for us to introduce
                the stranger.

(Note that the adverb movement test fails, so one could also argue that the
infinitive phrase modifies the adverb *there*.

Confirmation: *For us to introduce the stranger, they waited there politely.)

9. To admire the book is to admire the author.
   Noun   Noun

 Confirmation: To admire the book is to admire the author.
         It   it

10. We got a new external drive to run the new programs.
                 Adv modifying the verb

 Confirmation: To run the new program we got a new external drive.

11. I got a notice to pay my library fines.
          Adj

 Confirmation: I got a notice to pay my library fines.
              it

12. For me to explain the situation, I will need a pencil and some paper.
         Adv modifying the verb

 Confirmation: (Already moved to first position.)

13. We tried to correct Leon's weak backhand.
          Noun

 Confirmation: We tried to correct Leon's weak backhand.
             it

14. The effect of the ruling is to increase property taxes.
            Noun

 Confirmation: The effect of the ruling is to increase property taxes.
               it

15. Check the label to find the directions.
         Adv modifying the verb

 Confirmation: Check the label in order to find the directions.

16. We received the approval to start our project on Monday.
            Adj

 Confirmation: We received the approval to start our project on Monday.
            it

 (Note: The phrase *on Monday* is ambiguous; it could also be part of the infinitive phrase.)

17. It was very upsetting to be so late.
         Adv modifying the predicate adjective *upsetting*

 Confirmation: *To be so late, it was very upsetting.

18. I took piano lessons to please my mother.
         Adv modifying the verb

 Confirmation: I took piano lessons in order to please my mother.

19. To forgive is divine.
  Noun

 Confirmation: To forgive is divine.
      It

20. For them to refuse the offer was a big mistake.
  Noun

 Confirmation: For them to refuse the offer was a big mistake.
      It

Phrase Exercise #25: Diagramming Infinitives and Infinitive Phrases Used as Nouns

1. I needed to update my calendar.

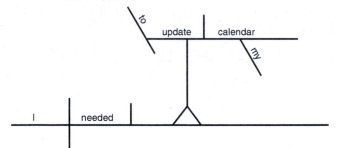

2. To start over was my last choice.

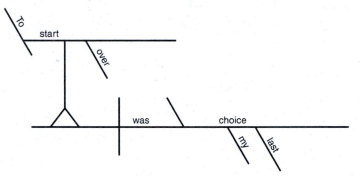

3. For them to make a fuss about it seemed unfair.

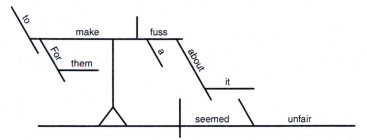

4. I like to swim.

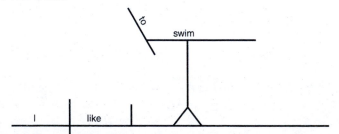

5. The answer to our problem was to be very creative.

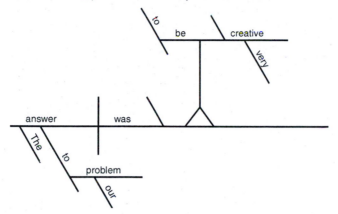

6. I hated to yell at them.

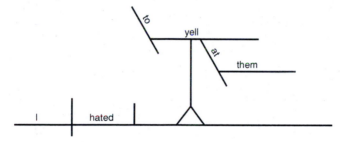

7. Their mission was to boldly explore space.

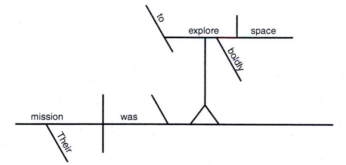

8. For me to finish on time was a real stretch.

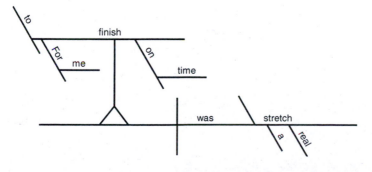

9. We need to increase our sales.

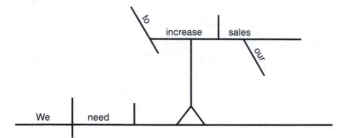

10. To stay still was difficult.

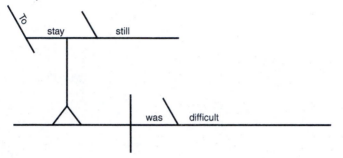

Phrase Exercise #26: Diagramming Infinitives and Infinitive Phrases Used as Modifiers

1. It was crazy to even try it.

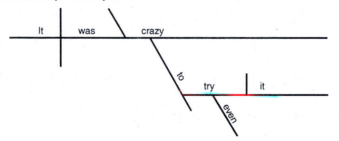

2. I went to the airport to meet a friend.

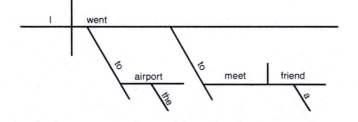

3. Congress passes a lot of bad bills in the rush to adjourn.

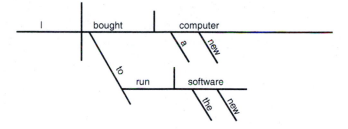

4. I bought a new computer to run the new software.

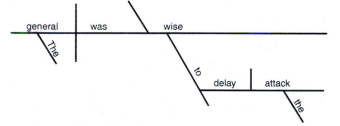

5. The general was wise to delay the attack.

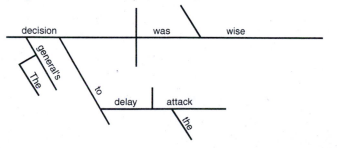

6. The general's decision to delay the attack was wise.

7. The general moved slowly to delay the attack.

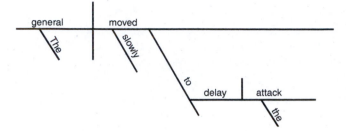

8. The desire to modernize seems irreversible.

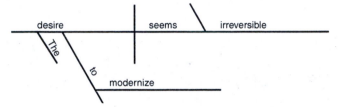

9. The country modernized to create more jobs.

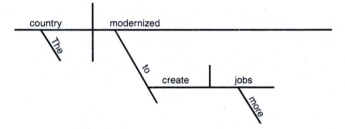

10. It is usually desirable to modernize.

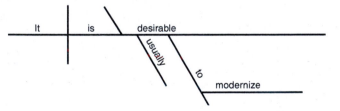

Phrase Exercise #27: Review of Verbals

1. <u>To further delay our plans</u> would be a big mistake.

> Infinitive phrase—noun playing role of subject

2. The farmers burned all the trees <u>infected by the insects</u>.

> Participial phrase—adjective modifying *trees*

3. A man <u>fingering his sword</u> welcomed them aboard.

> Participial phrase—adjective modifying *man*

4. <u>Organizing his work</u> is never easy.
> Gerund phrase—noun playing role of subject

5. It is very difficult <u>for me to do that</u>.
> Infinitive phrase—adverb modifying predicate adjective *difficult*

6. I began <u>to warm up</u>, <u>humming under my breath</u>.

Infinitive phrase	Participial phrase
noun playing role	adjective modifying *I*
of object of verb	

7. We bought an insecticide <u>intended for commercial use</u>.
> Participial phrase—adjective modifying *insecticide*

8. She came early <u>to finish her project</u>.
> Infinitive phrase—adverb modifying verb or adverb *early*

9. <u>Salting your food excessively</u> can be unhealthy.
> Gerund phrase—noun playing role of subject

10. The official abruptly terminated the conference, <u>ignoring the reporters' question</u>.
> Participial phrase
> adjective modifying *official*

11. He was the first person <u>to eat raw snails</u>.
> Infinitive phrase—adjective modifying *person*

12. <u>Shaking his burned fingers</u>, Rollo dropped the hot pan.
> Participial phrase—adjective modifying *Rollo*

13. It is a little late <u>to worry about that</u>.
> Infinitive phrase—adverb modifying the predicate adjective *late*

14. <u>For you to take the blame</u> was very honorable.
> Infinitive phrase—noun playing the role of subject

15. The building was ready <u>to be occupied</u>.
> Infinitive phrase—adverb modifying predicate adjective *ready*

Phrase Exercise #28: Review of Verbals

1. <u>Selecting his club carefully</u>, the golfer approached the tee.
> Participial phrase—adjective modifying golfer

2. Mr. Wilson gave a lecture about <u>investing in international bonds</u>.
> Gerund phrase
> noun used as object of preposition *about*

3. We bought a new computer <u>for Hugh to use</u>.
> Infinitive phrase—adjective modifying *computer*

4. She is certain <u>to take the job offer</u>.
> Infinitive phrase—adverb modifying predicate adjective *certain*

5. It began <u>raining heavily</u>.
> Gerund phrase—noun used as object of verb

6. We got some pizza <u>to take to the party</u>.
> Infinitive phrase—adjective modifying *pizza*

7. They heard a car <u>leaving the garage</u>.

   Participial phrase—adjective modifying car

8. <u>Touched by their plight</u>, Scrooge gave them some good advice.

   Participial phrase—adjective modifying Scrooge

9. The movie <u>playing at the local theater</u> was a real hit.

   Participial phrase—adjective modifying movie

10. I welcomed their ideas about <u>solving the problem</u>.

    Gerund phrase
noun used as object of preposition about

11. It was the first restaurant <u>to receive three stars</u>.

    Infinitive phrase—adjective modifying restaurant

12. It seemed petty <u>to raise the issue</u>.

    Infinitive phrase—adverb modifying predicate adjective petty

13. I regret <u>bringing you some bad news</u>.

    Gerund phrase—noun used as object of verb

14. <u>Avoiding every possible issue</u>, Senator Fogg concluded his lengthy talk.

    Participial phrase—adjective modifying Senator Fogg

15. <u>Taking a shortcut</u> can be very dangerous.

    Gerund phrase—noun used as subject

Chapter Six

Clause Exercise #1: Using the Pronoun Replacement Test to Identify Adjective Clauses

1. The scientists discussed the <u>issues that the conference had raised</u>.
   Confirmation: The scientists discussed <u>the issues that the conference had raised</u>.
   them

2. <u>Senator Fogg, who was up for re-election</u>, was for the bill.
   Confirmation: <u>Senator Fogg, who was up for re-election</u>, was for the bill.
   He

3. The company rejected the <u>parts whose design was defective</u>.
   Confirmation: The company rejected <u>the parts whose design was defective</u>.
   them

4. I rented a <u>movie that we had already seen</u>.
   Confirmation: I rented <u>a movie that we had already seen</u>.
   it

5. We found the <u>bird whose wing had been damaged</u>.
   Confirmation: We found <u>the bird whose wing had been damaged</u>.
   it

6. It was in an old <u>trunk that had belonged to my parents</u>.
   Confirmation: It was in <u>an old trunk that had belonged to my parents</u>.
   it

7. The <u>children whom you asked about</u> live next door.
   Confirmation: <u>The children whom you asked about</u> live next door.
   They

8. The <u>desserts that they serve</u> are really good.
   Confirmation: <u>The desserts that they serve</u> are really good.
   They

9. He passed the <u>exam that he was studying for</u>.
   Confirmation: He passed <u>the exam that he was studying for</u>.
   it

10. The <u>neighborhood where I live</u> is changing a lot.
    Confirmation: <u>The neighborhood where I live</u> is changing a lot.
    It

Clause Exercise #2: Identifying Adjective Clauses with Deleted Relative Pronouns

1. The doctor is treating the pain <u>I get in my knees</u>.
   Confirmation: The doctor is treating the pain <u>that I get in my knees</u>.

2. We put the pictures <u>the children draw</u> on the bulletin board.
   Confirmation: We put the pictures <u>that the children draw</u> on the bulletin board.

3. It is not the city <u>I used to know</u>.
   Confirmation: It is not the city <u>that I used to know</u>.

4. The students <u>he selected</u> did very well.
   Confirmation: The students <u>whom he selected</u> did very well.

5. They all appreciated the dinner <u>we served them</u>.
   Confirmation: They all appreciated the dinner <u>that we served them</u>.

6. The books <u>I put on reserve</u> have all been checked out.
   Confirmation: The books <u>that I put on reserve</u> have all been checked out.

7. We saw the movie <u>you told us about</u>.
   Confirmation: We saw the movie <u>that you told us about</u>.

8. We got the response <u>we expected</u>.
   Confirmation: We got the response <u>that we expected</u>.

9. It is a name <u>you can count on</u>.
   Confirmation: It is a name <u>that you can count on</u>.

10. The teacher <u>I had in the 6th grade</u> married my uncle.
    Confirmation: The teacher <u>whom I had in the 6th grade</u> married my uncle.

Clause Exercise #3: Using the Deletion Test to Distinguish Restrictive and Nonrestrictive Clauses

1. Napoleon, <u>who was actually from Corsica</u>, became a French patriot.
   Confirmation: Napoleon became a French patriot.
   Nonrestrictive (commas) because Napoleon is a proper noun.

2. They identified the person <u>who won the lottery</u>.

    Confirmation: They identified the person.
    Restrictive (no commas) because we do not know which person the sentence is about.

3. The first Sherlock Holmes story, <u>which was set in America</u>, made the author famous.

    Confirmation: The first Sherlock Holmes story made the author famous.
    Nonrestrictive (commas) because there is only one first story.

4. People <u>who live in glass houses</u> shouldn't throw stones.

    Confirmation: People shouldn't throw stones.
    Restrictive (no commas) because we do not know which people shouldn't throw stones.

5. The first question, <u>which was a math problem</u>, was the hardest.

    Confirmation: The first question was the hardest.
    Nonrestrictive (commas) because there is only one first question.

6. Anybody <u>who likes jazz</u> will love this CD.

    Confirmation: Anybody will love this CD.
    Restrictive (no commas) because modifier defines who the *anybody* is—just those who like jazz.

7. I found a place <u>where we could talk quietly</u>.

    Confirmation: I found a place.
    Restrictive (no comma) because modifier defines where the place is.

8. The milk <u>that is in the refrigerator</u> is getting too old.

    Confirmation: The milk is getting too old.
    Restrictive (no commas) because sentence implies that there is some milk that is not in the refrigerator.

9. My new computer, <u>which I bought through the university</u>, is a Mac.

    Confirmation: My new computer is a Mac.
    Nonrestrictive (commas) because there is only one new computer.

10. The woman <u>who sat in front of me</u> forgot her umbrella.

    Confirmation: The woman forgot her umbrella.
    Restrictive (no commas) because we don't know which woman the sentence is about.

Clause Exercise #4: Diagramming Adjective Clauses

1. The person who entered the tomb would die.

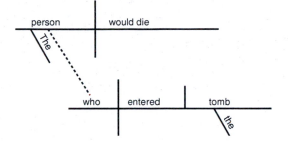

2. The cat that we found in the woods had kittens yesterday.

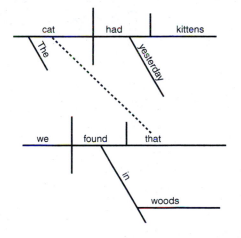

3. I like restaurants where the service is not rushed.

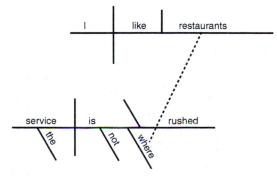

4. Adrian, whose parents were from Milan, speaks Italian.

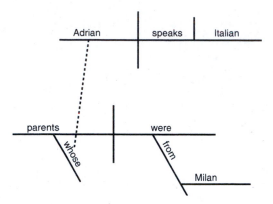

5. An article we featured in our last issue has won an award.

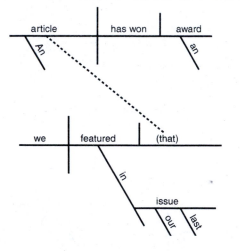

6. Watson found the revolver that Holmes had been looking for.

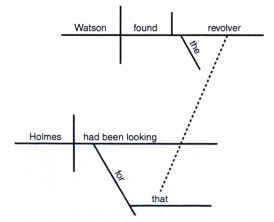

7. The barges that we had discussed earlier are now available.

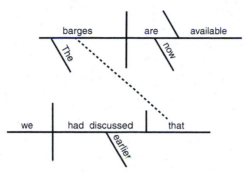

8. They rejected the suggestions we had offered.

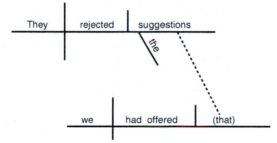

9. The union whose offer we accepted contacted their members.

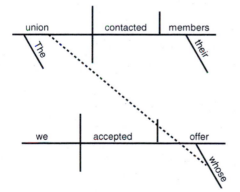

10. I finally found a doctor I like.

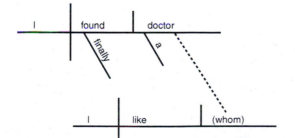

11. My parents thanked the students whose rooms they had used.

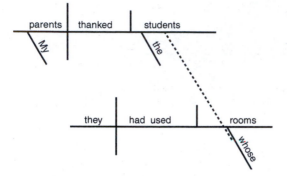

12. We really missed the things we had left behind.

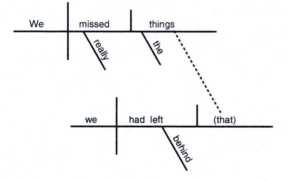

13. The Council, which meets on Tuesdays, will review your request.

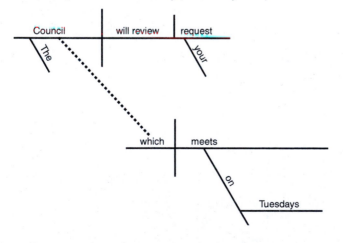

14. The campers checked the supplies that they had ordered.

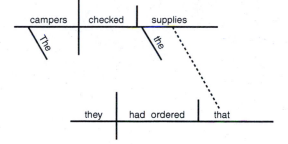

15. The coach took the names of the players who had missed practice.

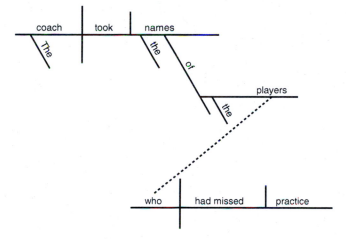

16. Everyone whose paper is finished may leave now.

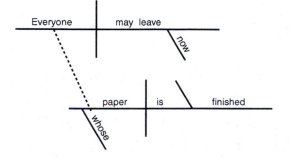

17. They listed the topics about which we might write.

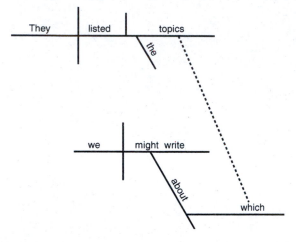

18. The employers we approached liked our ideas.

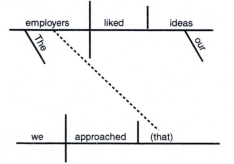

19. That was the place where we had planned to meet.

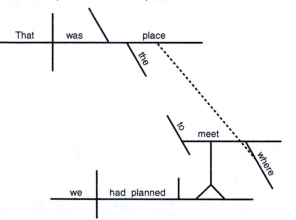

20. Give the man I told you about the package.

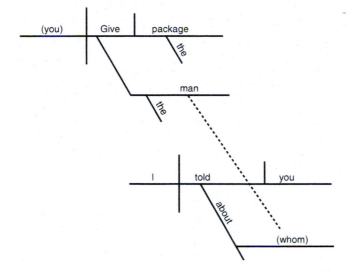

Clause Exercise #5: Identifying Adverb Clauses That Modify Verbs by the Adverb Clause Question Test

1. We completed the test <u>after we had lunch</u>.
   Confirmation: When did we complete the test? After we had lunch.

2. The bank will finance the development <u>after they approve the site</u>.
   Confirmation: When will the bank finance the development? After they approve the site.

3. We lost the game <u>because our quarterback got injured</u>.
   Confirmation: Why did we lose the game? Because our quarterback got injured.

4. He described the book <u>as though he had written it</u>.
   Confirmation: How did he describe the book? As though he had written it.

5. They complained <u>just because we got a little lost</u>.
   Confirmation: Why did they complain? Just because we got a little lost.

6. I'll get the paper <u>before you start breakfast</u>.
   Confirmation: When will I get the paper? Before you start breakfast.

7. The restaurant held the reservation <u>since they weren't very busy</u>.
   Confirmation: Why did the restaurant hold the reservation? Since they weren't very busy.

8. The roof leaks <u>every time it rains</u>.
   Confirmation: How often does the roof leak? Every time it rains.

9. They dropped the issue <u>as if it had been a hot potato</u>.
   Confirmation: How did they drop the issue? As if it had been a hot potato.

10. I'll tell you <u>since you asked</u>.
    Confirmation: Why will I tell you? Since you asked.

Clause Exercise #6: Identifying Adverb Clauses That Modify Verbs by the Adverb Clause Movement Test

1. We will cut off your phone <u>unless you pay your bill</u>.
   Confirmation: <u>Unless you pay your bill</u>, we will cut off your phone.

2. I am still gaining weight, <u>although I eat only carrot sticks</u>.
   Confirmation: <u>Although I eat only carrot sticks</u>, I am still gaining weight.

3. I bought my roommate a new ribbon <u>because I use her printer</u>.
   Confirmation: <u>Because I use her printer</u>, I bought my roommate a new ribbon.

4. I couldn't finish my paper <u>until I got all the references</u>.
   Confirmation: <u>Until I got all the references</u>, I couldn't finish my paper.

5. His dog followed him <u>wherever he went</u>.
   Confirmation: <u>Wherever he went</u>, his dog followed him.

6. I looked at the menu <u>before you came</u>.
   Confirmation: <u>Before you came</u>, I looked at the menu.

7. She liked the movie after all, <u>though she won't admit it</u>.
   Confirmation: <u>Though she won't admit it</u>, she liked the movie after all.

8. Fill these orders <u>as they come in</u>.
   Confirmation: <u>As they come in</u>, fill these orders.

9. I have spent a lot of time on the net <u>since I got my new computer</u>.
   Confirmation: <u>Since I got my new computer</u>, I have spent a lot of time on the net.

10. Watson tried to act normally, <u>although he was wearing a wig</u>.
    Confirmation: <u>Although he was wearing a wig</u>, Watson tried to act normally.

Clause Exercise #7: Identifying Adverb Clauses That Modify Adjectives and Adverbs

1. Aluminum bats can hit a ball <u>farther</u> <u>than wood bats can</u>.
   Adv

2. Airplane accidents are <u>rarer</u> <u>than the public believes</u>.
   Adj

3. The coach was <u>surprised</u> <u>(that) the goal counted</u>.
   Adj

4. The machine scans much more <u>accurately</u> <u>than the old one did</u>.
   Adj

5. Yellow objects are more <u>visible</u> <u>than red objects are</u>.
   Adj

6. My dog is <u>bigger</u> <u>than your dog is</u>.
   Adj

7. Buses during the day are more <u>frequent</u> <u>than buses are at night</u>.
    Adj

8. We are <u>confident</u> <u>you can do it</u>.
    Adj

9. Twins often talk <u>sooner</u> <u>than single children do</u>.
    Adv

10. The first dress was more <u>attractive</u> <u>than the second one was</u>.
    Adj

Clause Exercise #8: Distinguishing Subordinating Conjunctions from Conjunctive Adverbs

1. I was upset; <u>however</u>, there was nothing I could do about it.
    Conj Adv
    Confirmation: I was upset; there was nothing I could do about it, however.

2. I was upset <u>because</u> I had damaged the VCR.
    Sub Conj
    Confirmation: Because I had damaged the VCR, I was upset.

3. We are ready to leave <u>unless</u> there is anything else to do.
    Sub Conj
    Confirmation: Unless there is anything else to do, we are ready to leave.

4. We are ready to leave; <u>otherwise</u>, we will miss the bus.
    Conj Adv
    Confirmation: We are ready to leave; we will miss the bus, otherwise.

5. Aunt Sally has been depressed <u>because</u> she lost at Monopoly.
    Sub Conj
    Confirmation: Because she lost at Monopoly, Aunt Sally has been depressed.

6. Aunt Sally has been depressed; <u>moreover</u>, she lost at Monopoly.
    Conj Adv
    Confirmation: Aunt Sally has been depressed; she lost, moreover, at Monopoly.

7. The accident ruined the experiment; <u>thus</u>, we had to start all over.
    Conj adv
    Confirmation: The accident ruined the experiment; we had, thus, to start all over.

8. The accident ruined the experiment <u>while</u> it was still in process.
    Sub Conj
    Confirmation: While it was still in process, the accident ruined the experiment.

9. The doctor testified <u>inasmuch as</u> she had taken the X-rays.
    Sub Conj
    Confirmation: Inasmuch as she had taken the X-rays, the doctor testified.

10. The doctor testified <u>after</u> she had taken the X-rays.
    Sub Conj
    Confirmation: After she had taken the X-rays, the doctor testified.

Clause Exercise #9: Identifying Adverb Clauses

1. I <u>returned</u> the book <u>as soon as I was done with it</u>.
   Verb

2. The movie lasted much <u>longer</u> <u>than we had expected</u>.
   Adverb

3. I <u>get</u> a headache <u>whenever I am under a lot of stress</u>.
   Verb

4. I am <u>afraid</u> <u>that we must leave now</u>.
   Adjective

5. <u>Since we would be late</u>, we <u>called</u> them.
   Verb

6. The kids <u>began</u> to party <u>after their parents left for the weekend</u>.
   Verb

   (Note: The adverb clause could also modify the verb *party*.)

7. We finished <u>poorer</u> <u>than we had started</u>.
   Adjective

8. John <u>took</u> a taxi to the airport <u>so he wouldn't miss his flight</u>.
   Verb

9. <u>After the party was over</u>, we <u>began</u> cleaning the apartment.
   Verb

10. The movie was <u>funnier</u> <u>than the book was</u>.
    Adjective

11. <u>If you had led spades</u>, we <u>could have set</u> them.
    Verb

12. I <u>want</u> to finish my paper <u>before it is due</u>.
    Verb

    (Note: The adverb clause could also modify *finish*.)

13. We were <u>afraid</u> <u>that we would stick in the wet snow</u>.
    Adjective

14. I have <u>learned</u> a lot <u>since I began going to classes regularly</u>.
    Verb

15. <u>Although they won the battle</u>, they <u>have</u> not <u>won</u> the war.
    Verb

16. I answered more <u>calmly</u> <u>than I thought I could</u>.
    Adverb

17. The church is much <u>older</u> <u>than it appears on the outside</u>.
    Adjective

18. <u>If you look to your right</u>, you <u>will see</u> the river.
    Verb

19. Aunt Sally was <u>glad</u> <u>that you wanted to play Monopoly with her</u>.

Adjective

20. The test was hard; however, I had reviewed all the material.

(Trick question. There is no adverb clause in the sentence.)

Clause Exercise #10: Diagramming Adverb Clauses

1. I am sorry that we must leave now.

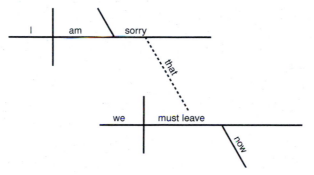

2. Since we would be late, we called them.

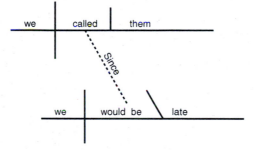

3. When their parents left, the kids ordered pizza.

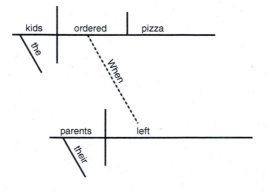

4. We finished worse than we had started.

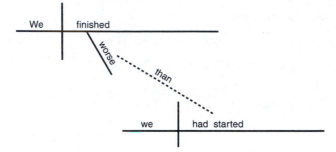

5. So that he would not miss his flight, John took a taxi to the airport.

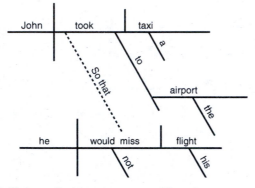

6. We began the job as soon as we got the order.

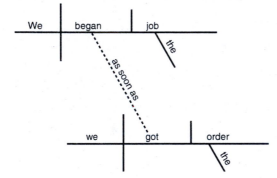

7. The movie was funnier than we had expected.

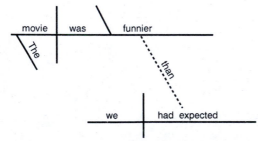

8. If you had led spades, we could have set them.

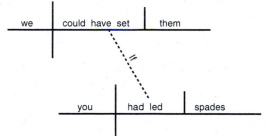

9. Since the undercoat was not dry, the finish was always sticky.

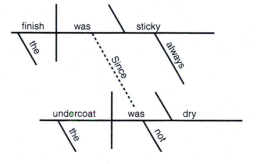

10. I finished my paper before it was due.

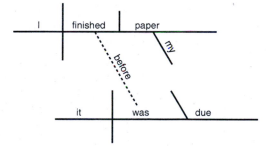

11. I was glad that it was finished.

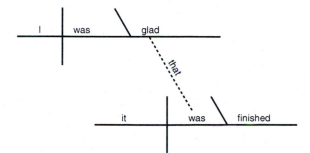

(Note: *was finished* can also be a passive.)

12. He was more upset than he should have been.

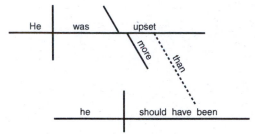

13. Although we won the battle, we have not won the war.

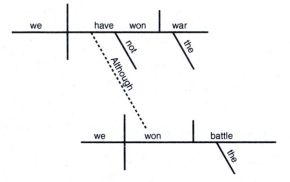

14. He is very snide whenever he discusses other people's work.

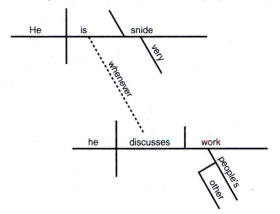

15. The church is older than it looks.

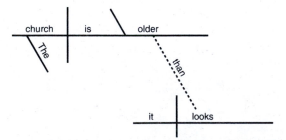

Clause Exercise #11: Identifying **that**-type Noun Clauses by the **it** Test

1. I don't think <u>that they believe you</u>.

                           it

2. <u>That the plan was already approved</u> squelched the opposition.

              it

3. The idea was <u>that we would get up early</u>.

                    it

4. They argued about <u>whether Dorothy should take her slippers</u>.

                            it

5. <u>That he was no friend of mine</u> was apparent to everyone.

             It

6. They should tell us <u>if they are coming</u>.

                    it

7. The question is <u>whether or not they can be trusted</u>.

                      it

8. <u>That he could diagram those sentences</u> strained credulity.

             It

9. I don't know <u>whether I can go</u>.

                  it

10. <u>That you are here</u> shows <u>that you are interested</u>.

          It

Clause Exercise #12: Distinguishing Adjective and Noun Clauses by the **Which** Test

1. I bet <u>that you can't diagram this sentence</u>.

                       Noun clause

Confirmation: *I bet <u>which</u> you can't diagram this sentence.

2. Did you fill out the questionnaire <u>that I gave you</u>?

                                    Adjective clause

Confirmation: Did you fill out the questionnaire <u>which </u>I gave you?

3. Bugsy denied <u>that he had fired the fatal shot</u>.

                       Noun clause

Confirmation: *Bugsy denied <u>which</u> he had fired the fatal shot.

4. I will personally guarantee <u>that there will be no problem</u>.

                                  Noun clause

Confirmation: *I will personally guarantee <u>which</u> there will be no problem.

5. Bugsy made him an offer <u>that he couldn't refuse</u>.

                            Adjective clause

Confirmation: Bugsy made him an offer <u>which</u> he couldn't refuse.

6. I hated <u>that I had become addicted to tic-tac-toe</u>.

                    Noun clause

Confirmation: *I hated <u>which</u> I had become addicted to tic-tac-toe.

7. I understood the hatred <u>that they felt</u>.
          Adjective clause
   Confirmation: I understood the hatred <u>which</u> they felt.

8. Romeo murmured <u>that he hated to leave</u>.
          Noun clause
   Confirmation: *Romeo murmured <u>which</u> he hated to leave.

9. I regret <u>that I have only one life to give to my country</u>.
          Noun clause
   Confirmation: *I regret <u>which</u> I have only one life to give to my country.

10. The regret <u>that I feel</u> can only be imagined.
          Adjective clause
    Confirmation: The regret <u>which</u> I feel can only be imagined.

Clause Exercise #13: Diagramming that-*Type Noun Clauses*

1. Whether we would succeed was a big question.

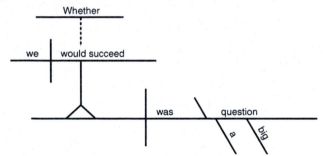

2. I believed that I was ready.

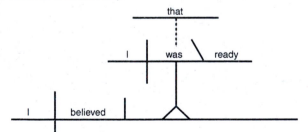

3. We didn't know if it would rain.

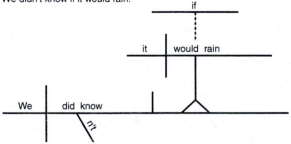

4. That the new program worked better was not a surprise.

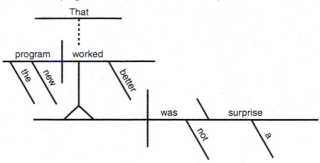

5. I knew we were in big trouble.

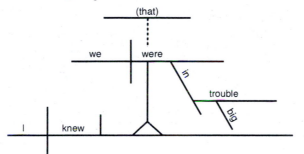

6. Whether or not you fail is your decision.

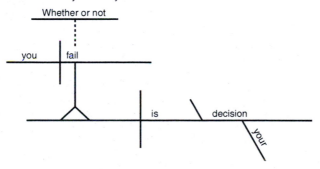

7. That the sun shines every day is true.

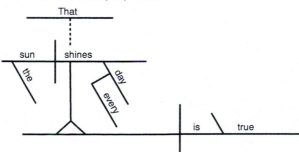

8. I couldn't decide if I should go.

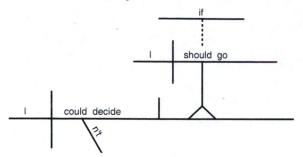

9. I wish we could quit now.

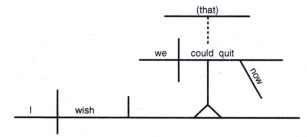

10. We thought it was time to quit.

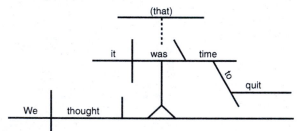

Clause Exercise #14: Identifying the Role of Noun Clauses and the Role of wh- Words Inside the Noun Clause

1. <u>What we did wrong</u> is obvious to us now.
   Subj
   What is object of verb

2. I know <u>why we should floss our teeth</u>.
   Verb Obj
   Why is an adverb of reason

3. I was worried about <u>which computer would be best</u>.
   Prep Obj
   which is an adjective

4. The problem was <u>what we should wear</u>.
   Pred Nom
   what is object of verb

5. I was surprised at <u>how they had behaved</u>.
Prep Obj
how is adverb of manner

6. <u>What they talked about</u> was a big secret.
Subj
what is object of preposition

7. Everyone asked <u>where you were</u>.
Verb Obj
where is adverb of place

8. He would not tell me <u>who he was</u>.
Verb Obj
who is predicate nominative

9. I asked <u>why the lights were left on</u>.
Verb Obj
why is adverb of reason

10. <u>What you see</u> is <u>what you get</u>.
Subj   Pred Nom
what is object of verb in both clauses

Clause Exercise #15: Identifying wh-*Type Noun Clauses by the* It *Substitution Test*

1. We did <u>what was necessary</u>.
it
what is the subject

2. <u>What Bugsy said</u> aroused the police's suspicion.
It
what is the object of the verb *said*

3. They relied on <u>what they had been told</u>.
it
what is the object of the verb *told*

4. <u>What they were serving for lunch</u> was fine with us.
It
what is the object of the verb *serving*

5. <u>Which shoes you take</u> matters a lot on a long hike.
It
which is an adjective modifying *shoes*

6. Our limited time restricted <u>where we could go for lunch</u>.
it
where is an adverb of place

7. <u>What you say</u> may be used in evidence against you.
It
what is the object of the verb *say*

8. We were surprised at <u>how Margie reacted to the news</u>.
it
how is an adverb of manner

9. I understood <u>why they felt that way</u>.

it

why is an adverb of reason

10. <u>Where Fred took his date</u> made a lasting impression.

It

where is an adverb of place

Clause Exercise #16: Diagramming **wh-***Type Noun Clauses*

1. They depend on what you give them.

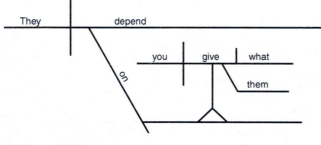

2. I know where you are.

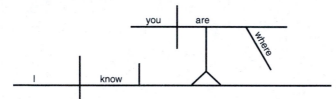

3. What they said really surprised us.

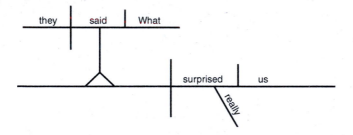

4. I'll have whatever you are having.

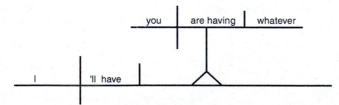

5. What they did is none of your business.

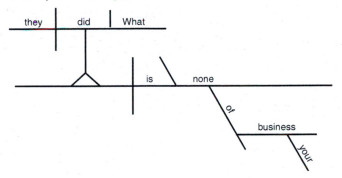

6. I sympathize with what they were feeling.

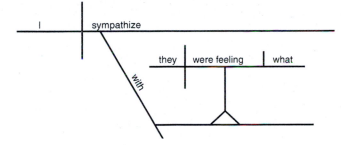

7. I gave them whatever they wanted.

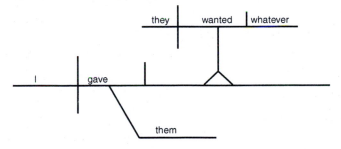

8. They had answers for whatever questions we asked.

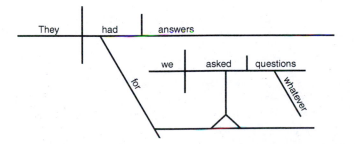

9. What you say may be used against you.

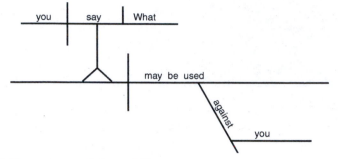

10. The answer was what you said it was.

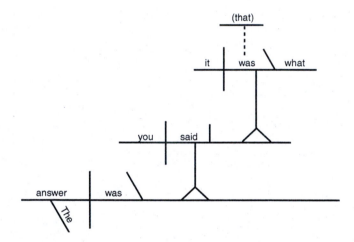

Clause Exercise #17: Changing **wh-**Type Noun Clauses Into **wh-** Infinitives

    1. I was concerned about <u>what I should tell Sally</u>.
                             what to tell Sally
    2. They told us <u>where we should park our cars</u>.
                        where to park our cars
    3. I figured out <u>how I could solve the problem</u>.
                     how to solve the problem
    4. <u>What we should do about the accident</u> was a major concern.
               What to do about the accident
    5. The staff talked about <u>whom we should hire</u>.
                   who(m) to hire
    6. We were confused about <u>when we should leave</u>.
                   when to leave
    7. They showed us <u>how we should use chopsticks</u>.
                how to use chopsticks
    8. <u>What we should say in this situation</u> is always a problem.
            What to say in this situation
    9. I don't understand <u>what I should do</u>.
                what to do

10. Our training taught us <u>how we should react to a crisis</u>.
    how to react to a crisis

Clause Exercise #18: Identifying Noun Clauses and wh- Infinitives

1. I know <u>who you are</u>.
   Object of verb

2. Aunt Sally has decided <u>that we should play Scrabble</u>.
   Object of verb

3. <u>Whomever you elect</u> will have a hard time.
   Subject

4. We learn <u>how to behave</u>.
   Object of verb

5. You will know <u>if you have a problem</u>.
   Object of verb

6. We argued about <u>whether we should get travelers' checks</u>.
   Object of preposition *about*

7. Their position was <u>that they would accept any valid offer</u>.
   Predicate nominative

8. <u>How she manages to stay thin</u> is a miracle.
   Subject

9. They took advantage of <u>whatever opportunity they found</u>.
   Object of preposition *of*

10. The slowest line is <u>whichever one I pick</u>.
    Predicate nominative

11. We hear <u>what we want to hear</u>.
    Object of verb

12. <u>What they said</u> seemed pretty unbelievable.
    Subject

13. I do not know <u>if I can get ready by then</u>.
    Object of verb

14. Nobody told me <u>where I should go</u>.
    Direct object

15. They were angry about <u>how the clerk had treated them</u>.
    Object of preposition *about*

16. <u>Whoever finishes the coffee</u> must make the next pot.
    Subject

17. Do you understand <u>how to do it</u>?
    Object of verb

18. <u>Whether or not he is right</u> is quite debatable.
    Subject

19. I heard <u>what you said about where the test was</u>.
    Object of verb
    I heard what you said about <u>where the test was</u>.
    Object of preposition *about*

20. I believe <u>that what you said is correct</u>.
Object of verb *believe*

I believe that <u>what you said</u> is correct.
Subject of noun clause

Clause Exercise #19: Identifying Dependent Clauses

1. I didn't like the program <u>that we were watching</u>.
Adj

2. <u>When I was your age</u>, I had never been outside River City.
Adv

3. Scratch it <u>where it itches</u>.
Adv

4. <u>If you think that you can do that</u>, you are mistaken.
Adv

If you think <u>that you can do that</u>, you are mistaken.
Noun

5. He was bitter <u>that Senator Fogg had defeated him</u>.
Adv (modifies *bitter*)

6. The kingdom became richer <u>than it ever had before</u>.
Adv (modifies *richer*)

7. <u>Since you asked about what I know</u>, I will tell you.
Adv

Since you asked about <u>what I know</u>, I will tell you.
Noun (object of *about*)

8. <u>What you said</u> surprised everyone <u>who was there</u>.
Noun   Adj

9. <u>After we ate</u>, I charged <u>what we had spent</u> on my credit card.
Adv   Noun

10. We saw the ad <u>everyone had been talking about</u>.
Adj (with understood *that*)

11. <u>While you were out</u>, Matthew called again.
Adv

12. Tell me <u>when you will be ready to leave</u>.
Noun (direct object)

13. The salesman talked faster <u>than I could follow</u>.
Adv (modifies *faster*)

14. The press viewed the story with suspicion <u>that verged on disbelief</u>.
Adj

15. I wrote about the French <u>who invaded England in 1066</u>.
Adj

16. <u>What we found</u> was hardly worth looking for.
Noun

17. I was a little disappointed considering all the work <u>we had done</u>.

Adj (with understood *that*)

18. We repeated <u>what we had heard over the radio</u>.

Noun

19. I gave a list of <u>what I needed</u>.

Noun (object of preposition *of*)

20. <u>As I was going to St. Ives</u>, I met a man <u>who had seven wives</u>.

Adv   Adj

Chapter Seven

Complement Exercise #1: Using the Passive to Identify Predicate Nominatives

1. <u>Moby Dick</u> was a white <u>whale</u>.

Confirmation: *A white whale was been by Moby Dick.

2. <u>Moby Dick</u> is also the <u>name</u> of a rock group.

Confirmation: *The name of a rock group is been also by Moby Dick.

3. <u>Jason</u> seemed a nice young <u>man</u>.

Confirmation: *A nice young man was seemed by Jason.

4. <u>Humpty Dumpty</u> was a good <u>egg</u>.

Confirmation: *A good egg was been by Humpty Dumpty.

5. <u>Alice</u> remains a close <u>friend</u> of mine.

Confirmation: *A close friend of mine is remained by Alice.

6. <u>Scrooge</u> became a better <u>person</u>.

Confirmation: *A better person was become by Scrooge.

7. The <u>proposal</u> seemed a good <u>idea</u> at the time.

Confirmation: *A good idea at the time was seemed by the proposal.

8. <u>He</u> is such an <u>alarmist</u>.

Confirmation: *Such an alarmist is been by him.

9. <u>I</u> felt a complete <u>fool</u>.

Confirmation: *A complete fool was felt by me.

10. <u>It</u> was the <u>best</u> of times.

Confirmation: *The best of time was been by it.

Complement Exercise #2: Identifying Adverbial of Place Complements

1. The men remained <u>in the dining room</u>.

Confirmation: *In the dining room the men remained.

2. The boat is staying <u>at the dock</u>.

Confirmation: *At the dock the boat is staying.

3. We parked <u>in their driveway</u>.
   Confirmation: *In their driveway we parked.

4. They live <u>next door</u>.
   Confirmation: *Next door they live.

5. The cereal is <u>above the refrigerator</u>.
   Confirmation: *Above the refrigerator the cereal is.

6. I have always lived <u>in Georgia</u>.
   Confirmation: *In Georgia I have always lived.

7. The next delivery is <u>close by</u>.
   Confirmation: *Close by the next delivery is.

8. Ralph stayed <u>behind</u>.
   Confirmation: *Behind Ralph stayed.

9. We all sat <u>on the couch</u>.
   Confirmation: *On the couch we all sat.

10. The suspect last resided <u>in Miami</u>.
    Confirmation: *In Miami the suspect last resided.

Complement Exercise #3: Review of Verbs With No More Than One Complement

1. The earthquake nearly destroyed <u>the building</u>.
   Noun phrase

2. They are <u>very good workers</u>.
   Predicate nominative

3. I have lived <u>here</u> for several years now.
   Adverbial of place

4. The audience laughed loudly.
   No complement

5. We rebuilt <u>the carburetor</u>.
   Noun phrase

6. They are <u>such good friends</u>.
   Predicate nominative

7. Sticks and stones will break <u>my bones</u>.
   Noun phrase

8. They stayed <u>at a motel near the freeway</u>.
   Adverbial of place

9. I am <u>really upset</u>.
   Predicate adjective

10. We discussed <u>the problem</u>.
    Noun phrase

11. The problem seemed <u>insurmountable</u>.
    Predicate adjective

12. The car hung <u>over the guardrail</u>.
    Adverbial of place

13. Several of my teachers have retired recently.
    No complement

14. We postponed <u>any decision</u>.
    Noun phrase

15. They really seem <u>strange</u>.
    Predicate adjective

16. That carburetor is missing again.
    No complement

17. At the time of the crime, Bugsy was <u>on a plane to Vegas</u>.
    Adverbial of place

18. Please begin any time.
    No complement

19. Tarzan became <u>a grammarian</u>.
    Predicate nominative

20. The train left <u>the station</u>.
    Noun phrase

Complement Exercise #4: Identifying NP1 + NP2 Complements

1. Save <u>me</u> <u>some dessert</u>.
   NP1   NP2
   Confirmation: Save some dessert for me.

2. The wizard granted <u>the knight</u> <u>his wish</u>.
             NP1   NP2
   Confirmation: The wizard granted his wish to the knight.

3. Hand <u>me</u> <u>a towel</u>.
     NP1 NP2
   Confirmation: Hand a towel to me.

4. Bugsy made <u>them</u> <u>a non-negotiable offer</u>.
         NP1   NP2
   Confirmation: Bugsy made a non-negotiable offer to them.

5. You can't teach <u>an old dog</u> <u>new tricks</u>.
           NP1   NP2
   Confirmation: You can't teach new tricks to an old dog.

6. Throw <u>the dog</u> <u>a bone</u>.
       NP1   NP2
   Confirmation: Throw a bone to the dog.

7. Don't do <u>me</u> <u>any favors</u>.
       NP1   NP2
   Confirmation: Don't do any favors for me.

8. They sent <u>us</u> <u>a bill</u>.
      NP1 NP2
   Confirmation: They sent a bill to us.

9. Order <u>me</u> <u>a tuna sandwich</u>.
        NP1   NP2

Confirmation: Order a tuna sandwich for me.

10. "Friends, Romans, countrymen, lend <u>me</u> <u>your ears</u>."
                                        NP1   NP2

Confirmation: Friends, Romans, countrymen, lend your ears to me.

Complement Exercise #5: Identifying NP + OC Complements

1. The committee rated <u>her</u> <u>the best applicant</u>.
                        NP   OC
Confirmation: her = the best applicant

2. Holmes proved <u>the butler</u> <u>an imposter</u>.
                    NP   OC
Confirmation: the butler = an imposter

3. The stock market made <u>them</u> <u>millionaires</u>.
                        NP   OC
Confirmation: them = millionaires

4. We elected <u>Marsha</u> <u>class president</u>.
               NP   OC
Confirmation: Marsha = class president

5. The jury believed <u>him</u> <u>the guilty party</u>.
                  NP   OC
Confirmation: him = the guilty party

6. I pronounce <u>you</u> <u>man</u> and <u>wife</u>.
              NP OC   OC
Confirmation: you = man and wife

7. They named <u>their first child</u> <u>Philip</u>.
              NP   OC
Confirmation: their first child = Philip

8. His decision proved <u>him</u> <u>an outstanding general</u>.
                  NP   OC
Confirmation: him = an outstanding general

9. I consider <u>myself</u> <u>a decent person</u>.
           NP   OC
Confirmation: myself = a decent person

10. She thought <u>him</u> <u>an older man</u>.
            NP   OC
Confirmation: him = an older man

Complement Exercise #6: Identifying NP + Pred Adj and NP + ADVplace Complements

1. Jason left <u>the fleece</u> <u>on the boat</u>.
          NP   ADVplace
Confirmation: *On the boat Jason left the fleece.

2. I like <u>my coffee</u> <u>really hot</u>.
            NP   Pred Adj

3. The cold snap turned <u>the leaves</u> <u>red</u>.
                         NP   Pred Adj

4. I put <u>the money</u> <u>in the bank</u>.
          NP   ADVplace
    Confirmation: *In the bank I put the money.

5. Get <u>it</u> <u>ready</u>.
   NP Pred Adj

6. She placed <u>the vase</u> <u>on the mantle</u>.
            NP   ADVplace
    Confirmation: *On the mantle she placed a vase.

7. It really made <u>me</u> <u>angry</u>.
              NP Pred Adj

8. They put <u>me</u> <u>on hold</u>.
        NP ADVplace
    Confirmation: *On hold they put me.

9. The Thermos keeps <u>the milk</u> <u>cold</u>.
                 NP   Pred Adj

10. The bank robbers left <u>the stolen vehicle</u> <u>at the airport</u>.
                      NP   ADVplace
    Confirmation: *At the airport the bank robbers left the stolen vehicle.

Complement Exercise #7: Identifying NP + VPpres Part Complements

1. We left <u>John</u> <u>studying for his test</u>.
        NP   VPpres part
    Confirmation: We left <u>John</u> <u>studying for his test</u>.
                      him

2. The contractor had <u>his crew</u> <u>tearing off the old shingles</u>.
                    NP   VPpres part
    Confirmation: The contractor had <u>his crew</u> <u>tearing off the old shingles</u>.
                              them

3. The coach caught <u>some players</u> <u>reading a book</u>.
                 NP   VPpres part
    Confirmation: The coach caught <u>some players</u> <u>reading a book</u>.
                       them

4. I felt <u>the walls</u> <u>shaking</u>.
          NP   VPpres part
    Confirmation: I felt <u>the walls</u> <u>shaking</u>.
                them

5. We really got <u>them</u> <u>thinking about it</u>.
              NP   VPpres part

6. Snow White overheard <u>the dwarves</u> <u>planning to go on strike</u>.
                        NP   VPpres part
    Confirmation: Snow White overheard <u>the dwarves</u> <u>planning to go on strike</u>.
                          them

7. The kids were watching <u>the kittens</u> <u>chasing each other</u>.
                        NP   VPpres part
   Confirmation: The kids were watching <u>the kittens</u> <u>chasing each other</u>.
                                  them

8. I left <u>the water</u> <u>running</u>.
              NP   VPpres part
   Confirmation: I left <u>the water</u> <u>running</u>.
                      it

9. Did you notice <u>the guy</u> <u>eating at the counter</u>?
                     NP   VPpres part
   Confirmation: Did you notice <u>the guy</u> <u>eating at the counter</u>?
                        him

10. The whole office heard <u>the boss</u> <u>chewing me out</u>.
                       NP   VPpres part
   Confirmation: The whole office heard <u>the boss</u> <u>chewing me out</u>.
                         him/her

Complement Exercise #8: Identifying Noun Phrase + VPinf Complements

1. Darth Vader forced <u>Luke</u> <u>to get a haircut</u>.
      NP   VPinf
   it test: *Darth Vader forced Luke it.
   Adv movement: *To get a haircut, Darth Vader forced Luke.

2. Allow <u>me</u> <u>to introduce a friend</u>.
      NP   VPinf
   it test: *Allow me it. (where *it* does not equal *to introduce a friend*)
   Adv movement: *To introduce a friend, allow me.

3. I found <u>them</u> <u>to be very helpful</u>.
        NP   VPinf
   it test: *I found them it.
   Adv movement: *to be very helpful, I found them.

4. Senator Fogg told <u>the reporters</u> <u>to mind their own business</u>.
                NP   VPinf
   it test: *Senator Fogg told the reporters it.
   Adv movement: *To mind their own business, Senator Fogg told the reporters.

5. Cinderella got <u>the mice</u> <u>to help her</u>.
            NP   VPinf
   it test: *Cinderella got the mice it.
   Adv movement: *To help her, Cinderella got the mice.

6. The password enabled <u>me</u> <u>to run the program</u>.
                  NP   VPinf
   it test: *The password enabled me it.
   Adv movement: *To run the program, the password enabled me.

7. The students wanted <u>their papers</u> <u>to be perfect</u>.
                                  NP   VPinf

   it test: *The students wanted their papers it.
   Adv movement: *To be perfect, the students wanted their papers.

8. The book really helped <u>me</u> <u>to understand the conflict</u>.
                             NP   VPinf

   it test: *The book really helped me it.
   Adv movement: *To understand the conflict, the book really helped me.

9. We encouraged <u>them</u> <u>to start over</u>.
                      NP   VPinf

   it test: *We encouraged them it.
   Adv movement: *To start over, we encouraged them.

10. The IRS requires <u>tax payers</u> <u>to file every year</u>.
                        NP   VPinf

    it test: *The IRS requires tax payers it.
    Adv movement: *To file every year, the IRS requires tax payers.

Complement Exercise #9: Review of Verbs with Multiple Complements

1. The jury found <u>them</u> <u>to be innocent</u>.
                  NP   VPinf

2. I found <u>the kids</u> <u>playing in the back yard</u>.
            NP   VPpres part

3. We found <u>the kittens</u> <u>a good home</u>.
            NP1   NP2

4. She put <u>the umbrella</u> <u>under her seat</u>.
           NP   ADVplace

5. Kit caught <u>William</u> <u>stealing his lines</u>.
            NP   VPpres part

6. We wanted <u>them</u> <u>to be more careful</u>.
           NP   VPinf

7. They sold <u>them</u> <u>their old car</u>.
          NP1   NP2

8. Bugsy placed <u>a gun</u> <u>on the table</u>.
           NP   ADVplace

9. We heard <u>them</u> <u>arriving during the night</u>.
           NP   VPpres part

10. The company named <u>him</u> <u>the new president</u>.
                 NP   OC

11. The company named <u>him</u> <u>to succeed the old president</u>.
                 NP   VPinf

12. I hate <u>John</u> <u>doing that</u>.
          NP VPpres part

13. Events proved <u>me</u> <u>wrong</u>.
                NP   Pred Adj

14. Stan made <u>Ollie</u> <u>the chairman of the board</u>.
            NP   OC

15. Tell <u>me</u> <u>the truth</u>.
     NP1   NP2

16. The Archbishop placed <u>the crown</u> <u>on his head</u>.
                    NP   ADVplace

17. We expected <u>you</u> <u>to do better</u>.
             NP   VPinf

18. The coach thought <u>the team</u> <u>ready</u>.
                NP   Pred Adj

19. I found <u>myself</u> <u>falling asleep in class</u>.
          NP   VPpres part

20. Keep <u>them</u> <u>in their seats</u>.
      NP   ADVplace

Complement Exercise #10: Identifying Adverb Complements

1. Snow White and Prince Charming broke <u>up</u>.
Confirmation: *Up Snow White and Prince Charming broke.

2. They were always butting <u>in</u>.
Confirmation: *In they were always butting.

3. I am going to have to drop <u>out</u>.
Confirmation: *Out I am going to have to drop.

4. Bugsy and his gang got <u>away</u>.
Confirmation: *Away Bugsy and his gang got.

5. Eventually, Snow White and Prince Charming made <u>up</u>.
Confirmation: *Eventually, up Snow White and Prince Charming made.

6. Everybody pitched <u>in</u>.
Confirmation: *In everybody pitched.

7. I really screwed up.
Confirmation: *Up I really screwed.

8. The old plant finally shut down.
Confirmation: *Down the old plant finally shut.

9. We had to start <u>over</u>.
Confirmation: *Over we had to start.

10. The batter struck <u>out</u>.
Confirmation: *Out the batter struck.

Complement Exercise #11: Identifying Adverb + NP Complements by the Phrasal Adverb Movement Test

1. Philip called <u>up</u> <u>his girlfriend</u>.
        Adv NP
   Confirmation: Philip called his girlfriend up.

2. We brought <u>back</u> <u>some pictures of our trip</u>.
           Adv   NP
   Confirmation: We brought some pictures of our trip back.

3. I finally cleaned <u>out</u> <u>the attic</u>.
             Adv NP
   Confirmation: I finally cleaned the attic out.

4. Susan dropped <u>off</u> <u>some of your books</u>.
            Adv   NP
   Confirmation: Susan dropped some of your books off.

5. Stan and Ollie figured <u>out</u> <u>the problem</u>.
                 Adv   NP
   Confirmation: Stan and Ollie figured the problem out.

6. They wandered up the path.
   Up the path is an adverbial prepositional phrase telling where they wandered.

7. The children made <u>up</u> <u>a new game</u>.
              Adv NP
   Confirmation: The children made a new game up.

8. The teacher pointed <u>out</u> <u>their mistake</u>.
               Adv   NP
   Confirmation: The teacher pointed their mistake out.

9. The company <u>laid off</u> <u>the temporary workers</u>.
            Adv   NP
   Confirmation: The company laid the temporary workers off.

10. I sent <u>back</u> <u>the defective part</u>.
        Adv   NP
    Confirmation: I sent the defective part back.

Complement Exercise #12: Identifying Preposition Complements

1. We jumped <u>at</u> <u>the chance</u>.
   Confirmation: *At the chance we jumped.

2. The students wondered <u>about</u> <u>the assignment</u>.
   Confirmation: *About the assignment the students wondered.

3. The whole class participated <u>in</u> <u>the experiment</u>.
   Confirmation: *In the experiment the whole class participated.

4. The drama students posed <u>as</u> <u>their favorite movie stars</u>.
   Confirmation: *As their favorite movie starts the drama students posed.

5. She was searching <u>for</u> exactly the right dress.
   Confirmation: *For exactly the right dress she was searching.

6. The firm specializes <u>in</u> solid-waste disposal.
   Confirmation: *In solid-waste disposal the firm specializes.

7. The kitten stared <u>at</u> the barking dogs.
   Confirmation: *At the barking dogs the kitten stared.

8. I'm studying <u>for</u> a big test.
   Confirmation: *For a big test I'm studying.

9. They take <u>after</u> their mother.
   Confirmation: *After their mother they take.

10. People are always messing <u>with</u> my stuff.
    Confirmation: *With my stuff people are always messing.

Complement Exercise #13: Identifying Prep + NP Complements

1. We disagreed <u>with</u> <u>their answer</u>.
                Prep   NP
   Confirmation: Their answer was disagreed with (by us).

2. You can count <u>on</u> <u>me</u>.
                  Prep NP
   Confirmation: I can be counted on (by you).

3. He looked <u>for</u> <u>the answer</u>.
             Prep   NP
   Confirmation: The answer was looked for (by him).

4. Sue hinted <u>at</u> <u>the problem</u>.
              Prep   NP
   Confirmation: The problem was hinted at by Sue.

5. The mechanic checked <u>on</u> <u>the battery</u>.
                        Prep   NP
   Confirmation: The battery was checked on (by the mechanic).

6. The accountant went <u>over</u> <u>the books</u>.
                       Prep   NP
   Confirmation: The books were gone over by the accountant.

7. Sam looked <u>at</u> <u>the proposal</u>.
              Prep   NP
   Confirmation: The proposal was looked at by Sam.

8. Everyone knew <u>about</u> <u>the problems</u>.
                 Prep   NP
   Confirmation: The problems were known about by everyone.

9. The receiver locked <u>onto</u> <u>the transmitter</u>.
                       Prep   NP
   Confirmation: The transmitter was locked onto by the receiver.

10. Our investigators will look <u>into</u> <u>the situation</u>.
                                Prep   NP
    Confirmation: The situation will be looked into by our investigators.

Complement Exercise #14: Distinguishing "separable" and "inseparable" Phrasal Verbs

1. The coach <u>used up</u> all their time-outs.
   separable
   Confirmation: The coach used all their time-outs up.

2. I <u>defer to</u> your opinion.
   inseparable
   Confirmation: *I defer your opinion to.

3. Portia just <u>got by</u> the bar exam.
   inseparable
   Confirmation: *Portia just got the bar exam by.

4. All the king's men <u>put together</u> Humpty Dumpty again.
   separable
   Confirmation: All the king's men put Humpty Dumpty together again.

5. Naturally, we <u>jumped at</u> the offer.
   inseparable
   Confirmation: *Naturally, we jumped the offer at.

6. <u>Keep up</u> the good work.
   separable
   Confirmation: Keep the good work up.

7. I think that they <u>lied about</u> the accident.
   inseparable
   Confirmation: *I think that they lied the accident about.

8. They are <u>living beyond</u> their means.
   inseparable
   Confirmation: *They are living their means beyond.

9. Can I <u>make up</u> the test?
   separable
   Confirmation: Can I make the test up?

10. I was <u>looking for</u> my keys.
    inseparable
    Confirmation: *I was looking my keys for.

Complement Exercise #15: Identifying NP +Prep + NP Complements

1. John lodged <u>a complaint</u> <u>against</u> <u>his noisy neighbors</u>.
   NP   Prep   NP
   Confirmation: *Against his noisy neighbors, John lodged a complaint.

2. The play portrayed <u>Elizabeth</u> <u>as</u> <u>a tough-minded politician</u>.
   NP   Prep   NP
   Confirmation: *As a tough-minded politician, the play portrayed Elizabeth.

3. Ralph got <u>himself</u> <u>into</u> <u>a lot of trouble</u>.
   NP   Prep   NP
   Confirmation: *Into a lot of trouble, Ralph got himself.

4. We talked <u>them</u> <u>out of</u> <u>their original plan</u>.
     NP   Prep   NP

Confirmation: *Out of their original plan, we talked them.

5. His help got <u>me</u> <u>out of</u> <u>a bad situation</u>.
     NP   Prep   NP

Confirmation: *Out of a bad situation, his help got me.

6. Holmes took <u>Watson</u> <u>as</u> <u>a bit of a simpleton</u>.
     NP Prep   NP

Confirmation: *As a bit of a simpleton, Holmes took Watson.

7. The librarian supplied <u>us</u> <u>with</u> <u>the necessary information</u>.
     NP Prep   NP

Confirmation: *With the necessary information, the librarian supplied us.

8. The fairy godmother turned <u>the pumpkin</u> <u>into</u> <u>a coach</u>.
     NP   Prep NP

Confirmation: *Into a coach, the fairy godmother turned the pumpkin.

9. He asked <u>me</u> <u>for</u> <u>a favor</u>.
     NP Prep NP

Confirmation: *For a favor, he asked me.

10. The recipe substituted <u>yogurt</u> <u>for</u> <u>sour cream</u>.
     NP Prep   NP

Confirmation: *For sour cream, the recipe substituted yogurt.

Complement Exercise #16: Review of Complements of Phrasal Verbs

1. Talk <u>to</u> <u>me</u>!
  Prep NP

2. The plane took <u>off</u>.
     Adv

3. Ruth takes <u>after</u> <u>her mother's side of the family</u>.
    Prep   NP

4. I have thought <u>over</u> <u>your proposal</u>.
     Adv   NP

5. The police have closed <u>the highway</u> <u>to</u> <u>traffic</u>.
     NP   Prep NP

6. The store is <u>out of</u> <u>computer ribbons</u>.
    Prep   NP

7. The hounds ran <u>down</u> <u>the fox</u>.
     Adv NP

8. The wizard turned <u>the prince</u> <u>into</u> <u>a frog</u>.
     NP   Prep NP

9. They ran <u>down</u> <u>the opposition</u>.
    Adv   NP

10. The knight was searching <u>for</u> <u>the princess</u>.
                                    Prep   NP

11. They set <u>aside</u> <u>their differences</u>.
               Adv   NP

12. Senator Fogg was working <u>against</u> <u>the bill</u>.
                                    Prep   NP

13. She put <u>across</u> <u>her ideas</u> very effectively.
               Adv   NP

14. We participated <u>in</u> <u>the review session</u>.
                         Prep   NP

15. The senate limited <u>debate</u> <u>to</u> <u>five hours</u>.
                        NP   Prep   NP

16. We were living <u>beyond</u> <u>our means</u>.
                     Prep   NP

17. Put <u>up</u> <u>your hands</u>!
      Adv   NP

18. We went <u>over</u> <u>the problem</u>.
             Prep   NP

19. We just dropped <u>by</u>.
                    Adv

20. Brush <u>up</u> <u>your Shakespeare</u>!
        Adv   NP

Complement Exercise #17: Review of All Complement Types

1. The movie really grossed <u>out</u> <u>the kids</u>.
   #13   Adv   NP

2. The pop star dedicated <u>the song</u> <u>to</u> <u>his agent</u>.
   #15   NP   Prep   NP

3. The remote control is <u>on the coffee table</u>.
   #5   ADVplace

4. Henry VII essentially proclaimed <u>himself</u> <u>king</u>.
   #7   NP   OC

5. We prayed <u>for</u> <u>rain</u>.
   #14   Prep NP

6. Ralph hurt <u>himself</u> <u>playing soccer</u>.
   #10   NP   VPpres part

7. We wanted <u>them</u> <u>to apologize</u>.
   #11   NP   VPinf

8. Sally broke <u>off</u> <u>their engagement</u>.
   #13   Adv   NP

9. She told <u>him</u> <u>about</u> <u>Harry</u>.
   #15   NP   Prep   NP

10. The wedding seemed very <u>tasteful</u>.
    #4   Pred Adj

11. I told <u>the children</u> <u>to leave</u>.
    #11   NP   VPinf

12. The Wicked Queen looked <u>into the mirror</u>.
    #5   ADVplace

    (Compare with *She looked into the situation.*)

13. The thieves got completely <u>away</u>.
    #12   Adv

14. The law limits <u>hunters</u> <u>to</u> <u>three ducks</u>.
    #15   NP   Prep   NP

15. They lied <u>about</u> <u>the situation</u>.
    #14   Prep   NP

16. We were living <u>beyond</u> <u>our means</u>.
    #14   Prep   NP

    (Compare with *We were living beyond the river.*)

17. I rushed <u>off</u> to pick up the kids.
    #12   Adv

    (*To pick up the kids* is an optional adverbial infinitive.)

18. We put <u>aside</u> <u>our differences</u>.
    #13   Adv   NP

19. Senator Fogg seemed <u>the perfect candidate</u>.
    #3   PredNom

20. His boss exerted <u>real pressure</u> <u>on</u> <u>him</u>.
    #15   NP   Prep NP

Complement Exercise #18: Review of All Complement Types

1. The missing text never turned <u>up</u>.
   #12   Adv

2. Carefully, she put <u>the full coffee cup</u> <u>on the counter</u>.
   #9   NP   ADVplace

3. Everybody thought <u>the Wright brothers</u> <u>foolhardy</u>.
   #8   NP   Pred Adj

4. Everyone responded <u>to</u> <u>the news</u>.
   #14   Prep   NP

5. Please convey <u>our sympathies</u> <u>to</u> <u>your friend</u>.
   #15   NP   Prep   NP

6. We felt <u>the building</u> <u>shaking in the wind</u>.
   #10   NP   VPpres part

7. Tell <u>him</u> <u>to stop</u>.
   #11 NP   VPinf

8. Senator Fogg withdrew <u>from the race</u>.
   #14   Prep   NP

9. They never caught <u>on</u>.
   #12   Adv

10. I cleaned <u>out the refrigerator</u>.
    #13   Adv   NP

11. I want <u>you to quit now</u>.
    #11   NP   VPinf

12. The union reacted <u>against the company's proposal</u>.
    #14   Prep   NP

13. It crossed <u>my mind</u>.
    #2   NP

14. He is still living <u>at home</u>.
    #5   ADVplace

15. She put <u>the baby</u> <u>in the crib</u>.
    #9   NP   ADVplace

16. Prince Charming noticed <u>Cinderella</u> <u>looking at her watch</u>.
    #10   NP   VPpres part

17. Igor threw <u>up his hands</u>.
    #13   Adv   NP

18. The jury found <u>Bugsy</u> <u>innocent</u>.
    #8   NP   Pred Adj

19. The teacher got <u>the students</u> <u>some new books</u>.
    #6   NP1   NP2

20. It rained all night.
    #1 (no complement)

Usage

Apostrophe Exercise #1: Placing Apostrophes in Contractions

1. I <u>wouldn't</u> do that if I were you.
   Confirmation: wouldn't = would not

2. <u>Didn't</u> you get my message?
   Confirmation: didn't = did not

3. <u>Let's</u> do it!
   Confirmation: Let's = let us

4. <u>Haven't</u> we met before?
   Confirmation: haven't = have not

5. I <u>can't</u> imagine why.
   Confirmation: can't = can not

6. <u>Don't</u> do it unless you have to.
    Confirmation: don't = do not

7. <u>I'm</u> not able to go.
    Confirmation: I'm = I am

8. <u>Aren't</u> you ready yet?
    Confirmation: aren't = are not

9. I <u>wasn't</u> watching.
    Confirmation: wasn't = was not

10. They <u>weren't</u> any friends of ours.
    Confirmation: weren't = were not

Apostrophe Exercise #2: Possessives and Plurals

1. cow: cow's, cows, cows'
2. girl: girl's, girls, girls'
3. mouse: mouse's, mice, mice's
4. wife: wife's, wives, wives'
5. farmer: farmer's, farmers, farmers'
6. niece: niece's, nieces, nieces'
7. nephew: nephew's, nephews, nephews'
8. goose: goose's, geese, geese's
9. aunt: aunt's, aunts, aunts'
10. ox: ox's, oxen, oxen's

Apostrophe Exercise #3: Identifying Possessives by the Possessive Pronoun Test

1. The children played the <u>queen's</u> helpers.
    Confirmation: <u>the queen's</u> helper
                   her

2. It's something that happens in every <u>child's</u> life.
    Confirmation: <u>every child's</u> life
                 his/her

3. The coach measured each <u>player's</u> height and weight.
    Confirmation: <u>each player's</u> height and weight
                 his/her

4. They appealed the <u>judge's</u> ruling.
    Confirmation: <u>the judge's</u> ruling
                 his/her

5. We had to memorize the <u>body's</u> major muscles.
    Confirmation: <u>the body's</u> major muscles
                 its

6. The program calculated all the <u>planets'</u> orbits.
   Confirmation: all <u>the planets'</u> orbits
   their

7. The <u>candidate's</u> press release ignored the issue.
   Confirmation: <u>the candidate's</u> press release
   his/her

8. The exam covered the entire <u>course's</u> content.
   Confirmation: <u>the entire course's</u> content
   its

9. I found them in my <u>grandmother's</u> basement.
   Confirmation: <u>my grandmother's</u> basement
   her

10. The <u>ship's</u> anchor began to drag in the heavy wind.
    Confirmation: <u>the ship's</u> anchor
    its

Apostrophe Exercise #4: Identifying Possessives by the Whose Test

1. The court ordered the <u>suspect's</u> release.
   Confirmation: Whose release? The suspect's release.

2. The <u>baby's</u> blanket is in the dryer.
   Confirmation: Whose blanket? The baby's blanket.

3. The <u>team's</u> goal was the first for the season.
   Confirmation: Whose goal? The team's goal.

4. I hated being called the <u>teacher's</u> pet.
   Confirmation: Whose pet? The teacher's pet.

5. <u>Newark's</u> airport is now the busiest in the New York area.
   Confirmation: Whose airport? Newark's airport.

6. We picked up <u>Philip's</u> toys.
   Confirmation: Whose toys? Philip's toys.

7. I ignored the tooth <u>fairy's</u> warning.
   Confirmation: Whose warning? the tooth fairy's warning.

8. They doubted the <u>economists'</u> dire predictions.
   Confirmation: Whose dire predictions? The economists' dire predictions.

9. The <u>referee's</u> whistle stopped the action.
   Confirmation: Whose whistle? The referee's whistle.

10. A <u>plumber's</u> snake is a flexible metal tool.
    Confirmation: Whose snake? A plumber's snake.

Apostrophe Exercise #5: Identifying Subjects of Gerunds

1. The <u>school's</u> offering soccer is something new.
   Confirmation: Their offering soccer. Whose offering soccer? The school's.

2. The <u>parrot's</u> knowing classical Greek was a surprise.
   Confirmation: Its knowing. Whose knowing? The parrot's knowing.

3. We hadn't expected the <u>company's</u> agreeing to the offer.
   Confirmation: Their agreeing. Whose agreeing? The company's agreeing.

4. The <u>light's</u> coming through the open window woke us up.
   Confirmation: Its coming. Whose coming? The light's coming.

5. We never got used to the <u>restaurant's</u> being open so late.
   Confirmation: Its being open. Whose being open? The restaurant's being open.

6. <u>Lincoln's</u> walking miles to return two pennies is probably a myth.
   Confirmation: His walking. Whose walking? Lincoln's walking.

7. The <u>broker's</u> recommending the stock made a difference.
   Confirmation: His/her recommending. Whose recommending? The broker's recommending.

8. We encouraged the <u>children's</u> participating in sports.
   Confirmation: Their participating. Whose participating? The children's participating.

9. Aunt <u>Bea's</u> selling her car turned out to be a mistake.
   Confirmation: Her selling. Whose selling? Aunt Bea's selling.

10. The <u>council's</u> approving the motion was a foregone conclusion.
    Confirmation: Its approving. Whose approving? The council's approving.

Apostrophe Exercise #6: Distinguishing it's and its by the Expansion Test

1. I think <u>it's</u> up to you.
   Confirmation: I think it is up to you.

2. The bank closed <u>its</u> drive-in window.
   Confirmation: *The bank closed it is drive-in window.

3. I think <u>it's</u> too cold to eat outside.
   Confirmation: I think it is too cold to eat outside.

4. The movie had <u>its</u> moments.
   Confirmation: *The movie had it is moments.

5. We planted a tree, and now <u>it's</u> blooming.
   Confirmation: Now it is blooming.

6. The ice cream is so cold that <u>it's</u> giving me a headache.
   Confirmation: That it is giving me a headache.

7. <u>It's</u> about dinner time.
   Confirmation: It is about dinner time.

8. A store's reputation is only as good as <u>its</u> employees.
   Confirmation: *As good as it is employees.

9. The cat refused to eat <u>its</u> food.
   Confirmation: *The cat refused to eat it is food.

10. <u>It's</u> an ill wind that blows no good.
    Confirmation: It is an ill wind that blows no good.

Apostrophe Exercise #7: Identifying Time Expressions Requiring Apostrophes by the of Paraphrase

1. It is a problem in <u>today's</u> fast-paced society.
   Confirmation: The fast-paced society of today.

2. I've got ten <u>days'</u> vacation coming to me.
   Confirmation: Vacation of ten days.

3. They are debating this <u>year's</u> budget.
   Confirmation: The budget of this year.

4. That's <u>tomorrow's</u> problem.
   Confirmation: The problem of tomorrow.

5. That's a whole <u>week's</u> work.
   Confirmation: The work or a whole week.

6. A <u>day's</u> wages back then was only about a dollar.
   Confirmation: The wages of a day.

7. I can't do it on a <u>minute's</u> notice.
   Confirmation: The notice of a minute.

8. I got the minutes of last <u>week's</u> board meeting.
   Confirmation: The board meeting of last week.

9. <u>Today's</u> lesson is from St. Paul.
   Confirmation: The lesson of today.

10. It is this <u>century's</u> first major crisis.
    Confirmation: The first major crisis of this century.

Apostrophe Exercise #8: Review

1. <u>It's</u> a valuable Swiss watch.
   Confirmation: It is a valuable Swiss watch.

2. Did you get <u>today's</u> menu?
   Confirmation: The menu of today.

3. He <u>doesn't</u> understand the question.
   Confirmation: He does not understand the question.

4. The <u>computer's</u> keyboard needed cleaning.
   Confirmation: Its keyboard needed cleaning.

5. Dracula replaced the <u>coffin's</u> lid.

    Confirmation: Dracula replaced its lid.

6. I appreciated the <u>clerk's</u> returning my call so quickly.

    Confirmation: I appreciated his/her returning my call so quickly.

7. <u>Somebody's</u> car was stuck in the ditch.

    Confirmation: Whose car? Somebody's car.

8. The hawk returned to <u>its</u> roost.

    Confirmation: *The hawk returned to it is roost.

9. We could hear the <u>churches'</u> bells.

    Confirmation: We could hear their bells.

10. I <u>didn't</u> catch what she said.

    Confirmation: I did not catch what she said.

11, The <u>store's</u> specials were not very impressive.

    Confirmation: Its specials were not very impassive.

12. Obviously, the bird had lost <u>its</u> way in the fog.

    Confirmation: *Obviously, the bird had lost it is way in the fog.

13. I was worried about the <u>children's</u> getting too much sun.

    Confirmation: I was worried about their getting too much sun.

14. After an <u>hour's</u> delay, the umpire postponed the game.

    Confirmation: The delay of an hour.

15. <u>You're</u> missing the point.

    Confirmation: You are missing the point.

16. We ordered the <u>chef's</u> special for dinner.

    Confirmation: We ordered his/her special for dinner.

17. The <u>voters'</u> rejecting the bond issue was a disappointment.

    Confirmation: Their rejecting the bond issue was a disappointment.

18. <u>It's</u> always fair weather when good fellows get together.

    Confirmation: It is always fair weather.

19. A <u>year's</u> delay will cost the company a fortune.

    Confirmation: The delay of a year.

20. We had to postpone the <u>author's</u> reception.

    Confirmation: We had to postpone his/her reception.

Article Exercise #1: Identifying Mass Nouns by the Abstract Category Test

1. New roads mean increased <u>traffic</u>.

    Confirmation: <u>Traffic</u> is a mass noun meaning all entire amount of vehicles on the road.

2. Russia has vast reserves of <u>oil</u>.

    Confirmation: <u>Oil</u> is a mass noun meaning all petroleum.

3. There was nothing but <u>junk</u> in the attic.
   Confirmation: <u>Junk</u> is a mass noun meaning a collection of trash.

4. <u>Carbon dioxide</u> may contribute to global warming.
   Confirmation: <u>Carbon dioxide</u> is a mass noun meaning a type of gas.

5. I learned the importance of <u>relaxation</u> in PE class.
   Confirmation: <u>Relaxation</u> is a mass noun meaning the state of being relaxed.

6. Everyone knows that <u>smoking</u> is bad for your heath.
   Confirmation: <u>Smoking</u> is a mass noun meaning the act of smoking.

7. Poor techniques affect the <u>reliability</u> of research findings.
   Confirmation: <u>Reliability</u> is a mass noun meaning the state of being reliable.

8. The accidents caused a great deal of <u>confusion</u>.
   Confirmation: <u>Confusion</u> is a mass noun meaning the state of being confused.

9. After what happened, his <u>distrust</u> was quite understandable.
   Confirmation: <u>Distrust</u> is a mass noun meaning the state of being distrustful.

10. He has been doing a lot of <u>walking</u> to reduce his blood pressure.
    Confirmation: <u>Walking</u> is a mass noun meaning the process of taking walks.

Article Exercise #2: Identifying Mass Nouns by Category

1. You should eat several servings of <u>fruit</u> each day.
   Confirmation: <u>Fruit</u> is a food.

2. The kids love playing <u>basketball</u>.
   Confirmation: <u>Basketball</u> is a sport.

3. At the peak of the storm, the sky was filled with <u>lightning</u>.
   Confirmation: <u>Lightning</u> is a weather term.

4. Would you like another helping of <u>chicken</u>?
   Confirmation: <u>Chicken</u> is a food.

5. When we went to Las Vegas, we really had good <u>luck</u>.
   Confirmation: <u>Luck</u> is an abstraction.

6. The engines were producing excessive <u>smoke</u>.
   Confirmation: <u>Smoke</u> is a weather term or a natural phenomenon.

7. Everything in the house was covered with <u>dust</u>.
   Confirmation: <u>Dust</u> is a weather term or a natural phenomenon.

8. The audience reacted with great <u>amusement</u>.
   Confirmation: <u>Amusement</u> is an abstraction.

9. The old battery couldn't produce enough <u>energy</u>.
   Confirmation: <u>Energy</u> is an abstraction or a natural phenomenon.

10. I am studying <u>literature</u>.
    Confirmation: <u>Literature</u> is an academic field.

Article Exercise #3: Using Indefinite Articles with Count and Mass Nouns

1. On <u>a</u> trip recently, we encountered <u>some</u> bad fog.
   Count-Sg   Mass

2. <u>Some</u> dogs were chasing <u>a</u> squirrel.
   Count-Pl   Count-Sg

3. I would like <u>some</u> bread and <u>some</u> butter.
                 Mass   Mass

4. With <u>some</u> luck, we should there in time for <u>a</u> nice dinner.
         Mass   Count-Sg

5. I have <u>a</u> class this afternoon.
          Count-Sg

6. <u>Some</u> situations are worse than others.
   Count-Pl

7. We got <u>some</u> gas at <u>a</u> filling station on the highway.
          Mass   Count-Sg

8. We took <u>some</u> friends to <u>a</u> soccer game.
           Count-Pl   Count-Sg

9. There was still <u>some</u> hot water left in <u>a</u> container.
                    Mass   Count-Sg

10. She has <u>some</u> information about the meeting.
            Mass

Article Exercise #4: Using Definite Articles

1. A truck pulled up beside us. Someone in <u>the</u> truck yelled at us.
                                            Prev Men

2. Some of <u>the</u> books on *The New York Times* list of best-selling books have not
           Mod
   yet been sold to the public.

3. I got into my car and turned on <u>the</u> radio.
                                    Norm Exp
   we expect cars to have radios

4. We went to a Little League baseball game. <u>The</u> players were not great, but
   they were fun to watch.   Norm Exp
   we expect games to have players

5. I switched on a light and <u>the</u> bulb promptly burned out.
                             Norm Exp
   we expect lights to have bulbs

6. My cat nearly caught a bird. <u>The</u> bird barely escaped with its life.
                                Prev Men

7. I went into a phone booth and picked up <u>the</u> receiver.
                                            Norm Exp
   we expect phone booths to have receivers

8. I found <u>the</u> book that you had recommended.
   Mod

9. We went to a football game in <u>the</u> new stadium.
   Norm Exp
   we expect a football game to be in a stadium

10. Most fantasy novels involve a conflict between <u>the</u> forces of good and evil.
    Mod

11. I have to hang up now; someone is at <u>the</u> door.
    Norm Exp
    we expect places to have doors

12. I had a strange dream last night. In <u>the</u> dream, I was diagramming sentences in Latin.
    Prev Men

13. <u>The</u> index in our textbook is pretty helpful.
    Mod

14. Most small meteors that hit our planet burn up in <u>the</u> atmosphere.
    Norm Exp
    we expect planets to have atmosphere

15. Did you see <u>the</u> headphones that I got yesterday?
    Mod

Article Exercise #5: Using Mass and Plural Count Nouns Without Articles for Generalizations

1. <u>Conflicts</u> are usually easier to start than to stop.
   Pl Ct
   Confirmation: Pres, No Mod, Adv Freq

2. <u>Transportation</u> is always hard to arrange.
   Mass
   Confirmation: Pres, No Mod, Adv Freq

3. Hardly ever do we eat <u>meat</u>.
   Mass
   Confirmation: Pres, No Mod, Adv Freq

4. <u>Ice cream</u> always gives me a headache.
   Mass
   Confirmation: Pres, No Mod, Adv Freq

5. <u>Discoveries</u> are often accidental.
   Pl Ct
   Confirmation: Pres, No Mod, Adv Freq

6. The discovery led to a big controversy.
   Discovery is not used to make a generalization—it has an article and the sentence is in the past tense.

7. Generally, <u>kitchens</u> recover the cost of remodeling.
   Pl Ct
   Confirmation: Pres, No Mod, Adv Freq

8. <u>Coffee</u> contains a lot of caffeine.
   Mass
   Confirmation: Pres, No Mod

9. <u>Tropical diseases</u> are poorly understood.
   Pl Ct
   Confirmation: Pres, No Mod

10. <u>Natural gas</u> is formed by the process of decay.
    Mass
    Confirmation: Pres, No Mod

Article Exercise #6: Review

1. I answered <u>an</u> ad in the newspaper.
   First mention of <u>ad</u>, a singular count noun

2. <u>Some</u> opinions usually don't count for very much.
   First mention of <u>opinions</u>, a plural count noun

3. I left <u>the</u> key to my room with the desk clerk.
   Modifier makes <u>key</u> an established noun

4. We saw <u>a</u> terrible accident on our way here.
   First mention of <u>accident</u>, a singular count noun

5. <u>The</u> winter that we had this year was unusually damp.
   Modifier makes <u>winter</u> an established noun

6. Do you have <u>a</u> card?
   First mention of <u>card</u>, a singular count noun

7. There must be <u>some</u> children next door.
   First mention of <u>children</u>, a plural count noun

8. I think it was in <u>a</u> play that Shakespeare wrote.
   First mention of <u>play</u>. The modifier doesn't make the noun established because Shakespeare wrote a number of plays.

9. (No art) Accidents can usually be prevented.
   <u>Accidents</u> is a plural count noun being used to make a generalization.

10. I just bought <u>a</u> new computer. <u>The</u> computer is a Mac.
    <u>Computer</u> is first mention of a singular count noun; second mention

11. There are <u>some</u> candles in the top drawer.
    First mention of <u>candles</u>, a plural count noun

12. <u>The</u> pressure of a new job can be pretty intense.
    Modifier makes <u>pressure</u> an established noun

13. <u>A</u> phrase is a group of related words.
    First mention of <u>phrase</u>, a singular count noun

14. I found <u>a</u> cat under my car. It looked like <u>the</u> cat hadn't eaten in days.
    First mention of <u>cat</u>, a singular count noun; second mention

15. We normally classify (No Art) words by part of speech.
    <u>Words</u> is a plural count noun used to make a generalization

Commas and Appositives Exercise #1: Identifying and Punctuating Appositives by the Appositive Deletion Test

1. Miss Manners, <u>a newspaper columnist</u>, advised against it.
   Confirmation: Miss Manners advised against it.

2. We took a train, <u>a new Amtrak sleeper</u>, across the county.
   Confirmation: We took a train across the country.

3. Mozart, <u>a child prodigy</u>, was already famous in his teens.
   Confirmation: Mozart was already famous in his teens.

4. In the tropics there are many coral islands, <u>usually atolls</u>.
   Confirmation: In the tropics there are many coral islands.

5. The most famous atoll, <u>Bikini</u>, was used for testing atomic weapons.
   Confirmation: The most famous atoll was used for testing atomic weapons.

6. Dorothy's enemy, <u>the Wicked Witch of the West</u>, suddenly appeared.
   Confirmation: Dorothy's enemy suddenly appeared.

7. Her first publication, <u>an autobiographical short story</u>, was in 1983.
   Confirmation: Her first publication was in 1983.

8. The theater, <u>a concrete warehouse</u>, had no air conditioning.
   Confirmation: The theater had no air conditioning.

9. We had dinner with the Smiths, <u>old friends of my parents</u>.
   Confirmation: We had dinner with the Smiths.

10. There was a rug, <u>a beautiful Persian</u>, in the attic.
    Confirmation: There was a rug in the attic.

11. A pickup, <u>a rusty old Chevy</u>, waited in the parking lot.
    Confirmation: A pickup waited in the parking lot.

12. Katy, <u>their youngest daughter</u>, took us around the garden.
    Confirmation: Katy took us around the garden.

13. I got a new bike, <u>an Italian racer</u>.
    Confirmation: I got a new bike.

14. Emergency vehicles, <u>an ambulance and two police cars</u>, were at the scene of the accident.
    Confirmation: Emergency vehicles were at the scene of the accident.

15. The judge, <u>a middle-aged woman</u>, came into the courtroom.
    Confirmation: The judge came into the courtroom.

16. Did you meet him, <u>Tom's college roommate</u>?
    Confirmation: Did you meet him?

17. SR 1008, <u>a bill introduced by Senator Jones</u>, deals with traffic congestion.
    Confirmation: SR 1008 deals with traffic congestion.

18. Watch out for that truck, <u>the yellow one in the left lane</u>.
    Confirmation: Watch out for that truck.

19. Cleopatra, <u>my weird cousin's pet snake</u>, was missing again.
    Confirmation: Cleopatra was missing again.

20. The coffee, <u>an expensive French roast</u>, tasted bitter to me.
    Confirmation: The coffee tasted bitter to me.

Commas and Coordinate Adjectives Exercise #1: Identifying Adjective Classes

1. ship a wooden old huge
   Answer: a <u>huge</u> <u>old</u> <u>wooden</u> ship
         General Age Material

2. primitive the societies first European
   Answer: the first <u>primitive</u> <u>European</u> societies
              General   Origin

3. sensitive pink some tissue new
   Answer: some <u>sensitive</u> <u>new</u> <u>pink</u> tissue
              General   Age Color

4. cape valuable feather red Sir Roderick's
   Answer: Sir Roderick's <u>valuable</u> <u>red</u> <u>feather</u> cape
                        General Color Material

5. evil that idol stone old
   Answer: that <u>evil</u> <u>old</u> <u>stone</u> idol
              General Age Material

6. finish popular new its satin
   Answer: its <u>popular</u> <u>new</u> <u>satin</u> finish
             General Age Material

7. continental innovative our design new
   Answer: our <u>innovative</u> <u>new</u> <u>continental</u> design
             General   Age   Origin

8. population entire urban the
   Answer: the <u>entire</u> <u>urban</u> population
             General Origin

9. broken several crates wooden
   Answer: several <u>broken</u> <u>wooden</u> crates
                General   Material

10. new problems these frightening technical
    Answer: these <u>frightening</u> <u>new</u> <u>technical</u> problems
                General   Age   Origin

11. pizza our sausage hot
    Answer: our <u>hot</u> <u>sausage</u> pizza
              General Material

12. annual the dinner German third
    Answer: the third <u>annual</u> <u>German</u> dinner
                   General   Origin

13. old our desks two massive oak

Answer: our two <u>massive</u> <u>old</u> <u>oak</u> desks
General   Age   Material

14. explorers the European known first

Answer: the first <u>known</u> <u>European</u> explorers
General   Origin

15. cotton my clean shirt white

Answer: my <u>clean</u> <u>white</u> <u>cotton</u> shirt
General Color   Material

Commas and Coordinate Adjectives Exercise #2: Identifying Coordinate Adjectives by the Switched Order Test and the **and** *Test*

1. He is a regular old crook.

Confirmation: *He is an old regular crook. *He is a regular and old crook.

2. Dracula had an <u>ordinary, normal</u> childhood.

Confirmation: Dracula had a normal, ordinary childhood.

Dracula had an ordinary and normal childhood.

3. He answered Holmes' questions in <u>halting, accented</u> English.

Confirmation: He answered Holmes' question in accented, halting English.

He answered Holmes' question in halting and accented English.

4. His suggestion provided an <u>effective, convenient</u> solution.

Confirmation: His suggestion provided a convenient, effective solution.

His suggestion provided an effective and convenient solution.

5. He was a proper English butler of the old school.

Confirmation: *He was an English proper butler of the old school.

*He was a proper and English butler of the old school.

6. He was a <u>difficult, obstinate</u> child.

Confirmation: He was an obstinate, difficult child.

He was a difficult and obstinate child.

7. She decided that her basic black dress was appropriate.

Confirmation: *She decided that her black basic dress was appropriate.

*She decided that her basic and black dress was appropriate.

8. Lady Mortock was smitten by the tall dark stranger.

Confirmation: *Lady Mortlock was smitten by the dark tall stranger.

*Lady Mortlock was smitten by the tall and dark stranger.

9. It is a <u>dirty, dangerous</u> job, but somebody has to do it.

Confirmation: It is a dangerous, dirty job. It is a dirty and dangerous job.

10. She toyed with her beautiful new pearls.

Confirmation: *She toyed with her new beautiful pearls.

*She toyed with her beautiful and new pearls.

11. We all noticed her <u>delicate, smooth</u> complexion.
    Confirmation: We all noticed her smooth, delicate complexion.
    We all noticed her delicate and smooth complexion.

12. Holmes fixed the cabby with a <u>steady, cold</u> eye.
    Confirmation: Holmes fixed the cabby with a cold, steady eye.
    Holmes fixed the cabby with a steady and cold eye.

13. Alexander had a <u>terrible, horrible</u> day.
    Confirmation: Alexander had a horrible, terrible day.
    Alexander had a terrible and horrible day.

14. The original American musical was changed into a British novel.
    Confirmation: *The American original musical was changed.
    *The original and American musical was changed.

15. We attended a <u>disorganized, unprofessional</u> performance.
    Confirmation: We attended an unprofessional, disorganized performance.
    We attended a disorganized and unprofessional performance.

Commas and Coordinating Conjunctions Exercise #1: Punctuating Coordinating Conjunctions by the Period Test

1. It was a great restaurant, <u>and</u> we had a wonderful meal.
   Confirmation: It was a great restaurant. We had a wonderful meal.

2. Helen got into the car, <u>and</u> she drove to the station.
   Confirmation: Helen got into the car. She drove to the station.

3. I'm sure you are right, <u>but</u> I can't help worrying about it.
   Confirmation: I'm sure you are right. I can't help worrying about it.

4. The children were playing outside <u>and</u> making a lot of noise.
   Confirmation: The children were playing outside. *Making a lot of noise.

5. My father saved his bonus money, <u>and</u> he bought a new boat.
   Confirmation: My father saved his bonus money. He bought a new boat.

6. Mary planned the wedding, <u>and</u> she made up the guest list, too.
   Confirmation: Mary planned the wedding. She made up the guest list, too.

7. They should hurry, <u>for</u> the game is about to start.
   Confirmation: They should hurry. The game is about to start.

8. Henry jumped to his feet <u>and</u> ran to the door.
   Confirmation: Henry jumped to his feet. *Ran to the door.

9. His family was poor <u>but</u> honest.
   Confirmation: His family was poor. *Honest.

10. My parents got a new car <u>and</u> a new camper at the same time.
    Confirmation: My parents got a new car. *A new camper at the same time.

11. It was time to go, <u>but</u> we weren't ready yet.
    Confirmation: It was time to go. We weren't ready yet.

12. The police posted a sign <u>and</u> closed the road to through traffic.
    Confirmation: The police posted a sign. *Closed the road to through traffic.

13. She set the table, <u>and</u> I lit the candles.
    Confirmation: She set the table. I lit the candles.

14. Jason answered the question <u>and</u> won a prize.
    Confirmation: Jason answered the question. *Won a prize.

15. Answer the question, <u>and</u> win a prize!
    Confirmation: Answer the question! Win a prize!

Commas and Coordinating Conjunctions Exercise #2: Sentence Combining

1. (a) The governor vetoed the bill, and he/she sent it back to the senate.
   (b) The governor vetoed the bill and sent it back to the senate.

2. (a) The performers dazzled the crowd, and they amazed the critics.
   (b) The performers dazzled the crowd and amazed the critics.

3. (a) The editor compiled a list of typographical errors, and he/she sent the list to the grateful author.
   (b) The editor compiled a list of typographical errors and sent the list to the grateful author.

4. (a) The workers stacked the crates in the warehouse, and they labeled them according to their contents.
   (b) The workers stacked the crates in the warehouse and labeled them according to their contents.

5. (a) The candidate invoked the names of the founding fathers, and he/she promised to follow in their footsteps.
   (b) The candidate invoked the names of the founding fathers and promised to follow in their footsteps.

6. (a) The Boy Scouts synchronized their watches, and they oriented their maps.
   (b) The Boy Scouts synchronized their watches and oriented their maps.

7. (a) The astrologer forecast the future of the stock market, and he called his broker.
   (b) The astrologer forecast the future of the stock market and called his broker.

8. (a) Dripping wet, Leon got out of the shower, and he answered the phone for the third time.
   (b) Dripping wet, Leon got out of the shower and answered the phone for the third time.

9. (a) A couple in a brand-new BMW wheeled into the filling station, and they paid for their gas with nickels and dimes.
   (b) A couple in a brand-new BMW wheeled into the filling station and paid for their gas with nickels and dimes.

10. (a) Holmes sent a wire to 221 Baker Street, and he told Watson to pack his service revolver.
    (b) Holmes sent a wire to 221 Baker Street and told Watson to pack his service revolver.

Commas and Introductory Elements Exercise #1: Punctuating Introductory Elements by the Introductory-Element Deletion Test

1. <u>Rummaging in the trunk</u>, the wizard pulled out an old hat.
   Confirmation: The wizard pulled out an old hat.

2. <u>As soon as I got your message</u>, I put in the order.
   Confirmation: I put in the order.

3. <u>Surely</u>, you must be joking.
   Confirmation: You must be joking.

4. <u>In Japan</u>, they drive on the left side of the road.
   Confirmation: They drive on the left side of the road.

5. Behind the brick was the coded message.
   Confirmation: *Was the coded message.

6. <u>After all</u>, what difference did it make?
   Confirmation: What difference did it make?*

7. There were several comma errors in the paper.
   Confirmation: *Were several comma errors in the paper.

8. <u>On Tuesday</u>, we visited an old monastery.
   Confirmation: We visited an old monastery.

9. <u>Recalling Lady Dedlock's mysterious words</u>, Holmes called for the upstairs maid.
   Confirmation: Holmes called for the upstairs maid.

10. <u>On Christmas day</u>, it began snowing in earnest.
    Confirmation: It began snowing in earnest.

11. <u>All too soon</u>, we had to leave.
    Confirmation: We had to leave.

12. <u>After eating a heavy meal</u>, I always get terribly sleepy.
    Confirmation: I always get terribly sleepy.

13. What they did next was a big mistake.
    Confirmation: *Was a big mistake.

14. <u>Thanks to their efforts</u>, Disneyland was safe again.
    Confirmation: Disneyland was safe again.

15. From Key West to Miami is about 150 miles.
    Confirmation: *Is about 150 miles.

16. <u>Since it was getting late</u>, we decided to head back.
    Confirmation: We decided to head back.

17. <u>In the poor light</u>, I could hardly read the sign.
    Confirmation: I could hardly read the sign.

18. There was really nothing I could say.
    Confirmation: *Was really nothing I could say.

19. <u>Somewhere over the rainbow</u>, skies are blue.
Confirmation: Skies are blue.

20. <u>When it rains</u>, it pours.
Confirmation: It pours.

Dangling Modifiers Exercise #1: Identifying Dangling Modifiers by the Understood Subject Test

1. <u>Waving good-bye to his mother</u>, Philip's eyes grew misty.
Correction: Waving good-bye to his mother, Philip began crying.
Confirmation: *Philip's eyes* did not wave good-bye.

2. <u>Piled on the floor</u>, I began sorting through my books.
Correction: Piled on the floor, my books were an unsightly mess.
Confirmation: *I* was not piled on the floor.

3. <u>Detouring through my old neighborhood</u>, our house looked the same as ever.
Correction: Detouring through my old neighborhood, we found our old house.
Confirmation: Our house was not detouring through the neighborhood.

4. Having matured, I now enjoy *The Flintstones*.
Confirmation: *I* is a valid subject of *having matured*.

5. <u>Being old Dodger fans</u>, the outcome of the game pleased us.
Correction: Being old Dodger fans, we enjoyed the game.
Confirmation: *The outcome of the game* was not an old Dodger fan.

6. <u>Once considered only an average player</u>, Don's game has improved enormously.
Correction: Once considered only an average player, Don has improved.
Confirmation: *Don's game* was not a player, *Don* was.

7. <u>Hoping for a league championship</u>, there was excitement in the air.
Correction: Hoping for a league championship, the team took the field.
Confirmation: *Excitement* was not hoping for a league championship.

8. Disappointed by the unexpected defeat, we applauded the team's efforts nonetheless.
Confirmation: *We* is a valid subject of *disappointed*.

9. <u>Working for old Mr. Green</u>, he really taught us the value of a good day's work.
Correction: Working for old Mr. Green, we learned how to look busy.
Confirmation: *He* (Mr. Green) did not work for Mr. Green, *we* did.

10. <u>Finishing in 2 hours and 57 minutes</u>, Ruth's first marathon was a terrific success.
Correction: Finishing in 2 hours and 57 minutes, Ruth was pleased.
Confirmation: *Ruth's first marathon* did not finish, *Ruth* did.

11. Shining in the sun, the water looked very inviting.
Confirmation: *Water* is a valid subject of *shining*.

12. Done with our project, we all went out for a pizza.
Confirmation: *We* is a valid subject of *done*.

13. <u>Running across the plowed field</u>, my ankle twisted.

    Correction: Running across the plowed field, I twisted my ankle.

    Confirmation: *My ankle* did not run across the field, *I* did.

14. <u>Made from a new plastic</u>, you cannot easily tell these artificial flowers from the real ones.

    Correction: Made from a new plastic, the flowers looked real.

    Confirmation: *You* were not made from plastic, the *flowers* were.

15. <u>Warped and twisted from the heat</u>, I realized that my records were ruined.

    Correction: Warped and twisted from the heat, my records were ruined.

    Confirmation: *I* was not warped and twisted, my records were.

Fragments Exercise #1: Identifying Fragments by the I Know That Test

1. I couldn't get started on my paper <u>because I had nothing to say</u>.

   Confirmation: *I know that because I had nothing to say.

2. While everyone waited, I looked for my library card, <u>which I had left at home in my rush to get to the library</u>.

   Confirmation: *I know that which I had left at home in my rush to get to the library.

3. We were awakened in the middle of the night <u>by the tornado-warning sirens</u>.

   Confirmation: *I know that by the tornado-warning sirens.

4. Bambi fled, <u>hearing the approach of the hunter</u>.

   Confirmation: *I know that hearing the approach of the hunter.

5. June 6, 1944, <u>the day the allies landed in Normandy</u>.

   Confirmation: *I know that the day the allies landed in Normandy.

6. We took the kids to Grumpyland, <u>part of the Seven Dwarfs amusement complex.</u>

   Confirmation: *I know that part of the Seven Dwarfs amusement complex.

7. I missed class because of a bad cold, <u>which was made worse by a sinus infection.</u>

   Confirmation: *I know that which was made worse by a sinus infection.

8. The conflict ended in 1987 <u>when the rebels signed a treaty with the government</u>.

   Confirmation: *I know that when the rebels signed a treaty with the government.

9. We heard about the engagement <u>when her brother called last night</u>.

   Confirmation: *I know that when her brother called last night.

10. He said he has stopped smoking <u>if you can believe what he says</u>.

    Confirmation: *I know that if you can believe what he says.

11. We went to Baltimore, <u>which has a restored inner harbor</u>.

    Confirmation: *I know that which has a restored inner harbor.

12. I finally found the office, <u>buried in the depths of a sub-basement</u>.
    Confirmation: *I know that buried in the depth of a sub-basement.

13. He was fined $5,000, <u>a huge sum at the time</u>.
    Confirmation: *I know that a huge sum at the time.

14. They didn't answer the phone, <u>even though they were home at the time.</u>
    Confirmation: *I know that even though they were home at the time.

15. We finally found the kids, <u>playing with the children next door</u>.
    Confirmation: *I know that playing with the children next door.

Participles Used as Adjectives Exercise #1: Identifying Participles by the doing Test

1. I thought it was a really <u>amused</u> movie.
   amusing
   Confirmation: The movie is doing the amusing.

2. It was certainly a terribly <u>embarrassed</u> accident.
   embarrassing
   Confirmation: The accident was doing the embarrassing.

3. The amusement park advertised its <u>thrilled</u> rides.
   thrilling
   Confirmation: The rides are doing the thrilling.

4. The <u>sprawled</u> suburbs went on for miles and miles.
   sprawling
   Confirmation: The suburbs are doing the sprawling.

5. The <u>soaked</u> rain brought the dry grass back to life.
   soaking
   Confirmation: The rain is doing the soaking.

6. I was really bothered by my <u>injuring</u> knee.
   injured
   Confirmation: The knee is NOT doing the injuring.

7. The diplomats issued the newly <u>redrawing</u> maps.
   redrawn
   Confirmation: The maps are NOT doing the redrawing.

8. We bought some <u>water-repelled</u> rain garments.
   water-repelling
   Confirmation: The rain garments are doing the water-repelling.

9. It was a very <u>amused</u> incident.
   amusing
   Confirmation: The incident was doing the amusing.

10. After the hike, I soaked my <u>blistering</u> feet.
    blistered
    Confirmation: The feet were NOT doing the blistering.

11. A <u>delaying</u> flight caused us to miss all of our connections.
      delayed
    Confirmation: The flight was NOT doing the delaying.

12. The crew asked the <u>remained</u> passengers to leave the plane.
                          remaining
    Confirmation: The passengers were the ones doing the remaining
                  (staying behind).

13. The policeman duly reported the <u>alleging</u> incident.
                                      alleged
    Confirmation: The incident was NOT doing the alleging.

14. There was a <u>revolved</u> restaurant at the airport.
                  revolving
    Confirmation: The restaurant is doing the revolving.

15. A <u>watching</u> pot never boils. (idiom)
      watched
    Confirmation: The pot is NOT doing the watching.

Progressive Usage Exercise #1: Identifying Stative Verbs by the Ongoing State Test

1. I <u>am believing</u> that the answer is wrong.
      believe
   Confirmation: Belief is an ongoing state.

2. It <u>is seeming</u> to be our best bet.
        seems
   Confirmation: Seeming (i.e., what something appears to be) is an ongoing state.

3. We <u>are staying</u> with some friends this weekend.
   Confirmation: Staying with something is a temporary condition.

4. The boss <u>is distrusting</u> all expense vouchers.
                  distrusts
   Confirmation: Distrust is an ongoing condition.

5. The train <u>is arriving</u> on Track 7 now.
   Confirmation: Arriving is a momentary event.

6. The solution <u>is sounding</u> pretty weak to me.
                    sounds
   Confirmation: The way that something sounds (i.e., appears) is its normal
                  ongoing state.

7. They <u>are wanting</u> us to approve their proposal.
             want
   Confirmation: Wanting something is an on-going condition.

8. It's <u>raining</u>.
   Confirmation: Raining is not an ongoing state because it can start and stop
                  at any time.

9. She is loving coffee ice cream.
   loves
   Confirmation: Loving something is an ongoing state.

10. I am returning your call.
    Confirmation: Returning a call is a momentary event.

11. My heart is belonging to Daddy.
    belongs
    Confirmation: Belonging is a continuous state.

12. He is certainly acting the part.
    Confirmation: Acting a part is a temporary event.

13. No one is believing in the gold standard anymore.
    believes
    Confirmation: Belief in something is a continuous state.

14. I am hating what I do.
    hate
    Confirmation: Hating something is a continuous state.

15. Thank you. I am appreciating your effort.
    Confirmation: Appreciating something is a continuous state.

Personal Pronoun Exercise #1: Identifying Correct Pronoun Form by the First-Element Deletion Test and the Plural Pronoun Replacement Test

1. They gave it to you and she.
   her
   1st element: They gave it to her.
   Pl pronoun: (Doesn't apply)

2. I hope that Fred and him can get along with each other.
   he
   1st element: I hope that he can get along.
   Pl pronoun: I hope that they can get along with each other.

3. The reason that we are late is that Harvey and me got lost.
   I
   1st element: The reason that we are late is that I got lost.
   Pl pronoun: The reason that we are late is that we got lost.

4. The gift was originally intended for Sally and he.
   him
   1st element: The gift was originally intended for him.
   Pl pronoun: the gift was originally intended for them.

5. Why did Mr. Smith ask you and I to leave?
   me
   1st element: Why did Mr. Smith ask me to leave?
   Pl pronoun: Why did Mr. Smith ask us to leave?

6. My brother and <u>me</u> used to be good friends.
                 I

1st element: I used to be good friends with my brother.
Pl pronoun: We used to be good friends.

7. John and <u>me</u> want to be partners.
             I

1st element: I want to be partners.
Pl pronoun: We want to be partners.

8. After Alice and he called, we had to change our plans.
1st element: After he called, we had to change our plans.
Pl pronoun: After they called, we had to change our plans.

9. Our visitors went with Alfred and <u>I</u> to the movies.
                               me
1st element: Our visitors went with me to the movies.
Pl pronoun: Our visitors went with us to the movies.

10. The outcome of the case surprised both Holmes and <u>he</u>.
                                                    him
1st element: (Does not apply.)
Pl pronoun: The outcome of the case surprised both of them.

11. Theo answered the phone because Louise and I had left already.
1st element: Theo answered the phone because I had left already.
Pl pronoun: Theo answered the phone because we had left already.

12. Ludwig proudly announced that Gretchen and <u>him</u> had won.
                                               he
1st element: Ludwig proudly announced that he had won.
Pl pronoun: Ludwig proudly announced that they had won.

13. Only Philip and <u>me</u> would have been home at the time.
                     I
1st element: Only I would have been home at the time.
Pl pronoun: Only we would have been home at the time.

14. Above Dorrie and <u>I</u> was an ornate ceiling.
                     me
1st element: Above me was an ornate ceiling.
Pl pronoun: Above us was an ornate ceiling.

15. Near Holmes and <u>I</u> was the dark tower that we had seen earlier.
                     me
1st element: Near me was the dark tower that we had seen earlier.
Pl pronoun: Near us was the dark tower that we had seen earlier.

Relative Pronoun Exercise #1: Choosing Between **who** *and* **whom** *by the verb–next Test*

1. I have teachers that love to diagram sentences.
   who

   Confirmation: *Who* is followed by the verb *love*.

2. We studied the Germans that invaded England in the 4th century.
   who

   Confirmation: *Who* is followed by the verb *invaded*.

3. The king met with the bishops that had opposed his policy.
   who

   Confirmation: *Who* is followed by the verb *had opposed*.

4. Donald became a wealthy banker that everyone envied.
   whom

   Confirmation: *Whom* is followed by the pronoun *everyone*.

5. They employed an executive secretary that really ran the business.
   who

   Confirmation: *Who* is followed by the verb *ran* (The adverb *really* does not count.)

6. The voters rejected the candidates that the party had nominated.
   whom

   Confirmation: *Whom* is followed by the noun phase *the party*.

7. The story had been filed by a correspondent that the bureau had hired.
   whom

   Confirmation: *Whom* is followed by the noun phrase *the bureau*.

8. The plot involved rural sheriffs that kept wrecking their police cars.
   who

   Confirmation: *Who* is followed by the verb *kept*.

9. Lady Lockheart graciously acknowledged the peasants that were permitted to watch their betters at play.   who

   Confirmation: *Who* is followed by the verb *were permitted*.

10. The manager called in the pitcher that they had recently acquired.
    whom

    Confirmation: *Whom* is followed by the pronoun *they*.

11. (They) turned on the dentist that had ridiculed their brushing habits.
    who

    Confirmation: *Who* is followed by the verb *had ridiculed*.

12. The young woman that answered the phone took my order.
    who

    Confirmation: *Who* is followed by the verb *answered*.

13. I called the couple that had answered the ad.
    who

    Confirmation: *Who* is followed by the verb *had answered*.

14. The clerk <u>that</u> I talked to found us a room.
     whom

     Confirmation: *Whom* is followed by the pronoun *I*.

15. The actors <u>that</u> were stage-front were blocking the other actors.
     who

     Confirmation: *Who* is followed by the verb *were*.

16. (It) needs the name of the mechanic <u>that</u> fixed your car.
     who

     Confirmation: *Who* is followed by the verb *fixed*.

17. Someone <u>that</u> I had met at the party called me up.
     whom

     Confirmation: *Whom* is followed by the pronoun *I*.

18. Writers <u>that</u> try to write completely outside their own experience
     who

     Confirmation: *Who* is followed by the verb *try*.

19. He played the part of an aristocrat <u>that</u> everyone considered
     whom

     Confirmation: *Whom* is followed by the pronoun *everyone*.

20. I know a person <u>that</u> would be perfect for the part.
     who

     Confirmation: *Who* is followed by the verb *would be*.

Run-On Sentences Exercise #1: Identifying Run-On Sentences by the Two Periods Test

1. English is a hybrid language; it is related to both German and French.
    Confirmation: English is a hybrid language. It is related to both German
                  and French.

2. I'm going to have to get a new car; my old one is in the shop again.
    Confirmation: I'm going to have to get a new car. My old one is in the shop again.

3. Don't eat your ice cream so quickly; you'll get a headache.
    Confirmation: Don't eat your ice cream so quickly. You'll get a headache.

4. Children shouldn't see scary movies; they have nightmares for weeks.
    Confirmation: Children shouldn't see scary movies. They have nightmares
                  for weeks.

5. The sale was a flop; we hardly sold a thing.
    Confirmation: The sale was a flop. We hardly sold a thing.

6. I don't like sitcoms on TV; they're all alike.
    Confirmation: I don't like sitcoms on TV. They're all alike.

7. He must have a cold; his nose is running all the time.
    Confirmation: He must have a cold. His nose is running all the time.

8. It was really cold this winter; the lake even froze over.
   Confirmation: It was really cold this winter. The lake even froze over.

9. I don't like that salsa; it is too hot for me.
   Confirmation: I don't like that salsa. It is too hot for me.

10. The forecast is for thunderstorms; we should close the downstairs windows tonight.
    Confirmation: The forecast is for thunderstorms. We should close the downstairs windows tonight.

11. I rarely watch the late show; I don't want to stay up that late.
    Confirmation: I rarely watch the late show. I don't want to stay up that late.

12. I have a copy of the book if you want to borrow it.
    Confirmation: I have a copy of the book. *If you want to borrow it.

13. My sister is going to UCLA; my brother is going to USC.
    Confirmation: My sister is going to UCLA. My brother is going to USC.

14. I can't take that class; I have a conflict with a required course.
    Confirmation: I can't take that class. I have a conflict with a required course.

15. Taking calculus is easy; understanding it is hard.
    Confirmation: Taking calculus is easy. Understanding it is hard.

16. They had a parfait, a dessert made with ice cream and syrup.
    Confirmation: They had a parfait. *A dessert made with ice cream and syrup.

17. She's going to miss a couple of games; she twisted her ankle in practice.
    Confirmation: She's going to miss a couple of games. She twisted her ankle in practice.

18. It is located near the Interstate, about an hour's drive from here.
    Confirmation: It is located near the Interstate. *About an hour's drive from here.

19. Las Vegas can't grow forever; if nothing else, it can't get enough water to keep expanding.
    Confirmation: Las Vegas can't grow forever. If nothing else, it can't get enough water to keep expanding.

20. Will Rogers said that you could always get a bank loan as long as you could show that you didn't need it.
    Confirmation: Will Rogers said that you could always get a bank loan. *As long as you could show that you didn't need it.

Subject–Verb Agreement Exercise #1: Identifying Subjects by the First Noun Test

1. In our last three games, the average <u>margin</u> of our losses <u>has</u> been two points.
   Confirmation: In our last three games, the average <u>margin has</u> been two points.

2. The <u>answers</u> for the problems in the first section <u>are</u> on page 312.
   Confirmation: The <u>answers are</u> on page 312.

3. Only one <u>finalist</u> out of several hundred contenders <u>is</u> selected.
   Confirmation: Only one <u>finalist is</u> selected.

4. In the last chapter, our <u>hero</u>, attacked by swarms of crazed bees, <u>was</u> swimming through the rat-infested sewers of New York.
   Confirmation: In the last chapter our <u>hero was</u> swimming. . . .

5. The <u>time</u> for cooking turkeys <u>depends</u> on the size of the birds.
   Confirmation: The <u>time depends</u> on the size of the birds.

6. <u>Speculation</u> about the actions of the committee <u>has</u> dominated the news lately.
   Confirmation: <u>Speculation has</u> dominated the news lately.

7. In any event, the simplest <u>solutions</u> to a complex problem <u>are</u> the hardest to carry out.
   Confirmation: In any event, the simplest <u>solutions are</u> the hardest. . . .

8. Three <u>mistakes</u> in a row <u>mean</u> that you are out.
   Confirmation: Three <u>mistakes mean</u> that you are out.

9. <u>Parking</u> in the marked spaces <u>is</u> forbidden by city ordinance.
   Confirmation: <u>Parking is</u> forbidden by city ordinance.

10. As is usually the case, the <u>people</u> seated in the back row <u>need</u> to move forward.
    Confirmation: As is usually the case, the <u>people need</u> to move forward.

11. The <u>number</u> of accidents caused by drunk drivers <u>increases</u> at night.
    Confirmation: The <u>number increases</u> at night.

12. According to the catalog, <u>one</u> of these three classes <u>is</u> required for your major.
    Confirmation: According to the catalog, <u>one is</u> required for your major.

13. The heavy fall <u>rain</u> in the mountains <u>has</u> washed a lot of soil away.
    Confirmation: The heavy fall <u>rain has</u> washed a lot of soil away.

14. The <u>boxes</u> in the back of the trailer <u>go</u> in the storage room.
    Confirmation: The <u>boxes go</u> in the storage room.

15. The <u>belongings</u> of the transit passenger <u>are</u> now available.
    Confirmation: The <u>belongings are</u> now available.

16. The <u>radio</u> shown in their new catalogs <u>was</u> just what we wanted.
    Confirmation: The <u>radio was</u> just what we wanted.

17. The <u>experts</u> that we polled at the university <u>have</u> confirmed our opinion.
    Confirmation: The <u>experts have</u> confirmed our opinion.

18. <u>Parking</u> in the downtown lots overnight <u>is</u> prohibited.
    Confirmation: <u>Parking is</u> prohibited.

19. <u>Pain</u> in the joints of the fingers and toes <u>signals</u> arthritis.

Confirmation: <u>Pain signals</u> arthritis.

20. A <u>group</u> of small children playing outside <u>delights</u> in keeping me from working.

Confirmation: A <u>group delights</u> in keeping me from working.

Subject–Verb Agreement Exercise #2: Identifying Subjects in Existential there Sentences

1. There <u>is</u> <u>dozens</u> of books piled on the carpet.
   are

Confirmation: Dozens of books are

2. There <u>was</u> many <u>jobs</u> still to do.
   were

Confirmation: Many jobs were

3. We discovered that there <u>is</u> some <u>tools</u> that we could use.
   are

Confirmation: Some tools are

4. There <u>is</u> an old <u>flashlight</u> and some <u>batteries</u> in the trunk.
   are

Confirmation: An old flashlight and some batteries are

5. There <u>was</u> some <u>dishes</u> that looked OK.
   were

Confirmation: Some dishes that looked OK were

6. There <u>appears</u> to be several possible <u>solutions</u> to the problem.
   appear

Confirmation: Several possible solutions to the problem appear

7. There <u>is</u> several <u>movies</u> that I would like to see.
   are

Confirmation: Several movies that I would like to see are

8. Suddenly, there <u>was</u> several bright <u>lights</u> shining in the trees.
   were

Confirmation: Several bright lights shining in the trees were

9. There <u>is</u> <u>lakes</u> all across this basin.
   are

Confirmation: Lakes are

10. There <u>seems</u> to be <u>noises</u> coming from the back yard.
   seem

Confirmation: Noises coming from the back yard seem

Index